Functions and Activities of the National Government in the Field of Welfare

A REPORT WITH RECOMMENDATIONS

PREPARED FOR

THE COMMISSION ON ORGANIZATION OF THE

EXECUTIVE BRANCH OF THE GOVERNMENT

by

The Brookings Institution

GREENWOOD PRESS, PUBLISHERS
NEW YORK

Originally printed in 1949 by the U.S. Government Printing Office.

First Greenwood Reprinting, 1969

Library of Congress Catalogue Card Number: 69-10072

Letter of Transmittal

WASHINGTON, D. C.,
13 January 1949.

DEAR SIRS: In accordance with Public Law 162, approved July 7, 1947, the Commission on Organization of the Executive Branch of the Government has undertaken an examination into the operation and organization of the executive functions and activities. In this examination it has had the assistance of various task forces which have made studies of particular segments of the Government. Herewith, it submits to the Congress a study prepared for the Commission's consideration of the Field of Public Welfare.

The study of each task force naturally is made from its own particular angle. The Commission, in working out a.pattern for the executive branch as a whole, has not accepted all the recommendations of the task forces. Furthermore, the Commission, in its own series of reports, has not discussed all the recommendations of an administrative nature although they may be of importance to the officials concerned.

The Commission's own report on Public Welfare is submitted to the Congress separately.

The Commission wishes to express its appreciation to the Brookings Institution for preparation of this task force study.

Faithfully,

Chairman.

The Honorable
The President of The Senate.

The Honorable
The Speaker of The House of Representatives.

CONTENTS

PART THREE. FEDERAL POLICY AND ORGANIZATION FOR EDUCATION

Letter of Submission

THE BROOKINGS INSTITUTION,
Washington 6, D. C., November 10, 1948.

Hon. HERBERT HOOVER,
Chairman, Commission on Organization of the Executive
Branch of the Government,
Washington, D. C.

MY DEAR MR. HOOVER. In compliance with an agreement between the Commission on Organization of the executive branch of the Government and the Brookings Institution dated January 12, 1948, I transmit herewith a report entitled "Functions and Activities of the National Government in the Field of Welfare."

The report is divided into six parts, as follows:

ONE. General Introduction and the Question of Departmentalization.

Two. Functions and Activities in the Field of Health.

THREE. Federal Policy and Organization for Education.

FOUR. Federal Activities and Organization in the Field of Employment.

FIVE. Relief and Social Security.

SIX. Recreational Activities of the Federal Government.

Each of the parts dealing with a distinctive function was prepared in first draft by a person specializing in that particular field, in some cases with assistants. The various parts were later read, revised, and in some cases condensed by other members of the staff. The persons who prepared the initial draft were:

Health.—George W. Bachman of the regular staff of the Institution, assisted by Miss Amy Tapping and in cooperation with the Committee on Medical Care of your Commission.

Education.—Hollis P. Allen, head of the Graduate School of Education at Claremont College, specially retained by the Institution for this study. He was assisted by Mrs. Janet D. Allen, John Edgerton, and in the condensation of the report by Gordon Lee, assistant professor of education at Claremont College.

Employment.—Avery Leiserson of the Department of Political Science of the University of Chicago, specially retained by the Institution for this project.

xiii

Relief and Social Security.—Lewis Meriam of the regular staff of the Institution.

Recreation.—Miss Amy Tapping, specially retained. The Federal Inter-Agency Committee on Recreation kindly supplied a large part of the material upon which this brief report was based.

Charles A. H. Thomson of the regular staff assisted in the review and revision of several of the parts.

Part III, Federal Policy and Organization for Education, as here submitted, is a condensation of a more detailed manuscript prepared by Dr. Allen. The full text of the original is available if the Commission desires it.

In transmitting this report I wish to express our appreciation of the cooperation and many courtesies extended to us by the staff of the Commission on Organization.

Yours very truly,

HAROLD G. MOULTON,
President.

Part One

GENERAL INTRODUCTION AND THE QUESTION OF DEPARTMENTALIZATION

Chapter I

GENERAL INTRODUCTION

According to the terms of the contract between the Committee on Organization of the Executive Branch of the Government and the Brookings Institution this report deals with the functions and activities of the Federal Government in the field of welfare which includes such activities as education, health, employment and relief, and social security.

Each of the terms thus used in defining welfare applies to a well-recognized, distinct, and in many respects separate function of government. A common practice in government—National, State, and local—in higher educational institutions and in professional writings is to treat each one as distinct. The four functions are, however, interrelated, at some points intimately. As the National Government has given more and more attention to these functions and has sought in part through grants-in-aid to stimulate, if not in some degree to control, State and local activities with respect to them the interrelationships have become of vastly increased significance.

Activities in each of these functions have a direct impact on the individual citizen. To no small extent his life is the resultant of the forces of health, education, employment, and social security. In the individual the interrelationships are so complex that separation is impossible. Thus it is becoming increasingly apparent that government must give thought to interrelationship. Thus the National Government in dealing with the States must have balanced programs in its efforts to help individuals attain and maintain social and economic balance.

In the present report each of these major functions, and recreations, is made the subject of a separate part. Each of the parts looks two ways: Outward toward other agencies and activities of government in fields related to it, and intensively inward at the agencies and activities of government in the specific field.

Part one of the report deals with a single over-all issue which affects all the welfare functions of government, "The Question of Departmentalization." The word "question" is used for two major reasons:

The first is that many issues with respect to departmentalization depend on the extent to which the Commission proposes to go in recommending the development of a general agency of administration under the President. Such an agency might be responsible for making recommendations to the President for coordinating the activities of the several departments. With such an agency strong and well staffed the number of separate departments would be much less important than it is when chief reliance for coordination is placed on departmentalization of the operating agencies. Our observations over the years have led us to the belief that coordination is primarily a problem of day-to-day management and could best be served by a well-developed staff agency under the President to make recommendations to him. Tradition, however, tends to favor reliance on departmentalization. In presenting "The Question of Departmentalization" we have attempted to set forth the issues and the arguments for and against.

The second reason for using "question" is that no definite clear-cut line divides the functions and activities of a Federal Security Agency from a Department of Labor. The location of the Employment Service and of Unemployment Compensation, to be specific, remains debatable so long as these two distinct departments are continued. Questions of distinctly political policy are involved which have only recently been passed upon by the Congress. A possible solution, again involving political policy, would be to combine the two departments. On such issues of political policy the factors may be clear but individuals will differ as to the relative weights to be attached to them. Under such circumstances our objective in a strictly institutional report is to define as clearly as possible the issues which have to be faced by officials charged with the duty of determining political policy.

One other matter requires emphases in the introduction to the report as a whole.

Three of the present reports, namely those on health, education, and relief and social security, deal with Federal grants-in-aid, made for special narrow programs or categories. In each of these fields, the conclusion was reached that better balance and better Federal-State relationships would be attained if the National Government made what are termed block grants for each of the fields—health, education, and public assistance—and if the States were given freedom, within reasonable restrictions, to determine the distribution of the grant by activities within the general field. In no instance did a member of the group favor a single grant covering all the welfare functions combined.

The present report does not go into the question of the ability of the several States independently to support the necessary functions and activities of government according to reasonable minimum standards; nor into the related question of how far the necessity for Federal grants could be reduced by a proper allocation of sources of revenue and taxes between the National Government and the States. It may be said, however, that preservation of the Federal form of Government, as distinct from a centralized government would be promoted by proper allocation of revenues and taxes. If national policy calls for minimum standards of activity by the States within a particular field, a Federal offset tax is to be preferred to a conditional grant-in-aid. If preservation of cooperative federalism is the objective, Federal grants-in-aid should be used primarily for enabling the financially poorest States to give services up to at least a reasonable minimum standard.

This concept of the use of grants-in-aid for equalization means that all grants whatever their purpose should be made in the light of the capacity of the several States to support all necessary functions of government according to a reasonable minimum standard. What the National Government needs in reaching decisions with respect to policy is a statement of current receipts and expenditures of the several States with appraisals on the revenue side of further capacity to pay, if any, and on the expenditure side of the extent and adequacy of the activities of the State and local governments. A single thorough report prepared by a single objective Federal agency should meet all needs for the basic facts. It is neither necessary nor desirable that each department or agency promoting a grant-in-aid program should make a separate independent appraisal nor should grant-in-aid laws be passed without real consideration of the need for extending help to the States.

If a general overhead coordinating agency of general administration is created it might well be responsible for these studies necessary for appraising the needs of the States. If not, the duties might well be assigned to the Treasury Department, or possibly to the Bureau of the Census. The present activities of the Census Bureau with respect to State and municipal finances should be carried on by the agency which is responsible for the investigations to determine the financial capacity of the States to support the necessary functions of government. In our judgment such studies as the census now makes should have a dual purpose, to supply general information and to furnish objective information which will throw light on the real need for grants-in-aid.

Chapter II

THE QUESTION OF DEPARTMENTALIZATION

Health, education, employment, and social security and relief are the major functions of the National Government dealt with in the present report. This chapter will consider the question of whether the principal agencies concerned with these functions should be grouped together in a department or whether the several major functions should each be entrusted to a unifunctional department or independent agency. Then upon the assumption that the National Government will adhere to its preference for a relatively small number of departments, the question of the organization of a single department will be discussed. This decision will necessarily include consideration of whether the present Department of Labor and the Federal Security Agency should be consolidated and if not where the dividing line should be drawn between them.

Functions of Agencies Summarized

The discussion of a single multifunctional type of department versus several unifunctional small departments or independent agencies can perhaps best begin by a summary of the salient facts from the chapters dealing with the several functions.

1. The four major functions: health, education, employment, and social security and relief, although interrelated, are essentially independent. The leadership and the fundamental work in each is professional, technical, or scientific. Each is the domain of a distinct profession, although in comparison with medicine, education, and social work, the knowledge and techniques of personnel or employment management (including wage administration and union relations as well as hiring and firing) have achieved only embryonic professional recognition.

2. Traditionally, under the American Federal system of Government the legislative powers over health, education, employment, and relief have been vested primarily in the several States with the exceptions of old age and survivors insurance and regulation of wages, hours, and child labor. The National Government operates in these

4

fields through grant-in-aid legislation or in the case of unemployment compensation through the device of an offset Federal tax. Under these arrangements the responsibility for operating is in the hands of the States. The national agencies are engaged primarily in seeing that the conditions prescribed by the National Government for grants-in-aid or for tax offsets are fulfilled, in conducting research, collecting and supplying information, and giving professional advice and leadership both substantive and administrative. During the past 15 years there has been a great expansion of Federal expenditures in all four fields, and particularly in employment and social security the Federal Government has assumed an unprecedented degree of initiative in program development. Nevertheless, the cooperative pattern of State administration under Federal standards for receiving financial aids does not seem likely to be supplanted or reversed in the near future.

3. In the States the functions of health, education, employment, and relief are almost completely separate. Separate State departments or agencies carry on each of these major functions, often with branches extending down into local governments—county and municipal. In the case of education the situation is further complicated by the practical application of the American traditional principle that the administration of education should insofar as possible be kept out of politics. The usual device has been separate governmental organization for education, often coupled with distinctive financing.

4. Since at the State level these functions are separate in legislation and administration, it appears that for many years to come, the National Government under a Federal system will have to legislate separately for each of the several functions if it continues to use conditional grants or offset taxes to raise the level of performance with respect to them. It seems extremely dubious that a single multifunctional department at the Federal level could have a single unified program. The departmental program would have to consist of separate programs for health, education, employment, and social security and relief. Both Congress and the State legislatures will presumably have to continue to legislate separately for the several functions.

Advantages and Disadvantages of a Single Department

In such a situation what would be the advantages and disadvantages of a single large multifunctional department?

With a large department a single officer, presumably a secretary of cabinet status, would report directly to the President and within the department carry out administration policies. In theory such an arrangement simplifies the administrative task of the President. It

5

must be noted, however, that department heads are usually laymen serving ordinarily for relatively short terms, frequently with little prior experience in the substantive work of the department. In the present instance the problems which will come to the President will apparently lie in distinctly professional fields and deal with substantive matters or broad issues of administration. Only under exceptional circumstances could a single department head deal competently with so diverse a range of technical activities. When the President has to consider substantive issues it would seem entirely possible that he might get more help from several heads of smaller departments than from the head of one big one because one could scarcely master the details in a reasonable period.

A single department head possessed of the requisite determination and aided by a competent corps of assistants could conceivably eliminate some duplication among the diverse agencies under his authority and develop a better integration of programs than at present exist. In our judgment the possibility for coordination of the activities of the several services so that each gives consideration to the programs of the others is the strongest and most valid argument for the single large multifunctional department.

It must be recognized, however, that the task is Herculean and only the department head with exceptional talents can be expected to be successful. The bureaus to be coordinated in this department are basically professional. The interests of the Government demand that the heads of the bureaus in health, education, employment, and relief and social security shall be leaders in their respective professions. To be successful they must have a substantial professional following. In grant-in-aid and tax offset programs their influence ramifies out into the States and often into local communities. State, local and Federal employees are organized into Nation-wide professional organizations which are frequently highly effective pressure groups. If a secretary attempts something to which these groups are opposed, he has a difficult fight on his hands even if the bureau chief is willing to go along with him or to remain neutral. These organizations may at times turn against the Federal agency and its leaders and defeat their proposals in Congress, partly because their organizations go down to the grass roots.

A department head of a large multifunctional agency, such as is here under consideration, cannot count on the support of the Congress and its committees. The grass roots organizations just mentioned are one factor in the situation. Another is that not infrequently a new department head has little knowledge of the diversified work of the agencies under him and little if any professional standing in the respective fields. The chances are that veteran Members of Congress who have followed the development of the agencies over the years are

6

far better informed than he is, and they may know the political forces that led to his appointment. On the other hand, Members of Congress frequently have high regard for the ability and technical competence of a bureau chief. In congressional hearings it is not unusual to find the relationships between the committee members and the bureau chief or the chief of a major division not unlike those between a board of directors and the officers of a corporation. A secretary serving for a few years often without prior specific experience can scarcely expect to have the close relationships with Congress that the best of the professional bureau chiefs have developed over the years.

The American system of government, it should be noted, results in this division of responsibility and authority between the Congress and the President and his department head. The position may be taken that a President should have undivided responsibility for and authority over the administrative departments and that through the secretary of his own choice he should control each department. In this view the assumption is that the Congress should pass the laws and make the appropriations in broad terms leaving administration to the President and his appointees. The National Government, however, has rarely worked in this way. The Congress has always exercised a large but a varying measure of control over administration, particularly through its appropriations committees. The principle of checks and balances applies here. Whatever the merits of the allegations sometimes made that Presidential control is more democratic than congressional control, and vice versa, the fact remains that the Constitution divides authority over Federal administration between Congress and the President.

In our judgment it cannot be guaranteed that grouping all these agencies under a single department head would result with certainty in effective coordination. Objectivity necessitates recognizing that the effort may result, as it has sometimes in the past, in difficulties that reach serious proportions and arouse controversies in Congress and in press and radio.

Three points deserve special emphasis in considering a multifunctional agency such as is here under discussion.

It is exceedingly difficult to select a head for it who will be acceptable to and have the confidence of the diverse professional interests involved and the various clienteles.

If great powers are vested in the secretary, and secretaries change frequently, there may be some vacillation in policy. The department, it may be recalled, will administer several grant-in-aid or tax-offset programs which involve State legislation, appropriations, and administration. For successful Federal-State cooperation a high degree of continuity in Federal administration is essential. One way of insuring such continuity is to reduce administrative discretion at the Federal level to a minimum.

To a greater degree than any other civilian department of the National Government this one will affect the lives of individuals. It will be providing, directly or indirectly, free public services, distributing social insurance benefits, and giving relief. The political potentialities are obviously great, especially since this department has no necessary responsibility for raising the funds to pay for the services and the benefits. As already noted, the agencies in the department have affiliates in the State and local governments that reach to practically every settlement. An intensely partisan politically minded secretary would have in his hands what might be made a powerful political implement. It may, however, be assumed that the Congress will be aware of this fact and will limit the discretionary authority of the secretary, and possibly continue to vest a considerable measure of the discretionary power in the bureau chiefs.

The Alternative of Several Smaller Unifunctional Agencies

Since it is by no means certain that the advantages of the great multi-functional department outweigh the disadvantages, consideration should be given to the possibilities of several smaller, more unifunctional departments or independnt establishments.

Any proposal of this type, if it be taken at all seriously, presupposes that the President will have immediately under him an agency of general administration, possibly an enlarged Bureau of the Budget. This agency would supply him with the information to facilitate his exercise of administrative control over the agencies in the Executive Branch of the Government. More important from the standpoint of the present discussion, it would provide a mechanism for the coordination of programs and policies that extend across departmental lines.

In this connection it should be pointed out that even the large multi-functional department here under consideration would not and could not embrace all the activities of the Government in the fields of health, education, employment, and relief and social security. Some of the activities in these fields will necessarily remain in other departments where they are byproducts or joint products of other activities and will have to be coordinated above the departmental level. More important, many major problems inevitably cut across departmental lines and likewise call for coordination above the departmental level. A few specific illustrations are perhaps in point here.

Real social security depends on the maintenance of high productivity, which in turn demands a high level of employment. Although the large multi-functional department under consideration would have an important role in any program for achieving these objectives,

8

especially on the informational and remedial sides, it would by no means play the dominant part. The Treasury, the Federal Reserve Board, Agriculture, Commerce, Public Works, Housing, and others would each have parts, and probably some coordinating agency would be required to make constructive decisions of timing and priority between the several programs and projects.

In a national emergency calling for full utilization of manpower and allocation of materials this department would perform essential service and probably control functions unless, as in the recent war, the employment and training agencies were transferred from it to special war organizations. Although its functions of recruiting and distributing manpower would give it a strategic and limiting, rather than a commanding role, this role would probably require direct integration of the operating agencies with the machinery for coordinating the civilian emergency effort.

The recent war has resulted in a degree of relationship between the agenices of the National Government and the research and educational institutions of the country that is unprecedented. Although Federal aid to these institutions may be a factor, the dominant fact is that National agencies want the institutions to supply them with personnel adequately trained to meet the needs of the service or else they want research carried on that will serve those needs. The United States Office of Education in the multifunctional department may conceivably be expected to ascertain and report the impact of these Federal demands on the educational institutions of the country, but it is inconceivable that the office or the department in which it is located can exercise any degree of control over the situation. Control must come from above the departmental level.

Health and physical well-being are in part dependent on food and nutrition, housing, clothing, etc., and the prices at which the essentials can be obtained. The departments of Agriculture, Commerce, and Interior, the Housing Administration, and the financial agencies of Government all have a part.

It seems to us clear that great attention should be focused on establishing under the President an effective organization for developing and coordinating policies and programs that cut across departmental lines. Through use of either standing or special interdepartmental committees with a representative of the President's staff as executive secretary or officer, administrative programs could be developed, either to be submitted to the Congress or, if the President has the authority, to be put into effect by Presidential order.[1] It is here assumed that

---

[1] In programs involving Federal-State relationships in professional fields it is often desirable to have representatives of the States, of the professions, or of the general public participate in program planning and in making recommendations for coordination. The law governing the overhead organization should make specific provision for such representation.

the agency under the President would be a staff agency advisory to the President and that it would have no independent authority to issue orders to department heads. It might be highly influential with department heads but it should neither direct them nor prevent them from urging the President to modify its recommendations.

If such an over-all staff agency were developed under the President, then careful consideration should be given to breaking up the big multifunctional agency into a number of separate more nearly unifunctional organizations.

1. Perhaps the experiment most worth trying would be to make the United States Office of Education an independent establishment with an advisory board constituted as is proposed in the part of the present report that deals with education. It is assumed that the American people will continue in their demands that control of education be kept in the hands of the State and local governments and that every effort be made to eliminate partisan political influence. A fear has often been expressed that increased Federal activity in this field would result in an undesirable centralization of educational authority. Some people believe that any action giving controlling powers to the head of the multifunctional department would increase that danger. A separate establishment with an advisory board would avoid some of that danger and probably would materially increase the influence of the Office of Education in giving nonpartisan, nonpolitic leadership to education in the States.

2. Another possible department or independent establishment might be concerned with health and directly related activities for promoting and preserving it.

3. The functions relating to employment, social security and relief constitute a third group which might be consolidated with the remaining functions of the Department of Labor. In connection with the latter possibility, revision of the act creating the Labor Department might help to make the plan more acceptable to the Congress and the public.

The reasons for suggesting the possibilities of these separate agencies is obviously to narrow the range of activities which the head of the department will have to cover and to minimize the frictions which appear inevitable if the distinctive professions are brought together under a single head. It should be repeated for emphasis that these suggestions are deemed practicable only if a strong coordinating organization is established under the President.

Internal Organization of a Multifunctional Department

If it be determined that the present multifunctional Federal Security Agency be retained with such minor additions or subtractions as may be desirable, there are several issues of internal organization that require consideration. The most important are: (1) The powers of the administrator; (2) the powers and the status of the bureau chiefs; (3) the nature and duties of the staff of the administrator; and (4) the organization of the field staffs of the agency or of its several bureaus.

THE POWERS OF THE AGENCY HEAD

In a unifunctional department it is not unusual for the essential powers to be vested in the head of the department. He may have authority to delegate power to subordinates, to determine internal organization, and to select and remove bureau chiefs. Responsibility and authority may be centered in him. Is such centralization of power desirable in the multifunctional Federal Security Agency?

The Federal Security Agency is a very loose supervisory mechanism, created in 1939, to which were transferred bureaus and agencies which were either independent, as in the case of the Social Security Board, or bureaus in other departments such as the Public Health Service, the Office of Education, the Children's Bureau, and the Food and Drug Administration. Each of these agencies operated under specific substantive laws, which defined their duties and responsibilities and generally vested administrative power in the bureau chiefs. The bureau chiefs, or their equivalent, are generally appointed by the President and confirmed by the Senate. Control of bureau chiefs by the head of the department in which the bureau was located was thus what may be characterized as informal. Naturally bureau chiefs would prefer to get along comfortably with the department head. Department heads often were aware that bureau chiefs had a status of their own, consisting of the respect and confidence of the President, strong supporters in Congress, standing with members of their professions, or a following among the clientele of their agency, and possibly all four combined. Under such conditions department heads had to proceed with a substantial degree of caution.

The bureaus or corresponding units of the Federal Security Agency, it should be again emphasized, are generally professional. More than that, each represents a different profession. The principal professions are health, education, and social welfare, each with its distinctive body of knowledge and techniques. Insofar as they are engaged in professional research and investigation and supplying consulting service and leadership to their clientele, a general overhead lay administrator is ill equipped to plan professional programs, to evaluate the product in its scientific aspects, or to judge of the technical competence of the workers. Because of these limitations it seems highly questionable whether power over professional matters should be vested in a lay department head. His powers, it would seem, should be confined

11

largely to matters of general administration, coordination of activities, and the housekeeping functions.

The Bureau Chiefs

In a multifunctional department the bureau chiefs are the real directing heads of actual operations, especially if the bureaus are engaged in professional or scientific fields. They should be and often are selected primarily on the basis of their professional attainments and standing. Often, but by no means invariably, they keep reasonably free from partisan politics, although they may be strong advocates of programs. The position of bureau chief may represent one of the high eminences in a professional career, perhaps the apex in a professional career in the government service. When the National Government is operating a grant-in-aid program, one of the objectives of which is to raise the level of administration in the States, it is of extreme importance that the State officials who are asked to follow should have great confidence in the integrity and professional ability of the person who is expected to lead. A partisan politician is not a good leader for States in which the majority of voters are on the other side.

Our recommendation would be that no steps be taken which would reduce the status and prestige of the chiefs of the professional bureaus in the Federal Security Agency. The positions should attract the best, and opportunity for professional leadership and influence is perhaps the most attractive feature of these positions.

The Nature and Duties of the Administrator's Staff

A proposal has been made that the head of the Federal Security Agency should have an assistant administrator for each of the professions—health, education, and welfare—so that each profession would be represented on his immediate staff.

In our judgment such an arrangement would prove highly unsatisfactory for the following reasons:

1. It would be unnecessary duplication as the bureau chiefs already represent the several professions.

2. The professional assistant administrators would have to be constantly on their guard lest they assume the duties of the bureau chief. Possibilities of conflict would be great.

3. The status of bureau chief would be reduced. They would rank not next to the department head but below the assistant secretaries in the line of authority.

The duties of the principal assistants to the head of the department are housekeeping, administration, and coordination. For coordination it would seem preferable to have staff assistants who work on a project basis, undertaking such studies and investigations as the head of the department may direct. These assistants would report to the head of the department. If orders are to be issued to the bureau chiefs they should come from the head of the department and not from the staff assistants.

In 1939 the Social Security Board, originally an independent agency, was transferred to the Federal Security Agency. In 1945 the Board was abolished and the title of the agency changed to the Social Security Administration. When the Children's Bureau was transferred from the Department of Labor to the Federal Security Agency it was made a subordinate bureau in the Social Security Administration.

If the Federal Security Agency is continued it might be well to abolish the Social Security Administration, making all its present constituent bureaus divisions of the Federal Security Agency. The Bureau of Employment Security already has been taken out from under the Social Security Administration and there appears to be no good reason why the Bureau of Public Assistance and the Bureau of Old Age and Survivors Insurance should not receive similar treatment. The head of the department would then be free to determine from time to time whether a bureau chief shall report directly to him in the first instance or whether the initial reports shall be made to an assistant he designates. Staff assistants of the head of the Federal Security Agency should make to him recommendations for action to promote coordination among the bureaus.

In case the Social Security Administration is not abolished, it is specifically recommended that the Children's Bureau be taken out of it and placed directly under the Federal Security Administrator. The basic function of that Bureau is to investigate and report on all matters pertaining to the welfare of children and child life among all classes of our population. Its success over the years has been largely due to the fact that it has established a position of leadership among both public and private agencies concerned with child welfare in all its phases and it is looked to for authoritative publications and advice by thousands of parents confronting the manifold problems that arise with respect to children. It has been a real force in adult education. One reason for its success has been that the position of Chief of the Children's Bureau has always been filled by a woman with high professional qualifications and outstanding reputation and it has been able to ceruit from the best in the field. In our judgment it was a mistake to reduce the status of the Bureau by making it a branch of the Social Security Administration instead of an independent bureau under the Federal Security Administration.

13

As previously noted, each of the major bureaus of the department administering a grant-in-aid program deals with a separate agency of State government, primarily health, education, employment, and welfare. Much of this work is professional or technical—consulting and advising with respect to the development of State plans, examining State plans and proposals for new State legislation to determine whether they meet the requirements of national law, and advising with respect to particular cases that raise new technical questions. The professional field representatives are also expected to bring to the State officers information as to practices which have proved successful in other States.

It seems perfectly clear to us that each regional office of the Federal Security Agency must have on its staff at least one well-qualified person in each of the special technical fields and as many more as the load really requires. Technical advice and leadership cannot be given satisfactorily by a single person in two distinct professional fields.

If representatives of each distinct field are required in the regional offices the question arises: Does the line of administrative authority over the several field representatives run to the respective professional bureaus or does it run to the head of the Federal Security Agency? Insofar as the work is professional or technical it would seem much simpler to have it run to the bureaus directly. Action would be quicker and simpler both incoming and outgoing and there would be less chance for inconsistent rulings in different States. If the Federal Security Administrator should be dissatisfied with the results he would deal through the bureau chief who is directly responsible. The bureau chiefs are in our opinion better qualified to appraise the work of professional field representatives than would the administrator and his assistants.

The administrator might have a representative at the head of each regional office to observe and report upon the general relationships between the National Government and the governor, the State legislature, and the several agencies operating a program with which the National Government is concerned. In our judgment, however, such a representative should not have authority to issue orders to the representatives of the several bureaus who are attached to that field office with respect to their professional work. If he is not satisfied with their activities he should so report to the administrator who would take up the matter with the bureau chief involved. Any orders for change would then come from the bureau chief. It seems essential to have clear-cut lines of responsibility and authority, and to avoid the confusion and possible inconsistencies that might result if bureau representatives in the field were uncertain as to who was in immediate authority over them and who was authorized to direct their professional activities.

The administrator and his assistants should, in our judgment, be responsible for the housekeeping activities of the regional offices, supplying quarters, supplies, telephone service, and general facilitating clerical personnel. An office manager presumably would be responsible in each regional office for seeing that the required housekeeping services were efficiently rendered and the office was not overstaffed with facilitating personnel.

Routine auditing of State accounts may advantageously be a function of the overhead administration. These would be technical advantages in an audit which was independent of the operating bureau. Two cautions, however, appear to be needed. Routine auditing ought to be reduced to minimum essentials to save expense and irritation. The Federal auditors should as a rule clear with the professional regional representative of the National Government on any matter involving professional or technical matters before reporting to Washington or to the State authorities. Prompt, cooperative, friendly adjustment of minor differences should be the practice, and only issues of substantial magnitude should go up the line to Washington.

The regional representative might also be responsible for coordinating the activities with respect to those laws of the National Government that require the State to make appointments under the merit system, especially with respect to clerical positions. Methods of selecting professional, technical, and scientific workers necessarily vary with the nature of the work. Health, education, relief, and employment each involve different problems with respect to professional and subprofessional personnel. Effective cooperation between the State operating departments and the professional bureaus in the Federal Security Agency are highly important with respect to developing required entrance qualifications and methods of testing and adequate classifications. At the Federal level progress seems to lie in decentralization of personnel functions with respect to professional, scientific, and technical workers. The same principle would seem to be desirable in Federal-State relationships in professional fields.

Relationships Between Labor and Federal Security

The next question that must be considered is the relationship between the present Department of Labor and the present Federal Security Agency. Should the two be kept separate or consolidated into a single department of health, education, relief and social security, and labor?

From the purely technical standpoint the two most significant points of contact and difficulty relate to (1) the employment service and unemployment compensation and (2) statistics of employment, wages, etc. Each of these situations will be reviewed and then certain others will be mentioned briefly.

EMPLOYMENT SERVICE AND UNEMPLOYMENT COMPENSATION

The present Employment Service is a Federal-State cooperative venture originally established under the grant-in-aid provisions of the Wagner-Peyser Act of 1933. Administratively it has had what may be termed a checkered career. The essential facts are in brief:

1. Before the service had become fully and firmly established the National Government embarked upon its program of operating work projects to furnish employment to unemployed employables. Under this program it was necessary for some agency to certify that applicants for the work projects were actually unemployed. The National Government established its own agencies for this purpose and had them administered by the Department of Labor and more specifically by the Employment Service within that Department. This action naturally retarded the development of the cooperative Federal-State system envisaged in the Wagner-Peyser Act.

2. In 1935 the Social Security Act provided that the States should utilize the public employment offices, established under the Wagner-Peyser Act, in passing upon unemployment compensation claims. The result was that an agency under the Department of Labor was performing an essential function in connection with the administration of unemployment compensation which was under the Social Security Board. Such a division of authority and responsibility was undesirable. President Roosevelt resolved the difficulty by transferring the Employment Service to the Social Security Board by executive order under the Reorganization Act of 1939.

3. When the United States entered the war, President Roosevelt requested the Governors of the several States to turn the public employment offices over to the National Government, which they did. The Employment Service thus temporarily nationalized was transferred to the War Manpower Commission. It was given mandatory powers and employers in many kinds of work had to get employees through it. Thus temporarily it played an important role in the allocation of manpower.

4. Following the war, some of the administrative agencies of the Federal Government believed that the Employment Service should remain nationalized and that unemployment compensation should likewise be nationalized. The Congress did not approve the idea of nationalizing the Employment Service and directed that the Service be returned to the States.

16

5. By Executive Order 9617, of September 19, 1945, President Truman transferred the Employment Service from the War Manpower Commission to the Department of Labor and in Reorganization Plan No. 1 of 1948 he proposed to transfer unemployment compensation from the Federal Security Agency to the Department of Labor. This, it will be recalled, was the exact reverse of the action taken by President Roosevelt in practically the identical matter. The Congress, however, rejected the President's reorganization plan in each House and by legislation directed the transfer of the Employment Service to the Federal Security Agency where it would be coordinated with unemployment compensation.[2]

What are the essential elements in respect to this controversy over the location of the Employment Service and unemployment compensation?

The weight of opinion is overwhelmingly in favor of having the two services not only in the same department but also under one administrative head. The States generally object to having to deal with two different agencies in two different departments when sound State administration requires at least coordination at the State level.

Use of the Employment Service by applicants for unemployment compensation is mandatory. All other uses except in emergencies are voluntary. Employers are not required to list open jobs with the Service and no one seeking a job and not an applicant for unemployment compensation is compelled to register. A relatively small percentage of hirings are made through the Employment Service even in times of full employment and a scarcity of workers. Often both employers and organized employees prefer other methods.

Before the Employment Service became the legal instrument to be used in the administration of unemployment compensation, the question of whether it was located in the Federal organization was a matter of little concern to most employers. They could use it or not as they saw fit, and most of them did not use it to a substantial extent. Not until it was coupled with unemployment compensation did its location become a real issue. Employers believe that the issue is basically the economical and unbiased administration of unemployment compensation. Labor organizations and the Labor Department insist that the real issue is whether unemployment compensation shall be integrated with other agencies concerned with employment conditions and employment information as part of the program of maintaining full employment.

Why is the location of unemployment compensation administration of concern to employers? In most of the States the pay-roll tax which supports unemployment compensation rests entirely upon employers. The Federal offset tax is levied on them. Almost all the

_____
[2] Act of June 16, 1948 (Pub. Law 646, 80th Cong., 2d sess.).

States have now introduced experience rating or merit rating whereby the tax is reduced in accordance with the employment record of the employer or the condition of the reserve fund. Lax administration which permits benefits to be paid to persons who are not actively seeking work and do not take advantage of available openings increases the costs and ultimately will affect the taxes under an experience rating plan.

A substantial body of opinion exists in opposition to experience rating. According to this view the tax should be uniform and constant, or should be changed for all employers simultaneously according to prescribed ratios between tax rates and size of reserve funds. As reserves grow to what is deemed a safe point, benefits should be increased in amount and duration or sickness benefits introduced. Not infrequently proponents of this view also favor nationalization of unemployment compensation, which would do away with the present variations among the States and presumably with experience rating.

The unemployment compensation system also leaves room for some exercise of administrative discretion. For example, what constitutes the relationship of employer and employee and makes the employer subject to the Federal tax? There are a host of border-line cases, perhaps not involving great numbers of persons but of extreme importance to the businessman. Is he subject to the tax? If he is subject to it, he may face the necessity of a radical reorganization of an essential part of his business, generally his methods of marketing. The success of some of these enterprises rests on a method of marketing that would be impracticable if the salesmen were classified as employees. Naturally the businessmen engaged in such enterprises are greatly concerned with the issue: What Federal agency is to exercise administrative discretion with respect to coverage?

The Department of Labor was originally created in response to the desires of organized labor. An argument at the time of its creation was that labor was entitled to a place in the President's cabinet. The objective of the Department, as stated in the organizational act, was "to foster, promote, and develop the welfare of the wage earners of the United States, to improve their working conditions, and to advance their opportunities for profitable employment." [3] Over the years since the Department was established the secretaries have been drawn from the ranks of organized labor or from persons reasonably acceptable to labor. At the time of the recent debates on the location of the Employment Service and unemployment compensation the Department had one assistant secretary from the American Federation of Labor, one from the Congress of Industrial Organizations, and one from an independent labor organization. Each was primarily responsible for the

---

[3] 37 Stat. 736.

18

relationships between the Department and the group with which he was affiliated.

Under these conditions it is not surprising that there are employers who regard the Department of Labor as one created to advance the interests of a particular group, a large and politically powerful group. In the general public are substantial numbers, moreover, who think of the Department of Labor in about the same way. The existence of this point of view possibly explains in part why the administration of unemployment compensation, old age and survivors insurance, and the three relief categories of the Social Security Act were entrusted to a newly established Social Security Board rather than to the existing Department of Labor. It may also help to explain the gradual diminution in the scope of the Depaartment since 1935.

Representatives of organized labor insist, however, that the statutory mission of the Department is a recognized Congressional policy, and that the advancement of wage earners' opportunities for profitable employment is a genuinely public purpose. Since 1933 the Secretary of Labor has not been a representative of organized labor. The Department of Labor sponsored the Federal-State system of employment offices established in 1933, and the Secretary of Labor was chairman of the Social Security Committee which recommended in 1935 the system of State responsibility for fixing the amount, duration, and eligibility of unemployment-compensation benefits under State laws. Lax administration of unemployment compensation, insofar as it exists, is a matter of State responsibility, except the Federal Security Administrator may have allotted insufficient funds for State administration. More than half the States on their own initiative have extended the coverage of unemployment compensation to employers of less than eight, and several have extended it to employers of one or more.

The Employment Act of 1946 recognized the threat of unemployment as a national problem, and established the policy of coordinating the functions and services of the Federal Government with the view to promoting and maintaining maximum employment opportunities under private enterprise. One method of furthering such coordination would be to bring the facilities and resources of all agencies concerned with employment information, employment conditions, and employment processes under a common administrative head. This would be a proper statutory function of the Department of Labor, and adequate devices of Congressional supervision and group consultation are available to foreclose any undue influence of either labor or management upon the administration of unemployment compensation.

The nature of this issue regarding the proper location of the Federal agency administering the Employment Service and unemployment compensation precludes its settlement on a purely factual basis. A

19

decision must be arrived at on the basis of judgment, and in last analysis this judgment must be exercised by the duly elected representatives of the people. The Brookings Institution is not submitting any formal recommendations on the subject because detailed facts alone do not determine the issue.

STATISTICS OF EMPLOYMENT

The separation of the Department of Labor from the present Federal Security Agency presents another difficulty with respect to statistics of employment, current, short-run, and long-run. The importance of these statistics under modern economic conditions is obvious. It can hardly be questioned that better and less costly statistics could be obtained if the Bureau of Labor Statistics, the Employment Service, unemployment compensation, and possibly old age and survivors insurance were in the same department. Then the head of that department could have a thorough study made of the whole problem, preferably in co-operation with the State agencies and with the assistance of the Statistical Standards Unit of the Budget Bureau, and recommend to Congress the arrangements best suited for an efficient and economical system.

The words "recommend to Congress" are used because the collection of much of the data should involve close cooperation among the Federal agencies, State and local agencies, and the thousands of employers whose activities have to be recorded and reported. The evidence justifies the conclusion that best results will be secured through the wide utilization of state agencies in collecting the material and probably in making the initial basic tabulations. Some changes in appropriations and possibly in basic law will be necessary to permit the development of a sound integrated cooperative system.

Although the location of the employment agencies and the statistics of employment are the major difficulties in having the Department of Labor separated from the Federal Security Agency, there are some lesser ones that deserve brief consideration.

EDUCATION

One of the essentials of education is that the youth be trained to support himself and his dependents under the conditions that will confront him when he leaves school. The various steps in the movement through school into successful gainful employment, insofar as the Federal Government is immediately involved, may be summarized somewhat as follows:

20

General education and professional education—	The Office of Education Federal Security Agency.
Vocational guidance—	The Office of Education, utilizing data from the Employment Service, now in Federal Security, and from bureaus in the Department of Labor.
Vocational education—	Same as in vocational guidance.
Aptitude testing and placement—	The Employment Service, utilizing school records.
Apprentice training—	The Department of Labor.

One other point requires mention. Youth who leave school without acquiring the degree of education, often necessary for success in maintaining a reasonable living for themselves and their dependents, still constitute a serious economic and social problem. Although improvement is being made with respect to each succeeding generation the country has the accumulations from the past. Labor, particularly organized labor, has a great concern for adult education to attempt to reduce the limitations that handicap these persons. The leaders believe that their interest is such that a program in this field should be developed in the Department of Labor. If the Department of Labor and the Federal Security Agency were consolidated into a single department better programming might conceivably result if the general public interest could prevail over special group interests.

Industrial Hygiene and Safety

The separation between the Department of Labor and the present Federal Security Agency presents another difficulty in the field of industrial hygiene and safety. Some of the hazards lie within the realm of medical science and call for the type of research and development that can best be supplied by the Public Health Service. Others call for the services of industrial engineers, and still others require only better management and enforced observance of fairly well established devices for ensuring safety. A distinction has to be drawn, moreover, between (1) research, development, and education and (2) factory inspection and the enforcement of standards established by law. In the States factory inspection for the enforcement of standards and general employee health and safety work has usually been in the Department of Labor or other comparable agency. Within recent years Federal appropriations for the Public Health Service have been used to stimulate State activities in industrial hygiene through State departments of health. The evidence suggests need for better coordination at the Federal level to prevent Federal grants from developing lack of coordination in the States and division of responsibility for enforcement.

The United States Children's Bureau, with its mandate to investigate and report upon all matters pertaining to the welfare of children and child life among all classes of the population, presents another difficulty for the reorganizer. Multifunctional, it overlaps health, education, labor, and public welfare. The outstanding service that it has rendered its clientele, the parents and children of the country and the child-welfare institutions, appear abundantly to have justified its maintenance. It could, of course, be fitted into a unified department made up by consolidating Labor and Federal Security, although problems of interbureau jurisdiction would remain. But with the two departments divided, the Children's Bureau does not fit neatly into either.

If a consolidated department should be set up, it is possible, perhaps even probable, that friction will develop between the secretary and the bureau chiefs. It may cause the President some difficulty and almost certainly will come before the Congress and its committees. That horn of the dilemma, however, seems preferable to vesting in the Secretary and associates of his own choosing the power to control the policies and administration of such large and heterogeneous activities. If major importance is attached to vesting controlling powers in the head of the department, the answer clearly seems to lie in having several smaller unifunctional departments and a strong central coordinating mechanism under the President.

In connection with the suggestion of consolidating Labor and Federal Security, a point previously made deserves repetition. The Department would be in no sense unifunctional. It would have many functions and require the services of several distinctive professions. It could not have a single program; at most it could have related and somewhat integrated programs. Under these circumstances, in our judgment, it would be hazardous to strip the bureau chiefs of authority and responsibility and vest maximum possible powers in the Department head upon the theory that he could weld the parts into a homogeneous whole. On the contrary, should the experiment of a single department be tried, it should be frankly and clearly recognized that the major bureaus in it, such as the Public Health Service, the employment agencies, the Bureau of Old Age and Survivors Insurance, and the Children's Bureau, should have a high degree of autonomy.

Part Two

FUNCTIONS AND ACTIVITIES IN THE
FIELD OF HEALTH

INTRODUCTION

The health functions and activities of the Federal Government are analyzed in this report, with the objective of detecting overlapping and duplications and recommending consolidation when feasible. Those activities which are recommended for retention are defined and limited.

The report is divided into three chapters.

The first is entitled "General Description and Summary of Recommendations." It includes data on the known obligations of the Federal Government for public health. Charts and tables are presented to clarify and condense the numerous health activities and to show the distribution of the financial obligations.

The second chapter attempts to bring together certain major interdepartmental public health programs, including (1) nutrition, (2) industrial hygiene, (3) international health, (4) environmental sanitation, (5) health education, (6) rural health, (7) migrant labor, (8) mental hygiene, (9) disaster preparation, (10) preventive medicine, including preventive medical aspects of the armed forces and Veterans' Administration, (11) grants-in-aid, (12) field offices of the Federal Security Administration, and (13) the value of preventive medicine.

The third chapter contains the body narrative describing functions and activities of the major agencies engaged in public health work.

Over 75 civilian agencies of the Federal Government are described as engaged in some form of health activity. The actual amount of overlapping and duplication of effort is not as large as would be expected—especially since some of these agencies are working independently. Much of the overlapping is unavoidable and in some instances desirable. Where actual duplication of activities exists, it is found to be frequently better than setting up new structural organizations as a device for the prevention of waste and inefficiency.

No attempt has been made to include within this report every possible health activity of the civilian agencies of the Federal Government. The agencies of the armed forces and the veterans are excluded except as they are covered in the section on preventive medicine. However, a complete picture of the health functions and activities of each civilian agency has been attempted where its activities have been considered of importance; not to give an impression of a diffused and scattered system of health services found throughout the departments and bureaus of the Government, but, intentionally, to show the extent to which public health has been made a part of the various agencies of the Government. Some of these health activities may appear to be only incidentally concerned with health per se, or even remotely related to public health.

Space has been given to descriptions of the legal basis for the various agencies giving health services; also to the organization of these agencies and their interrelationships with other agencies of the Government conducting health activities. This factual material often reveals the reasons for the present allocation of health activities and their development, considerations which are important in considering the reorganization of health services.

No attempt has been made to include the previous plans and proposals for effective correlation of public health activities. Such expressions have been made for the last 75 years. However, the ideas expressed that still have validity today are reflected in some of the recommendations.

Comments and recommendations, when found necessary, follow the description of the health activities under each agency.

In the chapter, "Summary and Recommendations," an effort is made to pull together comments and recommendations of this report. This consideration is intended to help in pointing the way for better understanding of the report.

The material for the compilation of the report has been secured through the courtesy of the various agencies, in reports, in bulletins, and by personal visits and interviews with Federal officers. References and footnotes are given for the various statements found pertinent to this report.

The work of this report was originally assigned on a contract basis to the Brookings Institution. Later, in order to avoid overlapping and duplication of treating Federal activities in the field of public health and medicine, the medical service committee (appointed by the Commission) and the Brookings Institution combined their work insofar as possible to prepare a joint statement to the Commission. To this end both task forces have contributed to its preparation.

Chapter I

GENERAL DESCRIPTION AND SUMMARY
OF RECOMMENDATIONS

The present chapter will start with a broad general description showing the distribution of health activities among the various agencies of the Government, with tables and charts showing the volume of obligations incurred for them. The descriptive matter will be followed by a summary of the recommendations. More detail with respect to specific problems in the field of health will be found in chapter II and with respect to specific departments and agencies in chapter III.

Distribution of Health Activities

Health activities of the Federal Government are found in many of its agencies. In chapter III the five executive departments and six independent agencies are described which are concerned directly or indirectly with some form of health activities, exclusive of the armed forces, and Veterans' Administration. These activities are administered by more than 75 civilian bureaus, divisions, and offices. Part of these fall within the field of environmental sanitation and sanitary engineering. Others are in the realm of basic and applied research in an effort to determine the causes, control, and prevention of disease.

Additional activities are in the field of health protection:

Industrial hygiene, which protects the industrial worker from industrial accidents and occupational diseases;

Foreign and domestic quarantine, which protects individuals and communities from the inroads of communicable and pestilential diseases;

Control of food and drugs, which protects the consuming public against adulterated foods, dangerous drugs, and cosmetics;

Activities directed toward helping States through grants-in-aid programs, assignments of personnel, and the preparation of materials to extend their health work.

Keeping abreast of the expanding frontiers in medical knowledge, especially in the field of psychosomatic medicine, health activities also operate in the development of programs in the mental hygiene field. The interest in international health problems and the recognition of the World Health Organization are further indications of the broadening activities of the Government in health.

TABLE I.—*Functional health service activities performed by various civilian agencies*

A—Primary; B—Secondary

Functional service	Public Health Service	Children's Bureau	Food and drug	Agriculture	Interior	Labor	Treasury	State	Housing	FWA	TVA	FTC	Atomic Energy
A. General health services:													
1. Facilities	A	B			B				B		B		B
2. Professional personnel	A	A	A										A
3. Administration	A	A											
B. Personal health services:													
1. Medical care	A	B			A								B
2. Foreign quarantine	A												
3. Categorical programs:													
a. Communicable disease control:													
(1) Tuberculosis	A				B								
(2) Venereal disease	A												
(3) Other	A										A		
b. Chronic disease control:													
(1) Cancer	A												
(2) Heart	A	A											
(3) Mental	A	B					B						
(4) Other	A	B											
c. Programs for special groups:													
(1) Maternal and child care		A											
(2) Indian wards					A								
(3) Other	B												
4. Noncategorical programs	A										B		
C. Environmental health services:													
1. Foreign quarantine	A				B				B	[a]			
2. Interstate control	A		A	A							A		
3. Water polution control	A				A					A	A		
4. Sanitation control	A		A	A	B					A			
5. Industrial hygiene	A				A	A							A
D. Research services:													
1. Research as an adjunct of medical care	A	A											
2. Research as a basis for control programs	A	A	A	A							A		
3. Research as a basis for environmental health	A				B	A			B		A		
4. Basic research	A	A		A	B								A
5. Social science research	A	A		A		A				B			
6. Vital and health statistics	A	A		A		A							
E. Promotional services:													
1. Negotiations, etc., on international front	A	B	B				A	A					
2. Public health education	A	A	A	A	A	A					A	B	A
3. Nutrition	A	A		A									
4. Field demonstrations	A	A		A	B						B		
5. Consultations	A	A		A		A					B		

To a less extent, grants are made to individuals for special training (and fellowships are granted) and to institutions for training and research. The activities in the field of nutritions have recently received considerable attention as it is regarded as "the most important environmental factor influencing health." The Government's interest in housing, especially for low-income groups and slum clearance, have extended health activities to various agencies of the Government. And again, other activities are directed to statistical studies and their relation to the progress of health programs and medical care programs.

This review of health activities does not imply that all these agencies of the Federal Government are primarily concerned with health as a major activity. In some instances the health work is carried

Functional health service activities performed by various civilian agencies

[Supplement to Table I]

Public Health Service:
Practically all the functional services listed on the chart are performed directly by the various organizational components of the Public Health Service.

Children's Bureau:
A1 Improvement in facilities for crippled children and infant care.
A2 Personnel for above.
A3 Development of administrative practices for above.
B1 Medical care for children through States.
B3b (2) Heart control for children.
B3b (3) Special mental hygiene for children.
B3b (4) Special dental program for children.
B3c (1) Maternal and child care program.
D & E Practically all research and promotional services listed on the chart are performed directly by the Children's Bureau in connection with its operating programs.

Food and Drug Administration:
A2 Develop technical personnel for food and drug inspection.
C2 Regulatory activity in relation to interstate commerce.
C4 Food and drug inspection.
D2 Research as basis for regulatory activities.
E2 Labelling and uses of foods and drugs.

Agriculture Department:
B3a (1) TB in animals.
C1 Inspection of animals and animal products.
C2 Inspection of animals, animal products and foods.
C4 Food inspection.
D2 Research for regulatory activities.
D3 Research for experimental stations, Brueau of Animal and Industrial Chemistry.
D4 Dairy, sanitation, animal industry, entimology, plant quarantine, nutrition, etc.
D5 Home Economics, etc.
D6 Bureau of Agricultural Economics.
E1 International cooperation on agricultural economics.
E2 Rural education, extension service, etc.
E3 Promotion of better nutrition on farms.
E4 Extension Service, Home Economics Demonstrations.
E5 Extension Service, Farm Bureau Agents.

Interior Department:
A1 Indian wards.
B1 Indian wards.
B3c (2) Indian wards.
C3 Indian wards and national parks.

Interior Department—Continued
C4 Rodent control and wildlife.
C5 Health and safety (Mines).
D3 Health and safety (Mines).
D4 Wildlife.
E2 Indians, mines and safety.
E4 Mines, safety.

Labor Department
C5 Health and safety, accidents, etc.
D5 Health and safety, accidents, etc.
D6 Bureau of Labor Statistics.
E2 In all fields related to labor.
E5 Field services to States.

Treasury Department
B 3b(3) Activity in connection with narcotics control.
C1 Activity in connection with narcotics control.
E1 Activity in connection with narcotics control.

State Department
E1 Negotiating agency on international front for all health problems.

Housing Agency
A1 Medical facilities in public projects.
C4 Slum clearance, public housing projects.
D3 Research on slum clearance.
D5 In connection with housing needs.

Federal Works Administration
C3 Cooperating with Public Health on water pollution.

Tennessee Valley Authority
A1 Medical facilities for personnel and families in TVA area.
B 3a(3) Malaria control.
B4 General health development for area.
C3 Malaria control.
D2 Malaria control.
D3 Broad research for area rehabilitation.
E2 In connection with above programs and plans for area rehabilitation.
E5 In connection with States and educational institutions in area.

Federal Trade Commission
C2 Control of advertising practices in connection with food and drug products.
E2 Control of advertising practices in connection with food and drug products.

Atomic Energy Commission
A1 Medical facilities in special areas.
A2 Training of medical personnel in atomic energy field.
B1 Training of medical personnel in atomic energy field.
C5 Radiological safety.
D4 Use of atomic energy in medicine, etc.
E2 Preventives in relation to atomic energy uses.

---

along with a major function of an agency, while in others public health constitutes one of the principal activities. In order to summarize the various agencies described as engaged in health work, and to show their primary and secondary health functions and activities, chart I and table I have been prepared.

In table I, above, with supplement of explanatory notes, 11 executive and independent agencies are presented to show that practically all the chief civilian health functions are grouped under the organizational units of the Public Health Service of the Federal Security Agency except those of maternal and child care and the health activities of the Indian wards. It will also be seen that a large percentage of (*a*) general health, and (*b*) personnel health services are centered within the Public Health Service, and that the disper-

29

sion of the health activities occurs in the fields of (c) environmental health services, (d) research services, and (e) the promotional services of the other Federal agencies. Many are grouped in the Departments of Agriculture and the Interior which overlap similar activities of the Public Health Service.

In table II, pages 31–38, an attempt is made to summarize the scattered health functions and activities of the various agencies into a comprehensive form for an easy grasp of a system of health services.

In addition to the health activities as summarized above, the Federal Government provides through the Public Health Service a number of hospitals and medical care services such as hospitals for merchant seamen, for Negroes, for mental patients, a leprosarium, two for drug addicts; and furnishes clinical psychiatric services to the District of Columbia juvenile court and assists Federal agencies in setting up health services programs.

Recently the health and medical care activities have been increased through the enactment of laws by the Eightieth Congress for specific health and medical projects such as:

HEART DISEASE [1]—to provide research, additional facilities for care and diagnosis, and for training of workers in the field of research and matters relating to heart disease;

MENTAL HEALTH [2]—for the expansion of the national health program;

DENTAL DISEASE [3]—For research and demonstrations;

WATER POLLUTION CONTROL act,[4] to eliminate stream pollution.

For a full description of the medical care and hospital services, see Medical Service Committee of Reorganization of the Executive Branch of the Government.

Financial Obligations for Health Activities

An attempt to give a monetary evaluation [5] to the numerous health activities of the Federal Government can best be only an estimation; partly because some of the agencies' health activities are incidental to their major functions and also because the funds to carry on this work are buried in an over-all cost of the major program. Consequently, the obligation given in table III, pages 39–42, cannot be considered overestimated.

---

[1] For this purpose Congress appropriated $3,144,088 for the fiscal year 1948–49.

[2] Grants-in-aid for the development and maintenance of community mental health service $3,550,000, and for research and training $2,000,000.

[3] Congress voted $1,000,000 for field demonstration, and $750,000 for research and treatment.

[4] The sum of $75,000 was appropriated as an initial amount for administration purposes.

[5] Obligations consist of orders placed, contracts awarded, services received, and all other transactions during a given period which legally reserve the appropriation for expenditure. Such amounts include expenditures not preceded by obligations and reflect the adjustments for the differences between obligations and the actual expenditures. See secs. 3 and 5 of Budget Treasury Regulation No. 1.

TABLE II

Public Health Activities in the Federal Government

Executive Departments

A. DEPARTMENT OF AGRICULTURE

Agency	Health functions and activities
1. AGRICULTURAL RESEARCH AND ADMINISTRATION.	Administers scientific research activities of the Department of Agriculture.
a. BUREAU OF HUMAN NUTRITION AND HOME ECONOMICS.	Conducts basic research on food values and other essentials to healthful living; dissemination of information on better living.
b. BUREAU OF ANIMAL INDUSTRY.	Conducts investigations in the causes, control, treatment, and prevention of animal diseases affecting man.
c. AGRICULTURAL AND INDUSTRIAL CHEMISTRY.	Conducts research in the field of chemistry and biology, drugs, and their uses as applied to animals and to humans.
d. OFFICE OF EXPERIMENT STATIONS.	Conducts research in the field of nutrition and public health protection; reviews and approves projects for grants-in-aid in support of research.
e. BUREAU OF DAIRY INDUSTRY.	Develops sanitary methods of handling milk; conducts research in dairy products.
f. BUREAU OF ENTOMOLOGY AND PLANT QUARANTINE.	Conducts investigations in the control, treatment, and prevention of plant diseases and plant parasites, some of which affect the health of humans.
g. BUREAU OF PLANT INDUSTRY, SOILS, AND AGRICULTURAL ENGINEERING.	Conducts research essential to the protection of general health and welfare through crop improvement, water supply, and better quality foods.
2. FARMERS HOME ADMINISTRATION.	Administers health programs in relation to environmental sanitation, improved diets, and assistance in obtaining needed medical care.
3. FARM CREDIT ADMINISTRATION.	Assembles information concerning specialized rural health cooperatives and other health programs in which farmers' cooperative associations participate.
4. PRODUCTION AND MARKETING ADMINISTRATION.	Establishes standards for various food products; responsible for administration of National School Lunch Act of 1946 through its food distribution branch program; administers services related to wholesomeness and purity of foods.
5. COOPERATIVE EXTENSION SERVICE.	Aims to improve the economic welfare, health, family and community life of rural population by making the results of its Department of Research available to farmers.
6. BUREAU OF AGRICULTURAL ECONOMICS.	Evaluates rural studies concerning farm accidents, medical care, and rural health needs.

31

A. Department of Agriculture—Continued

Agency	Health functions and activities
7. Soil Conservation Service__	Contributes only indirectly to health through a national program of soil and water conservation and to provide a better and more abundant food supply.
8. Forest Service_____	Provides facilities for safeguarding health, disposal of sewage and waste, policing and enforcing sanitary laws.
9. Rural Electrification Administration.	Supplies power for food preservation and sanitary facilities.
10. Office of Personnel_____	Renders medical services to the personnel of the Department of Agriculture in accordance with provisions of Public Law 658, 79th Cong. 2d sess.

B. Department of the Interior

1. Bureau of Mines_____	Makes investigations in methods of mining, especially in relation to the safety of the miners, appliances best adapted to prevent accidents, and improvements in environmental conditions.
2. Fish and Wildlife Service___	Conducts research related to nutritive values of fishery products and disease problems affecting wildlife, control over importation of diseased wildlife, rodent control, and medical and health services on the Pribilof Islands.
3. Office of Indian Affairs____	Promotes health and medical services among Indians and Eskimos.

C. Department of Labor

1. Bureau of Labor Statistics__	Conducts surveys on work injuries; compiles injury rates; conducts studies on accidents, workers' health, workmen's compensation, etc.
2. Women's Bureau_____	Formulates standards and policies concerning relations of conditions of work for women to health, accidents, etc. Advises States on labor legislation; health facilities for women in industry.
3. Bureau of Labor Standards__	Acts as service agency to State labor departments, State officials, to labor employers and others interested in improving working conditions in industry. It is authorized to develop desirable labor standards in industrial practice, labor legislation, and labor law administration.

D. Department of the Treasury

1. Bureau of Narcotics_____	Charged with duty of regulating, supervising, and controlling traffic in narcotic drugs; cooperates with State licensing privileges.
2. Bureau of Customs_____	Cooperates with Bureau of Narcotics in the detention and prosecution of smugglers of narcotic drugs.

32

E. Department of State

Agency	Health functions and activities
1. Division of International Labor, Social and Health Affairs.	Supports the interests and the foreign policy of the United States by developing and assuring the application of appropriate principles in our foreign relations so far as they affect * * * health matters, and promotes international cooperation in this field.
a. Health Branch.	Promotes international cooperation in the field of public health, especially in relation to the development of the World Health Organization.
2. Liaison Office on Narcotic Control.	Liaison between Bureau of Narcotics in Treasury Department and United Nations Commission on Control of Narcotic Drugs.
3. Institute of International Affairs.	Conducts cooperative health programs in South America.
Pan American Sanitary Bureau.[1]	Conducts health and sanitation work in the American republics and in the prevention of the spread of communicable diseases.

Independent Agencies

A. Federal Security Agency

1. Public Health Service:

a. Office of the Surgeon General.	Directs and coordinates all activities of the Public Health Service.
(1) National Office of Vital Statistics.	Collects, tabulates, analyzes, and publishes national statistics of births, deaths, marriages, divorces, and vital statistics having public health importance.
(2) Office of International Health Relations.	Coordinates and gives general direction to all Service activities on international health matters; directs programs on international health and supervises special health missions.
(3) Division of Sanitary Engineering.	Provides technical standards, advice, and guidance for all sanitary engineering and sanitation activities of the Service and to other Federal, State, and local authorities; conducts basic research in water pollution, sewage, and industrial waste.
(4) Division of Dentistry.	Provides technical standards and guidance for all dental activities in the Service; consultative service to Federal, State, and local authorities on improvement in dental health and facilities.
(5) Division of Nursing.	Prepares technical standards and gives guidance for nursing activities and supervision of nursing personnel; plans research in nursing service and provides consultative service to States.

---

[1] Independent agency to which funds are contributed by the Government through the State Department

Agency	*Health functions and activities*
(6) Division of Health Methods.	Evaluates national health problems through collection and analysis of morbidity and medical care statistics; develops statistical procedures, organization, and administrative methods to meet the problems involved in public health practices·
(7) Division of Commissioned Officers.	Coordinates commissioned corps policies of the Public Health Service with those of other agencies.
b. National Institutes of Health.	Coordinates scientific investigations in medical and related sciences; coordinates research activities of the institutes and other divisions of the Public Health Service and agencies of the Federal Government; administers research grants and fellowship program; develops and enforces the Biological Control Act.
(1) Division of Infectious Diseases.	Responsible for conducting laboratory investigations relating to the cause, prevention, and diagnosis of infectious diseases.
(2) Division of Tropical Diseases.	Responsible for research on the transmission and prevention of tropical diseases and the mechanism of drug action against parasites; supervises the malaria investigation station at Memphis, Tenn., and its malaria research laboratory at Columbia, S. C.
(3) Division of Physiology.	Conducts studies on the fundamental problems of physiology and the biochemical processes of diseases, physiology of aging processes, and synthesis of new drugs.
(4) Pathological Research Laboratory.	Conducts researches in pathology of various diseases and gives instructions in human and experimental pathology, pathological service to the Public Health Service, and other agencies.
(5) National Cancer Research.	Conducts and coordinates research related to the cause, prevention, diagnosis, and treatment of cancer; provides training and grants-in-aid to public and private laboratories; cooperates with and furnishes State consultative service and advice.
(6) Biologics Control Laboratory.	Responsible for the enforcement provisions for the control of biologics in interstate commerce and for improving the quality of existing products and developing new products.
(7) Division of Research Grants and Fellowships.	Responsible for preparing research grants for action by the National Advisory Health Council; analyzing and compiling data and administering research fellowship programs.

A. FEDERAL SECURITY AGENCY—Continued

Agency	*Health functions and activities*
(8) CHEMISTRY LABORATORY.	Conducts research on the public health aspect of drugs and chemicals.
(9) LABORATORY OF PHYSICAL BIOLOGY.	Responsible for the study of toxic properties of chemical and physical environment in current and prospective industrial practices as they affect health.
c. BUREAU OF MEDICAL SERVICES.	Includes Hospital Division; Freedmen's Hospital; Federal Employees' Health Division; medical care for Federal Security Agency personnel; medical care for all others. Administers hospitals and clinics providing medical care for beneficiaries of the Service, such as merchant seamen, Coast Guard personnel, and injured Federal employees.
(1) MENTAL HYGIENE DIVISION.	Administers the National Mental Hygiene Program; the Public Health Service hospitals and the National Institute of Mental Health; conducts research through grants-in-aid for inservice studies into the causes, diagnosis, prevention, and treatment of mental illnesses, including drug addiction.
(2) FOREIGN QUARANTINE DIVISION.	Carries out quarantine inspection at ports of arrival of sea and air conveyances; and applies measures to prevent the introduction of communicable diseases.
d. BUREAU OF STATE SERVICES.	Administers the Federal aspects of Federal-State cooperative programs for the strengthening of general health activities.
(1) VENEREAL DISEASE DIVISION.	Assists and cooperates with public authorities, scientific institutions, and scientists in the conduct of research for developing control programs through grants-in-aid and rapid treatment centers related to venereal disease.
(2) TUBERCULOSIS CONTROL DIVISION.	Assists in bringing about improvements in the diagnosis, treatment, control, and prevention of tuberculosis; aids States through grants; provides consultative services to States and other Government agencies concerning tuberculosis control.
(3) STATES RELATIONS DIVISION.	Assists States in establishing and maintaining adequate public health services through grants-in-aid; enforces interstate quarantine regulations and provides consultative services to State health agencies and manages the annual conference of State and Territorial health officers.

Agency	*Health functions and activities*
(4) Hospital Facilities Division.	Plans and assists States in the provision of adequate hospital and clinical services; administers grants to States for surveys of existing facilities and for planning and construction of hospitals and health centers; develops standards and provides consultation relative to hospital needs, design, construction, and operation.
(5) Office of Health Education.	Provides technical field supervision and coordination of health education.
(6) Office of Public Nursing.	Coordinates the public health nursing activities and gives professional supervision of the public health nurses of the Bureau and of certain divisions in other bureaus.
(7) Industrial Hygiene Division.	Promotes the development and application of means for protection and improvement of health of workers through direct services to industry; aids States through consultation and service of technical and administrative problems.

2. Social Security Administration:

a. Children's Bureau.	Directs all Bureau activities in the fields of health and welfare; develops Bureau programs; formulates policies; cooperates with National and State commissions and organizations concerned with children and youth; cooperates in international programs.
(1) Division of Research in Child Development.	Conducts research in the physical and emotional health, growth, and development of children; develops standards of maternal and child care for the use of professional workers; cooperates with Division of Health Services on administrative studies; in cooperation with Division of Reports prepares bulletins and leaflets on child care for parents, etc.
(2) Division of Health Services.	Plans programs and directs field operations in (1) maternal and child health, and (2) Crippled Children's Program, including the administration of grant-in-aid programs for these services; provides advisory service in medical, dental, nursing, physical-therapy, medical-social, administrative methods, and nutrition fields; provides regional consultation services to States in these fields.
(3) Division of Statistical Research.	Such part of statistical research and analysis as impinges on child health services, infant and maternal mortality, etc.

Agency	Health functions and activities
b. DIVISION OF RESEARCH AND STATISTICS IN THE OFFICE OF THE COMMISSIONER OF SOCIAL SECURITY.	Conducts studies and analyses of over-all adequacy of existing social security measures and problems connected with the development of a comprehensive program with particular reference to unmet needs for protection during illness and disability and for responsibility for the review and coordination of research and statistics throughout the Federal Security Administration.
3. U. S. OFFICE OF EDUCATION.	Directs educational surveys and collects and distributes information on education in the United States and foreign countries. Concerned with providing health instruction to school-age groups and to educational agencies of the community.
4. OFFICE OF SPECIAL SERVICES.	
a. OFFICE OF VOCATIONAL REHABILITATION.	Administers a broad program for rehabilitating the disabled persons in industry or otherwise and their return to remunerative employment. Establishes standards and certifies funds to States to provide the above necessary services.
b. FOOD AND DRUG ADMINISTRATION.	Controls quality of foods and drugs; functional research to form background for law enforcement.
(1) COSMETIC DIVISION.	Develops, coordinates, and directs technical work involved in the examination of cosmetics; develops methods for identifying and analyzing natural and synthetic coloring matters in foods, drugs, and cosmetics.
(2) MICROBIOLOGY DIVISION.	Develops and applies bacteriological and microanalytical methods for detecting filth and decomposition in foods and drugs; studies causes and develops methods of preventing food poisoning and identifying foods and drugs by microscopical techniques.
(3) VITAMIN DIVISION.	Develops facts and methods necessary for enforcement of the act as it applies to biochemical and nutritional problems; develops control procedures related to food and drugs for special dietary use and the routine examination of foods and drugs for vitamins or other nutritional values.
(4) MEDICAL DIVISION.	Responsible for determining the medical policy of the Food and Drug Administration with respect to the therapeutic efficacy of safety for man and animals in food and drug devices and cosmetics.
(5) PENICILLIN CERTIFICATIONS AND IMMUNOLOGY DIVISION.	Develops and directs technical work involved in the certification of penicillin products and streptomycin; tests all antibiotics, antiseptics, and germicidal preparations for safety and efficacy.

A. FEDERAL SECURITY AGENCY—Continued

Agency	*Health functions and activities*
(6) PHARMACOLOGY DIVISION.	Develops and directs technical work involved in the biological analysis of certain drugs and glandular products; certifies insulin-containing drugs; determines toxicity of drugs and causes of food poisoning; develops pharmacological and analytical methods.
(7) FOOD DIVISION.	Responsible for developing and establishing methods, including chemical tests for examining foods for determining their identity, quality, and freedom from adulteration.

B. FEDERAL TRADE COMMISSION

1. BUREAU OF MEDICAL OPINIONS.	The prevention of unfair and deceptive practices in the handling of foods, drugs, cosmetics, and medical devices.

C. TENNESSEE VALLEY AUTHORITY

1. DIVISION OF HEALTH AND SAFETY.	Conducts malaria control and research in malariology, prevention of stream pollution, public health education among people served by its utilities. Employs medical care and health program.

D. FEDERAL WORKS AGENCY

1. BUREAU OF COMMUNITY FACILITIES.	Engineering programs in cooperation with Public Health Service in the control of stream pollution and the construction of public health clinics and hospitals.
E. ATOMIC ENERGY COMMISSION.	The use of atomic energy for the improvement of public welfare, increasing the standards of living, and providing for medical and biological research.
F. HOUSING AND HOME FINANCE AGENCY.	Responsible for the principal housing programs and functions of the Federal Government; insofar as these programs aid in the solution of our current housing problems, they have a direct effect on national standards of health.
COMMUNICABLE DISEASE CENTER.	Administers field operations for the control of communicable diseases with special emphasis for those caused by insects and other animals.
CONFERENCE OF STATE AND TERRITORIAL HEALTH OFFICERS.	The conference is called annually by the Surgeon General to discuss matters of interest in the field of public health. The conference is designed to provide opportunity for mutual consultation between State authorities and Public Health Service officials.

TABLE III.—*Total obligations for health and medical care activities in civilian agencies*

1940

Agency	Total obligations	State aid, including administrative costs		Research				Regulatory	Medical care,[1] including administration hospitals, clinics			All others, including over-all administration
		State grants	Direct operations	Direct activities	Grants to institutions and individuals	Fellowships	Training		Narcotic	Marine	All others	
Total Federal Government	²$66,560,251	$23,865,151	$2,035,462	$2,259,739	$92,689	$69,850	$83,524	$9,457,166	$2,387,097	$12,528,243	$6,896,832	$6,228,498
Total Executive Departments	²19,049,495	1,973,853		346,110				6,809,210			5,099,413	4,164,909
Department of Agriculture	11,544,004	1,973,853		301,740				5,633,180				3,635,231
Agricultural Research Administration	5,770,748	29,008		301,740				5,440,000				
Bureau of Human Nutrition and Home Economics	155,040			155,040								
Bureau of Animal Industry	5,433,000							5,433,000				
Office of Experiment Stations	29,008	29,008										
Bureau of Dairy Industry	90,700			83,700				7,000				
Bureau of Entomology and Plant Quarantine	63,000			63,000								
Farmers Home Administration	3,577,803											3,577,803
Farm Credit Administration												
Production and Marketing Administration	250,608							193,180				57,428
Cooperative Extension Service	1,944,845	1,944,845										
Bureau of Agricultural Economics												
Office of Personnel												
Department of the Interior	²5,799,783			44,370							5,099,413	
Bureau of Mines	²656,000											
Fish and Wildlife Service	55,613			44,370							11,243	
Office of Indian Affairs	5,088,170										5,088,170	
Bureau of Reclamation												
Department of Labor	290,485											290,485
Bureau of Labor Standards	290,485											290,485
Department of the Treasury	1,306,700							1,176,030				130,670

[1] Includes only the medical care of those agencies covered in this report. The armed forces and Veterans' Administration are not included.

² Distribution of $656,000 for Bureau of Mines is not available.

TABLE III.—*Total obligations for health and medical care activities in civilian agencies*—Continued

1940

Agency	Total obligations	State aid, including administrative costs		Research			Training	Regulatory	Medical care, including administration hospitals, clinics			All others, including over-all administration
		State grants	Direct operations	Direct activities	Grants to institutions and individuals	Fellowships			Narcotic	Marine	All others	
Department of State	$108,523											$108,523
Total Independent Agencies	47,510,756	$21,891,298	$2,035,462	$1,913,629	$92,689	$69,850	$83,524	$2,647,956	$2,387,097	$12,528,243	$1,797,419	2,063,589
Federal Security Agency	44,111,901	21,891,298	1,997,029	1,913,629	61,380	69,850	83,524	2,625,316	2,387,097	9,514,659	1,546,865	2,021,254
Public Health Service	32,898,242	13,689,105	1,721,029	1,874,629	61,380	69,850	83,524	52,850	2,387,097	9,514,659	1,546,865	1,897,254
Children's Bureau	8,641,193	8,202,193	276,000	39,000								124,000
Food and Drug Administration	2,572,466		2,572,466					2,572,466				
Federal Trade Commission	22,640							22,640				
Tennessee Valley Authority	362,631		38,433		31,309						250,554	42,335
Federal Works Agency	3,013,584									³ 3,013,584		
Atomic Energy Commission												
Housing and Home Finance Agency												

³ Construction purposes.

1947

Agency	Total obligations	State grants	Direct operations	Direct activities	Grants to institutions and individuals	Fellowships	Training	Regulatory	Narcotic	Marine	All others	All others, including over-all administration
Total Federal Government	$187,816,510	$96,263,201	$16,601,181	$10,572,727	$11,504,327	$156,653	$13,429,292	$16,771,149	$2,935,360	$23,966,739	$14,449,478	$11,166,403
Total Executive Departments	33,377,190	2,994,780		1,688,935	5,861,231			12,007,900			7,174,526	3,649,818
Department of Agriculture	15,302,653	2,994,780		738,360				10,711,900			8,842	848,771
Agricultural Research Administration	11,167,650	37,790		711,460				10,418,400				
Bureau of Human Nutrition and Home Economics	487,960			487,960								
Bureau of Animal Industry	10,400,000							10,400,000				
Office of Experiment Stations	37,790	37,790										
Bureau of Dairy Industry	193,800			175,400				18,400				
Bureau of Entomology and Plant Quarantine	48,100			48,100								
Farmers Home Administration	230,723											230,723
Farm Credit Administration	2,367											2,367

Agency	1	2	3	4	5	6	7	8	9	10	11	12
Production and Marketing Administration	910,681			1,500				293,500				615,681
Co-operative Extension Service	2,956,990	2,956,990										
Bureau of Agricultural Economics	25,400			25,400								
Office of Personnel	8,842											8,842
Department of the Interior	10,340,494		960,575								7,165,684	2,224,235
Bureau of Mines	3,053,990		875,130									2,178,860
Fish and Wildlife Service	91,723		75,445								16,278	
Office of Indian Affairs	7,131,400										7,086,025	45,375
Bureau of Reclamation	63,381										63,381	
Department of Labor	295,916											295,916
Bureau of Labor Standards	295,916											295,916
Department of the Treasury	1,440,000						1,296,000					144,000
Department of State	5,998,127			5,861,231								136,896
Total Independent Agencies	154,439,320	63,268,421	16,601,181	8,883,792	5,643,096	156,653	13,429,292	4,763,249	2,935,360	23,966,739	7,274,952	7,516,585
Federal Security Agency	147,032,691	63,268,421	16,579,011	5,783,303	3,524,563	156,653	13,429,292	4,733,495	2,935,360	23,520,375	5,768,933	7,324,285
Public Health Service	112,536,443	34,230,226	16,008,011	5,751,303	3,524,563	156,653	13,429,292	113,442	2,935,360	23,520,375	5,768,933	7,098,285
Children's Bureau	29,867,195	29,038,195	571,000	32,000								226,000
Food and Drug Administration	4,620,053							4,620,053				
Federal Trade Commission	29,754							29,754				
Tennessee Valley Authority	590,022		22,170		20,533						435,019	112,300
Federal Works Agency	446,364									446,364		
Atomic Energy Commission	6,249,000			3,000,000	2,098,000						1,071,000	80,000
Housing and Home Finance Agency	100,489			100,489								

1948

Agency	1	2	3	4	5	6	7	8	9	10	11	12
Total Federal Government	$208,261,883	$64,619,923	$16,974,548	$19,376,047	$22,693,902	$520,000	$9,648,674	$17,860,106	$3,391,475	$25,626,598	$16,034,731	$11,515,879
Total Executive Departments	34,949,972	3,041,120	2,237,370	6,012,605				12,880,900			7,387,081	3,390,896
Department of Agriculture	15,596,013	3,041,120	873,700					11,593,900	45,000			42,293
Agricultural Research Administration	12,252,500	194,000	833,100					11,225,400				
Bureau of Human Nutrition and Home Economics	628,400		628,400									
Bureau of Animal Industry	11,200,000							11,200,000				
Office of Experiment Stations	194,000	194,000										
Bureau of Dairy Industry	185,800		160,400					25,400				
Bureau of Entomology and Plant Quarantine	44,300		44,300									

TABLE III.—*Total obligations for health and medical care activities in civilian agencies*—Continued

1948

Agency	Total obligations	State aid, including administrative costs		Research			Training	Regulatory	Medical care, including administration hospitals, clinics			All others, including over-all administration
		State grants	Direct operations	Direct activities	Grants to institutions and individuals	Fellowships			Narcotic	Marine	All others	
Farmers Home Administration	$8,413											$8,413
Farm Credit Administration	3,880											3,880
Production and Marketing Administration	417,100			$18,600				$368,500				30,000
Co-operative Extension Service	2,847,120	$2,847,120										
Bureau of Agricultural Economics	22,000			22,000								
Office of Personnel	45,000										$45,000	
Department of the Interior	11,422,581			1,363,670							7,342,081	2,716,830
Bureau of Mines	3,919,920			1,303,090								2,616,830
Fish and Wildlife Service	89,319			60,580							28,739	
Office of Indian Affairs	7,315,300										7,215,300	100,000
Bureau of Reclamation	98,042										98,042	
Department of Labor	249,486											249,486
Bureau of Labor Standards	249,486											249,486
Department of the Treasury	1,430,000							1,287,000				143,000
Department of State	6,251,892				$6,012,605							239,287
Total Independent Agencies	173,311,911	61,578,803	$16,974,548	17,138,677	16,681,297	$520,000	$9,648,674	4,979,206	$3,391,475	$25,626,598	8,647,650	8,124,983
Federal Security Agency	155,129,128	61,578,803	16,958,155	9,054,677	11,423,711	520,000	8,548,674	4,944,106	3,391,475	24,733,328	6,368,568	7,607,631
Public Health Service	129,443,463	41,523,838	16,411,155	9,023,677	11,423,711	520,000	8,548,674	128,406	3,391,475	24,733,328	6,368,568	7,370,631
Children's Bureau	20,869,965	20,054,965	547,000	31,000								237,000
Food and Drug Administration	4,815,700							4,815,700				
Federal Trade Commission	35,100							35,100				
Tennessee Valley Authority	543,413		16,393		17,586						392,082	117,352
Federal Works Agency	893,270									893,270		
Atomic Energy Commission	16,595,000			7,968,000	5,240,000		1,100,000				1,887,000	400,000
Housing and Home Finance Agency	116,000			116,000								

42

The total obligations of the various civilian agencies,[6] of the Federal Government for health activities and medical care services amounted to $66,560,251, in 1940; $187,816,510, in 1947; and $208,-261,883 [7] in 1948, or an increase of 213 percent in the 9-year period. The executive departments have increased their obligation for public health 265 percent since 1940. For details of the total obligations for the 3 years, see table III.

The total Public Health Service's obligations for 1940 amounted to $32,898,242, as compared to $129,443,463 in 1948, an increase of 293 percent in about 9 years. For a complete statement, see chapter III, Public Health Service.

Of the total health obligations for 1948 by civilian agencies, out of every public health dollar, 62 cents is obligated for Public Health Service, 10 cents for the Children's Bureau, 8 cents each for the Department of Agriculture and Atomic Energy Commission, and 6 cents each for the Department of Interior and for the combined remaining agencies.

Of the total health dollar, obligated by functions or activities, 39 cents goes for State aid, 22 cents for medical care, 20 cents for research, 9 cents for regulatory activities, 5 cents for training, and 5 cents for all other costs including administration. (See chart I, page 44.)

In the distribution of the public health dollar by civilian agencies for specific purpose, fiscal year 1948 (see chart II, page 45), it will be noted that, generally speaking, only a few agencies participate or account for most of the obligations for each specific purpose, and many participate in only one function.

Out of every dollar for State aid, 71 cents comes from Public Health Service, 25 cents from the Children's Bureau, 4 cents from the Department of Agriculture, 1 cent from others. Out of every dollar for regulatory functions, 65 cents comes from the Department of Agriculture, 27 cents from Food and Drug Administration, 7 cents from the Treasury Department, and 1 cent from others. Out of every dollar spent for research, 49 cents comes from Public Health Service, 31 cents from Atomic Energy Commission, 14 cents from the State Department, 6 cents from others. Of the dollar spent for training, 89 cents comes from Public Health Service, and 11 cents from the Atomic Energy Commission.

Table IV gives a complete summary of the agencies for public health activities in 1948.

---

[6] The armed forces and Veterans' Administration are not included.

[7] Of this amount ($200,261,883), $45,195,000 is for medical care services, obligated chiefly for the marine hospitals administered by Public Health Service, Indian Wards, Department of the Interior, and the Medical Care Service of the Atomic Energy Commission. It should also be understood that $45,195,000 does not include the medical care obligations of the armed forces and the Veterans' Administration.

CHART I—The Public Health Dollar, Civilian Agencies, 1948

WHO SPENDS IT?

HOW IS IT SPENT?

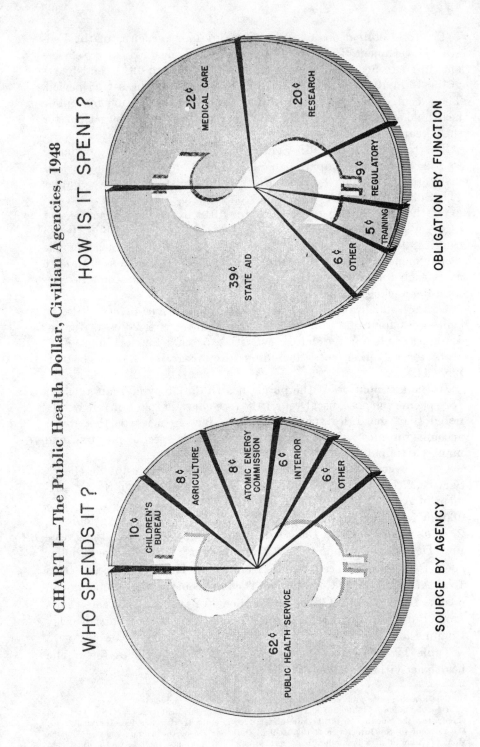

SOURCE BY AGENCY

OBLIGATION BY FUNCTION

44

CHART II—Distribution of Public Health Dollar, Civilian Agencies, 1948

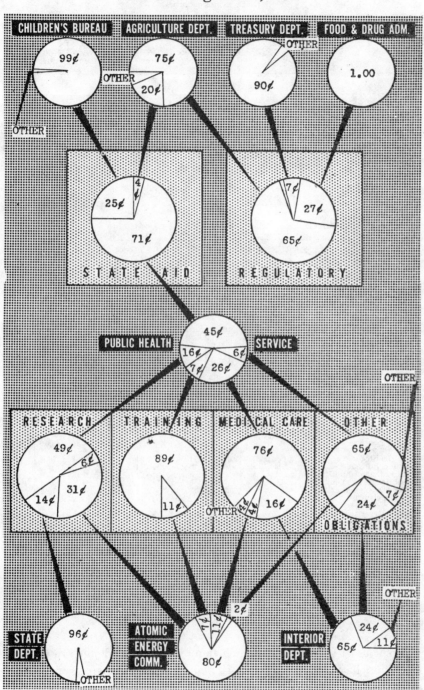

CHILDREN'S BUREAU — 99¢ — OTHER — OTHER

AGRICULTURE DEPT. — 75¢ — OTHER — 20¢

TREASURY DEPT. — OTHER — 90¢

FOOD & DRUG ADM. — 1.00

STATE AID — 25¢ — 4¢ — 71¢

REGULATORY — 7¢ — 27¢ — 65¢

PUBLIC HEALTH — 45¢ — 16¢ — 6¢ — 7¢ — 26¢ — SERVICE

RESEARCH — 49¢ — 6¢ — 14¢ — 31¢

TRAINING — 89¢ — 11¢

MEDICAL CARE — 76¢ — 16¢ — OTHER

OTHER — 65¢ — 24¢ — 7¢ — OTHER — OBLIGATIONS

STATE DEPT. — 96¢ — OTHER

ATOMIC ENERGY COMM. — 2¢ — 80¢

INTERIOR DEPT. — 65¢ — 24¢ — 11¢ — OTHER

TABLE IV.—*Obligations by civilian agencies for public health activities, fiscal year 1948*

[In thousands of dollars]

Agency	Total obligations	Type of obligation					
		State aid	Research	Training	Regulatory	Medical care	Other
AMOUNT							
All agencies	208,261	81,594	42,591	9,649	17,860	45,195	11,372
Public Health Service	129,443	5,7935	20,967	8,549	128	34,493	7,371
Children's Bureau	20,870	20,602	31				237
Food and Drug Administration	4,816				4,816		
Agriculture Department	15,596	3,041	874		11,594	45	42
Interior Department	11,423		1,364			7,342	2,717
Labor Department	249						249
Treasury Department	1,430				1,287	143	
State Department	6,252		6,013				239
Housing Agency	116		116				
Federal Works Administration	893					893	
Tennessee Valley Authority	543	16	18			392	117
Federal Trade Commission	35				35		
Atomic Energy Commission	16,595		13,208	1,100		1,887	400
PERCENT BY TYPE OF OBLIGATION							
All agencies	100.0	39.2	20.4	4.6	8.6	21.7	5.5
Public Health Service	100.0	44.8	16.2	6.6	.1	26.6	5.7
Children's Bureau	100.0	98.7	.2				1.1
Food and Drug Administration	100.0				100.0		
Agriculture Department	100.0	19.5	5.6		74.3	.3	.3
Interior Department	100.0		11.9			64.3	23.8
Labor Department	100.0						100.0
Treasury Department	100.0				90.0	10.0	
State Department	100.0		96.2				3.8
Housing Agency	100.0		100.0				
Federal Works Administration	100.0					100.0	
Tennessee Valley Authority	100.0	2.9	3.3			72.3	21.5
Federal Trade Commission	100.0				100.0		
Atomic Energy Commission	100.0		79.6	6.6		11.4	2.4
PERCENT BY AGENCY							
All agencies	100.0	100.0	100.0	100.0	100.0	100.0	100.0
Public Health Service	62.2	71.0	49.2	88.6	.7	76.3	64.8
Children's Bureau	10.0	25.3	.07				2.1
Food and Drug Administration	2.3				27.0		
Agriculture Department	7.5	3.7	2.1		64.9	.1	.4
Interior Department	5.5		3.2			16.2	23.9
Labor Department	.1						2.2
Treasury Department	.7				7.2	.?	
State Department	3.0		14.1				2.1
Housing Agency	.05		.3				
Federal Works Administration	.4					2.0	
Tennessee Valley Authority	.3	.02	.04			.9	1.0
Federal Trade Commission	.02				.2		
Atomic Energy Commission	7.8		31.0	11.4		4.2	3.5

Summary of Recommendations

Agencies of Government which include health and welfare in their functions have never been static entities but growing organisms. Additional programs have always been developed within their structure as the will of the people, expressed in congressional action, has demanded Government action on new phases of the public health. Such is the history of the inclusion of foreign quarantine, health and safety protection for industrial workers, and the tuberculosis control, among many others, in the development of the Public Health Service. Other services have been included as our frontiers of knowledge have broadened and as a result of experimental research in the control and prevention of disease.

Many other agencies of Government operate under broad congressional mandates which allow some health activities to be carried out within their structure. This inherent quality of our Government structure precludes the making of fixed Government blueprints for health programs which develop out of our growing needs for health protection in new areas.

The inclusion of both these direct and indirect health activities in many agencies of Government may seem to a casual observer to produce overlapping and unnecessary duplication. However, on closer examination and as a result of this study, such apparent overlapping is frequently unavoidable and even necessary. Also this study reveals that, within the framework of Government, it is possible to enhance our public health protection by interrelating the health functions of the various Government agencies into a coordinated plan. At the present time where overlapping or duplication of services occurs, conferences and even agreements between the agencies concerned add to the efficiency of the services involved and prevent unnecessary waste as a result of mutual understanding. In general, emphasis should be placed upon close interdepartmental and interagency cooperation, rather than upon fixing existing health activities into a new system reconstructed solely on the basis of design.

In the following pages, specific recommendations are made for efficiency of operation. These may include transfer of agencies and coordination of services. A plan for coordinating the major health services of the Federal Government is herewith recommended.

COORDINATION OF HEALTH ACTIVITIES

From this study, it is evident that at the present time there is no well-developed plan for coordinating the health activities within the Federal Government.[8] If our national health program is to be developed in accordance with the present trends in the field of positive

---

[8] In 1935 the President reestablished the Interdepartmental Committee (Executive Order 7481) to coordinate health and welfare activities, and to sponsor cooperative working agreements among various Government agencies in the health and welfare field. It ceased to function in 1939. Also the Office of Defense, Health and Welfare Services was established Sept. 3, 1941 (Executive Order 8890), to supersede the Office of the Coordinator of Health, Welfare and . . . to coordinate all health, medical, welfare, nutrition . . . under the Federal Security Agency. It was abolished Apr. 29, 1943.

health,[9] health, and particularly public health, cannot be attacked by one agency of the Government, nor even by the Government alone, but by a concert of those agencies and private organizations, primarily interested in public health activities.

Therefore, the development of a committee organization, or secretariat, seems necessary if an efficient, integrated, over-all health program is to be carried out. Such a committee system should necessarily (1) bring about mutual understanding between member agencies of their individual health programs, (2) correlate facts about their programs in a simple, comprehensive reporting system for the public information, (3) take action to prevent undue duplication and overlapping of programs, (4) plan research and programs based on such research in areas yet untouched by present health activities, and (5) give consideration to our international health obligations.

The committee system would also provide for the appointment of subcommittees to investigate and report on their special activities which make contributions to a national health program.[10] It would coordinate groups now working on the operation level, such as committees and advisory councils which are composed of representatives of both Government and non-Government agencies and organizations concerned with their particular areas of interest. These groups have already demonstrated their sufficient usefulness to warrant their continuation as subcommittees under a general secretariat.

Such a committee undoubtedly should be placed where it could carry out its functions adequately and where the purpose and type of work will best serve the interests of the committee. As the Public Health Service is entirely dedicated to health activities, it therefore seems logical that the development of such a committee, located in a Bureau of Health of the Department of Health, Education and Welfare, would be the simplest plan for coordination of the Federal health activities. The question may arise as to whether the responsibility for setting up such a committee should be in the hands of the Secretary of Health, Education and Welfare (or even in his office) rather than being the legal responsibility of the Surgeon General. As such a committee will be entirely devoted to health activities, and in view of the available facilities in the Bureau of Health, we believe the committee should be located where the committee's functions will not be sidetracked by a mass of educational and other welfare problems.

---

[9] Health is defined as "a state of complete physical, mental and social well-being, not merely the absence of disease and infirmity."

[10] The National Board of Health, organized by an act of March 3, 1879 (20 Stat. L. 484), was authorized merely to obtain information on all matters affecting public health and to devise a plan for a national health organization. The board functioned until 1884, after which the act creating it was repealed.

There is now established under the office of the Federal Security Agency Administrator an Office of Interagency and International Relations, which is concerned with health, education, welfare, and social insurance.

Provision should be made for the coordination of Federal and State health activities. The Association of State and Territorial Health Officers has been a useful coordinating mechanism. It might be improved by some representation from local health officials and perhaps other State officials responsible for operating health programs not under the health departments. Likewise it may be beneficial for the coordination of Federal health activities with those of voluntary activities where it seems that the Federal Government should play an active role as members of the National Health Council along with the voluntary health agencies, as for instance, the American Public Health Association, etc.

The assignment of technical health personnel from the Bureau of Health to other agencies would certainly assist in coordinating the health activities of the Federal Government. With a corps of trained personnel in various public health fields and professions, the Public Health Service, through its service group, should be able to promote coordination by assigning such personnel to other Federal agencies, State local health departments, universities, foreign countries, World Health Organization, etc. In the Federal Government this would permit the administration of health functions to remain with the agency performing them and would provide that agency with skilled personnel in the knowledge of public health programs.

COORDINATION OF HEALTH, EDUCATION, AND WELFARE

The suggestion often arises that there should be also an over-all committee or secretariat to coordinate the health, education, and welfare activities of the Federal Government. The Federal Security Agency is entirely dedicated to the welfare of human beings, therefore the development of such a committee under the secretariat of health, education, and security is a possibility, or, better still, it might be placed in an expanded Executive Office of the President with liaison with other agencies of the Government.

Public Health Service

Until recently the functions of the Public Health Service were related solely to sanitation and the prevention of disease. Public health problems were attacked in the belief that the absence of disease and infirmity connoted health. Gradually, we have come to appreciate the fact that social and mental factors are related to the health of the individual and his community. Today we define health as "a state of physical, mental, and social well-being." This concept of health has been developed on the basis of our expanding knowledge in such fields as psycho-somatic medicine, nutrition, etc.

Various agencies of the Federal Government have implemented their services with those directly or indirectly related to health. These health activities were started independently of the Public Health Service. They operate in agencies of Government where they are related to the basic functions of the agency, such as in Agriculture, Education, Indian Affairs, etc. To isolate these health activities from their parent agency would rob them of their effectiveness. They serve health better where they are now placed.

In accordance with the present concept of positive health the activities of the Public Health Service are closely interwoven with the activities of the other bureaus of the Federal Security Agency which operate in the broad social and educational fields of human welfare.

If the Government decides to depend primarily on departmentalization to achieve coordination of the programs of these several agencies, the Public Health Service is properly placed in the Federal Security Agency. Proposals for an independent department of health should be considered only in the event that the Government establishes an effective central agency of overhead administration directly under the President to obtain coordination of programs that extend across departmental lines.

Personnel assigned by the Public Health Service should be chosen for assignment to other Federal agencies on the basis of their training, experience, and personal qualifications for this particular assignment, so that their special knowledge and technique of public health methods may apply more effectively to this assignment.

In the past the uncertain tenure of service, frequently short, has prevented these officers from becoming an integral part of the agency to which they have been assigned. Their knowledge and skills have not had an opportunity to be given full play, nor have they had the personal satisfaction of planning and developing a program. They should remain in an agency long enough to permit them to become an integral part of the agency.

Proper organization of *Federal field services* is highly important in public health where a major Federal function is that of providing technical assistance and stimulation to State and local health departments. Decentralized authority and simple, clear-cut lines of communication are essential. It is quite possible to separate scientific competence from responsibility for the "housekeeping" aspects of office management, which the new FSA regional plan is intended to accomplish. It should also be possible to separate the work of specialist consultants from that of grant-in-aid administration, thereby broadening the vision of the administrator and sharpening the competence of the specialist; this is an objective of the Public Health Service Committee on Organization.

Probably the outstanding function of the Children's Bureau is that of presenting everlastingly and persistently the needs of the whole child in the fields of health, welfare, and education. The "team" approach has been useful though representation of the field of education in the Bureau has been minimal. If individual persons could be found or trained who would be able to represent the whole child in the regional offices as do the chief and associate chief of the Bureau in Washington, it should be possible for the Bureau to do an even more effective job than at present. The "team" has certain obvious disadvantages when it comes to dealing with State and local people, which would not be true of an individual.

If field offices are to function effectively, sufficient travel funds must be provided to allow headquarters and field to maintain close liaison, and to permit field personnel actually to work with State and local governments. If travel money is inadequate, the district office tends to operate behind an iron curtain with only the mail "air lift" as a channel for communication.

Recommendations in Specific Fields

1. Decentralization of authority and simple lines of communication with the field should be constant objectives. The regional office plan of the FSA now being set up is generally sound and implements these aims.

2. Separation of "housekeeping" administrative responsibility and scientific activities is desirable in the regional offices. It should be possible under the new FSA plan.

3. Channels of communication between program bureaus in Washington and their representatives in the regional offices must be clear without the interposition of administrative checks by regional directors. This does not mean that the regional director should be frustrated in well-considered attempts to coordinate agency programs and to integrate the health, welfare, and educational work of the agency.

4. Specialist consultants in the health field should be available to regional offices, but assigned to duties enabling them to pursue their specialized work actively most of the time, rather than being stationed directly in the regional office. Recommendation of the Public Health Service Committee on Organization regarding district offices should be carried out; it should also be applied to the Children's Bureau.

5. Field representatives of the Children's Bureau should embody in the highest possible degree the coordinated approach to all the problems of children. A policy should be followed of placing a single individual conversant with the broadest possible range of childhood problems to represent the Children's Bureau in regional offices.

6. Centralization of fiscal and merit system audits by the FSA is thoroughly justifiable, but it is highly important that the bureaus

responsible for program operations retain opportunities to determine policy within their particular fields in matters involving professional judgment.

7. Adequate travel funds are essential to the efficient operation of field offices.

DISASTER PREPARATIONS

Acts of nature, such as floods, hurricanes, epidemics, etc., often assume disastrous proportions that require public health assistance.

The American Red Cross as a quasi-governmental organization and the National Foundation for Infantile Paralysis play an indispensable role in mobilizing health resources in time of disasters. Both these organizations are demonstrating the importance of teamwork with governmental and voluntary health agencies in areas where public health catastrophe service are needed—service that has frequently been inefficiently applied in the past, due to the lack of cooperation between Government and local health agencies.

The Public Health Service has recently set up the Health Emergency Planning Unit in the Office of the Surgeon General to correct this deficiency and to "plan for a coordinated program for safeguarding public health during a national emergency."

To this end the Health Emergency Planning Unit in the Public Health Service has a useful function in planning for public health participation in disasters and should be continued, its staff being augmented as may be required.

GRANTS-IN-AID

Grants-in-aid have been in existence almost as long as our Government, but the first important grant for health work appeared as part of the Social Security Act of 1935. Subsequently, a number of others were enacted into law and about a dozen are now in operation.

Laws Not Uniform

1. The laws setting up the several grants-in-aid are not uniform in their underlying philosophy as to the Federal-State relationship in public health administration. Some specifically state their purpose to be an "enabling" one, while others tend to emphasize operation by a Federal agency. Economy and efficiency call for clarification of this point.

It is recommended that the Congress reexamine the laws which have set up grants-in-aid with a view toward codifying and unifying them. This would require a determination as to the role of the Federal health agency in the administration of public health; whether it is to be a supervisory agency with powers to control practices in the various

States, or whether, at the other extreme, it is to be merely a dispensing agent with no authority to set even minimum standards. The best stand would be at an intermediate point, instructing the Federal health agency to permit as much administrative autonomy in the States as possible, so that the latter may use the funds most effectively. The Federal agency on the other hand must be satisfied that the State has a plan for a program in which the funds are to be used, and that plan is sound from the point of view of local needs, effectiveness of proposed procedures, and judicious use of the funds. Beyond this, the State health authority should be the determining factor in the administration of the program, so long as the approved plan is carried out.

Classes of Grants

2. The grants may be classified chiefly as pertaining either to a group of persons or to a disease. The trend in recent years has been to add categories as interest was aroused, and the continuation of this trend indefinitely will result in a further accumulation of heterogeneous laws, varied administrative practices, and deleterious effects on grantees and public. Each State has its own health problems with considerable variation from one State to another, and emphasis of attack must differ. Categorical grants tend to be too restrictive as regards determination of use by the State health authority. The granting of "block" funds to a State for all purposes combined, such as health, welfare, education, roads, etc., is condemned as tending to foster political juggling of use of these funds. Any consolidation of categories should not go beyond a classification of grants for general health purposes as an extreme.

It is recommended that Congress reconsider the categorical versus the general approach in the promulgation of grant-in-aid programs. Fewer categories would increase the determinative powers of the State health authority, allowing it to concentrate more upon the public health problems which exist in that locality.

Carrying Out Grant-in-Aid Laws

3. The responsibility for carrying out the provision of each act having to do with grants-in-aid is definitely placed, but with no uniformity. The Public Health Service carries most of the current programs and three categories are now outside of it. Though consolidation is not indicated, the three agencies involved should coordinate their grant-in-aid programs.

With several new acts, additional advisory councils have been set up, seemingly a top-heavy organization. Either with or without the categorical system, a general advisory council (with specialized consultant committees) would facilitate the administration of these

53

programs. The use of the same council by the Children's Bureau and the Office of Vocational Rehabilitation would bring the programs of all three agencies closer together.

It is recommended that the Congress codify the laws which provide funds for grants-in-aid with a view towards unifying their provisions and their placing of administrative responsibility. The present categorical councils should be transformed into consultant committees to the National Advisory Health Council.

Apportionment of Funds

4. The funds in most of the programs are apportioned through the use of a formula which weighs: (*a*) Population, (*b*) financial need, and (*c*) extent of the problem. Others consider one or more of these factors, but not all of them. In one instance (dental) the entire matter is left up to a recommendation of the advisory council. Unification in this respect, whether or not the categorical system is retained, would clarify many issues.

It is recommended that the Congress review the modes of apportionment as written into the present acts and codify these provisions so that there is unification. Mode of apportionment on the basis of (*a*) population, (*b*) extent of the problem, (*c*) financial needs of a particular State, (*d*) such other factors as the advisory council may recommend, would be equitable and reasonable. "Financial needs" should receive more relative weight, in accordance with the basic philosophy of grants-in-aid.

Qualifications of Recipient

5. The conditions that the recipient must meet in order to qualify for a grant vary from one act to another. Especially confusing is the requirement in some that the State match the funds, in others that they pay one-third, in others there is no mention of the proportion. Here, too, more rational provisions in the legislation are indicated.

It is recommended that the Congress revise the acts with respect to the conditions that the recipients of grants must meet in order to rationalize these requirements. It is recommended that these requirements be general rather than specific, and that the Surgeon General be required to consult with the State and territorial health officers and with the National Advisory Health Council before he promulgates any regulations which govern the conditions which should be met by the States, and that the administrators of other programs consult analogous bodies.

Administration of Program

6. Some acts specify that the State health authority shall administer a grant-in-aid program, some specify a State agency, others

54

make no specific requirement. In order that the standards of public health work be maintained, and even advanced, health work must be the responsibility of a group professionally qualified to do the job. The State health authority is the agency best qualified for this purpose, and the Federal Government, in the interest of raising standards, should foster the channeling of health grants-in-aid through it insofar as is possible.

It is recommended that all grants-in-aid relating to health work be administered within a State by the constituted health authority of that State. Merit system requirement should be a legal provision and not a regulatory one.

In-Government Grant Administration

7. Within the Public Health Service, grants are administered by five divisions within the Bureau of State Services and by three divisions elsewhere. In addition, two other grants operate within the Children's Bureau and one other in the Office of Special Services. Obviously, this situation requires reorganization.

It is recommended that the Public Health Service reorganize its grant-in-aid functions in order to place the administration of these funds in one unit of the Service, namely a Grants Division to be established in the Bureau of State Services, with the "technical" divisions acting in an advisory capacity. The Children's Bureau and Office of Vocational Rehabilitation should coordinate their grant-in-aid programs with those of the Public Health Service.

Statutory Definition

8. Rules and regulations define and interpret the terms used in the legislative acts. There is some diffusion here, but codification of the acts would lead to simplification of the regulations. The extent to which specific requirements are made of the recipients is nicely balanced and places most of the responsibility for planning and execution upon the State (where it belongs)..

It is recommended that new rules and regulations be written in accordance with the content of any codification of existing laws on grants-in-aid or any consolidation of the responsibilities pertaining thereto. These new regulations should keep the same balance of responsibility between the Federal agency and the respective States.

Supervisory Functions

9. District officers of the Public Health Service (and of the other two Federal agencies herein mentioned) act in an advisory and consultative capacity to State health (and other) agencies. There are,

in their relationships, some aspects of the supervisory function, but this could and should be minimized as much as possible.

It is recommended that with relation to the States, the consultative and advisory functions of the district offices should be emphasized and their supervisory functions minimized.

Progress of Grants-in-Aid

10. Grants-in-aid have been responsible for: (*a*) An increase in the number of local health units; (*b*) coverage of a greater proportion of the population with local health services; (*c*) the promotion of training and placing of large numbers of well-qualified public health workers in positions where they could best serve the public; (*d*) the stimulation of interest in public health and the participation of State and local funds; (*e*) research, both basic and applied; (*f*) etc.

In short, grants-in-aid have made possible the extension of more and better health services to the people. Further progress is anticipated.

It is recommended that grants-in-aid be considered to have evolved through the "experimental" phase, and recognized as a reasonable and just function of the Federal Government.

HEALTH EDUCATION

1. The Federal Government should engage aggressively in health education of the people, coordinating its activities with national voluntary health agencies and with State and local health departments.

2. The Public Health Service because of its very broad interests and duties should take primary responsibility for the coordination of all health education carried on by agencies of the Federal Government to avoid overlapping and duplication as well as to promote complete coverage of the field. Agencies other than the Public Health Service with important health programs may use health educators and health education techniques advantageously in serving the people, but their work should be correlated with similar work by other Federal agencies.

3. The Office of Health Education in the Public Health Service should advise with all other units of the service on health education matters.

4. The Office of Education should develop an active program of school health education to assist State and local departments of education.

5. The Federal Government should consider the teaching of preventive medicine to medical students as the field of medical education in which Federal subsidy has the greatest possibility of usefulness.

6. Federal subsidies to institutions and field centers training public health workers should be provided.

Rural Health

Remedies without number have been suggested, and only a few will be mentioned here. Improvement in farm income is basically important and this has been accomplished to some extent. Extension of full-time well organized local health units throughout the rural areas is fundamental, and there is little question in the minds of those familiar with the development of such units that some Federal subsidy is necessary to stimulate their extension to provide the entire population with basic health services. Upon this structure additional services may be built readily. Community hospitals and health centers must be provided in rural and semirural areas to attract medical personnel. Modern health workers have been trained rightly to realize that they cannot bring the benefits of present-day medicine to their patients without minimum facilities. Methods of mobilizing purchasing power for medical care through prepayment plans in which the consumers have a voice must be developed and adapted to rural problems. All preventive and treatment services must be coordinated through local health councils and similar devices.

The answer to the problem of rural health is complex but it can be found. Particularly in States with a high percentage of rural population, the Federal Government has an essential role to play in finding this answer.

It is recommended that the Federal Government through grants-in-aid, technical assistance and other means should increase its participation in solution of the rural health problem. Grants are needed especially to promote the extension and improvement of full-time local health departments and to assist in the building and maintenance of hospitals and health centers.

Mental Hygiene

Preventive mental hygiene services are conducted by several agencies of the Federal Government and, through Federal subsidies, by the several States and other public and private agencies. Federal programs have usually been a part of general health services, and have been implemented by mental health education among Government employees (including military personnel). In addition, the National Institute of Mental Health has begun a research program, and plans for demonstration mental hygiene programs have been formulated.

State plans have stressed mental hygiene clinics, mental health education programs in cooperation with community agencies, training of personnel, and a certain amount of research. Grants-in-aid have helped institutions and individuals in training and research. Because the Mental Hygiene Division works so closely with States, its position in the Bureau of Medical Services is somewhat anomalous.

A more logical administrative arrangement would place it in the Bureau of States Services where it could work more closely with the Division of Grants.

Since mental hygiene is a relatively new activity in public health practice, much about it remains to be defined. The meaning of mental well-being (individual, community, national), cause and effect relationships, host versus environment (to borrow an epidemiological concept), administrative considerations; these and others need to be worked out through experience and critical evaluations.

It is recommended:

1. That the National Institute of Mental Health be responsible for integration of research projects carried on by States, universities, hospitals, other institutions or agencies, and by its own staff.

2. That the administration of the two hospitals now operated by the Division of Mental Hygiene be transferred to the proposed Medical Care Service of the National Health Administration.

3. That the Division of Mental Hygiene be transferred from the Bureau of Medical Services to the Bureau of State Services.

4. That the Division of Mental Hygiene in the Public Health Service be responsible for carrying out demonstration programs, in coordination with the activities of State and local agencies and with the National Institute of Mental Health.

5. That the Division of Mental Hygiene supply consultant services to States and other agencies through the district offices of the Public Health Service, and continue to study the programs evolved by these agencies critically and analytically.

6. That grants-in-aid to States and other agencies and individuals be continued, being administered by a Division of Grants with the Division of Mental Hygiene acting in an advisory capacity.

7. That training of personnel continue in effect to meet the problems of shortage and poor distribution of qualified specialists.

8. That the Mental Hygiene Unit of the Employees' Health Service expand its work to extend to all employees and place additional emphasis on the job and family relationships of the individuals.

INTERNATIONAL HEALTH

International control of narcotics began with the Shanghai conference on opium in 1912, and of pestilential and contagious diseases about 100 years ago. These controls confirm the fact that in the field of health, nations can meet together in a spirit of understanding and friendship and arrive at firm decisions which are carried through to an effective conclusion for the betterment of mankind. It also confirms the fact that within the United States, various Government agencies and private organizations can work together to attack health problems, international as well as national in scope.

The newly created World Health Organization gives top priority to other health problems such as communicable diseases (tuberculosis, venereal diseases, malaria), maternal and child health, sanitation, and nutrition, problems capable of being attacked internationally, but which must be controlled nationally if we are to raise the level of our own health and efficiency.

The Interim Quarantine Commission of World Health Organization not only made possible the control of the cholera epidemic in Egypt in 1947 but pushed forward our frontiers of knowledge on quarantine control to the benefit of every nation in the world.

Experience has therefore shown that the solution of these far-ranging national and international problems cannot be immediately obtained. The control of narcotic drugs was 37 years in the making. The first law for the control of "pestilential diseases" in the United States was enacted in the "Province of Carolina" in 1712—237 years ago. The world, however, is smaller and moves much faster today. The ability to work together in these areas is basic to our very existence, our health and efficiency, and is almost imperative today. Real progress points to the need for intensified cooperation with other countries of the world through the World Health Organization.

ENVIRONMENTAL SANITATION

The report on a Nation-wide inventory of sanitation needs [11] gives considerable information on the extent of work yet to be done if everyone is to have a safe and healthy environment. The report recognizes the fact that the country's sanitation needs are far beyond an immediate goal and that they all depend upon changes in the economic, cultural, and social pattern of the community. An effective organization for the practical solution of community sanitary problems must take into consideration the local attitudes and desires of the community as well as the economic conditions.

To provide an environment conducive to better social and physical health, educational work and technical advice are needed, as well as cooperative effort of Federal, State, and local agencies. This will require additional personnel, financial assistance where advisable, and cooperative long-time planning. Although there is considerable duplication of sanitary services in the various agencies, this duplication is unavoidable as these services can best be given by these agencies as part of their major functions.

---

[11] Supplement No. 204 to the Public Health Report, April 1948.

The problem of controlling the sanitary quality of milk has been a source of friction between the agricultural and health branches of government at all levels. The agricultural interests have been concerned primarily with the economic aspects and those in the health field have focussed their attention on control of disease. As both approaches have value, it is recommended:

That production on the farm be the chief concern of Agriculture, and that health agencies concern themselves primarily with control of processing and distribution phases of milk sanitation.

INDUSTRIAL HYGIENE

Proposal for consideration of the overlapping jurisdiction between the Departments of Labor and Industrial Hygiene Division of the Public Health Service in regulatory powers in State departments of labor and health.

The State departments of labor operate under State laws which, in every instance, have given them powers to inspect and to enforce regulations for the control of industrial health hazards in conformity with the State law.

The industrial hygiene divisions in State departments of health have been greatly augmented through grants-in-aid to their State programs. Inasmuch as Federal funds become available for this purpose without necessity of excessive State matching, the States, as might be expected, have tended to reduce or to discontinue appropriations to State labor departments for factory inspection and enforcement of industrial health and safety laws.

Under their augmented programs, State industrial hygiene units in State public health departments are now sponsoring legislation in individual States which give them regulatory powers for the control of industrial health and safety in industry. In the seven states where they have succeeded in passing this legislation, there are two sets of inspectors with overlapping jurisdiction giving orders to management for the correction of working conditions in their plants. This problem is discussed in the chapter on Industrial Hygiene.

The solution which has seemed reasonable to the State of California (by informal agreement between directors of industrial relations and public health), the Bureau of the Budget, and Bureau of Labor Standards would be to establish, on the Federal level, a functional division between safety problems, including accident prevention, and health problems, including the control of occupational diseases. States should be encouraged to unify their industrial health codes to avoid conflicts, and if they wish to place their inspection service on a unified basis, this should also be encouraged.

60

It also seems as logical to assist State departments of labor in their training of personnel, enforcement programs, and improved administration of State laws regulating conditions of employment, by a grant program as to assist State health departments through grants in developing an industrial hygiene program.

MIGRANT LABOR

Migrant labor has been defined as referring to those workers who are engaged in seasonal or temporary employment, and who do not have the status of residents. The health of these migratory workers involves not only the workers themselves but also those people with whom they have transitory contacts. These conditions are favorable to the spread of communicable disease and control measures are required.

There is little doubt that many of these health aspects of the problem require Federal action and to this end it is recommended that:

1. The Federal Government should take the initiative in focusing attention on the health problems created by interstate movement of migrant labor, and should enlist whatever aid is possible from State and local government and employer groups involved.

2. Grants-in-aid should be made available to States affected by the migrant labor problem to assist in building up and maintaining strong health services to control communicable disease and provide medical care for such of these workers as cannot be cared for otherwise.

NUTRITION

This section on nutrition will deal first with consideration of what the broad policies should be and then with the methods and procedures through which they can be effected.

The policies should include:

1. Obtaining the necessary data for the formulation of national nutrition policies and the planning of programs.

This would include compilation and evaluation of information from nongovernmental sources as well as stimulation and carrying on of original research. Complete and impartial information in a form to be understood by representatives of the public without intensive scientific training would be available to the legislative arm of the Government. Data in technical form would be used by agencies concerned with health, welfare, education, and agriculture.

2. Planning and carrying out programs directed toward attainment of optimal nutritional status for the people of the country.

These would include educational and service programs through which nutritional knowledge would be made to function in the every-

61

day living of the people; and such agricultural programs for the production and adequate distribution of foods essential to health as shall make them available to all families of the Nation within their purchasing power. The Federal Government would support and encourage activities undertaken by State and local governments and non-governmental agencies. It would also assume immediate responsibility for certain activities which could not otherwise be dealt with efficiently. For example, measures for safeguarding the nutritional status of migrants.

3. Cooperation in intergovernmental efforts to free the world from hunger and undernutrition.

This would include working through such specialized agencies of the United Nations as the Food and Agriculture Organization, World Health Organization, UNESCO, of the International Children's Emergency Fund.

Recommendations

To carry out such a broad policy will involve:

a. Research, service, and educational programs

Efforts to improve nutrition must be an integral part of agricultural, health, welfare, and educational programs of the Government and nonofficial agencies and organizations. Each of the agencies working in these fields should have adequately staffed nutrition units to see that that aspect of the program is dealt with efficiently. This is the philosophy underlying the wide distribution of nutrition personnel through Federal agencies at the present time.

One of the major functions of each of the governmental agencies employing nutrition workers would be to carry out its objectives in cooperation with nongovernmental organizations concerned with nutrition. For this purpose any agency, within the broad policies of the national nutrition program, would be free to work independently with outside groups in the field of its special interest. For example, the agency or agencies concerned with the administration of school-lunch programs would carry on detailed conferences with manufacturers of equipment for school kitchens. The agency or agencies concerned with public health would work with professional organizations setting standards for workers in this field and with the educational institutions providing courses of instruction meeting these standards.

Joint planning would be needed for the satisfactory execution of certain overlapping activities of Federal agencies in the nutrition field. For example, research on the relation of soil to the vigor and nutritive content of plant and animal products grown in a given area and to the nutritional status of the human beings subsisting on these products would require cooperation between agricultural and health agencies. It would be expected that these agencies would enter into such agreements as are necessary without involving agencies not immediately concerned with this program.

In summary, much of the nutritive work of the Federal Government would be carried out by the respective agencies in the broad fields to which nutrition makes a contribution. Certain activities would call for joint planning and cooperation between two or more governmental agencies or between a single Federal agency and a nongovernmental organization.

b. Coordination of service, and education programs

The Federal agencies that carry on educational and service programs in fields related to nutrition have already discovered that they have interlocking interests that call for clearance and coordination. The so-called Nutrition Planning Committee provides a partially satisfactory answer to this need in that it gives an opportunity for the agencies carrying on field programs to meet regularly and to exchange information on current and proposed activities at the Federal and State levels. The principal handicaps to the effective functioning of this committee in the limited scope that it has set for itself are: (1) The lack of complete independence related to the fact that nutrition programs which provide the secretariat for the committee are directed at least nominally by the director of one of the member agencies of the committee; and (2) the lack of technical training on the part of any member of the secretariat. Even so a coordinating body of this nature has demonstrated sufficient usefulness to warrant recommendation of its continuation, and placement in an administrative setting that would facilitate well-balanced handling of the interests of the member agencies.

Since most of the Federal agencies carry on most of their educational and service programs in nutrition through grants-in-aid to State agencies, they recognize the need for encouraging coordination at the State level through State nutrition committees, which are active in some States and exist in most. The Nutrition Planning Committee has attempted to maintain contact with these State committees through the designation of a field worker in one of the member agencies as a liaison officer. Although shortages in field staff and in travel funds have interfered with the smooth operation of this plan, it seems to have potentialities that justify its further development. On one hand, field workers of Federal agencies who are confronted with the total nutrition activities and problems in the State, of whose committee they serve as a liaison officer, see their own program in true perspective and bring back to Washington the breadth of understanding that makes for true Federal cooperation. On the other hand, State agencies have been impressed

63

favorably by this concrete evidence of harmonious working relationships among their Federal counterparts.

c. Joint action at the policy-making level

It is at the level where planning, standard-setting, and the formulation of policies are carried on that the nutrition interests of the country receive least adequate consideration. Only in the research field, where the Food and Nutrition Board of the National Research Council has provided a meeting place for national leaders in nutrition and related sciences, has a considerable measure of success along this line been achieved. The effectiveness of the Food and Nutrition Board has been hampered by the precariousness of its financial backing, entirely from nongovernmental sources. Moreover, in the absence of a similar organization of those correspondingly expert in aspects of nutrition work other than research, the Food and Nutrition Board has diverted some of its energies to matters on which it cannot speak with the full authority desired.

The creation of a National Nutrition Council has long been under consideration and has been recommended most recently by the Nutrition Section of the National Health Assembly in May of this year. It is assumed that such a body would provide not only for coordination of existing nutrition endeavors of all kinds but would also give governmental and nongovernmental bodies an opportunity to consider jointly the total national needs together with our international obligations and to plan on the best way to deal with specific problems. Such a body could present the importance of an adequate supply of expertly trained workers in the various fields of nutrition and the desirability of making explicit provision for such workers in any program of Federal aid for scientific training. Within the National Nutrition Council, there would be room for such bodies as the Food and Nutrition Board and for a parallel group of specialists in the application of nutrition knowledge to the national welfare. There would be a place for the committee that would realize the potentialities of the present Nutrition Planning Committee in coordinating the field services in nutrition of the various operating agencies; there would also be arrangements for joint planning by the policy-making officials of these same agencies. A Nutrition Council would function most effectively set up as a part or section of the Health Council which is suggested in the recommendations. Distinguished specialists in nutrition, both in government service and in private organizations have had wide experience in guiding the development of interagency nutrition committees. They know both the resources and the problems inherent in setting up a broad national program.

Also, good nutrition practices are of sufficient importance in carrying out many public-health programs, such as communicable disease control, mental health, industrial hygiene, institutional and hospital programs, health services to Government workers, etc., to give division status in the Public Health Service to a nutrition program.

PREVENTIVE MEDICINE

Preventive medicine as applied to the individual and his family and public health as applied to the community are integral parts of a balanced health program. Other activities included are health promotion, medical care and rehabilitation. All are supported by research and education. Only by support of all phases can the best and most economical results be achieved.

1. Generous support of preventive measures and those which promote health will reduce the costs of medical care for disease and injury.

2. As the wards of the Federal Government comprise one-seventh of the total population, expenditure of Federal funds for general health promotion and disease prevention among the population as a whole will produce more than general health benefits for the Nation. Very considerable savings will result in the Federal Government's obligations to its own wards for medical care.

3. Very intensive preventive measures are financially justifiable for Federal wards. There is every reason to expect that expenditures for such measures will be repaid many times over by savings in medical care costs.

THE CHILDREN'S BUREAU

During its 37 years of operation, the Children's Bureau has developed services in those areas in which the rights of children have needed protection, such as: Children living under improper home conditions, juvenile delinquents, crippled children, and children working in industry. It has been responsible for legislation to protect children. It has a research program, but is not allowed to make research grants. It operates, under title V of the Social Security Act, three grant-in-aid programs: (1) For maternal and child care, (2) for crippled children, and (3) for child welfare services.

When the Children's Bureau was in the Department of Labor it enjoyed a remarkable degree of autonomy, with the Chief being directly appointed by the President. At present the Bureau is administratively under the Social Security Administration and the Chief does not have direct access to the Federal Security Administrator. This arrangement makes it administratively difficult for the Bureau to perform its assigned functions of concerning itself with all the problems of children; of developing plans to meet these problems;

and, in general, making sure that children are considered in all the planning of the FSA.

It is therefore recommended that, in order to perform this broad function properly, the Bureau should be placed in the organization of the proposed Department of Health, Education, and Security in a general staff capacity where it can advise the Secretary of the new Department as well as the Directors General of Health, Education and Security.

It is also recommended that the scope of the Bureau be broadened somewhat beyond its present fields so that it may be equipped to deal more adequately with problems in the educational field.

The grant-in-aid programs for which the Children's Bureau is responsible have been administered admirably. Tremendous strides have been made in making maternal and child health available to people, though much remains to be done. Nevertheless, there is no unanswerable reason for leaving the grant-in-aid programs indefinitely with the Children's Bureau. Its primary functions should be those of research, planning, and promotion. A large administrative responsibility is inconsistent with the maximum performance of the Bureau's proper functions. Unquestionably, funds should be available for demonstrations, for training personnel, and for research conducted on a direct and a grant basis. It is therefore recommended that as soon as the Public Health Service develops a more unified approach to the administration of its own grant-in-aid programs, and as soon as the promotional phase is passed in the grant-in-aid programs now operated by the Children's Bureau, the health grant-in-aid programs should be transferred to the Public Health Service.

Office of Vocational Rehabilitation

It is recommended that the medical services aspect of vocational rehabilitation should be retained as part of the over-all program of the Office of Vocational Rehabilitation, though at the State level there are strong arguments for the administration of medical services by the agency responsible for the development of services to crippled children.

Assignment of medical officers from the Public Health Service to the Office of Vocational Rehabilitation to advise on the medical service activities is a wise procedure and should be continued. (See Public Health Recommendation.)

Food and Drug Administration

As the Food and Drug Administration is designed by law for the protection of health, it should be transferred to the Public Health Service in the proposed Section of Health Standards and Inspection in order to strengthen its law-enforcement powers. Furthermore, regulatory powers within the Department of Agriculture which are in any way related to health should be consolidated under the Food and Drug Administration.

The research facilities of the Food and Drug Administration are established by law to implement its enforcement powers. Some research is vital in obtaining the knowledge necessary for law enforcement.

Under the National Biologics Act, the Biologics Control Laboratory operates in the National Institute of Health, Public Health Service, and the Virus, Serum, Toxin Act is administered by the Bureau of Animal Industry, Department of Agriculture. Both the Public Health Service and the Bureau of Animal Industry are chiefly concerned with the therapeutic value of biologics. Both are regulatory activities, one affecting man and the other animal. The control of animal biologics should be retained in the Bureau of Animal Industry, Department of Agriculture. The control of biologics dealing with man should be transferred from the Biologics Control Laboratory, National Institute of Health, to Food and Drug Administration. The control of both human and animal biologics has been sustained through professional channels of both the physician and veterinarian.

Under existing law, the Food and Drug Administration in the Federal Security Agency, has control over the misbranding, false labeling, and adulteration of foods, drugs, cosmetics, and devices, while the Federal Trade Commission is given specific authority over misleading advertising of these same products.

For a period of years there has been need for the clarification of the functions of these two agencies in these closely related areas. The problems presented in this controversy are not directly related to the public health nor is this controversy wihin the province of this study. However there is abundant evidence of the need for a clarification of the functions of both these agencies by a codification of all the laws which pertain to the falsification of information in relation to foods, drugs, cosmetics and devices.

TENNESSEE VALLEY AUTHORITY

Division of Health and Safety.—In areas where TVA operates, it has assumed health obligations similar to those of both local and State agencies but always cooperatively with such agencies. This was necessary in the beginning of TVA's construction work as the impounding of streams and the shifting of population groups created health problems beyond the control of local health authorities. Thus it became necessary for TVA to provide health protection for people living in the Valley States who were exposed to the hazards of its construction and operational programs.

Through the cooperation of Federal, State, and local health agencies working with TVA, great advantages in the technical developments of the Valley States' health program have accrued. However, as the local and State health agencies are able to extend their services to meet the usual functions of State health needs of this area, the health activities of TVA should then be responsible for only those health conditions which its activities have created and which are beyond the normal control and responsibility of the local and State Governments.

All usual types of local health activites should be carried out on a local and State level with complete responsibility resting with the authorities of State and local governments. To meet this end, TVA has admirably assisted for it has consistently withdrawn its support as rapidly as other agencies could assume the burden. Moreover, it has sought and is still seeking the development of methods and relationships by which problems concerned with its own responsibilities can be dealt with under the administrative management of cooperating health agencies of the Valley.

TVA has unique opportunities to stimulate and initiate the development of projects in special fields related to public health problems of the Valley. For example, in nutrition its studies and developmental work stop short of human nutrition, yet this is related to plant and animal nutrition.

It is recommended:

1. That TVA should continue those activities which prevent adverse effects created by its activities on the region and its people.

2. That it should continue to operate in the development of those health activities which will enable the region to realize complete health protection.

3. That insofar as it is possible within the framework of its cooperative relations with health agencies of the area, it should consider the desirability of appropriate activity in this and other fields when opportunities for constructive collaboration in useful projects occur.

FEDERAL WORKS AGENCY

It is recommended that the actual construction of hospitals should be a function of the Federal Works Agency.

Public Health Service may well be responsible for studying needs, indicating hospital standards, and types of construction in the field of health.

Agencies such as the Public Health Service should not operate such facilities as the Federal Government maintains in other agencies for direct services, as in the field of construction.

Cooperative construction programs when the Federal Government participates on the grant-in-aid basis or as a lending agency and where the actual construction is carried on by the State and locality are in a somewhat different category from Federal construction per se. Under such circumstances the administrative rules of the Federal Works Agency or the Public Health Service should be determined by decision as to whether the major role of the Federal Government is that of construction or assistance with the determination of needs and priority and the fixing of standards. For general discussion between the functions of Federal Works Agency and Public Health Service, see section on Federal Works Agency.

DEPARTMENT OF AGRICULTURE

The Department in its postwar health planning anticipates the promotion of its health-protection program among rural people. It is logical that this program should have the benefit of the medical and health services of the Public Health Service. In this respect it is recommended:

1. That since the Public Health Service has assumed the responsibility and leadership in all areas of public health activities, the initiative and direction should rest with the Public Health Service and not with Agriculture.

2. That insofar as possible the Department of Agriculture should work in cooperation with the Public Health Service and keep it informed on all health problems within rural areas.

3. That the regulatory functions now in the Department of Agriculture regarding human health should be transferred when feasible to the Food and Drug Administration. (See Food and Drug Administration.)

4. That as the Biologics Act is concerned principally with the therapeutic value of serum, toxins, and viruses in the treatment and control of animal diseases, it should remain in the Bureau of Animal Industry, Department of Agriculture.

The Bureau of Human Nutrition and Home Economics.—The Bureau of Human Nutrition and Home Economics, as far as its health activities are concerned is well placed in the Department of Agriculture. While there is some overlapping in the nutritional studies of the Bureau with Public Health Service and other agencies of the Government, it is small in comparison with the interrelations of the Bureau's scientific cooperative work with the Experiment Station Extension Service of the Department of Agriculture, and with land grant colleges that work closely with the Department of Agriculture. As has been stressed, the Bureau cooperates in a wide field of activities with Federal and State agencies, as well as with nongovernment agencies. This cooperative service should be exercised, especially with

69

the Public Health Service, Office of Education, Children's Bureau, and other agencies concerned with general health and welfare. For complete statement see section under "Nutrition."

Department of the Interior

Bureau of Mines.—It is recommended that:

1. Use should be made of legal powers of the Bureau of Mines "to inspect and investigate . . . for prevention of accidents . . . and to cooperate with . . . States and Territories . . . and utilize their services in relation to health inspection" in order to avoid duplication of inspection, raise standards of inspection and thereby reduce costs of the total operation.

2. The proper role of the Bureau of Mines, Division of Health and Safety should eventually be transformed from one of direct inspection of mine property to one of advice and assistance to State administrating agencies by (*a*) improving their State mining laws, (*b*) administering grants to States for training State mine inspectors under adequate merit systems. (It is suggested that in those States in which the mine inspection service is performed under a State administrating agency which also inspects other industries in the State than mining, as for instance the State department of labor, the cooperation of the Federal Bureau of Labor Standards be invoked for assistance in codifying these State laws.)

3. During a transitional period, trial experiments might be conducted by those State bureaus which are nonpolitical, operate under broad persuasive legislation, and a merit system of civil service. The Federal agency might enter into agreements with these States to perform the inspection under Federal supervision.

4. That Federal inspection be continued until Congress provides funds and authority for the proposed change in program.

5. That Federal inspectors be employed under civil service.

6. The trend in Public Health Services is toward the definition of health incorporated in the constitution of World Health Organization. "Health is a state of complete physical, mental, and social well-being, and not merely the absence of disease and infirmity."

With its attention on the control of industrial diseases and industrial hazards, industrial hygiene is now primarily operating in the field of ". . . the absence of disease and infirmity."

In the light of our newer medical knowledge, however, there is need for industrial hygiene programs to take into consideration the broader aspects of positive health for industrial workers; and to relate the environmental factors surrounding industrial workers such as housing, nutrition, community water supplies, etc., to his susceptibility to occupational accidents and disease.

Fish and Wildlife Services.—The apparent overlapping of activities within the services of Fish and Wildlife seem unavoidable. A number of agencies in the Department of the Interior, such as the Forest Service, Park Service, the Bureau of Indian Affairs, etc., which control large tracts of land, perform activities incidental to health protection in the administration of their lands, waterways, and forests. Overlappings are bound to occur. However, it is recommended that these health and medical care activities though indirect, are of value and should be continued. Emphasis should, however, be placed upon cooperation with other Federal and State agencies directly concerned with the promotion of health.

Office of Indian Affairs.—The direction of the health and medical care program for the Indians should be in line with the purposes of our total Federal aid program for them. This program of financial assistance and related services is being directed toward the development of a self-sustaining economy for them within their cultural pattern and is one which guarantees them the rights of American citizenship. Under the same policy, the present health and medical care programs should be transferred as rapidly as possible to the State department of health of their residence. In other words, our Indian citizens should have the same rights and privileges as any other American citizen.

Since this recommendation involves congressional action, during a transitional period the following programs should be carried out:

1. The Federal Government should utilize the facilities of State departments of health and other health agencies to extend services to the Indians with such subsidies as are necessary for this purpose.

2. The present program of direct operations of services for the Indians by the Federal Government could be materially improved if the Public Health Service were responsible for these services on a similar basis as that now in operation through the Bureau of Prisons, Department of Justice.

Chapter II

MAJOR INTERDEPARTMENTAL HEALTH PROGRAMS

In an effort to emphasize and bring together some of the major activities in the field of health and preventive medicine, the following sections have been prepared. Some of these programs cover a wide field of activity and are carried on simultaneously by several agencies of the Government. They are:

1. A National Nutrition Program.
2. Industrial Hygiene Programs in the Federal Government.
3. International Health.
   a. United States Cooperation in International Health.
4. Environmental Sanitation.
5. Health Education.
6. Rural Health.
7. Migrant Labor.
8. Mental Hygiene.
9. Public Health Disaster Preparation.
10. Preventive Medicine Activities of the Veterans' Administration.
11. Preventive Medicine Divisions of the Armed Forces.
12. Grants-in-aid in Public Health.
13. Federal Field Offices for Public Health.
14. The Value of Preventive Medicine.

A NATIONAL NUTRITION PROGRAM[1]

Nutrition is probably the most important environmental factor in the attainment of health.

Many common diseases are closely related to deficiencies in the diet. In spite of our abundant food resources, considerable segments of our population, on all income levels and in every part of our country, are suffering from food deficiencies, which are potentially serious, but which can be alleviated on the basis of our present knowledge.

Every agency of Government that deals with the problems of human welfare and public health needs a knowledge of nutritionally adequate diets. Such knowledge is needed in industrial health programs for industrial workers; in the prevention and treatment of such deficiency diseases as tuberculosis, the anemias, pellagra; in mental health programs; in budget plans of the bureau of public assistance programs for the aged, dependent children, and the blind; in services to mothers and children; in school health programs and school lunches; in mass feeding operations (Government cafeterias, institutional programs, armed forces); in health services to Government workers; and in rural life programs.

At the first United Nations Conference on Food and Agriculture, held in Hot Springs, Va., in May 1943, the United States and 43 other nations formally endorsed the democratic principle that everyone is entitled to an opportunity to secure a diet adequate for health, that it is the responsibility of governments to assure this basic human right, and that agricultural policies, both nationally and internationally, must be directed toward this end.

---

[1] References on National Nutrition Program:

Report of United Nations Conference on Food and Agriculture.
Department of State, Conference Series 52.
Consultation and reports, Departments of Agriculture and Education.
Public Health Service, and Children's Bureau.
Report on Food and Nutrition work of the Federal Agencies represented on the Interdepartmental Nutrition Coordinating Committee, Department of Agriculture, April 1948.
"Coordination of Federal Nutrition Programs," Bureau of Budget, May 1945.
National Research Council, Food and Nutrition Board, March 1948.
Manual for the Study of Food Habits.
National Research Council.
National Academy of Sciences.
Reprints from Nutrition Reviews, Vol. 6, No. 4.
Currents in Biochemical Research, "Social Aspects of Nutrition," 1948.
Round Table discussion on Nutrition and Deficiency Disease, Journal of Pediatrics.

Goals in Nutrition

The goal of a nutrition program can be reached by organized effort along the following lines:

By encouraging and carrying on research on food values, food habits, nutritive needs of individuals for optimum health, and for the prevention and alleviation of disease in order that: (*a*) Such measures may be fostered for the production and distribution of foods essential to health as shall make a nutritionally adequate diet available to all families of the Nation within their purchasing power; and (*b*) the knowledge gained through research in food and nutrition can be brought to the people in such a way as to enable and encourage them to obtain the maximum benefits from our national food supplies.

Important developments have already been made, both within the Government and through private institutions and agencies, toward reaching this goal. There are four areas on which this goal impinges:

1. *Agriculture.*—Agricultural production should be adapted to yield the supplies most needed by consumers. The food produced should be available to all people.

Methods for attaining these agricultural goals are discussed in the Report of the UN Conference on Food and Agriculture of May 18 to June 3, 1943, Department of State, Conference Series 52.

2. *Research.*—Research extends the frontiers of our knowledge of nutrition. Both basic and applied nutrition research are undertaken in several agencies of Government and by the Food and Nutrition Board of the National Research Council and under private auspices. Compared with research in other physical and biological sciences, research in food and nutrition has only begun.

Malnutrition is one of the most important problems of preventive medicine. Therefore, it is within the province of the public health to share in the responsibility for nutrition research and in conducting surveys or studies to define existing nutrition problems, including the diagnosis, prevention, and treatment of specific dietary-deficiency diseases.

It is important that knowledge achieved through research should be quickly transmitted to the consuming public, producers, teachers, and educators.

3. *Professional training.*—There is a dearth of trained nutritionists and allied workers in the nutrition field to meet even present needs. An improvement in the quality of professional training in the science of nutrition, and the subjects related to it, is necessary to use most effectively the current knowledge of nutrition.

4. *Education of the public.*—The general goal of nutrition education is the establishment of good food habits in every individual, by

bringing him the knowledge necessary to select a good diet and helping him understand the relationship between an adequate diet and good health. Education in nutrition is being carried out to some extent in Government agencies concerned with health and welfare needs. There is a plethora of nutrition literature and radio publicity. Some of it is authentic and some highly colored by advertising. This publicity should be evaluated for the benefit of the consuming public.

Following is a brief summary of the work already being carried on in the Federal Government agencies whose programs include one aspect or another of nutrition and in which a nutrition program is consistent with its basic purpose. These summary statements are designed primarily to identify the type of program and the organizations or parts of organizations which exist to administer or further it.

Research in Nutrition

BUREAU OF HUMAN NUTRITION AND HOME ECONOMICS

Human nutrition was first recognized as a Government function when in 1894 Congress appropriated $10,000 "to enable the Secretary of Agriculture to investigate and report upon the nutritive value of the various articles and commodities used for human food, with special suggestions of full, wholesome, and edible rations, less wasteful and more economical than those in common use. . . ." Thus began the research work of the Bureau of Human Nutrition and Home Economics. Since 1943 this Bureau of Human Nutrition and Home Economics has been an integral part of the Agricultural Research Administration of the Department of Agriculture.

An appropriation of $407,000 (one-half the total appropriation for the Bureau of Nutrition and Home Economics) is currently available for research in human nutrition. This amount sinks into insignificance in comparison with the total research appropriation in the Agricultural Research Administration of about $40,000,000.

Current research in this Bureau comprises studies into the inherent nutritive values of food and how these are affected by soil, production practices, processing, and other handling, including home food preparation; the food and nutritional requirements of people; the levels of consumption of various commodities by different population groups; what affects these levels; and how consumption compares with requirements. Much that is learned about nutrition of other animals also has an implication for human beings. Consequently, the research under way in the laboratories of the Department of Agriculture and of the State experiment stations on nutrition of man and other animals is continuing to contribute greatly to building the science of nutrition.

PUBLIC HEALTH SERVICE

Some research in experimental nutrition has for many years been conducted as a part of the research program of the Division of Physiology of the National Institute of Health.

In 1946, at the request of the Conference of State and Territorial Health Officers, a section on nutrition was organized in the State Relations Division of the Bureau of State Services to assist the State health departments in developing demonstration nutrition programs which would implement the basic research activities conducted in the NIH. The present program of this section is conducting field studies on the prevalence of nutritional deficiency diseases from medical and public health standpoints and testing and developing remedial and preventive measures of practical value to local and State public health organizations. Under the chief of this section there is a medical officer in charge of demonstrations, a budgeted position for a chief nutritionist, and a consulting nutritionist. Four field demonstration units have been set up to work with official health units usually on a county basis, and to cooperate with other agencies in the community such as schools, agricultural agents, universities, etc.

In general, the staff of a nutrition field unit consists of a medical officer in charge, a public health nurse, a nutritionist, a biochemist, a laboratory technician, and a clerk.

The central office of the Nutrition Section, in addition to its functions of general supervision and coordination of the field units, is developing a program of aid and consultation to State health departments and other agencies interested in nutrition.

FISH AND WILDLIFE SERVICE

The Division of Commercial Fisheries maintains extensive laboratories for research in vitamins A and D. Experimental studies are done in these laboratories to determine the nutritive value of fishery products and the effect of storage, freezing, processing, cooking, and other handling methods on the vitamin content.

BUREAU OF LABOR STATISTICS

Investigational studies are made by this Bureau on prices and the cost of living. Studies are also made of consumer income and expenditure. The objective of these studies is to provide data on the relative importance of the individual commodities and services purchased by families of wage earners and clerical workers. This type of study provides data on the proportions of families in the country whose purchases of consumer goods determine American standards of well-being.

Conversely, it points out the danger spots in the country's total consumption pattern, one of which is the proportion of families who do not have adequate diets.

Professional Training for Nutrition

The most effective use of the current knowledge of nutrition in a national health program is contingent upon an improvement in the quality and quantity of professional training in the science of nutrition and the subjects related to it. Such an improvement will also help to advance the research which aims to clarify the relation of food and nutrition to health and to disease. No health or research program, however well-conceived and organized, can succeed without adequate trained personnel to supply leadership. Nutrition or the science of food in its relation to health is a comparatively new field. Up to now the investigator in the laboratory and the health worker with his knowledge of human needs have been far apart. The investigator is responsible for getting information, the health worker for interpreting it. The distance between them can be bridged by bringing the results of investigation to the health worker by means of a thorough professional training. Such training is needed for the following personnel: Undergraduate and graduate students in the basic sciences; medical undergraduates and graduates (hospital, house officers, and practicing physicians); dental undergradutes and graduates; health officers; nutritionists; dieticians; nurses; health educators; social workers; and teachers. At present, the land-grant colleges and universities are the chief groups training leaders in nutrition and home economics. A few private universities such as Columbia, Chicago, Johns Hopkins, Yale, and Harvard are also outstanding.

Educational and Leadership Programs

Department of Agriculture Nutrition Program

Early in 1943, responsibility for interdepartmental nutritional program coordination was transferred from the wartime National Nutrition Division set up by Executive Order No. 8890 to the War Foods Administration in line with its general responsibility for the war food program. The Nutrition Division then became the WFA Nutrition Program Branch, now a part of the Food Distribution Program Branch of the Production and Marketing Administration. The function of the Nutrition Program Branch derives from pertinent terms of Executive Order 8890 as follows: "Makes available to States and localities upon request the service of specialists in . . . nutrition . . . activities to assist in the planning and execution of local and state programs." Representatives of 20 agencies interested in food and nutrition comprise an interdepartmental Nutrition Coordinating Committee, which antedates the Program Planning Branch but is closely related to it. The objective of this committee is to achieve long-range objectives in raising nutrition levels ˅throughout the country. It has attempted to maintain contact with State and local nutrition committees through the designation of a field worker in one of the member agencies as a liaison officer. During the war trained nutritionists were assigned by the Federal Government to act as secretaries for many State nutrition committees, directly under the supervision of the State committee chairman.

At the end of the war these Federal nutritionists were withdrawn. However, through the wartime impetus given to these State and local committees, 40 State committees are now in operation and about one-half of them function actively. Several employ nutritionists as State officers. Otherwise, these activities are carried on by State or local committees under local professional leadership. Many of these State committees, such as in West Virginia, under local professional leadership, are developing indigenous programs suited to their own needs. The North Carolina Nutrition Committee, organized in 1940, has a well developed program.

The increase in the number of trained nutritionists in State agency programs and on regional staffs that supervise State programs (see the extension of the nutrition programs under Children's Bureau), the assistance given to these State committees by members of the Interdepartmental Nutrition Coordinating Committee, the Federal nutrition program office, nutritionist of the Agricultural Extension Service, as well as strong leadership in individual States are factors which have made these State and local nutrition committees active forces for nutrition education throughout the country.

OFFICE OF EDUCATION

1. The Office of Education cooperates with the State departments of education and other educational agencies and organizations in the promotion of nutrition education as an integral part of the public school program.

2. The Division of Vocational Education operates through field agents and consultants working chiefly through State departments of education and teacher training institutions on the various problems relating to nutrition education.

3. The Home Economic Education assists through State departments of education in the development of nutrition education as part

of: (*a*) The total home making education program and (*b*) the home economics teachers' contribution to school-wide nutrition education programs.

4. Agricultural education assistance in relating the problems in production and distribution of agricultural products to human nutrition through all the available educational avenues.

5. Distributive education emphasizes nutrition education in its training program for food service workers and for store workers who need better nutritional practice on their job.

CHILDREN'S BUREAU

The nutrition unit of two members is attached to the Health Service Division of the Children's Bureau to frame the policies of the Division in relation to maternal and child nutrition and a nutrition program for crippled children. These staff nutritionists, through regional nutrition consultants, assist the nutritionists in the child health service divisions of State and local departments of health and in agencies for crippled children to relate a nutrition program to the other health services for children through maternal and well-baby clinics, institutions, hospitals, health programs for families, etc. The nutritionists in the State departments of health cooperate with other State and local agencies, organizations, and committees interested in developing good health through nutrition. The growth of the nutrition service in State and local health departments is impressive. When the Health Service Division of the Children's Bureau was organized in 1935, there were 9 nutritionists in 3 State or local health departments. In December 1947 there were 170 budgeted nutrition positions in 50 State and local Territorial health departments, most of whom were in the child-health services of those departments.

AGRICULTURAL EXTENSION SERVICE

Educational work in foods and nutrition has, from the beginning of this service, held an important place in the educational programs of the Extension Service. State specialists in nutrition and extension nutritionists are responsible for the nutrition work of the county home-demonstration Agents who assist individual farm families and organize the nutritions programs in home-demonstration clubs, participate in the school-lunch and food-conservation programs, nutrition clinics, and in other methods of demonstration. The American Red Cross, a quasi-governmental agency, as part of its service conducts classes and demonstrations in nutrition, prepares manuals for the use of chapter nutrition committees for basic teaching outlines and other aids for instructors; general informational and promotional materials, mostly news letters and bulletins to chapter nutrition committees, directors and authorized instructors.

Proposals for Nutrition Activities

1. *Obtaining the necessary data for the formulation of national nurition policies and the planning of programs.*—This would include compilation and evaluation of information from nongovernmental sources as well as stimulation and carrying on of original research. Complete and impartial information in a form to be understood by representatives of the public without intensive scientific training would be available to the legislative arm of the Government. Data in technical form would be used by agencies concerned with health, welfare, education, and agriculture.

2. *Planning and assisting with programs directed toward attainment of optimal nutritional status for the people of the country.*—These would include educational and service programs through which nutritional knowledge would be made to function in the everyday living of the people; and such agricultural programs for the production and adequate distribution of foods essential to health as shall make them available to all families of the Nation within their purchasing power. The Federal Government would support and encourage activities undertaken by State and local governments and nongovernmental agencies. It would also assume immediate responsibility for certain activities which could not otherwise be dealt with efficiently. For example, measures for safeguarding the nutritional status of migrants.

3. *Cooperation in intergovernmental efforts to free the world from the age-long burden of hunger and undernutrition.*—This would include working through such specialized agencies of the United Nations as the Food and Agriculture Organization, World Health Organization, UNESCO, and the International Children's Emergency Fund.

BASIC REQUIREMENTS

For carrying out these policies it would be necessary to have:

1. *Research, service, and educational programs.*—Efforts to improve nutrition must be an integral part of agricultural, health, welfare, and educational programs of the Government and nonofficial agencies and organizations. Each of the agencies working in these fields should have adequately staffed nutrition units to see that the nutritional aspects of the program is dealt with efficiently. This is the philosophy underlying the wide distribution of nutrition personnel through Federal agencies at the present time.

One of the major functions of each of the governmental agencies employing nutrition workers would be to carry out its objectives in cooperation with nongovernmental organizations concerned with nutrition. For this purpose, any agency, within the broad policies of the national nutrition program, would be free to work independently with outside groups in the field of its special interest. For example, the agency or agencies concerned with the administration of school-lunch programs would carry on detailed conferences with manufacturers of equipment for school kitchens. The agency or agencies concerned with public health would work with professional organizations setting standard for workers in this field and with the educational institutions providing courses of instruction meeting these standards.

Joint planning would be needed for the satisfactory execution of certain overlapping activities of Federal agencies in the nutrition field. For example, research on the relation of soil to the vigor and nutritive content of plant and animal products grown in a given area and to the nutritional status of the human beings subsisting on these products would require cooperation between agricultural and health agencies. It would be expected that these agencies would enter into such agreements as are necessary without involving agencies not immediately concerned with this program.

In summary, much of the nutritive work of the Federal Government would be carried out by the respective agencies in the broad fields to which nutrition makes a contribution. Certain activities would call for joint planning and cooperation between two or more governmental agencies or between a single Federal agency and a nongovernmental organization.

2. *Coordination of service, and education programs.*—The Federal agencies that carry on educational and service programs in fields related to nutrition have already discovered that they have interlocking interests that call for clearance and coordination. The so-called "Nutrition Planning Committee" provides a partially satisfactory answer to this need in that it gives an opportunity for the agencies carrying on field programs to meet regularly and to exchange information on current and proposed activities at the Federal and State levels. The principal handicaps to the effective functioning of this committee in the limited scope that it has set for itself are: (*a*) The lack of complete independence related to the fact that nutrition programs which provide the secretariat for the committee are directed at least nominally by the director of one of the member agencies of the Committee; and (*b*) the lack of technical training on the part of any member of the secretariat. Even so a coordinating body of this nature has demonstrated sufficient usefulness to warrant recommendation of its continuation, and placement in an administrative setting that would facilitate well-balanced handling of the interests of the member agencies.

Since most of the Federal agencies carry on most of their educational and service programs in nutrition through grants-in-aid to State agencies, they recognize the need for encouraging coordination at the State level through State nutrition committees, which are active in some States and exist in most. The Nutrition Planning Committee has attempted to maintain contact with these State committees through the designation of a field worker in one of the member agencies as a liaison officer. Although shortages in field staff and in travel funds have interfered with the smooth operation of this plan, it seems to have potentialities that justify its further development. On one hand, field workers of Federal agencies who are confronted with the total nutrition activities and problems in the State to whose committee they serve as a liaison officer see their own program in true perspective and bring back to Washington the breadth of understanding that makes for true Federal cooperation. On the other hand, State agencies have been impressed favorably by this concrete evidence of harmonious working relationships among their Federal counterparts.

3. *Joint action at the policy-making level.*—It is at the level where planning, standard-setting, and the formulation of policies are carried on that the nutrition interests of the country receive least adequate consideration. Only in the research field, where the Food and Nutrition Board of the National Research Council has provided a meeting place for national leaders in nutrition and related sciences, has a considerable measure of success along this line been achieved. The effectiveness of the Food and Nutrition Board has been hampered by the precariousness of its financial backing, entirely from nongovernmental sources. Moreover, in the absence of a similar organization of those correspondingly expert in aspects of nutrition work other than research, the Food and Nutrition Board has diverted some of its energies to matters on which it cannot speak with the full authority desired.

The creation of a National Nutrition Council has long been under consideration and has been recommended most recently by the Nutrition Section of the National Health Assembly in May of this year. It is assumed that such a body would provide not only for coordination of existing nutrition endeavors of all kinds but would also give governmental and nongovernmental bodies an opportunity to consider jointly the total national needs together with our international obligations and to plan on the best way to deal with specific problems. Such a body could present the importance of an adequate supply of expertly trained workers in the various fields of nutrition and the desirability of making explicit provision for such workers in any program of Federal aid for scientific training. Within the National Nutrition Council, there would be room for such bodies as the Food and Nutrition Board and for a parallel group of specialists in the application of nutrition knowledge to the national welfare. There would be a place for the committee that would realize the potentialities of the present Nutrition Planning Committee in coordinating the field services in nutrition of the various operating agencies; there would also be arrangements for joint planning by the policy-making officials of these same agencies.

A nutrition council would function most effectively set up as a part or section of the Health Council which is suggested in these recommendations. Distinguished specialists in nutrition, both in government service and in private organizations have had wide experience in guiding the development of interagency nutrition committees. They know both the resources and the problems inherent in setting up a broad national program. Among the group that should be called upon for guidance in policy making and program planning are such specialists in government services as Dr. Martha Eliot, representing the Children's Bureau; Dr. W. H. Debrill, Medical Director, Public Health Service; Dr. Hazel K. Steibeling, Bureau of Human Nutrition and Home Economics, and Dr. M. L. Wilson, Chief, Nutrition Programs, Production and Marketing Administration, both of the Department of Agriculture.

Also, good nutrition practices are of sufficient importance in carrying out many public-health programs, such as communicable disease control, mental health, industrial hygiene, institutional and hospital programs, health services to government workers, etc., to give division status in the Public Health Service to the nutrition program.

INDUSTRIAL HYGIENE PROGRAMS

Industrial development in the United States antedated by many years Federal participation in industrial problems. The introduction of the textile industry early in the last century resulted in the exploitation of child labor. Pennsylvania passed the first child labor law in 1848. Massachusetts adopted mandatory laws in 1877 for fire protection in factories and safeguards for industrial machinery. New York passed its first laws in 1886 to regulate industrial employment of women and children. By the turn of the century other States had followed these pioneering industrial regulations. Massachusetts' State Department of Health in 1905 was first to develop an industrial hygiene program which was later transferred to the State department of labor.

A forward step was taken in 1910 when New York State adopted a workmen's compensation act. During the next 10 years practically every State with industrial problems had adopted some form of workers' compensation. There is, however, little uniformity, State by State, in their provisions. Occupational diseases are recognized by law in almost two-thirds of the States and in the Federal Compensation Act.

The large insurance companies, particularly those that deal in industrial group insurance, have done more to improve the health of the industrial worker than any other agency, government or otherwise. Industry has an incentive to protect the worker by suitable means in order to lower its insurance premiums.

Many large industrial plants have developed comprehensive health programs for their workers. These may include among other services complete medical examinations, aid in the correction of remedial defects, clinic services, and a health education program dealing not only with the health and accident hazards of the particular industry but also information on individual hygiene and the promotion of community health, recreation, etc. They have also developed modern engineering and safety devices.

However, the smaller industries, with less than 250 employees, obviously have difficulties in providing comprehensive industrial hygiene and safety programs.

These small plants are generally in need of guidance from the Federal Government's industrial hygiene programs. Investigation has shown that at least 70 percent and perhaps as much as 85 percent of the annual total of work-connected injuries and deaths throughout the country come from small establishments and undertakings that generally do not participate in any phase of the organized safety movement. This multitude of plants constitute the national occupational accident problem today.[2]

Industrial workers are subjected to two special types of hazards. First, occupational diseases or diseases arising out of or in the course of a particular occupation. These occupational diseases account for about 2 percent of the total disabilities from industrial causes. Secondly, disabling injuries, of which nearly 11 million are estimated to occur annually in American industries. Industries spent 5 billion dollars during 1947 because of industrial accidents.[3]

In recognition of these two major types of industrial hazards, both State and Federal legislation for the protection of industrial workers has been enacted under the broad title of "Health and Safety" or "Health and Welfare." While "safety" may be technically considered only an indirect health function, to the industrial worker a "health and safety program" represents his protection from both occupational diseases and disabling incidents which equally incapacitate him for gainful employment in the industrial field. After all, the impetus for the inclusion of so-called health and safety programs as government functions has come primarily from workers themselves and to a much lesser degree from industry. More recently, as a result of the interest and research in occupational diseases by medical and health agencies, there has emerged a distinct public health category commonly referred to as "Industrial Hygiene and Sanitation."

Patterns Within the Government

The Federal Government is concerned with the administration of industrial hygiene on three broad fronts and "under three different patterns of government administration." (See table V, page 87.)

Department of Labor.—The act of March 4, 1913 (C–14; 1–7 Stat. 736) empowers the Department of Labor to encourage and assist individual States to develop and promote desirable labor standards in industrial practices, labor legislation, and labor law administration.

The Bureau of Labor Standards, with the cooperation of the Women's Bureau and the Bureau of Labor Statistics, performs these functions with a small professional staff in the Federal Bureau, but without recourse to a grant-in-aid program to assist State labor departments in developing and promoting labor standards and labor legislation.

---

[2] Statistics, Department of Labor (1947), p. 74.
[3] Statistics, Department of Labor.

TABLE V.—*Patterns of industrial hygiene programs in Federal Government*

As developed in—	Function by law or regulation	Professional and administrative staff	Cost of administrative program, 1947-48	Grants-in-aid to States	Administrative relationship to State programs	State industrial hygiene program		Relationship to industry	Administrative cooperation between Federal agencies
						Legal authority	Activities		
Department of labor: Bureau of labor standards.	Act of Mar. 4, 1913, C.141.1-37, Stat.736.—"To foster, promote and develop the welfare of wage earners. To promote their working conditions."	25 professional staff to service State departments of labor directly. To promote uniformity in labor legislation and labor law administration, etc.	$249,486	None	Service agency to State departments of labor. Service only.	Under State laws which vary widely in their powers to give safety protection to industrial workers.	To enter, inspect, industrial plants for safety of operation with enforcement and regulatory powers.	Directly through State departments of labor. Indirectly in cooperation with State departments of labor to industry.	Need for clarification of functions of these two agencies on State level, especially in relation to enforcement and regulatory powers.
Federal security agency: Public Health Service: Division of industrial hygiene.	Under general Provisons Pub. Health Law 410, 78th Cong., sec. 314.—Supervises industrial hygiene phases of total Federal-State cooperative program.	32 PHS officers cooperate with State divisions through professional staff attached to regional FSA offices.	$658,557	Approximates $1,000,000 annually for development of State programs; research demonstration and training.	Since 1935 supervised development of State divisions of industrial hygiene with general uniformity of program, implemented by grants-in-aid.	Generally under broad powers of State health laws. 5 State divisions have been responsible for passage of legislation with regulatory powers.	Focus upon reduction of disease incidences among industrial workers.	Directly through State departments of health; directly to industry on special health studies.	
Department of Interior: Bureau of Mines: Division of health and safety.	Organic act, Bureau of Mines 1910. (36 Stat. 369) Coal Mine Inspection Act of 1941 (55 Stat. 177, 30 U.S.C. 4 F.) Power to inspect all mines in relation to health and safety hazards to miners.	36 administrative staff. Operates through 3 headquarters offices, 11 district, and 11 subdistrict offices.	$3,054,990 (research $875,130; administration and others, $2,178,860).	None	None [1]	23 coal mine bureaus; 21 bureaus otherwise with regulatory powers for health and safety protection. Legal powers differ widely in individual States.	In general, to enter and inspect all mines in relation to health and safety hazards with enforcement powers. In general, no merit system for employment of mine inspectors.	Directly to industry and industrial workers.	No administrative co-operation. This program impinges on mining industry only.
						Federal-State inspection powers.		Duplicated not coordinated.	

[1] Public Law 47, 77th Cong., sec. 7. "In order to promote sound and effective coordination * * * bureaus shall cooperate with mine and safety inspectors or safety agencies of the several States and Territories * * * and may utilize service of such agencies in connection with the administration of the act."

Department of Interior, Bureau of Mines, Division of Health and Safety.—Under the organic act of the Bureau of Mines, 1910 (36 Stat. 369), and subsequent acts as the Coal Mine Inspection Act of 1941 (55 Stat. 177, 30 U. S. C. 4 F.) the Bureau of Mines, Department of Interior, is charged with the inspection and investigation of health and safety hazards in mines, the products of which are produced for and are transported in interstate commerce. The Division of Health and Safety inspects mining operations directly in the States and Territories, not through Federal-State cooperation.

Public Health Service, Bureau of State Services, Industrial Hygiene Division.—Under the general health provisions of title 6 of the Social Security Act of 1935, the Industrial Hygiene Division of the Public Health Service has fostered and aided industrial hygiene divisions in State departments of health.

DEPARTMENT OF LABOR

Three bureaus in the Department of Labor cooperate in the responsibility for the health and safety of industrial workers as a part of the basic purpose of the Department "to foster, promote, and develop the welfare of the wage earners of the United States and to improve their working conditions . . ."[4] In all industrial countries without exception supervision of the safety and health of workers in manufacturing and mechanical establishments is the responsibility of the agency set up to promote the welfare of wage earners. The pattern in the United States closely follows the world pattern. The earliest legal provisions, enacted for the protection of industrial workers, were in the realm of safety protection. In the highly industrialized States, Labor Departments were in operation before the turn of the century. Their creation covers a span of about 90 years. These departments were created under different titles such as Industrial Relations Board, Department of Labor and Industry, etc.

Today the health and safety protection afforded industrial workers differs widely State by State. In the highly industrial States, the laws creating the departments of labor were usually written with broad powers under which programs affecting the health, safety, and welfare of industrial workers could be expanded to meet expanding needs. In other States, especially those primarily agricultural in character, very limited powers were written into the labor legislation. As these States are becoming more highly industrialized they are seeking the assistance of the Bureau of Labor Standards to help them to develop more adequate legislation.

In order to assist these State departments of labor at the various levels of their development and with the particular legal, financial,

---

[4] Act of March 4, 1918, 37 Stat. 736.

and other problems of operation, the United States Department of Labor uses the resources of three of its bureaus.

Bureau of Labor Statistics.—This Bureau makes investigations and studies in the broad field of labor of which the health phases of industry constitute only a part. However, in the health and safety areas the Bureau conducts annual and quarterly surveys, on work injuries in large number, of manufacturing industries, and publishes quarterly and annual injury rates for all injuries covered. National estimates are prepared annually on all disabling work injuries, by the extent of disabling for major groups of industrial activity. Special studies are made from time to time in industries with high accident rates to determine accident causes. The purpose of such studies is to stimulate accident prevention in these industries. Technical services are extended to individual State labor departments to assist them in developing better accident statistics.

The Bureau also conducts studies of the effects of various types of working conditions on accidents, workers' health, etc., and problems in the field of workmen's compensation. It frequently serves as medium for publishing studies of industrial diseases and hygiene.[5]

Bureau of Labor Standards.—The Bureau of Labor Standards, established by departmental order in 1934, is a service agency to State labor departments, to State officials, and to labor, employers, and civic groups interested in the improvement of working conditions. The Federal Bureau is authorized to develop desirable labor standards in industrial practice, labor legislation, and labor-law administration.

The Bureau is charged with coordination of Federal and State activities relating to safety and health legislation for purpose of reducing duplication of inspection and providing for most effective use of Federal and State staffs.

The Bureau is responsible for assistance to States in developing and promoting standards of safety and heath, providing technical advice and service on safety and health to State labor departments, trade unions, etc. It conducts safety training programs; assists in preparation of State industrial safety codes; provides upon request technical assistance to individual State labor departments in adapting approved standards of legislation and administration; prepares technical articles and bulletins on all phases of labor legislation and administration of labor laws and populr publications.

As a service agency to State labor departments, the Bureau of Labor Standards acts as a clearing house for safety and health information. It makes use of the research, studies, and standards developed by the Bureau of Labor Statistics. It assists States to make the best use of their own resources and to develop indigenous

---

[5] U. S. Government Manual, p. 329.

health and safety programs modeled on the best health and safety practices but adapted to the particular labor situation in each State.

The Bureau of Labor Standards operates at the present time with a professional staff of about 20 who are used both in the Washington office and as field consultants. There is neither sufficient headquarters staff nor budget to place professional staff in the regional offices of the Department of Labor. The Bureau of Labor Standards has no appropriation to use for grants-in-aid to the States.

Appropriations available for current fiscal year 1948 are as follows:

	Positions	Net amount
Appropriations available	83	$343, 900
Less Union Registration Division	38	93, 486
Estimate	45	$249, 486

Professional staff respond to calls from State labor departments, from industry, etc.

Women's Bureau.—The protection of women in industry was first undertaken by the Department of Labor during the First World War as a war emergency measure. Out of the continuing need for such services the Women's Bureau was created at the end of the war. It formulates standards and policies concerning the relation of conditions of work for women to their health. It analyses individual State laws regarding health facilities for women. It gives field services to State and to industry on the administration of the minimum-wage laws, the enforcement of safety and health laws for women, and advises States on labor legislation and health for women in industrial plants. Its pattern of service for women in industry follows the general pattern of Federal-State relationships developed by the Bureau of Labor Standards for industry in general.

The Protection of Children in Industry

In 1917 the Children's Bureau was designated as the enforcing agency for the act of Congress prohibiting shipment of goods in interstate commerce from establishments employing children contrary to the standards of the act. The Child Labor Division of the Children's Bureau organized in May 1937 did preparatory work until this act went into effect and enforced the law during the 9 months of its operation. In 1938 the bureau was given responsibility for the enforcement of the child labor provisions of the Fair Labor Standards Act. This function was carried out on a broad program of Federal-State relations with optimum standards for the health and welfare of children and with efficiency of operation.

Under Administrative Order 15, effective July 16, 1946, this function was delegated to the Bureau of Labor Standards. In 1948, by administrative order, the function was transferred to the Fair Labor Practice

Division. Because of staff inadequacies in this division, this function is at present practically dissipated, although in the opinion of individuals and groups who have closely followed the mounting abuses in child practices, the need for a strong functioning of the child labor provisions is as acute as it has ever been.

Public Health Service, Bureau of State Services, Industrial Hygiene Division

The Workmen's Compensation Law, passed in 1910 in New York State and extended during the next 10 years to practically every other State, highlighted the need for giving assistance to individual industrial plants to combat the disease hazards peculiar to industry. A Division of Industrial Hygiene and Sanitation was, therefore, organized in the Public Health Service in 1912 to meet these needs. The first staff of this division consisted of a field group that dealt directly with industry, since there were only two States at that time with industrial hygiene divisions in their State health departments. The findings of this field staff developed a need for laboratory service in order to analyze contaminated dust, etc. An Industrial Hygiene Laboratory was, therefore, established under the aegis of the National Institute of Health.

Grants-In-Aid to States

As late as 1935, there were still only five industrial hygiene divisions operating in State health departments. Then by the terms of the Social Security Act in 1935, grants-in-aid were allocated to individual States to foster and develop such divisions throughout the country. The war years, with new industrial plants mushrooming everywhere over the United States, gave impetus for this development and brought extra responsibilities to this division and a need for a more adequate professional staff.

The appropriation to the Division of Industrial Hygiene for its grant-in-aid program approximates 1 million dollars annually. In all but three States and in many of the larger cities divisions or bureaus of industrial hygiene have been developed. It has been possible to achieve general uniformity of pattern in these divisions since they have all been developed over a brief span of years with sufficient funds to implement their programs and unhampered by restrictive legislation, as the State departments of labor have been. Grants-in-aid are allotted to these States on the basis of the population in hazardous industries weighted by the financial index. This method of allocation will probably be changed to a basis of the total industrial population in each State. The present basis seems to the Director of the Division

91

more logical since it does not penalize States with smaller financial resources.

The grants are used for the development of State programs, general field services to States, assistance in health education, and special or supplemental training for recruits to the program or for the present State staff members. The district consultant attached to the Southern States, for instance, has taught industrial hygiene courses in medical schools and recruited students financed by scholarship funds from the grants-in-aid allocation. The Director of the Division believes that industrial hygiene courses could well be part of the curricula of schools of technology and courses added to the medical schools for the training of physicians to serve in industrial plants.

State departments of industrial hygiene focus upon the reduction of disease incidence among industrial workers. They determine environmental factors conducive to illnesses associated with particular types of employment and recommend measures for control of those elements. These factors constitute the usual industrial hygiene approach to this problem.

Functions of Division

Under the general provisions of Public Health Law 410, Seventy-eighth Congress, section 314, "Grants and Services to States, the Division of Industrial Hygiene," functions are as follows:

This division supervises the industrial hygiene phases of the total Federal-State cooperative health program, with special reference to the control of occupational diseases and the promotion of health among industrial workers. It provides consultant services and technical aid to the States, especially to State industrial hygiene units, as well as to industrial establishments and labor organizations. It sponsors and promotes the establishment and maintenance of industrial hygiene service in State governments.

Surveys of industrial hygiene problems within particular areas or industries; laboratory analysis of substances believed to be hazardous; investigation of occupational disease outbreaks, especially of occupational dermatoses, to determine the causes and to recommend methods for the elimination or control of the hazards; collection, analysis, and publication of occupational morbidity and mortality statistics. The several units of the division deal with, and offer technical assistance in the various elements of an industrial hygiene program, as: medical, engineering, and chemical control of hazards; industrial dentistry and nursing; morbidity records and reports.

At the present time a laboratory within the division concerns itself with laboratory analyses, such as examinations of dust, air, etc., which are part and parcel of the operation of the industrial hygiene program. There still remains in the National Institute of Health a laboratory of physical biology which undertakes pure research in fields which are allied to the problems of industrial hygiene.

Through the Industrial Health Information Service, attached

directly to the office of the Director, it prepares and disseminates industrial health information especially for workers in specific industries.

The Industrial Hygiene Division maintains in the 10 district offices of the Federal Security Agency sanitary engineers who make program audits for the industrial hygiene divisions of State health departments on the basis of its grant-in-aid allocations. Through the professional regional staffs, arrangements are made for the Federal professional and technical staff to give service to State divisions as well as to private industrial plants.

Various industries request the services of the professional staff of the Division to assist them in ferreting out the causes of special occupational disease or hazard. Teams of professional workers are, therefore, loaned to the industry. Trailer trucks are available for such field studies; one for dental services; one as a field laboratory. Professional staff members of the State divisions of industrial hygiene concerned, work directly with these Federal teams. Such studies often result in a solution of problems hitherto untouched in the field of industrial hygiene.

Federal Staff

Thirty-two public health surgeons, engineers, sanitarians, and nurses are assigned to this Division from the Office of the Surgeon General. Their staff of experts operate through the regional offices directly to State divisions of industrial hygiene.

Bureau of Mines, Health and Safety Division

The special factors that were most effective in calling attention to the advisability of action by the Federal Government for a Bureau of Mines were disasters in coal mines and a growing realization of the waste of both life and resources in the varied mining and metallurgical interests of the country. As a result, Congress passed the Organic Act of the Bureau of Mines, May 16, 1910 (36 Stat. 369). One of its main provisions is the following:

That it shall be the province of said bureau and its director, under the direction of the Secretary of the Interior, to make diligent investigation of the methods of mining, especially in relation to the safety of miners, and the appliances best adapted to prevent accidents, the possible improvement of conditions under which mining operations are carried on, the treatment of ores and other mineral substance, the use of explosives and electricity, the prevention of accidents, and other inquiries and technologic investigations pertinent to said industries, and from time to time make such public reports of the work, investigations, and information obtained as the Secretary of said department may direct, with the recommendations of such bureau.

According to this provision there was set up in the Department of the Interior, Bureau of Mines, a Division of Health and Safety to carry out the health and safety functions of the act.

Operations

The office of the divisional headquarters in Washington coordinates and directs the operations of the three branches constituting the Health and Safety Division.

The total staff of the operating division comprises 500 persons (engineers, coal mine inspectors, chemists, physicists, safety instructors, clerk, etc.), working in or out of 22 offices or laboratories in 18 States and Alaska, and functioning to some extent in every State and in Alaska.

This staff operates through three branches, as follows:

Health Branch.—Headquarters, Pittsburgh, Pa. This branch operates through a laboratory doing fundamental research on amount and composition of dust, determination of toxic and explosive gases encountered in mining, to prevent poisoning, occupational diseases and explosions; the development of respiratory protective devices, etc. Samples of dust, etc., are routinely sent by field inspectors to this laboratory for examination, if they cannot be made in the field by subdistrict engineers.

Safety Branch.—Promotes safety in the mineral industry by educational methods; conducts engineering investigations on which recommendations of Bureau are based; gives instructions in first aid, etc.; assists in rescue work; tests electrical equipment, etc.

Coal Mine Inspection Branch.—Operates under the Coal Mine Inspection Act of 1941 (55 Stat. 177, 30 U. S. C. 4f) which authorizes and empowers the Bureau to make, or cause to be made, inspections and investigations of certain types of coal mines in the States, in order to reduce accidents and ill health among employees.

The Safety and Coal Mine Inspection Branches operate directly to the mining industry through 11 district headquarters with supervising engineers in charge and 11 subdistrict headquarters with engineers in charge. At present, about 200 inspectors work under the immediate direction of the engineers in charge of the subdistrict offices.

The act (sec. 9) requires only "basic qualification of 5 years' practical experience in the mining of coal" for inspectors. There are no educational requirements. More efficient service would be secured if inspectors were chosen on the basis of a merit system or civil service.

Inspection of mines.—The Coal Mine Inspection Act gives power of entry to and inspection of coal mines. It includes no regulatory powers. Miners themselves want such powers exercised by the Federal

Government; operators do not. In the neighborhood of 5,000 inspections are made yearly.

About 10,000 coal mines are under the inspectional jurisdiction of the Coal Mine Inspection Branch. Two thousand five hundred mines employ more than 25 men each. The others, in the neighborhood of 7,500, are small mines which employ less than 25 men, produce only about 5 percent of coal mined, but have a high percent of fatalities and accidents. These small mines need much more service than the present number of inspectors have time to give to them.

The Director of the Bureau believes that mining accidents and fatalities could be decreased with a larger staff of Federal inspectors. A bill is before Congress for increased appropriation for this staff.

Mine safety committees.—Under bituminous coal wage agreement of 1947: "At each mine there shall be a mine safety committee selected by local union, to inspect any mine development or equipment, to recommend to manager dangerous conditions, etc." These committees are trained by subdistrict inspectors.

Publicity and Educational Work

The Bureau has the power to compile, analyze, and publish the inspectional reports and make such recommendations as will improve safety and health of miners, and to prepare and disseminate reports, studies, statistics, and other educational material that will advance safety, prevent accidents and disease.

The headquarters office in Washington maintains a complete file of all inspectional reports, including recommendations. Copies are routinely sent to owners, superintendents, State bureaus of mines, national and local unions, etc. When violations of the safety code are indicated, special letters are written to owners. This very careful follow-up has been developed because the basic act (36 Stat. 369) gives no regulatory powers to the Bureau but does give it power to issue reports with recommendation. In many instances recommendations have been complied with.

Reports of inspectors, under this category, are prepared for newspaper release in local papers, etc., by the Information Service in the Bureau of Mines.

Continuous educational material in regard to safety, accident prevention, mine rescue, first aid is being prepared by the division. This includes a series of pamphlets, on both coal and metal mine accident prevention, which are used as textbooks for classes of officials in accident prevention, and to serve as general reference material.

Special handbooks have been prepared for the use of miners, such as The Coal Miners' Safety Manual and a Manual of Frst-Aid In-

95

struction. Thousands of mine workers and officials are thus trained yearly in first aid and mine safety.

A national bituminous wage agreement was executed on May 29, 1946, at the White House in Washington. This agreement, made between the Federal Government as administrator of the coal mines and the United Mine Workers of America, provides for a mine safety program including the development of a Federal mine safety code, a mine safety committee, coverage of employees with the protection of workmen's compensation and occupational disease laws, a health and welfare program including a medical and hospital fund and various welfare activities.

This code includes all of the known features and requirements of safe operations of mines based on the experience and observation of years. It is significant that it was continued in effect as part of the new contract for 1948 between the operators and the union.

Housing and Sanitary Conditions

In 1946 a survey and study was made for the Secretary of the Interior, by a medical survey group of the Navy, of the sanitary and housing conditions in the bituminous coal mining areas. The report of this survey and recommendations were published in 1947. In view of this report and the housing conditions surrounding many miners and their families which are not conducive to health and efficiency, the question might be raised as to whether our present industrial hygiene programs really protect men from industrial hazards and occupational diseases. These programs are concerned only with "absence of disease and infirmity;" they do not take into account the newer concept of health that it is a "state of complete physical, mental, and social well-being, and not just an absence of disease and infirmity." Under this concept some recognition might be given to the part that home surroundings, physical and mental conditions, nutrition, the fear of strikes and lay-offs play in the susceptibility to accidents and disease. The most modern safety devices cannot save a worker from an industrial accident if he is conditioned to accidents by lack of nourishing food, emotional insecurity, or the results of a contaminated water supply at home.[6]

---

[6] Sources of information:

Industrial Hygiene in Public Health Service

Toby, National Government and Public Health.
Smillie, Public Health Administration.
Public Health Reports: Outline of an Industrial Hygiene Program, supplement No. 171 to Public Health Reports; Distribution of Health Services in the Structure of State Government, chapter VIII, Industrial Health Activities by State Agencies, Reprint No. 2439 from Public Health Reports, vol. 58, No. 2, Jan. 8, 1943; Personal Interview

(Continued)

Budgets for industrial hygiene programs

Year	Department of Labor, Bureau of Labor Standards, over-all administration	Child labor	Public Health Service, States Relation, Industrial Hygiene Division			Department of Interior, Bureau of Mines, Division of Health and Safety		
			Total obligation	Direct operation	State grants	Total obligation	Over-all administration	Research
1940	$290,485		$167,668	$167,668		$656,000		
1947	295,916	$604,830 −308,914	1,658,557	658,557	$1,000,000	3,054,990	$2,178,860	$875,130
1948	249,486		1,628,445	663,779	964,666	3,919,590	2,616,830	1,303,090

Recommendations

The preceding review discloses undesirable overlapping jurisdictions in the field of industrial hygiene. In summary:

The State departments of labor operate under State laws which, in every instance, have given them powers to inspect and to enforce regulations for the control of industrial health hazards in conformity with the State law.

The industrial hygiene divisions in State departments of health have been greatly augmented through grants-in-aid to their State program. Inasmuch as Federal funds become available for this purpose without necessity of excessive State matching, the States, as might be expected, have tended to reduce or to discontinue appropriations to State labor departments for factory inspection and enforcement of industrial health and safety laws.

Under their augmented programs, State industrial hygiene units in State public health departments are now sponsoring legislation in individual States which give them regulatory powers for the control of industrial health and safety in industry. In the seven States where they have succeeded in passing this legislation, there are two sets of

(Note: continued)

with Dr. Townsend, director of Division of Industrial Hygiene and Sanitation, June 21, 1948, plus information on his functional and staffing charts.

Department of Labor

Material submitted by Bureau of Labor Standards, May 14, 1948.
Bureau of Labor Statistics, Series No. R–775, reports.
National Safety Council.
Annual Report, Secretary of Labor, 1947, p. 74.
Personal Interviews.

Department of Interior, Bureau of Mines

The material for the report was secured directly from the Health and Safety Division of the Bureau of Mines either (1) compilations of laws sent directly, (2) personal interviews with Mr. J. J. Forbes, Director, Division of Health and Safety; functional charts prepared in his office and educational material submitted.
Also Annual Report for 1947, Secretary of the Interior.
Medical Survey of Bituminous Coal Industry, Department of Interior, 1947.

inspectors with overlapping jurisdiction giving orders to management for the correction of working conditions in their plants. This problem is discussed in the section on labor.

The solution which has seemed reasonable to the State of California (by informal agreement between directors of industrial relations and public health), the Bureau of the Budget, and Bureau of Labor Standards would be to establish, on the Federal level, a functional division between safety problems, including accident prevention, and health problems, including the control of occupational diseases. States should be encouraged to unify their industrial health codes to avoid conflicts, and, if they wish, to place their inspection service on a unified basis.

It also seems as logical to assist State departments of labor in their training of personnel, enforcement programs, and improved administration of State laws regulating conditions of employment, by a grant program as to assist State health departments through grants in developing an industrial hygiene program.

It is recommended:

1. Use should be made of the powers invested in the Bureau of Mines under Public Law 47, Seventy-seventh Congress, section 7, which states: "In order to promote sound and effective coordination . . . bureaus shall cooperate with mine and safety inspectors or safety agencies of the several States and Territories . . . and may utilize service of such agencies in connection with the administration of the act." It should be invoked in order to avoid duplication of inspection, raise standards of inspection and thereby reduce costs of the total operation.

2. The proper role of the Federal agency should eventually be transformed from one of direct inspection of mine property to one of advice and assistance to State administrating agencies by (a) improving their State mining laws, (b) administering grants to States for training State mine inspectors under adequate merit systems. (It is suggested that in those States in which the mine inspection service is performed under a State administrating agency which also inspects other industries in the State than mining, as for instance the State department of labor, the cooperation of the Federal Bureau of Labor Standards be invoked for assistance in codifying these State laws.)

3. During a transitional period, trial experiments might be conducted by those State bureaus which are nonpolitical, operate under broad persuasive legislation, and a merit system or civil service. The Federal agency might enter into agreements with these States to perform the inspection under Federal supervision.

4. That Federal inspection be continued until Congress provides funds and authority for the proposed change in program.

5. That Federal inspectors be employed under civil service.

6. The trend in public health services is toward the definition of health incorporated in the constitution of World Health Organization: "Health is a state of complete physical, mental and social well-being, and not merely the absence of disease and infirmity."

With its attention on the control of industrial diseases and industrial hazards, industrial hygiene is now primarily operating in the field of ". . . the absence of disease and infirmity."

In the light of our newer medical knowledge, however, there is need for industrial hygiene programs to take into consideration the broader aspects of positive health for industrial workers; and to relate the environmental factors surrounding industrial workers, such as housing, nutrition, community water supplies, etc., to his susceptibility to occupational accidents and diseases.

INTERNATIONAL HEALTH

"Health is a state of complete physical, mental, and social well-being, and not merely the absence of disease and infirmity." Definition of health, incorporated in the constitution of the World Health Organization.

United States Cooperation

For nearly 100 years the world has been moving toward a collaboration between all the nations of the world on an international health front. The dramatic consummation of these international health endeavors came during an International Health Conference in 1946 in New York City, calling on the initiative of the United Nations. On July 22, 1946, a constitution for a World Health Organization was signed by representatives of 61 nations, probably the largest number of nations in the history of mankind ever to agree simultaneously on a set of principles.

Unfortunately, the Congress of the United States had not, up to that time, passed enabling legislation so that the United States could accept charter membership in this organization—in spite of the fact that health forces in these United States have been among the most vigorous proponents of and active participants in international health.

This 1946 International Health Conference appointed an interim commission as a preparatory body only, to continue the former international health organizations and, if necessary, to solve urgent health problems pending the coming into existence of the permanent World Health Organization. Eighteen nations were elected to appoint representatives on the Interim Commission. The pressure of circumstances was such that the Interim Commission became in effect an operating agency.

It has reestablished the epidemiological reporting services of the League of Nations and has revived the technical work of that organization and the Office Internationale d'Hygiene Publique in such fields as vital statistics, the standardization of drugs and biologicals, the fight against important epidemic diseases, the supervision of international quarantine measures, and the adaptation of the sanitary conventions to conform with modern scientific knowledge and to meet new needs. Three World Health Organization health missions are continuing work initiated by UNRRA in China, Greece, and Ethiopia, and medical liaison officers in Italy and Poland are now giving more limited health advisory services. All possible resources were mobilized through the Interim Commission to assist the Egyptian Government in successfully combating a cholera epidemic in the autumn of 1947.

The World Health Organization, to all intents and purposes, formally came into existence as a specialized agency of the United Nations early in 1948 when 21 member nations of the United Nations had ratified the World Health Organization constitution and legislative action by 8 other member nations had been completed. Therefore, the first World Health Assembly was called for on June 24, 1948, in Geneva, Switzerland. Ten days before the assembly met, the President of the United States signed Public Law Numbered 643, enabling the United States to accept membership in World Health Organization.

The World Health Organization is more than an international health agency. It challenges historical precedents in the field of health which have been largely negativistic and defensive. The World Health Organization is a positive, creative force with broad objectives reaching forward to embrace nearly all levels of human activity related to health. Its constitution is truly the Magna Charta of health and constitutes one of the most powerful international instruments designed to help man attain a better standard of living. Its creed proclaims that "the health of all peoples in fundamental to the attainment of peace and security and is dependent upon the fullest cooperation of individuals and States."

The World Health Organization has inherited the half century of experience of the International Office of Public Health of Paris, the Pan-American Sanitary Bureau, and the League of Nations Health Organization—all of them organizations which have won splendid reputations for productive international health work.

Based on the agenda submitted to the World Health Organization by its Interim Commission during these 2 years of study, the World Health Organization during its first assembly gave top priority to a concentration of its efforts on the control of malaria, tuberculosis, venereal diseases, and maternal and child health, with its next priority on nutrition and environmental hygiene. These are not only widely and urgently needed health programs but also programs that lend themselves to international health action.

Shortly before the adjournment of this first World Health Organization assembly, it endorsed the United Nations Appeal for Children Fund and directed "its Director General to . . . discuss common interests of the World Health Organization with the United Nations Appeal for Children Fund." A dramatic result of this decision is the largest mass tuberculosis immunization program ever undertaken—sponsored by the United Nations International Children's

Emergency Fund, the World Health Organization, the Danish Red Cross, and its Scandinavian associates—which calls for the testing of between 40 million and 50 million children in Europe this fall. A state serum institute on research in Copenhagen will be involved in this undertaking. Millions of records will be gathered which, it is predicted, will form the basis of one of the greatest epidemiological studies ever made.

In preparation for the first assembly of World Health Organization, the Interim Commission was confronted by the task of absorbing preexisting international organizations in the health field into this body. In developing this section of the constitution, specific consideration was given to the Pan-American Sanitary Bureau. This pioneer inter-American health agency was formed in 1902. The United States has actively participated in its operation since its inception. The bureau, through the past 44 years, has played such a significant part in the health programs of the American republics that no one desired to destroy it or see it lose its identity. Realizing that regional isolation in health is no longer effective and desiring to expand the scope of the bureau and also utilize its strength for the benefit of all, a special article (No. 54) was unanimously adopted providing for its integration in due course with the World Health Organization. Under this authority, an integrating agreement was so drawn that the bureau may serve as a regional office of World Health Organization without interruption of its work.

UNITED STATES ACTIVITIES

In the health field the United States has many obligations, some having a treaty status, which are the basis for programs of exchange of students between the United States and other countries and for the loan to other countries of scientific and technical personnel. The United States functions directly in the international health field through the Department of State, the Public Health Service, and the Children's Bureau. The operation of the Bureau of Narcotics, Treasury Department, has also public health implications in its control of legal and illicit trade in habit-forming and habit-sustaining drugs. (See section on narcotic drugs.)

Department of State

The department has a Health Branch within the Division of International Labor, Social, and Health. The purpose of this health branch is "to support the interest and the foreign policy of the United States by developing and assuring the adoption and application of appropriate principles in our foreign relations so far as they affect ... health matters, and to promote international cooperation in this field."

The major activity of this branch during the last 2 years has been the United States participation on the Interim Commission for World Health Organization.

The Institute of Inter-American Affairs

The institute was established during the Second World War by Executive Order 9710 of April 10, 1942, and now a part of the Department of State has accomplished much of permanent value. Through cooperative programs with nearly all of the other American republics, the institute has constructed health centers, hospitals, sewage and water plants, and has promoted general sanitation and health improvement. Eighteen Latin-American countries have participated in these cooperative health and sanitation programs. The agreements with 6 countries are still continuing (as of September 1, 1948). To implement its programs the institute has granted a large number of fellowships.

Recent Legislation

The Smith-Mundt Act.—The recent passage of this act by the Eightieth Congress establishes a world-wide exchange of persons program. The potentialities of this act are very great.

The Fulbright Act.—This act passed by the Seventy-ninth Congress is slowly getting under way. A large number of countries owe the United States for surplus property, in some cases quite large sums. Those countries which agree to do so may pay off these debts in local currencies by supporting United States students studying in their universities. It will be possible for some foreign students wishing to study in the United States to receive travel assistance if transportation companies will accept the foreign currencies. Fulbright funds are not subject to annual appropriations and the program is being planned for a period of 20 years.

Foreign Missions

Liberian Mission.—As a war measure, the State Department at the request of the Government of Liberia asked the Public Health Service to send a public health mission to Liberia. This mission, all Negro, is engaged in training Liberian personnel in nursing, sanitary inspection, technical laboratory work, etc., and in building up the Liberian Health Department.

Philippine Mission.—The Public Health Service has also a mission in the Philippines under the Philippine Rehabilitaton Act passed by the Seventy-ninth Congress. Under this act 25 Filipino physicians are now doing postgraduate work in public health methods and administration in this country and some 22 are expected to commence work during 1948.

Greek Mission.—The American Mission for Aid to Greece has a public health division from the Public Health Service. Approximately 15 physicians, engineers, and nurses are in this division. It is anticipated that this division will be continued under the European Cooperation Act passed by the Eightieth Congress.

Nongovernmental Agencies

The earliest endeavors were those of the various church missions and medical missionaries from the United States, today to be found in the most distant and remote areas. Nonmissionary groups with health interests include the American Bureau for Aid to China, the Greek War Relief Association, the Near East Relief, and many others of importance.

Many philanthropic foundations have international interests. The Rockefeller Foundation has engaged in health work in almost all countries of the world in the four decades of its existence. The Kellogg Foundation offers fellowships for Latin-American physicians in certain fields.

Public Health Service

Operations in other countries, in addition to foreign quarantine (see section on foreign quarantine), are conducted in the Public Health Service by:

1. Office of International Health Relations (Greece, Liberia, variout projects in Latin America).

2. Bureau of State Services (Philippines).

3. Office of Vital Statistics (various American countries).

4. National Institute of Health (various countries).

Fellowships in the United States for foreign health workers are being awarded by these three offices within the Public Health Service:

1. Office of International Health Relations.

2. Office of Vital Statistics.

3. National Institute of Health.

Office of International Health Relations.—The Office of International Health Relations was established in the Office of the Surgeon General, Public Health Service, in August 1945.

This office supervises and coordinates all activities of the Service in the international health field. It maintains liaison with agencies in this field; represents the Service in international health conferences;

Public health officers and civil service personnel on duty outside continental United States, through Office of International Health Relations

Missions and active projects	Commissioned officers	Civil service employees
Missions:		
Liberian Mission	14	5
American Mission for Aid to Greece	14	3
Active projects:		
Pan American Sanitary Bureau	6	8
Institute of Inter-American Affairs	1	2
Peru Research Project—Coca Leaves Chewing Habit	1	2

Obligations of the Department of State for international health activities

Item	Appropriations [1]		
	1940	1947	1948
Research: Grants to institutions and individuals:			
Cooperation with American Republics	0	$361,231	$212,605
Institute of Inter-American Affairs	0	5,500,000	[2] 5,800,000
All others, including over-all administrative costs:			
Contributions to international organizations:			
Pan-American Sanitary Bureau	$58,523	63,584	145,397
International Office of Public Health	0	2,553	[3] 5,105
World Health Organization [4]	0	0	0
Gorgas Memorial Laboratory	50,000	50,000	50,000
International Activities: Attendance at meetings	0	5,500	70,000
Cost of United States Representative at ICWHO	0	6,570	7,000
Administrative Costs: Departmental	0	8,689	11,785

[1] Appropriations for international health services of other agencies of the Government are included in the budgets of those agencies.
[2] References:

International Health Affairs

Public Health Service (conferences and material).
Health Branch, International Labor, Social, and Health, State Department (conferences and material).
World Health Organization by C. E. A. Winslow, Carnegie Endowment, March 1948, No. 437.
Congressional Record, August 17, 1948, A 5414.
State Department, Division of Public Liaison, Reports to Organizations on World Health Organization.
[3] Amount appropriated—no payment to be made.
For 1949–1950, $1,950,000.

directs the Public Health Service part of the Department of State's program of international exchange of health personnel and educational material; drafts sanitary conventions and regulations, and health reports required by international agreements; collects and distributes data relating to foreign medical and health institutions; supervises special health missions to foreign countries; and advises the State Department upon request regarding plans, programs, and policies in connection with the World Health Organization. The office advises the Surgeon General on international health matters.

Specifically, the office is now engaged in receiving and in preparing educational programs for a rapidly increasing number of public health workers from foreign countries referred to the Service by local embassies, the Department of State, by other agencies of the Federal Government, by the Interim Commission of the World Health Organization, by the Pan American Sanitary Bureau or by private foundations; preparing replies to requests for information on technical public health matters for the United Nations and certain specialized agencies, as well as for private organizations and citizens; operating a public health mission in Liberia; procuring personnel for and advising the Department of State regarding public health activities of the American Mission for Aid to Greece; arranging for public health representation at official and unofficial international conferences and preparing background material and reports for those in which the Service participates; representing the Surgeon General on a number of interagency committees dealing with international health problems; and collecting data regarding health facilities, personnel, and problems of foreign countries.[7]

Foreign Quarantine

Foreign quarantine in the United States was originally a function of State or municipal authorities. It remained thus from the passing of the first legal enactment in the "Province of Carolina" in 1712 relating to quarantine, until the Federal act of 1879 (21 Stat. L. 5), which created a national board of health "to have charge of interstate and foreign quarantine" for a period of 4 years. Many States had been reluctant to relinquish their quarantine authority to the Federal Government, believing thereby their States' rights were being violated.

Public opinion, however, tended to press for National action to prevent the importation of communicable disease from abroad because of the constant recurrences of yellow-fever epidemics and cholera outbreaks during the years from 1796 to 1866. Shipping interests, too, expressed themselves as greatly discommoded by the varying and sometimes arbitrary quarantine regulations that existed in many ports of the United States of America, operating through the regulations made by individual States.

The Quarantine Act of February 15, 1883 (27 Stat. L. 449), passed 4 years after the Federal Act of 1879, is still in force. It gives authority for all domestic and marine quarantine regulations. (Now Public Health Law 410, Part 8, Secs. 361–69.) This law states that "it shall be unlawful for any merchant ship or other vessel from any foreign port or place to enter any port of the United States except in accordance with the provisions of this act and with such rules and regulations of State and municipal authorities as may be made in pursuance of or consistent with this act." This act neither prohibited States or municipalities from maintaining quarantine stations, nor gave the Marine Hospital Service general powers to establish stations in localities where they were already operating under local authorities, unless the local work did not provide adequate protection. Gradually the State and local authorities have realized the advantages of a national quarantine system, and have surrendered quarantine functions to the Federal Government.

---

[7] Children's Bureau.

This same law prohibits the admission, among others, of "idiots and insane persons—persons likely to become a public charge, and persons suffering from a loathsome or a dangerous contagious disease."

Foreign Quarantine Functions

Quarantine as related to passenger ships and planes is the function of the Surgeon General of the Public Health Service through the Bureau of Medical Services, Division of Foreign Quarantine. Quarantine as related to cargoes and commerce is primarily the function of the Secretary of Agriculture through the Bureau of Animal Industry with the special cooperation of the Bureau of Customs, Treasury Department.

Functions of the Public Health Service.—The Division of Foreign Quarantine, Bureau of Medical Services, is responsible for the administration of the quarantine laws and regulations of the United States.

There are three lines of defense against quarantinable diseases:

1. Medical officers of the service are stationed abroad in many of the major ports, and working in conjunction with the consular officers, to prevent diseased persons from entering ships bound for the United States. They make a medical inspection of all prospective immigrants. Medical inspection of aliens has been undertaken by the Public Health Service since 1890 under the provision of an act of Congress of 1882 (20 Stat. 214), as a service to the Bureau of Immigration, Department of Justice.

2. A system of inspection is carried out on all ships and planes from any foreign port at the port of entry to the United States. Both passengers and crews are inspected and the ship quarantined if necessary. The Entomological Section of the Division of Quarantine is responsible for the entomological surveillance of airplanes.

Improved technique has made possible the more rapid handling of vessels. Passenger-carrying vessels may be cleared by a system of radio pratique at some of the larger ports; and, whenever possible, ships undergoing quarantine inspection and treatment are handled at the docks rather than in midstream as was the common custom in former years.

3. A system of cooperation is organized with State and municipal health officers, particularly at ports of entry, in the follow-up of diseases that are nonquarantinable by Federal authorities. For example, diphtheria cases are released at the port of arrival by Federal authorities but quarantined by the local health authorities.

The diseases under Federal quarantine jurisdiction are: Cholera, yellow fever, typhus, smallpox, leprosy, plague, and anthrax. The threat of most of these diseases entering the United States has been lessened by the international control of quarantinable diseases exercised by the Division of Sanitary Conventions and Quarantine of the World Health

107

Organization, set up at Geneva, Switzerland. Epidemiological information concerning the occurrence of pestilential diseases flows into this center from every country of the world. This information is transmitted throughout the world in a weekly epidemiological and vital statistics report and more rapidly to the affected countries through telegram and radio. This service is of vital importance in maintaining the free movement of sea and air traffic without undue risk of transmission of disease.

The great advances in medical science at the end of the nineteenth century when insects became known as the vectors of disease made possible the development of effective quarantine measures. The gradual elimination of disease-infested areas has also had a direct bearing on the efficacy of international quarantine.

Constant vigilance is exerted in relation to recurrences of all pestilential diseases. For instance, no serious outbreak of cholera had threatened the world for 40 years. In 1947 a very serious outbreak occurred in Egypt that cost many lives and millions of dollars. The epidemiological service at Geneva kept the ports of the world constantly and reliably informed on the course of this epidemic. The speedy and concerted intervention by the Interim Committee of World Health Organization was an important factor in stemming the tide of this outbreak. By using its technical knowledge and its command of medical resources in cooperation with the work of the Egyptian Government, cholera did not enter either Europe, or America, in 1947 as it did in epidemic proportions five times during the nineteenth century.

Smallpox epidemics are ever-present menaces. At present, the United States enjoys the lowest rate of morbidity and mortality from this disease ever known. Tightening quarantine regulations by enforcement of vaccination before aliens and visitors enter the United States has helped to maintain these present low rates.

Bubonic plague, another menace, is transmitted through the combined agency of rats and their fleas. Plague protection consists primarily in a system of inspection and deratization of ships, especially those coming from known plague-infested ports. This work has been so successful on a world-wide basis that a recent survey of 4,000 ships entering United States ports showed only 8 percent rat infestation.

Yellow fever and malaria.—Both of these diseases are transmitted by mosquitoes. Yellow fever was not considered a serious menace from about 1915 to 1936. However, jungle yellow fever was discovered in South America. Airplane service had developed with all South American countries. Persons infected with yellow fever in South America may reach airports in the United States before they show signs of the disease.

"Surveillance" is maintained at all international air fields in the United States by officials of Public Health Service, Immigration and Customs Authorities. Planes from foreign countries are allowed to land only when such officials are present. Surveillance is maintained by an interdepartmental committee representing these three agencies, using the following methods:

1. Disinfectation of airplanes arriving from Africa or South America.

2. Examination, at port of entry, of all passengers arriving from South America.

3. Determination of their itinerary for 9 days after arrival.

4. Vaccination against yellow fever of all airplane personnel that travel through South America.[8]

Quarantine has been defined as "the limitation of freedom of movements of persons or animals who have been exposed to communicable disease for a period of time equal to the longest usual incubation period of the disease to which they have been exposed."[9] "Quarantine procedures applicable to rapid air transit have not yet been able to cope with the problem because detention periods must be measured in terms of transit time. It has already forced us to place principal reliance upon 'surveillance.' . . . This is a compromise with realism, which robs quarantine of its effectiveness. But of more significance, it is useless in that many diseases are most contagious in their prodromal, nonsymptomatic phase."[10] However, this problem is already being attacked under the aegis of the World Health Organization, as was cholera by the Interim Commission.

Quarantine as related to commerce.—Federal laws relating to the entry and transportation of animals, animal products and food and drugs which affect the public health of the nation are administered cooperatively by various agencies of the Government.

The Department of Agriculture.—Upon authorization given in the various tariff acts, the Secretary of Agriculture through the Bureau of Animal Industry is charged with prohibiting the importation into the country and the shipment across State lines of diseased cattle; the diseases of cattle which may be transmitted by grain, hay, and bedding used by the animals on voyage by the fumigation of vessels and destruction of infected animals from countries where foot-and-mouth diseases are prevalent, and by the proper certification by consular offices abroad of hides, wool, skins, etc.

Inspectors of the Bureau of Animal Industry are employed to board incoming cargo ships at ports of entry to prevent the introduction of

---

[8] 39 Stat. L., 885–892, 896. Compilation of Public Health Service Regulations, Sup. No. 1, Title 8.

[9] Toby, Public Health Law, p. 138.

[10] L. L. Williams, M. D., "World Health Organization," Southern Medical Journal, Vol. 40, No. 1, January 1947.

109

diseased livestock and contaminated animal byproducts. They are assisted by officials of the Customs Service and Public Health Service. There is no indication of unnecessary duplication or overstaffing here. The Public Health Service works cooperatively with the Department of Agriculture and does not duplicate the large inspectional force of that department which is engaged in the protection of our food supply.

The research division of the Bureau make laboratory studies of methods of infection.

The Department of Agriculture cooperates with the Customs Division of Treasury, the Post Office Department, and the Food and Drug Administration in controlling the importation of veterinary biologic products such as toxins, viruses, and medicines.

The Public Health Service through its division of foreign and domestic quarantine prohibits the entrance of disease-bearing species of wildlife such as the parrot family that suffers from a virus disease, psittacosis. This disease is frequently transferred to man whenever there is a contact of man with birds of this family. The case fatality from this disease is high.

Department of the Interior is involved since all other species of wildlife come into the United States on the basis of permits granted to importers by the Secretary of the Interior through the director of Fish and Wildlife Service. Copies of these permits are sent to the collector of customs at the port of entry, who verifies the shipments and is responsible for allowing or prohibiting entrance.

Appropriations for the administration of Division of Foreign Quarantine, Bureau of Medical Services, Public Health Service, are as follows:

Year	Total cost
1940	$1, 546, 865
1947	2, 438, 496
1948	2, 688, 725

The cost of foreign quarantine as functions of the Departments of Agriculture, Treasury, Interior, and the Food and Drug Administration cannot be estimated.[11]

Narcotics: Their Control and Regulation

"Employment of narcotic drugs for purposes other than medical and scientific has been recognized throughout the world as abuse.

[11] References:
Public Health Service.
Department of Agriculture.
Department of the Interior.
Toby, National Government and Public Health.
Smillie, Public Health Administration in the United States.
L. L. Williams, Jr., "World Health Organization," Southern Medical Journal, Vol. 40, No. 1, January 1947.
International Organization in the Field of Public Health, Carnegie Endowment for International Peace, February 1, 1947.

Any traffic in such drugs conducted without specific governmental authority is, therefore, uniformly regarded as illicit."—Department of State Memorandum, November 1, 1938.

DEVELOPMENT OF INTERNATIONAL CONTROL

After the Philippines had become a possession of the United States, an American Bishop of the Episcopal Church, Charles Brent, viewed with alarm the mounting number of drug addicts in Manila and the ease with which they could procure opium. Back in America he discussed this matter, and what seemed to him its world-wide implications, with his friend Theodore Roosevelt, then President of the United States. On such a slender thread as this the first International Opium Commission was called at Shanghai in 1909 on the initiative of the United States Government. Thirteen nations participated in this conference but had no power to sign agreements. This conference could only lay down basic principles which individual nations might or might not carry out. From this slender thread there has developed during the intervening 36 years an international cordon encircling the globe for the suppression and control of illicit traffic in narcotic drugs. Two world wars have not destroyed its present effectiveness.

We have come to learn through the years that national control of certain matters such as epidemic diseases, postal services, even of icebergs, and now of atomic energy is not fully effective without international collaboration. Narcotic drugs, small in bulk but high in value, belong in this category. The development of the rather complicated machinery for international control of the production, the manufacture, and the traffic in habit-forming and habit-sustaining drugs has been slow, difficult, but continuously progressive. It has consisted of a series of international conferences, each building on the conventions of its predecessor, plus the unstinting labor of individuals and groups in many countries who have diligently labored between these conferences to further their international control. See chart III, page 112.

The existing system of international cooperation rests on three basic treaties: The Hague Opium Convention of 1912, the Geneva Drug Convention of 1925, and the Narcotics Limitation Convention of 1931.

In brief, the three treaties provide a system whereby neither raw opium nor coca leaves, nor derivatives manufactured from either of these materials, can move from one country to another without governmental permission to import and also governmental permission to export in the case of each shipment; and the quantities of narcotic drugs which may be manufactured in any 1 year are limited to those which, after careful investigation and study, have been determined

111

CHART III—United States and International Cooperation on Narcotics

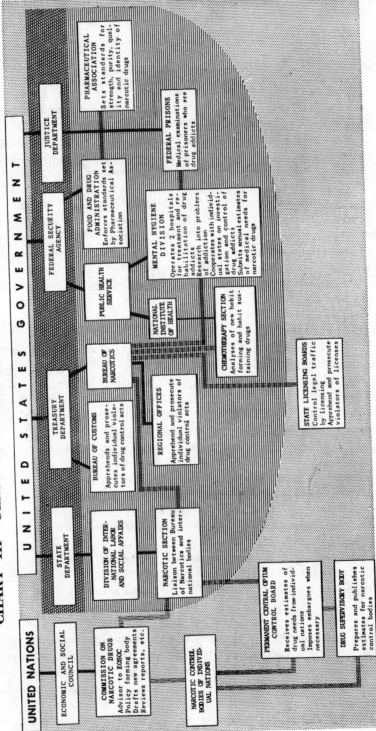

to be the quantities necessary for medical and scientific purposes only. The treaties require that the lawful distribution of raw material and of manufactured drugs be submitted to rigid supervision and accounting. However, in some countries national interests have resisted international control .

Perhaps the most flagrant abuser, Japan, though continuing to collaborate with the Advisory Council on Opium Control, encouraged the consumption of opium and manufactured drugs during its occupation of China during the Second World War, and increased the area of poppy cultivation, to debilitate the Chinese Army and people. Their profit from the illicit sale of narcotics, during the war years, has been estimated at $300,000,000.

In Iran, Mexico, and other agricultural nations the cultivation and trade in opium is an important part of the country's economy, and therefore inimical to international interests.

However, the vigor and effectiveness of the international controls developed through the League of Nations, in Geneva, was demonstrated when, at the first session of the Economic and Social Council of the United Nations, on February 15, 1940, it established the United Nations Commission on Narcotic Drugs. United Nations Document 2/20, February 15, 1940, pages 9–10 reads:

This Commission shall assist the Economic and Social Council in exercising supervision over the application of international conventions and agreements dealing with narcotic drugs; carry out such functions entrusted to the League Advisory Committee by Narcotic Conventions as the Council may find necessary; advise the Council on all matters pertaining to the control of narcotics; prepare draft conventions; consider what changes may be required in the existing machinery and submit proposals therein to the Council; and perform such other functions relating to narcotic drugs as the Council may direct.

PARTICIPATION OF THE UNITED STATES

The Treasury Department is specifically charged with carrying out of the functions of the Federal Narcotic Act, according to title 21, section 197 of the United States Code (Porter Act). ". . . the Secretary of the Treasury shall cooperate with the Secretary of State in the discharge of the international obligations of the United States concerning the traffic in narcotic drugs . . ." on the basis of the "Convention and Final Protocol Between the United States and Other Powers: Suppression of the Abuse of Opium and Other Drugs, Signed at The Hague, January 23, 1912, and July 9, 1913," Treaty Series 612, Washington, Government Printing Office, 1922, 32 pp. (38 Stat. 1912) ; and augmented by the Protocols of May 28, 1926, c. 411, Sec. 1, 44 Stat. 669, and June 17, 1930, c. 497, Title IV, Secs. 518, 649, 46 Stat. 737, 762.

Within the State Department there is set up a liaison office with the following functions:

To formulate departmental policy regarding the international control of narcotics, and to perform the duties imposed by statute and treaty obligations in relation to international cooperation for suppression of the abuse of narcotic drugs.

Federal Control of Habit-forming and Habit-sustaining Drugs

Contrary to what might be expected, the international conventions have little to say on the medical aspects of narcotic drug control. However, one of the conventions implies that the Drug Supervisory Board, in considering a country's estimate of needs must, of necessity, consider its medical and scientific needs. The international conventions must be considered as restrictive commodity agreements rather than health measures, since widespread drug addiction could have serious effects not only on domestic economy but also on security.

Interestingly enough, the United States Government has set up machinery to control the traffic and the abuse of narcotic drugs on both fronts—on its restriction through the Bureau of Narcotics in the Treasury Department, and on its medical aspects through the Mental Hygiene Division of the Public Health Service.

Bureau of Narcotics of the Treasury Department.—The Bureau of Narcotics was established within the Department of the Treasury primarily to safeguard the revenue of the United States and to protect the health of its people against illicit traffic in harmful drugs.[12] Under the Narcotic Drug Import and Export Act of 1922, the Marihuana Tax Act of 1937 (U. S. C., title 26, sec. 1399), and the Opium Poppy Control Act of 1942, additional controls over dangerous drugs are imposed. Thus, the primary function of the Bureau of Narcotics is the enforcement function over both the legal trade and illicit traffic in dangerous drugs.

State licensing boards.—Licensed practitioners and pharmacists may purchase narcotic drugs for bona fide medical purposes only.

The Bureau cooperates with the various State licensing boards by reporting to them for appropriate disciplinary action, practitioners and pharmacists who have violated the Federal narcotic law or who have been discovered to be addicted to narcotic drugs. The purpose of this report to the State licensing boards is to secure suspension or withdrawal of the professional license privilege in the interest of the public health and welfare.

---

[12] The Bureau was created in the Department of the Treasury by the act of June 14, 1930 (46 Stat. 585; U. S. C. 282–82A) to be known as the Bureau of Narcotics. The law provides that a Commissioner of Narcotics be in charge to carry out its functions and duties. The new organization assumed the obligation of the abolished Narcotic Unit of the Bureau of Prohibition.

Illicit traffic in narcotic drugs.—With the cooperation of the Bureau of Customs, Federal agents search for smuggled narcotic drugs at ports of entry into the United States.

The Bureau of Narcotics operates through its staff in 15 regional offices for the apprehension and prosecution of individual violators of the above-mentioned narcotic exclusion acts.

Narcotic control is also maintained in the United States zone in Germany, but not too successfully because of long borders that offer good opportunity for smuggling and the lack of experienced personnel to cope with the situation.

Legal trade.—The Bureau estimates annually the amount of narcotic drugs needed for both medical and scientific purposes. This estimate is conveyed to the Permanent Central Opium Control Board in Geneva, Switzerland. On the basis of this estimate the United States is privileged to purchase from abroad sufficient quantities of crude drugs to meet its medical and scientific needs. The importation of derivative drugs is absolutely prohibited.

The Bureau of Narcotics receives the cooperation of the Mental Hygiene Division of the United States Public Health Service, which is required by statute to furnish annually an estimate of the medical needs of the country for narcotic drugs to aid the Bureau of Narcotics in making its total estimates.

Public Health Service, Division of Mental Hygiene.—One of the main purposes of the act authorizing the establishment by the United States Public Health Service of hospitals for the confinement and treatment of drug addicts was the provision of an extensive research program into the nature, causes, and treatment of drug addiction.[13] As a result of these investigations, it was found that a majority of persons addicted to habit-forming drugs are mentally ill, "although not psychotic." This fact led the Congress of the United States to recognize the importance of changing the Narcotics Division of the Public Health Service to the Division of Mental Hygiene.[14] This division supervises the administration of two narcotic farms, one at Lexington, Ky., and the other at Forth Worth, Tex.[15] Formerly, drug addicts who are equally offenders against the United States were lodged in Federal prisons. These farms have a combined capacity of 2,400 patients. They provide facilities to rehabilitate drug addicts, to restore them to health, and to train them to be self-supporting. They also carry on extensive research into the nature, causes, and treatment of drug addiction.

This division also supervises (*a*) the study of drug addiction, rehabilitation, and investigations on the causes and prevention of mental

---

[13] Sec. 4–b of H. R. 11143.

[14] Public Law No. 357, 71st Cong., H. R. 11143, sec. 4–a.

[15] These narcotic farms are under the Hospital Division, Public Health Service, since October 1, 1948.

and nervous diseases, (*b*) the cooperation with States in the control and investigation of drug addicts, and (*c*) the provision of medical and psychiatric care to Federal prisons (Department of Justice) by loaning United States Public Health Service psychiatrists to direct their medical services.

The responsibility of the Public Health Service with respect to mental health was further increased by the National Health Act of 1946 (P. L. 410, 79th Cong.) which provides for the establishment of a National Institute of Mental Health and for grants-in-aid to States for psychiatric services. Consequently, out of the Narcotics Division of the Public Health Service, now defunct, in cooperation with the Bureau of Narcotics with its regulatory powers, has come provision for the prevention and treatment of mental and nervous diseases.

Public Health Service, National Institute of Health.—The National Institute of Health makes laboratory analyses of narcotic drugs. The Chemotherapy Section in the Division of Psychology cooperates with the Bureau of Narcotics, in the matter of securing tests of the habituating qualities of new synthetic analgesics which it may be found necessary to bring within the purview of existing narcotic laws covering derivative drugs from opium and coca leaves, and other habit-forming and habit-sustaining drugs.

Food and Drug Administration.—The United States Pharmaceutical Association (a private association) publishes the United States Pharmacopoeia, which contains standards set by the association for the strength, purity, quality, and identity of drugs, including narcotic drugs.

These standards were adopted as the standards for the country in the Food and Drug Act of June 30, 1906, and enforced by the Food and Drug Administration. Any infringement of these standards in narcotic drugs are therefore handled by the Food and Drug Administration.

One test of the efficacy of international and national control of narcotics is a comparison of the number of addicts at the time when such control began with the number in recent times, making due allowance for some of the factors which prevent complete accuracy. About 20 years ago, shortly before international control had become effective, an estimate of the ratio of drug addicts in the United States to the general population gave the figure as 1 in 1,000. A recent estimate gives the figure as 1 in 3,000, a reduction of two-thirds. However, the most reliable indication of the impressive decrease in drug addiction is the following from draft figures of the two world wars. In the First World War, 1 in 1,500 registrants was rejected from military service primarily because of drug addiction, whereas in the Second

116

World War, in the age group from 18 to 38 years, 1 in 10,000 such registrants was rejected.[16]

Cost of Narcotic Drug Control in 1947

Department of Treasury, Bureau of Narcotics

Appropriations for narcotic law administration	$1, 430, 000. 00
Revenue accruing to the Government from application of the Federal narcotic drug and marihuana laws	1, 749, 181. 56
Appropriations for Mental Hygiene Division, Public Health Service, for the medical care (including administration) for narcotic control	2, 935, 360. 00

Obligations: Treasury department for narcotic control

Items	1940	1947	1948
Regulatory	$1, 176, 030	$1, 296, 000	$1, 287, 000
All other including all over administrative costs	130, 670	1, 440, 000	1, 430, 000
Total	1, 306, 700	2, 736, 000	2, 717, 000

RECOMMENDATIONS ON NARCOTIC CONTROL

The president of the Permanent Central Opium Board, which is attached in an advisory capacity to the Commission on Narcotic Drugs of the Economic and Social Council of the United Nations, considers that the United States enjoys one of the most efficient national administrations (for drug control) in the world.

The impressive decrease in drug addicts in the United States is shown in the following figures: One registrant in every 1,500 in the First World War was rejected for military service primarily because of drug addiction, whereas in the Second World War the figure was one in 10,000 selective service registrants examined for military duty in the age group from 18 to 35 years.

In 1947 the revenue accruing to the Government from the application of the Federal narcotic drug and marihuana laws was $1,749,181.56 and the appropriation for narcotic law administration was $1,430,000. The funds, therefore, accruing to the Government from this service was $319,181.56, or nearly one-third of a million dollars. This plus the estimated reduction in the number of drug addicts over a period of about 21 years makes an impressive showing for this Bureau of Government.

---

[16] References: Annual Report of the Federal Security Agency, 1947. The Work of the United States Public Health Service, supplement No. 152 to the Public Health Report, 1940. Opium and Narcotic Laws, compiled by Elmer A. Lewis, Document Room, House of Representatives, 1941. United States Treasury Department Report, Protection Against Habit-forming Drugs, December 1936. Traffic in Opium and Other Dangerous Drugs, December 1947. International Agencies in which the United States Participates, U. S. Government Printing Office, Washington, 1946. Revised Edition, Public Health Law, James A. Toby, the Commonwealth Fund, 1947. Public Affairs Bulletins, Medical and Surgical Activities of the Federal Government, Charles A. Quattlebaum, General Research Section, Library of Congress, Bulletin No. 36, 1945. Narcotic Drug Control, Carnegie Endowment for International Peace, May 1948, No. 441.

117

International control of narcotics began with the Shanghai conference on opium in 1912, and of pestilential and contagious diseases about 100 years ago. These controls confirm the fact that, in the field of health, nations can meet together in a spirit of understanding and friendship and arrive at firm decisions which are carried through to an effective conclusion for the betterment of mankind. It also confirms the fact that within the United States, various Government agencies and private organizations can work together to attack health problems, international as well as national in scope.

The newly created World Health Organization gives top priority to other health problems such as communicable diseases (tuberculosis, venereal diseases, malaria), maternal and child health, sanitation and nutrition, problems capable of being attacked internationally, but which must be controlled nationally if we are to raise the level of our own health and efficiency.

These far ranging national and international problems, however, cannot be solved at once. The control of narcotic drugs was 37 years in the making. The first law for the control of "pestilential diseases" in the United States was enacted in the Province of Carolina in 1712; 237 years ago. The world, however, is smaller and moves much faster today. The ability to work together in these areas is basic to our very existence, our health and efficiency, and is almost imperative today. It is also necessary for the United States to give careful and detailed study to all the elements of these important health problems in order to mature recommendations on them.

International Cooperation in Maternal Child Health and Welfare

The international activities of the Children's Bureau are well established, having as their aim the exchange of information and experience with other nations of the world on all matters pertaining to child life.

Under authority of Public Law 355 (76th Cong.; 53 Stat. 1290), and Public Law 402 (80th Cong.), the Bureau lends technical advisors to other countries on request and brings specialists from other countries to the United States for training. These activities are financed by funds transferred to the Children's Bureau through the Federal Security Agency by the Department of State and are part of a broad program in which more than 50 Federal agencies are participating under the general direction of the Interdepartmental Committee on Scientific and Cultural Cooperation.

The Children's Bureau carries additional responsibilities incident to membership of the United States in various international organizations.

These responsibilities and activities are carried out by the Office of the Chief and the International Cooperation Service, the administrative unit in the Bureau through which many of these activities are directed or coordinated. Its functions include foreign research and exchange of scientific and technical information on maternal and child health and social services for children; advisory service to official agencies as requested by other governments and arrangements for training and observation by specialists in maternal and child health and welfare to whom special grants are made by the Bureau under the above-mentioned programs or who are referred to the Children's Bureau by such other agencies as the Specialized Agencies of the United Nations.

The field staff, which is administratively responsible to the International Cooperation Service, has included, as occasion demanded, specialists in pediatrics, orthopedics, public health nursing and midwifery, nutrition, and social services for children. Types of services requested by other governments have included studies and recommendations looking toward the establishment or reorganization of basic health and welfare services; the establishment of schools of social work and organizing of special demonstration training courses for health and child welfare workers; nutrition studies and education; advisory service with relation to children's institutions; advisory service in connection with the development of programs for crippled children.

The Children's Bureau has assigned personnel to nearly all of the American Republics. A special mission was sent to the Philippines in 1946 and assistance was given to India in 1946 in the field of medical social work.

In cooperation with the Pan American Sanitary Bureau and Mexican health agencies, the Children's Bureau has participated in the program of the Mexico-United States Border Public Health Association, which now includes a special section on maternal and child health and welfare.

The training grants awarded by the Children's Bureau to specialists from other countries provide for 6 months of study and observation in the United States. Each program is individually planned with a view to the particular needs of the country and the field of interest of the individual. In addition, the Bureau gives assistance to foreign visitors referred by other agencies. More than 250 individuals received this type of service in the fiscal year 1948.

The Children's Bureau carries major responsibility for planning participation of the United States in the Pan American child congresses which have been held periodically since 1916 and which cover the fields of pediatrics and child health, child welfare, and education. The Chief of the Children's Bureau is the technical delegate of the United States on the Directing Council of the American International Institute for the Protection of Childhood, an official agency with headquarters at Montevideo, Uruguay. Since 1948, she has been vice president of the Directing Council. The Institute, which is concerned with all phases of child life, including health, education, and social welfare, was created as the result of recommendations of the II, III, and IV Pan American child congresses. The United States had been a member of the Institute since 1928.

The Chief of the Bureau is United States representative on the Executive Board and the program committee of the International Children's Emergency Fund, established by the United Nations General Assembly, December 11, 1946. The fund is authorized to provide emergency assistance for the benefit of children, adolescents, and pregnant and nursing mothers in countries that were victims of aggression and countries receiving help from UNRRA, and for child-health purposes generally.

The Chief of the Bureau is alternate representative of the United States on the Social Commission of the United Nations Economic and Social Council, and is a member of the United States Commission for UNESCO.

The Associate Chief of the Bureau was advisor on the United States delegation to the Fifth Session of the Interim Commission of the World Health Organization and vice chairman of the United States delegation to the First World Health Assembly.

Other staff members have from time to time been designated as members of, or advisors to, United States delegations to international conferences and international agencies.

The Children's Bureau participates in the formulation of policy recommendations through the representative of the Federal Security Agency on the Interdepartmental Committee on International Social Policy and its Subcommittees on Health, Social Welfare, Labor, Human Rights, and Non-self-governing Territories, and in connection with refugees and displaced persons where such policies are related to the health and social welfare of children and youth.

Requests for such services come to the Bureau from various organizational units within the Department of State. A recent illustration relates to implementation of the United States military government law authorizing adoption of German children by American nationals officially stationed in Germany; immigration of unaccompanied minor refugee children to the United States; problems with the Canadian Government and State agencies in connection with the adoption of Canadian children by Americans; and individual problems relating to the legal status, adoption, immigration, claims of paternity or for benefits in the case of children of unmarried mothers in other countries resulting from the residence of American nationals or presence of troops in such countries.

In the case of international agencies, the Children's Bureau gives technical consultation and assistance, including on occasions the loan of personnel, through direct relations with international agencies, through the channels of the Social Security Administration or the Federal Security Agency, or through certain organizational units of the Department of State. Such services are being given in connection with programs and activities involving children and youth operated by Food and Agriculture Organization; Social Activities Division of the United Nations Secretariat; World Health Organization; United Nations Economic and Social Council; International Refugee Organization; International Labor Organization; Pan-American Sanitary Bureau; Mexico-United States Border Public Health Association; Pan American Union; Inter-American Commission of Women; Inter-American Indian Institute; in addition to the International Children's Emergency Fund and the American International Institute for the Protection of Childhood, mentioned above.

OTHER PROGRAMS

Environmental Sanitation

Control of the environment is fundamentally important in the prevention of disease and the promotion of community health. Environment, as it is usually defined, is concerned with the physical world in which we live—its climate, its topography, the changes brought about by man himself, such as housing, clothing, transportation, agriculture, water supply, sewage disposal, city planning—and the change that new discoveries constantly make in our methods of living. These conditions influence our lives for better or for worse. However, in the broad conception of the term, environment also includes such social influences as traditions, religious attitudes, cultural backgrounds, personal cleanliness, and our social heritage, which make up our social environment and bring about conditions that may influence health to an even greater degree than our physical environment.

ACTIVITIES

The following résumé of the sanitary activities of the various Federal agencies is designed to show the type and extent of the work done and the cooperative efforts put forth among the various agencies. The Government early in its history recognized its responsibility in the promotion of sanitation and the control of community disease. In 1692, the Province of South Carolina and the Massachusetts Bay Colony enacted laws for the prevention of infection associated with polluted air from garbage and slaughterhouses.[17] Since then, sanitary legislation with regulatory powers has been enacted in all States. State and local health departments include these activities in their divisions of sanitation that deal with waste disposal, water supply, and the prevention and abatement of nuisances.

While the Federal Government has no jurisdiction over State sanitary control measures, it nevertheless enters into a program of sanitation through establishing standards as they relate to water supply, the prevention of stream pollution, and other health engineering problems. These functions are chiefly discharged through the services of the United States Public Health Service in its relation to interstate commerce.

Many other Federal agencies also conduct sanitary engineering programs. Their sanitary work is related to their functional activities

---

[17] James A. Toby, Public Health Laws, Commonwealth Fund (1947), p. 217.

122

and is, in most cases, carried on with the technical and advisory assistance of the Sanitary Engineering Division of the Public Health Service. The principal Federal agencies that function in the sanitary engineering field are:

The Public Health Service.—The Sanitary Engineering Division, Office of the Surgeon General, of the Public Health Service directs all engineering and sanitation activities of the Service and is chiefly concerned with (*a*) the technical supervision and consultant services that are given to Federal, State, and local health agencies, (*b*) the establishment of standards and uniform sanitary engineering policies and programs, and (*c*) enforcement of Federal laws covering sanitation involving interstate and foreign commerce. These functions are administered through six sections covering the sanitation problems of land, air, and water; transportation facilities; milk and foods; and a general sanitation section dealing with housing sanitation, bathing beaches, and garbage and refuse disposal. There is also a section of water and sanitation investigation which conducts studies on stream pollution, sewage disposal, and other sanitary projects. These researches are general in their application. They cover studies related to bacteriological problems of stream pollution and sewage disposal, and to laboratory researches on disease-producing bacteria in milk.

In the field of milk and food sanitation, functions of this Division include research, advisory, and consultative service to local and State officials and to industry. It also has supervision of sanitation on interstate commerce carriers. Its program is, therefore, to assist State authorities to carry out their legal authority. The basic researches in the field of chemistry are conducted to determine the usefulness of known methods in determining the rates of biochemical oxygen demanded in sewage and polluted streams.

The Public Health Service conducts survey and fact-finding studies on sanitary problems and develops standard ordinances and sanitation codes, such as the Standard Milk and Food Ordinance.

Housing and Home Finance Agency.—This agency is primarily concerned with researches into the building codes and various phases of housing design and sanitation including the use of septic tanks and sewerage systems as well as improvement of the neighborhood.[18]

Department of Agriculture.—In the Department of Agriculture several agencies conduct sanitary programs. The Farmers Home Administration makes possible, through its supervised credit or loans to low-income farmers, sanitary facilities, adequate water supply, and insect-pests control. Also, the Cooperative Extension Service program includes general sanitation, modern plumbing, drainage, and the disposal of waste for the prevention of disease. These activities

---

[18] Personal communication, July 18, 1948.

are developed in cooperation with local health authorities and in accordance with State and local needs. Incidentally, the Rural Electrification Administration provides electric power to rural areas which make possible modern sanitary facilities. The Forest Service also provides sanitary facilities including the disposal of sewage and the enforcing of sanitary laws. The Division of Dairy Inspection encourages State agencies to institute better methods for the improvement of the sanitary quality of milk and for handling milk. The Food Inspection Division of the Department of Agriculture has regulatory powers to control food in interstate commerce, to inspect meat, and the sanitary methods of handling food products. As a part of an environmental sanitary program, the United States Bureau of Entomology and Plant Quarantine directs activities that control mosquitoes and other insect pests.

The Tennessee Valley Authortiy.—This agency likewise conducts sanitary engineering programs in relation to stream pollution. Where excessive pollution loads are discharged into the valley's streams, damage is done and conflict, therefore, arises with other Federal and State interests, as for example, Fish and Wildlife Service, recreational bureaus, and agencies dealing with sources of water supply. TVA's method in the furtherance of stream sanitation has been cooperation with Federal and State agencies and private and industrial organizations.

Federal Works Agency.—This agency, in cooperation with Public Health Service, assists in conducting a program for the elimination of stream pollution and improving the sanitary conditions of surface and ground water. It also extends Federal aid in the construction of sewage-treatment plants. Under Law No. 845, Water Pollution Control Act, the Federal Works Agency and the Public Health Service have undertaken an important cooperative project for the abatement of pollution of our water resources. This bill hase been recently passed and an appropriation of $75,000 for 1949 has been made for an initial administrative budget.

Department of the Interior.—Within the Department of the Interior, the Bureau of Mines conducts considerable research for the improvement of sanitation of mines and for the control of dangerous dusts and gases injurious to the health of the miners. Its operational staff of engineers and inspectors conduct field inspections of the health and safety conditions in mines.

In the Office of Indian Affairs their health program includes the encouragement of the Indians toward sanitary living and the promotion of better sanitary conditions on the reservations.

The Fish and Wildlife Service has considerable interest in the control of stream pollution in its efforts to protect and propagate fish and wildlife.

The protection of oyster beds from pollution is the responsibility of the Sanitary Engineering Division of the Public Health Service in cooperation with State and local health officials.

The National Park Service takes upon itself a sanitation program of considerable magnitude in its work of waste disposal, pure water, and improvement of general sanitary conditions in park areas.

Department of Labor.—In the Department of Labor, three bureaus cooperate in their responsibility for the health and safety of industrial workers. These bureaus work toward a better environmental condition to foster, promote, and develop the welfare of wage earners. In their promotional work, sanitation and ventilating engineers, chemists, and health authorities provide the necessary knowledge to meet this end. The Walsh-Healey Act (49 Stat. 2036, 41 U. S. C. 35–45) makes provision of safety and health in industrial plants operating in States where persons are employed on work involving Government contracts.

Other agencies of the Federal Government are concerned with problems of environmental sanitation within their own agency, as for example, the United States Maritime Commission conducts public health and sanitation programs of Government-owned shipyards and of other industrial plants engaged in construction work. Abatement of noises, smoke nuisances, and odors that cause discomfort have likewise received attention from the Government.

Expenditures

No definite monetary value can be attached to these sanitary control measures as they have been supported along with related projected programs. However, in the Public Health Service it is possible to attach values that are significant. In 1947, in the Bureau of Sanitary Engineering, Public Health Service, the obligations were $1,173,701, of which $294,250 were for direct operations including administrative costs, $181,467 for research, and $697,984 for all others including an over-all administration. In 1948, the total obligations for the Bureau were $1,062,210, of which $330,899 were for direct operations, $245,384 for research, and $485,927 were for all other health activities including administration.

The report on a Nation-wide inventory of sanitation needs [19] gives considerable information on the extent of work yet to be done if everyone is to have a safe and healthy environment. The report recognizes the fact that the country's sanitation needs are far beyond an immediate goal and that they all depend upon changes in the economic, cultural, and social pattern of the community. An effective organization for the practical solution of community sanitary prob-

---

[19] Supplement No. 204 to the Public Health Report, April 1948.

lems must take into consideration the local attitudes and desires of the community as well as the economic conditions. To provide an environment conducive to better social and physical health, educational work and technical advice are needed, as well as cooperative effort of Federal, State, and local agencies. This will require additional personnel, financial assistance where advisable, and cooperative long-time planning. While there is considerable duplication of sanitary services in the various agencies, this duplication is unavoidable as these services can best be given by these agencies as part of their major functions.

RECOMMENDATIONS

1. Sanitary Engineering Division now in Office of the Surgeon General, Public Health Service, should be transferred to the Bureau of State Services, as it is an operating unit with activities deeply involved in Federal-State relations.

2. The problem of controlling the sanitary quality of milk has been a source of friction between the agricultural and the health branches of government at all levels. The agricultural interests have been concerned primarily with economic aspects, and those in the health field have focused their attention on control of disease. Both approaches have value. A reasonable solution to the conflict and overlapping would be to agree that the agricultural group have primary jurisdiction over the production of milk on the farm, and that those concerned primarily with health come into the picture at the stage when milk is being processed and prepared for distribution to the consumer. Provision would also be needed for authorization of the health agencies to investigate actual or potential disease problems on the farms.

3. There should be a much closer liaison between Federal agencies concerned with sanitation so that conflicting bulletins are not published and to develop a coordinated program.

Health Education

Health education is defined [20] as the sum of experiences which favorably influence knowledge, attitudes, ad behavior relating to individual, family, and community health. Its purpose is to close the gap between scientific knowledge and the application of this knowledge to daily life. It includes:

[20] This definition is based largely on the following references: Wood, Thos. D., Fourth Yearbook of the Department of Superintendency of the National Education Association, 1926. Hiscock, Ira V., Ways of Community Health Education, New York, Commonwealth Fund 1939. Report of Committee on Terminology of the Health Education Section of the American Physical Education Association (now a department of the National Education Association), Definition of Terms of Health Education. J. Health and Physical Education 5: 16 December 1934.

a. School health education, concerned with providing health instruction of the school-age population (and sometimes their parents). This takes place in the school through efforts organized and conducted by school personnel, and is primary responsibility of the educational agencies of the community.

b. Public health education concerned, directly or indirectly, with all ages of the population, functioning through both public and private agencies in the homes of the people or in the community. It aims to achieve both personal and community health and to provide support for the general public health program through informed public opinion.

ACTIVITIES

With the above definition in mind, even superficial investigation shows that the majority of Federal agencies concerned with public health carry on health educational activities. The Office of Education is concerned with school health education primarily. Public health education is centered in the Office of Health Education, Bureau of State Services, Public Health Service. It is a primary function of the Children's Bureau in the fields of maternal and child health and the care of crippled children; the Food and Drug Administration; the Department of Agriculture through its Extension Service, Home Economics demonstrations, etc.; the Department of the Interior in the Office of Indian Affairs and the Bureau of Mines; the Department of Labor in fields related to labor; the Tennessee Valley Authority in its geographic area cooperating with State and local health departments; the Federal Trade Commission in connection with advertising of food and drugs; the Atomic Energy Commission in relation to preventive measures needed where atomic energy is employed; to a great degree in the armed forces; and so on.

Nutrition education, really a segment of broad health education, is considered elsewhere in this report.

The Office of Health Education in the Public Health Service has as its stated objective "the promotion in State and local health departments of sound health education programs which will effectively reach and motivate to acceptable health practices every individual in all groups of a community. This objective is accomplished largely through the field consultation service, which is rendered through the district offices and is designed to assist States in developing new health education programs and in improving the effectiveness of existing programs." A health education consultant is attached to the staff of the district director, and works, through the State health officer, with the health educators of the State health agency. This consultation service is similar to that conducted by other specialists of the district office, including temporary assignment of personnel to the State (or

127

local) health agency. In addition, the Office of Health Education holds occasional national and regional meetings, at which problems of general interest and methods of meeting them are discussed, and participates closely in numerous in-service training programs. Personnel of the Office of Health Education are assigned to several other divisions of the Bureau of State Services, such as tuberculosis, venereal disease, etc., in order to facilitate this aspect of the respective operating programs.

Closely associated with its consultative and advisory activities are the interests in qualifications and training of personnel by this office. The director and his associates are active in professional circles which attempt, among other activities, to establish minimum qualifications for workers in this and allied fields. Another training activity of this office has to do with the fellowship program financed by the National Foundation for Infantile Paralysis. The Office of Health Education administers these funds, which provide stipends and tuition for health educators at schools of public health. These trainees represent one of the chief sources of new personnel entering the field of health education, either with official or voluntary health agencies. Grants are also made to physicians and engineers.

An important phase of the work of the Office of Health Education is the demonstration and evaluation of health education programs. One example of such an activity is the interviewing of a sample of population before and after a selected chest X-ray campaign to learn the educational results therefrom. Another is the study of effectiveness of educational material sent to pharmacists upon the latter and their clients.

Through its programs of (a) consultation to States, local communities voluntary organizations, and other divisions of the Public Health Service, and coordination of their programs; (b) training of health educators and other health workers, and administration of fellowships; and (c) demonstration and evaluation of health education programs, the Office of Health Education performs functions on a national scale which are similar to those performed by a State division of health education. However, in some States, the latter has certain responsibilities with respect to schools which are not within the scope of this office, but are a function of the Office of Education.

School health education is a function of the Inter-Divisional Committee on School and College Health Services, Health Instruction, Physical Education, and Athletics, composed of representatives from several divisions of the Office of Education (namely, elementary, secondary, higher education, and auxiliary divisions). This committee offers consultant services to States, local school districts, and universities on the several phases of school health programs, and conducts research along professional lines in this field. Consultation is

128

usually on (*a*) health services, (*b*) curricula and methods of health instruction, (*c*) curricula and methods of physical education, and (*d*) health subjects in education of teachers. In addition, workshops and in-service training institutes, on a regional basis, are conducted by this committee. The Office of Health Education of the Public Health Service patricipates fully in the above programs, especially in the workshops and institutes. The Office of Education has appointed a member of its staff as consultant to the Office of Health Education of the Public Health Service and the latter in turn has reciprocated. It is therefore possible for staff members of either unit to visit both health and education departments at the State level in an official capacity. This is a simple mechanism which helps to minimize possible conflicts between the two units.

In the Office of the Federal Security Administrator there is an Office of Publicity and Reports which is the internal information point for the agency as a whole and which is concerned with the dissemination of general information to the public. It may be considered chiefly a publicity unit, not conflicting with the work of the agencies mentioned above.

There is also a Division of Reports in the Children's Bureau, the main function of which is the preparation of publications and bulletins, consultation on writing techniques to professional workers in the bureau, news releases, etc. Some of these functions may be considered health education, but it is generally on an operational rather than consultative level, and does not duplicate the work of the Office of Health Education.

There has been a tendency to curtail rigidly health education activities of the Federal Government. This is unfortunate, and restricts legitimate and desirable work that could be highly useful in promoting health and preventing disease. Educational media of Nationwide coverage such as radio (as used by the Farm and Home Hour) and periodicals could well be employed by the Federal Government to great advantage without interfering with prerogatives of the States. The so-called workship technique of education has proved merit as an educational method, and under proper safeguards should be encouraged rather than proscribed. At the National Health Assembly, May 1948, the section on rural health presented the following:

One of the greatest problems in rural areas is getting technical information and guidance for the development of plans and programs to improve health services. Since the congressional investigation of health workshops, professional health workers from the Federal Government have not been available to lay groups to provide technical information. To remedy the situation, the rural health section unanimously adopts the following resolution:

Problems affecting the health of the people can be best solved by local groups meeting together. Government and other agencies at all levels should be free to present to these groups the factual and technical information which, by virtue of their function, they have assembled.

TEACHING PREVENTIVE MEDICINE

The practicing physician has great opportunities to provide a preventive type of service and health education under most favorable circumstances for his patients. In fact, prevention and treatment are so indissoluably interwoven as to be almost inseparable. Prevention will be stressed if the practitioner has a preventive point of view, which he is most likely to have if it was inculcated during his medical education.

The teaching of preventive medicine in medical schools is very uneven and in the majority of schools inadequate. A study in 1946 [21] showed that only 15 of the 79 4-year schools in the United States and Canada devoted at least the recommended 4 percent of total teaching hours to preventive medicine.

The Federal Government has already entered the field of subsidizing medical schools in providing funds for cancer and mental health education. It would be even wiser to provide assistance in the general field of preventive medicine teaching.[22]

TRAINING OF PUBLIC HEALTH PERSONNEL

The need for public health personnel is discussed in the report dealing with the problem of all personnel in the medical and health fields. However, it is pertinent to point out here that the amount of training facilities for public health workers is inadequate, and that recent estimates indicate an urgent need for doubling present academic facilities and expanding to an even greater degree facilities for field training. None of the schools of public health serves a single State, all are regional or national and most of them have a large number of foreign students as well. It is a well-established fact that training of foreign students in public health has been one of the best investments in international good will which this country has ever made.

---

[21] Leavell, H. R., The Teaching of Preventive Medicine, J. Ass'n Am. Med. Coll., July 1947.

[22] Cancer Teaching. Public Law 410 as amended, which authorizes the National Cancer Institute (title IV, sec. 402) to:

a. Conduct, assist, and foster researches, investigations, experiments, and studies relating to the cause, prevention, and methods of diagnosis and treatment of cancer;

c. Provide training and instruction in technical matters relating to the diagnosis and treatment of cancer;

f. Cooperate with State health agencies in the prevention, control, and eradication of cancer.

Federal Security Agency Appropriation Act 1949, P. L. 639:

To enable the Surgeon General, upon the recommendations of the National Advisory Cancer Council, to make grants-in-aid for research and training projects relating to cancer, * * * to cooperate with State health agencies, and other public and private nonprofit corporations, in the prevention, control, and eradication of cancer by providing consultative services, demonstrations, and grants-in-aid.

Mental Health Teaching. Public Law 487, 79th Cong., National Mental Health Act, sec. 7, amending pt. A of title III, Public Health Service Act, sec. 303: To provide such training and instruction, and demonstrations, through grants, upon recommendation of the National Advisory Mental Health Council, to public and other nonprofit institutions, but only to the extent necessary for the purposes of such training and instruction.

130

The cost of training a student in public health is vastly greater than the tuition charged. The problem is one in which the Federal Government has a great stake, and legislation might well be considered providing grants-in-aid for public health training. Such grants should be made direct to the institutions, rather than being channeled through State health departments.

RECOMMENDATIONS

1. The Federal Government should engage aggressively in health education of the people, coordinating its activities with national voluntary health agencies and with State and local health departments.

2. The Public Health Service, because of its very broad interests and duties, should take primary responsibility for the coordination of all health education carried on by agencies of the Federal Government to avoid overlapping and duplication, as well as to promote complete coverage of the field. Agencies other than the Public Health Service with important health programs may use health educators and health education techniques advantageously in serving the people, but their work should be correlated with similar work by other Federal agencies.

3. The Office of Health Education in the Public Health Service should advise with all other units of the Service on health education matters.

4. The Office of Education should develop an active program of school health education to assist State and local departments of education.

5. The Federal Government should consider the teaching of preventive medicine to medical students as the field medical education in which Federal subsidy has the greatest possibility of usefulness.

6. Federal subsidies to institutions and field centers training public health workers should be provided.

Rural Health

Any discussion of public-health problems in the United States which failed to emphasize the needs of rural areas would be derelict in its duty. The following statement published recently summarizes the health situation concisely:

For practically every category of service, with the exception perhaps of the dubious benefits of midwives and patent medicines, the rural population receives services smaller in quantity and lower in quality than the urban and far less adequate than would be warranted by the burden of illness and impairment that it bears.[23]

---

[23] Mott, F. D., and Roemer, W. I., Rural Health and Medical Care, New York, McGraw-Hill, 1948.

The same authors quoted above highlight the fact that the rural health problems vitally affect the urban population as well:

The perennial bumper crop of farm children and the harvesting of nearly half that crop by our cities result in a disproportionately low number of persons in the prime of life in rural areas, and if tomorrow's urban citizens are to have the opportunity to build sound bodies and alert minds in infancy and childhood, the benefits of scientific health care must be extended to the country as well as the city.[24]

Some comparative figures are shown in the following table, quoted from both the sources named in the footnote.

Almost limitless other citations might be given to illustrate the point that rural health problems are generally more serious and improvement is taking place more slowly than in our cities due to inadequacies of health facilities and personnel.

Rural versus urban health [1]

	Rural	Urban
Mortality rate per 100,000 population, 1940:		
Typhoid and paratyphoid fevers	1.5	0.4
Diphtheria	1.5	.5
Pellagra	2.4	.5
Measles	.7	.2
Scarlet fever	.6	.4
Whooping cough	3.2	1.0
Malaria	1.9	.2
Percentage decrease in mortality, 1900-1940	29.0	45.0
Infant mortality 1942 (infant deaths per 1,000 live births)	43.3	34.3
Maternal mortality 1941 (maternal deaths per 1,000 live births)	3.5	2.6
Cases of illness (committee costs medical care) (per 1,000 population per year)	830	790
Academy of Pediatrics Survey:		
Ratio physicians per 1,000 children	1.8	4.1
Ratio dentists per 1,000 children	1.0	2.3
Beds in general hospitals per 1,000 children	8.4	15.4

[1] Sources: (1) Mott, F. D. and Roemer, M. I., Ibid; (2) Hubbard, J. P., Pennell, M. Y., and Britten, R. H., Health Services for the Rural Child, Chicago, American Medical Association, 1948.

Remedies without number have been suggested, and only a few will be mentioned here. Improvement in farm income is basically important and this has been accomplished to some extent. Extension of full-time well-organized local health units throughout the rural areas is fundamental, and there is little question in the minds of those familiar with the development of such units that some Federal subsidy is necessary to stimulate their extension to provide the entire population with basic health services. Upon this structure additional services may be built readily. Community hospitals and health centers must be provided in rural and semirural areas to attract medical personnel. Modern health workers have been trained rightly to realize that they cannot bring the benefits of present day medicine to their patients without minimum facilities. Methods of mobilizing purchasing power for medical care through prepayment plans in which the consumers have a voice must be developed and adapted to rural problems. All

[24] Hubbard, J. P., Pennell, M. Y., and Britten, R. H., Health Services for the Rural Child, Chicago, American Medical Association, 1948.

preventive and treatment services must be coordinated through local health councils and similar devices.

The answer to the problem of rural health is complex but it can be found. Particularly in States with a high percentage of rural population, the Federal Government has an essential role to play in finding this answer.

RECOMMENDATIONS

The Federal Government through grants-in-aid, technical assistance and other means should increase its participation in solution of the rural health problem. Grants are needed especially to promote the extension and improvement of full-time local health departments and to assist in the building and maintenance of hospitals and health centers.

Migrant Labor

Between 1 and 5 million workers and their dependents lead a nomadic life dependent on seasonal employment in agriculture and industry, going from one State to another. There are three principal "belts" in which migrant workers follow maturing crops from south to north: One on either coastal region and one in the central west. Many of these people have lost all legal residence and are therefore ineligible for many benefits available to other citizens of the United States, including health protection.

Our economy requires a certain amount of migrant labor to meet seasonal needs of agriculture, transportation, and industry. During depressions this type of labor becomes abundant, but during the past war domestic workers were so scarce that some 200,000 foreign workers were imported from Mexico and the British West Indies. Intergovernmental contracts were made guaranteeing these foreign workers many benefits unavailable to our own citizens, including provisions regarding wages, transportation, housing, health and medical services, continuity of employment and repatriation.

During the war the Public Health Service supervised work to protect the health of foreign migrant labor and to provide medical care. The job was done well.

In May 1946 a Federal Interagency Committee on Migrant Labor was established under authority of title III, section 302, War Mobilization and Reconversion Act of 1944 (Public Law 458, 78th Cong.), including representatives of the Agriculture and Labor Departments, Federal Security Agency, National Housing Agency, and Railroad Retirement Board. The Committee was directed "to review existing legal authority and administrative machinery of the various Government agencies to determine how living and labor standards of migrant workers in industry, transportation, and agriculture can be developed and improved" and "to submit appropriate recommendations as to the necessary corrective action."

"Migrant labor" was defined as referring to those workers who occasionally or habitually move, with or without their families, to seek or engage in seasonal or temporary employment, and who do not have the status of residents in the localities of expected job opportunity or employment. The health of these migratory workers involves not only the workers themselves but also residents of the various States with whom they have transitory contacts as they move about. Conditions favorable to the spread of communicable disease exist and control measures are required.

The Committee emphasized the need for broad handling of the problem by employer groups, States and the Federal Government. Needs were set forth: Safe transportation, adequate housing, provision for hospital and medical care as well as health services, facilities for child care and education, elimination of child labor (agricultural work is now more or less exempt from child labor laws) as well as measures to give migrant workers protection under workmen's compensation and social security laws. Efforts should be made to reduce to a minimum the number of migrant workers needed by diversified production, maximum mechanization, and fullest possible use of local workers. Federal grants-in-aid should be made available to States in accordance with their needs to assist in providing necessary health, education, welfare, and related services.

There is little doubt that many aspects of the problem require Federal action, and that unless stimulation is provided in the form of leadership and some technical and financial assistance, the migrant laborers and their families will continue as a minority group deprived of their rights of citizenship and serving as a menace to the health of communities in which they work. The Rural Health Section of the National Health Assembly May 1948 recommended that "a Federal tax-supported program to provide health services and medical care for migratory agricultural workers should be enacted."

RECOMMENDATIONS

1. The Federal Government should take the initiative in focusing attention on the health problems created by interstate movement of migrant labor, and should enlist whatever aid is possible from State and local government and employer groups involved.

2. Grants-in-aid should be made available to States affected by the migrant labor problem to assist in building up and maintaining strong health services, to control communicable disease, and to provide medical care for such of these workers as cannot be cared for otherwise.

134

Mental Hygiene

Since the newer concepts of public health imply the "mental and physical well-being of the people," it is fitting that mental hygiene [25] is now an integral part of governmental function. For a long time the isolation of the mentally ill was the only activity of governments with regard to this category of individuals, but with the advance of knowledge certain methods of empirical treatment were added to the custodial care. Later, progress in diagnosis and treatment resulted in the clinic or out-patient type of service. At the present time, medical science has gone one step further and is adapting psychiatric methods to man's everyday experiences in an effort to prevent future symptoms of mental illness.

There is little scientific proof that the person with an emotional disturbance of today will become, if unchecked, the psychotic case of tomorrow. It is well known, however, that such individuals tend to become neurotic, and by their attitudes and personality patterns to exert an unfavorable influence upon their associates, especially the young. The concentration of neuroticism in a population can be attacked by mental hygiene and public-health methods. Mental, as well as physical, well-being are the desirable goals.

The Federal Government has long been active in the care of persons who are mentally ill, concentrating especially upon certain categories of individuals. Among the latter are military personnel, other groups of Federal employees, merchant seamen, veterans, Indians, narcotic addicts, residents of the District of Columbia, etc. In many of these programs, there has been cooperation with the mental institutions of the several States; in some, notably the Veterans' Administration, an extensive program of care and treatment has been in effect. In addition to institutional care, several Federal agencies operate psychiatric clinic services (often in conjunction with general medical, surgical, or employee health clinics). The two mental hospitals in the Public Health Service are operated by the Mental Hygiene Division of the Bureau of Medical Services. Their attachment to the Hospital Division would be administratively sounder.

Both of these types of programs, hospitalization or out-patient clinics (or dispensaries), tend to emphasize the diagnosis and treatment of mentally ill (or potentially mentally ill) patients—that is, the clinical approach. A study of the Federal activities in this respect has been made by another group and will not be duplicated here.

Preventive mental hygiene is implicit in many activities other than clinical services per se. The so-called morale talks in the armed serv-

---

[25] The terms "mental hygiene," "mental well-being," and "preventive psychiatry" are used synonymously in this report, as a contrast to curative psychiatry or treatment of mentally ill patients, though obviously there are differences in definition.

ices, improved interpersonal relationships in an administrative hierarchy, health education activities of various groups, general betterment of socioeconomic situations, the sum total of human environment, all of these have effect on people which may be termed, in a sense, mental hygiene. It is clear that no organized program of government has touched all of these elements of preventive psychiatry nor is it likely that there will be such a program. At any rate, a study of such scope is neither intended nor possible here at this time. However, there have been some steps taken by the Federal Government which aim toward improvement of the mental health of the people. These will be touched upon.

ACTIVITIES

Under the Public Health Service, there has been established a National Institute of Mental Health (Public Law 487, July 3, 1946). This is a recent development and its program has been in operation only a short time, but already its plans are well formulated. Here, coordinated studies will be conducted in the many sciences which bear upon the problem of mental health. These will be aided by the appointment of research fellows who, it is hoped, will contribute to the present knowledge in this field. With respect to this research, certain advances are to be expected which may clarify the relationship between cause and effect in psychiatric disorders. Though such knowledge will be applicable in large measure to persons with symptoms, a better understanding of causation will perhaps point the way toward more effective preventive measures. At any rate, research in mental illness is a necessary activity from which may stem answers to one of today's serious public-health problems.

The Public Health Service has plans for setting up demonstrations for the purpose of stimulating mental hygiene activities in areas where they are deficient and of attempting to determine improved methods of conducting such activities. This aspect of the total field will probably not assume very large proportions, though just a few such demonstration units may possibly contribute much to public-health practice in mental hygiene.

The Public Health Service has operated, since July 1943, an Employees' Health Service which provides coordinating and consultative services regarding methods, scope, and standards for operating health programs within those Government agencies which request services in these matters. One of the units of this health service is that devoted to mental hygiene, whose program is truly preventive insofar as its emphasis is primarily on the solution of various problems that interfere with satisfactory job adjustment. In addition to consultative and instructional services to physicians and nurses of the health service, this unit conducts lectures and classes for employees and instructs personnel officers, supervisors, and counselors in emotional hygiene. Although this program reaches a limited number of the population, the experiences relating to job adjustments, supervisor-employee relationships, scientific personnel management, and, in fact, the entire field of industrial mental hygiene have demonstrated the advantages of such an approach. Progress in counselling and guidance in other fields and under other circumstances (considering now the population as a whole) is indeed closely related to the work of the Mental Hygiene Unit of the Employees' Health Service.

The direct activities of the Federal Government in mental hygiene are limited to research, demonstrations, and preventive services to certain employees (including similar programs in the military forces). However, the broader application of the knowledge gained in these activities is utilized in furthering mental health among all of the population.

Federal Subsidies

The Mental Health Act of July 1946 provides for the granting of funds to States and other political subdivisions and to universities, hospitals, laboratories, other public or private institutions, and individuals for research, training, and developing the most effective methods of prevention, diagnosis, and treatment of psychiatric disorders. These grants-in-aid are administered through the Division of Mental Hygiene of the Bureau of Medical Services of the Public Health Service, the largest proportion of the money going to the States which have submitted plans for establishing and improving the mental health services in their communities. Table VI, page 138, shows the 1949 budget of the Division of Mental Hygiene.

In keeping with the general philosophy of advocating administrative self-determination by State and local agencies (insofar as consistent with sound practices), the States are required to submit plans for establishing mental hygiene programs. The plans submitted by several States have shown diversity in principal objectives, points of emphasis, and organizational development. Since public-health practices in mental hygiene have not yet been established to the same degree as in other fields, it is perhaps wise to encourage these and other different approaches. Among the items for which some States are using the money granted to them (and matched from State funds) is the establishment or expansion of mental hygiene clinics. This is an attempt to bring integrated psychiatric teams to communities where such services are inadequate to meet the needs of the public. In general, such clinics tend to be treatment centers, but the preventive attitude is involved in the services to persons with mild emotional or behavior symptoms (these being often no different from what, in another, would be considered "normal").

137

TABLE VI.—*Division of Mental Hygiene (Bureau of Medical Services of U. S. Public Health Service) Budget for Fical Year 1949*

Community Services		$3, 888, 820
Grants to States	$3, 550, 000	
Consultative services	130, 820	
Demonstration clinics	132, 500	
District of Columbia Juvenile Court	15, 000	
Administration of Community Services Section	60, 500	
	3, 888, 820	
Hospital Services		3, 708, 000
Fort Worth, Tex	1, 706, 500	
Lexington, Ky	2, 001, 500	
	3, 708, 000	
Research		731, 100
Grants	470, 000	
Fellowships	100, 000	
National Institute of Mental Health	89, 000	
Publications, reports, statistics	72, 100	
	731, 100	
Training and standards		1, 696, 085
Graduate training	1, 430, 000	
Demonstrations in professional education	107, 935	
Institutes	20, 450	
Administration of Training and Standards Section	137, 700	
	1, 696, 085	
Administration		303, 340
Total budget		$10, 327, 345

The integrated staff of such a clinic (psychiatrist, psychiatric social worker, psychologist, psychiatric nurse) has functions other than that of seeing patients. Consultant services for private physicians, hospital clinics, health department physicians and nurses, when competently furnished, have their obvious benefits. This staff can participate in a community educational program in cooperation with such agencies as schools, colleges, civic organizations, parent-teacher associations, social workers, and other public and private agencies.

Another important use of the money by the State health authority is in facilitating training of professional personnel, chiefly psychiatrists, psychiatric social workers, clinical psychologists, and psychiatric nurses. This aspect of the program attempts to alleviate the well-known shortage of trained mental hygiene workers as well as their equally well-known maldistribution over the Nation as a whole.

Training and research are also facilitated by grants-in-aid to universities, hospitals, clinics, and other teaching centers, and by the award of stipends and fellowships to qualified individuals. The extent to which these research activities are integrated with one another is not yet evident because of the relative newness of the program, but every effort should be made to achieve coordination.

SUMMARY

Preventive mental hygiene services are conducted by several agencies of the Federal Government and, through Federal subsidies, by the several States and other public and private agencies. Federal programs have usually been a part of general health services, and have been implemented by mental health education among Government employees (including military personnel). In addition, the National Institute of Mental Health has begun a research program, and plans for demonstration mental-hygiene programs have been formulated.

State plans have stressed mental hygiene clinics, mental health education programs in cooperation with community agencies, training of personnel and a certain amount of research. Grants-in-aid have helped institutions and individuals in training and research. Because the Mental Hygiene Division works so closely with States, its position in the Bureau of Medical Services is somewhat anomalous. A more logical administrative arrangement would place it in the Bureau of States Services where it could work more closely with the proposed Division of Grants.

Since mental hygiene is a relatively new activity in public-health practice, much about it remains to be defined. The meaning of mental well-being (individual, community, national), cause and effect relationships, host versus environment (to borrow an epidemiological concept) administrative considerations—these and others need to be worked out through experience and critical evaluation.

RECOMMENDATIONS

1. That the administration of the two hospitals now operated by the Division of Mental Hygiene be transferred to the proposed Medical Care Service of the National Health Administration.

2. That the Division of Mental Hygiene be transferred from the Bureau of Medical Services of the Bureau of State Services.

3. That the Division of Mental Hygiene be responsible for carrying out demonstration programs, in coordination with the activities of State and local agencies and with the National Institute of Mental Health.

4. That the Division of Mental Hygiene supply consultant services to States and other agencies through the district offices of the Public Health Service, and continue to study the programs evolved by these agencies critically and analytically.

5. That grants-in-aid to States and other agencies and individuals be continued, being administered by the proposed Division of Grants, with the Division of Mental Hygiene acting in an advisory capacity.

6. That sponsorship of training of personnel continue in effect in order to meet the problems of shortage and poor distribution of qualified specialists.

7. That the Mental Hygiene Unit of the Employees' Health Service expand its work to extend to all Federal employees and place additional emphasis on the job and family relationships of the individuals.

Public Health Disaster Preparation

It is not the province of this report to discuss health problems of civil defense in wartime, which are being studied by the Medical Advisor to the National Security Resources Board (Public Law 253, 80th Cong.) and by the Medical Section of the Office of Civil Defense Planning set up under the National Military Establishment. It is important to suggest, however, that in omitting the Federal Security Agency from representation on the National Security Resources Board the civilian health problems that would be so serious in war apparently have been slighted.

Even during peacetime, floods, hurricanes, explosions, epidemics, and the like often assume disaster proportions and require public-health organization to protect the people. The American Red Cross, as a quasi-governmental organization, plays an indispensable role in mobilizing health resources through voluntary contributions, as does the National Foundation for Infantile Paralysis in its special field. Both these organizations are demonstrating much greater recognition of the importance of teamwork with governmental and other voluntary health agencies in areas where disasters occur than has too often been the case in the past. Part of the difficulty in cooperation has undoubtedly resulted from imperfect planning by governmental health agencies. The Public Health Service has recently set up the Health Emergency Planning Unit with a small staff in the office of the Surgeon General, thereby taking its rightful place of leadership in correcting this deficiency. The purposes of this unit are to "draw plans for more comprehensive public-health catastrophe service to be offered in response to peacetime emergency requests from States" and to "plan a coordinated program for safeguarding public health during a national emergency."

There must be joint planning by all Federal and national voluntary agencies which may be involved in providing services in disasters, as well as planning to mobilize fully the resources which the Public Health Service may itself be able to make available. This involves:

1. Communicable Disease Center, Atlanta.

2. Development of a group of Reserve officers in the Commissioned Corps, subject to emergency mobilization for disaster service.

140

The Communicable Disease Center is operated under the Bureau of State Services in the Public Health Service. It represents a relatively new and important development in that all types of medical and auxiliary personnel equipped to deal with epidemics are available for emergency duty upon call by the States. Necessary mobile equipment is at hand. The Center grew out of the program of malaria control in war areas which the Public Health Service conducted so effectively in World War II and which resulted in reducing the incidence of malaria in the armed forces in the continental United States very materially below that which prevailed in World War I.

RECOMMENDATIONS

The Health Emergency Planning Unit in the Public Health Service has a useful function in planning for public-health participation in disasters and should be continued, its staff being augmented as may be required.

PREVENTIVE MEDICINE ACTIVITIES OF VETERANS ADMINISTRATION AND THE ARMED SERVICES

Both the Veterans Administration and the armed services have to be considered with respect to activities in preventive medicine. There is, however, no organic connection between the two and each will be taken up separately.

The Veterans Administration

The Veterans Administration is not legally permitted to carry on preventive activities, but must await the development of actual disease before making its medical facilities available to veterans in the opinion of its legal staff. No special division of preventive medicine is maintained, but certain activities of the department of medicine and surgery are preventive in nature. It is fundamentally true that when the best possible medical treatment is provided a patient early in his disease, it can be shown readily that complications, sequelae and often death are prevented, and the period of illness and convalescence shortened.

Activities

In certain special areas there are activities of a preventive nature in the more commonly accepted sense of the term:

1. *Neuropsychiatry.*—Mental-hyiene clinics are operated at regional offices and some hospitals and definite attempts made to get patients under treatment early. Members of a veteran's family may be contacted by psychiatric social workers, but, if found to be in need of care, they cannot be treated by the Veterans Administration. They must be referred elsewhere even if contributing to the veteran's mental problems. There is no reason, however, why the Veterans Administration could not contract with a health-department mental-hygiene clinic where one existed, and agree to pay for the care of a veteran so that he and his family might be treated by the same psychiatrist.

2. *Venereal Disease.*—At the time of discharge at separation centers numerous veterans were found to have syphilis, and many were not previously diagnosed or had received inadequate treatment. The follow-up of this group has been far from adequate. A sample of

142

such cases studied has shown: (*a*) 10,000 positive or doubtful spinal fluid; (*b*) 150,000 treated, but spinal fluid not examined; and (*c*) 40,000 positive on separation, but not treated.

The armed forces have not maintained a syphilis register though the Hawley committee has recommended that they do so in the future. Such a register would facilitate greatly the venereal-disease control work of the Veterans Administration. Up to the present time, it has been impossible to discover and follow a great many veterans with syphilis who should be receiving treatment.

The problem of "service connection" is often a knotty one in the venereal-disease field, even though to establish service connection it must be shown that the disease was contracted while in service, that the earliest manifestation was reported, and that treatment was continued until the approved conclusion thereof.

Up to 1940 following World War I, the Veterans Administration spent $83,000,000 for medical care of venereal disease. The cost of a case of paresis was estimated at $40,000. At present over a million dollars a year is being paid as compensation to venereal-disease cases. I? the results following World War II are comparable with World War I, the medical care costs alone of venereal disease are estimated at $328,000,000 and compensation would increase the total to over a billion dollars. (It is too early to predict whether newer treatment methods used in World War II will reduce materially the late complications of syphilis which are so costly.)

3. *Tuberculosis.*—Some very useful preventive measures are in operation which will undoubtedly reduce the costs of providing medical care for tuberculosis veterans. Chest X-rays are being made to determine whether tubreculosis is present on all admissions to veterans' hospitals and "homes," all veterans examined in regional offices, hospital patients if institutionalized more than a year, and hospital personnel annually. New cases of tuberculosis among veterans are being reported at the rate of 450–500 per month now.

Tuberculosis case registers are maintained in each of the 67 regional offices to facilitate follow-up; contacts are listed and health departments notified so that contacts may be followed.

Hospitalization is discussed in another section.

4. *Rehabilitation and job placement.*—This may be considered in many respects a preventive type of program, and it has great importance. It will be discussed elsewhere.

5. *Examinations for evidence of tropical disease.*—Fortunately, the incidence of tropical disease among veterans has been considerably lower than was anticipated, but it has been important as a preventive measure to search for evidence of such disease.

1. Preventive measures such as venereal disease control, tuberculosis control and mental hygiene, which are likely to save great sums that might otherwise be spent for medical care including hospitalization, should be available readily to veterans. This may be accomplished in several ways:

a. Authorize and establish preventive measures to be carried on by the Veterans Administration, at least in certain fields where it can be shown the savings to the Federal Government would be enormous.

b. Authorize and establish a very efficient referral and follow-up system to be operated by the Veterans Administration to make sure that veterans receive the benefits of preventive measures that may be available through private physicians or local community facilities. This is an added reason for strengthening local health service to make such services available to veterans financially unable to employ a private physician.

2. Syphilis registers should be established and maintained by the armed forces and made available to the Veterans Administration.

3. The medical staff of the Veterans Administration should be encouraged in every possible way to have a major interest in prevention, health promotion and rehabilitation. These three approaches to health are relatively inexpensive and productive. Treatment and alleviation of disease and injury are important, but they are costly.

The Armed Forces

The Army, Navy, and Air Force each has a preventive medicine division serving in essentially similar roles in each branch of the armed services. All of these preventive medicine divisions recommend policies, standards and procedures for the control of disease, particularly communicable disease, insect and pest control, sanitation and industrial health. None of them has important operating functions, all serving in a staff capacity. The size of the preventive medicine divisions has been markedly curtailed since the close of the recent war.

ARMY PREVENTIVE MEDICINE DIVISION

This division operates under the Surgeon-General and is divided into five branches as follows:

1. Laboratory Branch.
2. Infectious Diseases Branch:
    a. Epidemiology Section.
    b. Immunization Section.
    c. Venereal Disease Section.

3. Nutrition Branch.
4. Environmental Sanitation Branch:
    a. Sanitation Section.
    b. Sanitary Engineering Section.
    c. Occupational Hygiene Section.
5. Medical Intelligence Branch:

    a. Analysis Section.
    b. Archives Section.

The division is staffed with six Army medical officers, one Army nutritionist, one Army entomologist and one Army sanitary engineer. There are two civil-service technical people in the division, one serving as Assistant Chief of the Laboratory and the other as Chief of Medical Intelligence. Both these were Army officers during the last war.

Research activities for the Army in the preventive medicine field are conducted largely by the Army Epidemiological Board, now administered by the Research and Development Board. This arrangement works quite satisfactorily.

The Army has a definite policy of sending officers to schools of public health for training. During the prewar years, this was done at the rate of about two to four per year. Since the war the number of men trained in public health schools has increased markedly: 1945–1946, 19; 1946–1947, 11; 1947–1948, 14; 1948–1949, 12. Most of these men so trained have been kept in preventive medicine work rather than being assigned to nonrelated duties. There is one in each Army area in the United States (6). Men are also assigned to the Army in Japan, Germany, Korea, Okinawa, etc., and to civil government in Japan and Germany. Some of them are assigned to work in foreign ports.

The actual operating work in preventive medicine is the responsibility of medical officers assigned to various Army areas and units under the direction of the commanding officer.

NAVY DIVISION OF PREVENTIVE MEDICINE

This division is set up in the Bureau of Medicine and Surgery of which the Surgeon General of the Navy is Chief, under the direct supervision of the Assistant Chief of the Bureau for Research and Medical Military Specialists.

In this Bureau, there are four divisions:

1. Research.
2. Atomic Defense.
3. Special Weapons.
4. Preventive Medicine Division.

Under the Preventive Medicine Division there are three branches:

1. Communicable Disease Control:
   a. Acute Communicable Disease—Epidemiology.
   b. Tuberculosis.
   c. Venereal Disease Control.
2. Quarantine Liaison Branch.
3. Sanitation and Health Branch:
   a. General Sanitation.
   b. Pest and Insect Control.
   c. Rodent Control.
   d. Industrial Hygiene.
   e. Accident Prevention.

There are five medical officers in the central Preventive Medicine Division; four additional doctors work in the communicable disease epidemiological unit, investigating epidemics as they arise and carrying on various kinds of research in the interim. At the naval district level, the general medical officer has a nonmedical man assigned to him to carry on preventive medicine activities.

The Navy has sent about eight men per year to schools of public health on a voluntary basis; not all of the men so trained have been kept in preventive medicine work in the Navy.

The Navy is particularly proud of the results of tetanus-toxoid immunization done in 1941. There were only four cases and two deaths in the Navy from tetanus, a much lower rate than existed in the World War I records. The Navy, early in the war, began preinduction X-rays for tuberculosis and this was placed on an annual basis for all men in the Navy beginning 1944 and 1945.

AIR FORCE—PREVENTIVE MEDICINE DIVISION

There are only two men in this division, the chief and a sanitary engineer. The Air Surgeon exhibited a great deal of interest in the discussion of preventive medicine activities of the Air Force. It was pointed out that, in the Air Force, preventive medicine activities fall in three major divisions:

1. *Communicable disease control and sanitation.*—Here principles developed by the Surgeon General of the Army are followed in most instances. The Air Force is given opportunity to comment on proposed new policies before they become effective and may either concur or not as seems appropriate. Certain special problems peculiar to aviation medicine such as the disinsectization of planes and problems relating to personnel engaged where no Army or Navy forces are operating are handled on a separate basis by the Air Force. The immunization requirements are identical with those of the Army. There are some difficulties at the present time in getting morbidity

146

figures separate from the Army figures. Perhaps this is because of the fact that the Air Force Medical Corps has not yet been separated entirely from the Army.

2. *Industrial medicine.*—Seven depots are maintained at present by the Air Force, carrying on engineering and supply functions and employing from 1,500 to 9,000 employees each. Here the program is to provide a hygienic working environment on the job, medical service for all civilian employees and education of personnel on employment hazards, accident prevention and proper health habits. Civilian physicians are used in cases where there are many civilian employees.

3. *Aviation medicine.*—Aviation medicine itself is essentially preventive, and the importance of having medical officers familiar with flying conditions is considered great. The development by the Air Surgeon's office of body armor in the European theatre of operations shows an actual record of having saved 500 crewmen of planes operating in this area. The ditching procedure developed by the Air Surgeon for planes having to land in the North Sea and the English Channel may also be cited. Prior to the development of these procedures, only 1.8 percent of the men were being saved. After the medical service of the Air Force developed a definite procedure and the men were trained in this operation, the saving increased to 46 percent. There were actually 2,500 men saved by this procedure.

The problem of frost bites was also one which engaged the attention of the medical service. Mental health problems were handled by the development of 40 rest homes on English estates where men were sent for a 1 week's period of rest as soon as premonitory symptoms of battle fatigue developed. It is pointed out that the medical officers needed to actually live with the men in order to be able to detect these premonitory symptoms at an early time when rest treatment could be made most effective. At present, a civilian commission is outlining criteria for the diagnosis of combat fatigue and is developing suggestions regarding methods for handling it.

The Air Force has trained six men in schools of public health since the war; only three of these now remain in the Force, including one teaching at the school of aviation medicine. Regular medical officers now receive 8 months of training at this school, Randolph Field, San Antonio. The Air Force would like to shorten this course by 4 months and have all medical officers take a course of the full academic year in schools of public health. About half of the training in the school of aviation medicine is now comparable to that which would be given in schools of public health.

GRANTS-IN-AID IN PUBLIC HEALTH

The principle of grants-in-aid [26] to State and local governments has been known and used throughout practically all our national history. The first grant-in-aid is said to be the provision (in 1785) that a portion of Federal domain be set aside in each township for the maintenance of public schools. Later, a percentage of funds derived from the sale of Federal lands within a State was turned over to the State, generally for educational purposes. Still later, the donation of Federal land to States was modified into a system of actual cash grants. A significant step was taken in 1889 when States were required to match Federal funds as a condition for receiving them (for disabled soldiers and sailors in State homes). Federal inspection or administrative audit with potential sanctions of withholding grants was a more recent development.

Thus, the pattern of grants-in-aid was laid down over a long period of time, gradually evolving through realization of needs and through changing concepts of Federal-State relationships. The implications of Federal versus State powers have been ever present in connection with grants-in-aid and are a prime consideration in a discussion of the entire problem, though not presented in all their ramifications in this report.

The Chamberlain-Kahn Act of 1918 for the control of venereal disease introduced national grants to the field of public health. In 1921 grants to the States for maternal and child-health programs were begun under the Sheppard-Towner Act. Both programs were short-lived and died through dwindling of interest and because of conflicts over the whole philosophy of grants-in-aid. With the passage of the Social Security Act of 1935, grants for maternal and child-health work were reestablished, and general public health grants inaugurated. Later, as part of the same act and under separate acts, venereal disease, tuberculosis, cancer, mental hygiene, heart disease, and other programs were provided for in grants to States. The Hospital Survey and Construction Act of 1946 authorized a program of grants to aid in the building of public and private nonprofit hospitals and health centers.

In addition to the grant programs enumerated above, there are several others, primarily in the field of research, which are considered

---

[26] The terms "grants" and "grants-in-aid" are used synonymously in this report, though their exact definitions may be somewhat different from each other. No distinction is made here as to whether or not a recipient is participating with his own funds, unless such qualification is specifically stated.

CHART IV

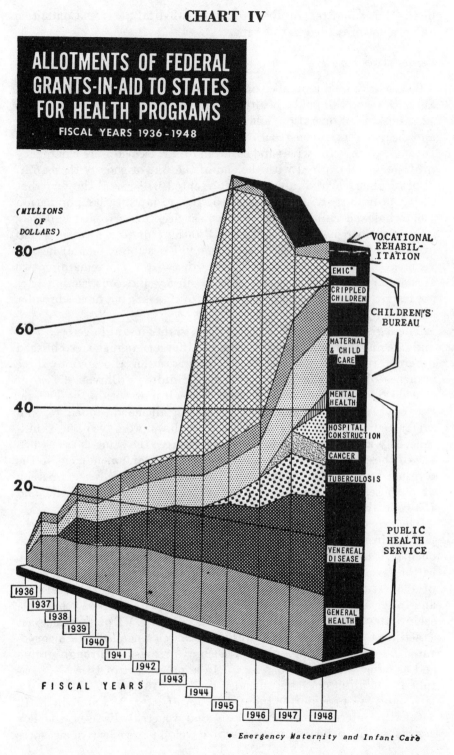

ALLOTMENTS OF FEDERAL GRANTS-IN-AID TO STATES FOR HEALTH PROGRAMS

FISCAL YEARS 1936-1948

(MILLIONS OF DOLLARS)

80

60

40

20

VOCATIONAL REHABIL-ITATION

EMIC*

CRIPPLED CHILDREN

CHILDREN'S BUREAU

MATERNAL & CHILD CARE

MENTAL HEALTH

HOSPITAL CONSTRUCTION

CANCER

TUBERCULOSIS

PUBLIC HEALTH SERVICE

VENEREAL DISEASE

GENERAL HEALTH

FISCAL YEARS

1936
1937
1938
1939
1940
1941
1942
1943
1944
1945
1946
1947
1948

* Emergency Maternity and Infant Care

149

by the Subcommittees on Research of the Medical Services Committee and are not presented in this report.

LEGISLATION

There have been a number of legislative acts authorizing grants-in-aid with respect to public health work. At the present time, there are 12 programs in operation, since the Lanham Act funds for hospital and health center construction and the Emergency Maternal and Infant Care Act for wives and children of servicemen were emergency provisions and expired with the end of the war or shortly thereafter. A brief glance at the categories represented will reveal the fact that they apply largely either to a specific group in the population (maternal and child health services, services for crippled children, industrial hygiene, vocational rehabilitation) or to a disease, group of diseases, or allied conditions (tuberculosis, cancer, mental health, venereal diseases, dental research, heart disease). The remaining two (general public health work, hospital survey and construction) are not restricted with respect to population or diseases, but have a broader and wider application.

The legislative acts establishing these grants-in-aid have been promulgated at different times, written in different language, established different requirements, and their administration allocated to three branches of the Federal Government (Children's Bureau, Office of Special Services, Public Health Service—all now within the Federal Security Agency). Some laws have been amended, added to, and subtracted from. In several instances, laws were written simultaneously and there is uniformity to a degree; the same is true when one of these categories was added to another as an amendment to the original law. But in most cases there is diversity in (a) expression of purpose, (b) specific provision, (c) mode of apportionment, and (d) conditions required to be met by the recipient.

The expression of purpose in a legislative act usually influences the policies in administration of the specific provisions thereof. Consequently, it is worth while to examine purposes as stated in the language of the several laws here under discussion. The Social Security Act of 1935 (title V, which refers to maternal and child health services and to services for crippled children) states as its purpose "to enable each State to extend and improve . . . ." Title VI of the same act (relating to general public health work, later amended and incorporated into P. L. 410 of July 1, 1944) says "to assist through grants and as otherwise provided . . . ." In another part of title V (vocational rehabilitation, later amended as P. L. 113 of July 6, 1943), the law states "to provide for the promotion of . . . ." Later, in P. L. 410, with reference to tuberculosis and venereal diseases, the law asserts that its primary purpose is "to develop more effective measures

150

for the prevention, treatment, and control of . . ." and only secondarily "to assist through grants and as otherwise provided . . . ." The most recent laws, mental, dental, and heart, are worded alike (though each is a separate act) : "to improve the health of the people of the United States through the conducting of researches . . . to assist and foster such researches . . . provide training . . . and promote the coordination of all such researches . . . ." However, the recent Hospital Survey and Construction Act proposes "to assist the several States . . . ."

There is a question whether these few observations may be interpreted as indicating a trend in Federal grant-in-aid philosophy from one of assistance to one of actual performance. There is no question, however, that no consistent philosophy regarding the role of Federal agency in the administration of public health in this country has prevailed. The effect on a State health agency of a relatively free hand in one category and close Federal supervision and participation in another is likely to be one of confusion, and in many instances has led to relatively ineffective use of the funds. In the interest of better administration of public health, clear statements of purpose are greatly needed.

The present system of grants-in-aid has developed through a consideration by Congress of the several categories mentioned in the preceding paragraphs, with one of these categories including general public health work not otherwise specifically provided for. If this categorical approach to public health problems is continued, additional groups of the population or attacks on other groups of diseases will likely be the objects of future laws. This would undoubtedly accentuate the inconsistencies herein observed with increased disadvantages in administrative practices. Then, too, public health problems existing in the several States vary considerably and the emphasis in each locality must be different. Best results can be obtained through more local determination of needs and measures calculated to meet these needs. A modification or consolidation of the categorical approach toward the general and away from the specific grant-in-aid is indicated.

On the other hand, funds appropriated by the Congress have traditionally been for specific purposes. A departure from this policy would mean less determination by the Federal Government of the methods of using these monies. Furthermore, appropriations in categorical fields have frequently resulted from stimulation by strong and active pressure groups with special interests. Unquestionably, this has led to larger appropriations and earlier action than would have been realized with a general approach. Methods must be found to retain the interest of these special groups in a balanced program by assuring adequate attention to the categorical problems.

The dimensions of each problem under a specific category is such that the relatively small amount of money heretofore available to meet it could be wisely spent. However, as funds become larger, this may no longer be true and a more balanced program will become increasingly important. For these reasons, definite policy should be developed as a guide for future legislative action and administration of grants-in-aid for public health work.

These acts specifically provide for grants-in-aid to be made to States, universities, hospitals, laboratories, individuals, and/or other private and public agencies (not all acts include all these as potential recipients). They emphasize research, training, construction or lease of facilities, purchase of equipment, and/or administrative activities. Some require prior recommendation by the National Health Council or its counterpart, others do not. The result of all this is that policies, regulations, and procedures become varied to a marked degree, with consequent confusion and frustration among the recipients. The diversity of aims in these various acts is perhaps justified, and provisions must be made for an experimental approach in some categories, a training approach in others, a straight administrative approach in still others, or combinations of any of these. Over-all codification, however, should provide for unified administration with enough flexibility to permit varying degrees of emphasis.

Several of the laws providing for grants-in-aid within a specific category (cancer, mental health, dental research, heart disease) have also set up special advisory councils to advise the Surgeon General in these specific fields and to recommend the grants. If the categorical approach is to be modified in the direction of general public health work, it would be wiser to abolish these categorical councils in favor of an over-all National Health Advisory Council and to have consultants in the various specialities assist the Council in technical matters (as special panels or committees). This Council would continue to advise in the general field of health as it now does.

Grants are apportioned in different ways, as specified in the legislation which established them. A minimum amount for each State is mentioned in three of them (maternal and child health services, services for crippled children, hospital survey and construction), but not in the others. Population of the State is specified as a factor in certain instances, but not in others. The extent of the problem under attack bears weight in some acts, but not in others. The financial need of the State receives consideration in several cases, but not in others. And in one instance (dental research) the entire matter is left up to a recommendation of the National Advisory Dental Council. As a contrast to the latter provision, the law on hospital survey and construction specified that a certain complicated formula be applied.

Greater uniformity of policy in the method of allocation of funds would provide for better and more efficient administration of the program, better understanding on the part of the individual States as to what the intentions of Congress are, and readier compliance by the States with the conditions they are required to meet in order to qualify for grants.

Under conditions to be met by recipient, considerable variation is again observed. Several acts require that the funds be administered by a State health agency, others by a State agency, others do not specify. Participation with State and local funds is required in most of the acts, though only two mention the extent to which Federal funds must be matched. In one act, Federal funds match those of the States, rather than vice versa. In most of the laws, the requirements are general, leaving specific items for regulation by the Surgeon General.

An important requirement of some laws is that a State agency which receives Federal grants shall establish and maintain a merit system of personnel administration. (In other grants, this requirement is included in regulations of the Surgeon General, and is therefore subject to change.) This provision has done much to promote better qualifications of public health workers and should be incorporated into law.

Unification of these provisions would permit the formulation of clearer administrative policies and procedures, and would enable the respective States to improve their own planning of public health programs.

The diversity and variation of the entire grant-in-aid program in public health is directly due to the lack of uniformity in the several acts of Congress which established these programs. In order to unify these acts and thereby improve the administrative machinery needed to carry out their provisions, Congressional action is indicated.

Organization for Administering Grants-in-Aid

The several legislative acts which authorize grants-in-aid place responsibility for their administration upon a specific person (Federal Security Administrator, Surgeon General, etc.), requiring the delegation of such duties to an organizational hierarchy. In the Public Health Service, where the majority of grants relating to health are handled, the set-up already existed and simply adopted the new duties imposed upon it without much upheaval or "expansion pains," that is, as far as the actual allocation of money is concerned. However, some of the factors which tend to disperse the activity and thus influence its effectiveness need to be discussed.

Within the Bureau of State Services of the Public Health Service are several divisions which administer grants-in-aid. The State Relations Division has the general public health grants, the Tuberculosis Division controls its funds, as do Hospital Facilities, Venereal

Disease, and Industrial Hygiene Divisions. (The latter is responsible for a grant-in-aid program, the funds for which are derived from the general grants for public health, not set up by separate congressional act.) Within this Bureau, therefore, there is duplication of administrative functions, and, although the cost of such organizational practice is not easily determined, duplication of functions is known to be expensive. The consolidation of grant-in-aid programs within one division under the direction of the chief thereof, would improve the efficiency of these programs. It is important that the administration of grants-in-aid be a professional function, not one which is delegated to accountants or other fiscal officers.

In addition to the programs within the Bureau of State Services, other grant-in-aid funds are administered in other sections of the Public Health Service. For instance, in the National Institute of Health, the Division of Research Grants and Fellowships administers the program corresponding to its title; in the National Institute of Health, the National Cancer Institute provides grants relating to cancer research, education, and control; in the Bureau of Medical Services, the Mental Hygiene Division allots grants-in-aid in this field (though the Division of Research Grants and Fellowships in the National Institute of Health acts as a clearing house in processing the latter). As a contrast to all the above, the Division of Dentistry (in the Office of the Surgeon General) acts in an advisory capacity to the States Relations Division (Bureau of States Services) with respect to grants-in-aid in dental research.

In other words, within the Public Health Service (without considering for the moment the programs in the Children's Bureau and the Office of Special Services) there are diversification, duplication, and some variation of policy in the administration of these funds. Reorganization is clearly indicated, and perhaps the best set-up would be one similar to that for dentistry. All health grants-in-aid, including those that might be transferred to the Public Health Service from other Federal agencies, should be administered by a Division of Grants, with the various "technical" divisions acting in advisory capacities. The National Advisory Health Council (with the assistance of its specialized committees) should give general approval to the methods by which these funds are allocated.

Within the States receiving these funds, the most important organizational problem is one of simplification. Hitherto, a new categorical act has sometimes forced a State to develop a new organizational unit, frequently not needed in that State. Sometimes a unit outside of the State health authority has been created to administer Federal funds in a health grant, thus producing a less unified health administration in that State. The elimination of categories and the concentration of responsibility for health grants in one Federal agency would set a pattern which the States might well follow in building their own organ-

154

izations for health administration. At present, no less than 14 different types of agencies in State government (such as welfare, agriculture, labor, education, special boards or commissions, etc., in addition to health departments) have major responsibility in the various States for specific health activities.[27] The United States Public Health Service could still act in its capacity as advisor and thus promote this more effective organizational scheme. The same practices would then filter down to local units, with consequent benefit to the public.

REGULATIONS AND POLICIES

The rules and regulations of the Public Health Service relating to grants-in-aid are promulgated after consultation with the State and Territorial health authorities, and insofar as is practicable the Surgeon General obtains their agreement prior to the issuance of such regulations or amendments. This assures participation in planning by State health officers and their staffs. The rules and regulations may be considered not only an expression of policy but also a guide for procedure in administering the funds. Terms used in the legislative acts are defined and interpreted; for example, "financial need" of a State is defined as the relative per capita income for the most recent 5-year period. This definition is used to determine the basis of allotment, in conjunction with definitions of population and extent of problem.

There are six factors listed under venereal disease which are to be taken into consideration in determining the extent of the problem, three under tuberculosis, three under special health problems, and two under mental health. (The other grant-in-aid programs are not mentioned in these regulations.) Among the factors are: Morbidity and mortality rates, diagnostic and treatment needs, special conditions which create unequal burdens in administration, etc. These factors are objective in character, and, used judiciously according to the weights assigned to them, should result in an equitable distribution of the available funds. However, the original purpose of grants-in-aid should be kept in mind, namely, one of assistance to those who need it most. The financial need of the State should receive a high "weight" in determining allocations.

The question of the categorical approach to grants-in-aid again arises. Different criteria are used in formulating policies and procedures for the several categories of funds, and rightly so under the present restrictions set down by Congress in its acts, but combination into a general public health program would eliminate many of the unnecessarily complex administrative procedures.

The rules and regulations express, too, the requirements which a State shall meet in order to receive funds. Specifically the State must

---

[27] Moutin, J. W., and Flook, E., "Guide to Health Organization in the U. S.", Pub. H. Serv. Misc. Publication No. 35 (1947).

describe the current organization and functions of health services and proposals for extending, improving, and otherwise modifying such organization and function. This regulation places the planning phase of the administrative process where it properly belongs, upon the State health authority. Of course, the plan must be approved by the Public Health Service before the funds are given, but the fact that the State is responsible helps improve ability to plan on that level.

Other financial requirements (matching) are given, and general procedures for audits, reports, fiscal affairs, etc., are listed. These are standardized, and necessarily so, for if 48 or more different reports or systems were in use, the Public Health Service could not effectively keep track of the money and see to it that it is expended according to the provisions of the law. Regulations of the Children's Bureau with respect to its grants-in-aid and of the Office of Vocational Rehabilitation in its program are similar to those discussed.

In general, the rules and regulations are extensive enough to assure proper administration of the law, but yet not so restrictive as to destroy initiative and autonomy on the part of the State health authority, although the prerogatives of the latter are preserved to a very considerable extent.

These regulations would, of course, be rendered obsolete if Congress adopts the recommendations to consolidate the categories now in existence. New regulations would be needed, but if they are written in the same spirit as the current ones, the program should proceed even more effectively than hitherto.

Administrative Relationships

The district officers of the Public Health Service are the field representatives of the Surgeon General, and are now to be coordinated with the regional offices of the Federal Security Agency. When a State plan is submitted to the district office, it is there reviewed and conferences are held with the State health agency in an attempt to bring the plan into conformance with sound practices. It is then forwarded to Washington, where approval and allotment of funds are handled. The district office then continues as the consulting and advisory agency to the State in administering the plan.

The district director is consultant to the director of the State health agency on matters of general public health, and, through the latter, the specialists on the staff of the district director confer with and advise the chiefs of divisions in the State with respect to their fields of interest. Part of this function is supervisory rather than consultative in that the Public Health Service officers inquire into the progress of the program, check to see whether it conforms to the plan, and note whether the expenditure of funds is appropriate. There is some variation in the extent of this supervision from place to place, but it is generally recognized that this Federal supervisory relationship should be minimized insofar as possible, recognizing, however, the Public Health Service as the responsible agency in the administration of the grant-in-aid program.

The elimination of categorical grants would have no visible effect upon the administrative relationships between the Public Health Service and the State health agencies. The latter would have more responsibility in determining the functional allocation of funds, but approval of the plan and grant of the money would proceed in the same way as at present, as would the consultative activities of the district office, both general and specialized. However, there might be some decrease in necessity for as close supervision, since the State health agency would be able to exercise more flexibility in the use of funds.

The Children's Bureau and the Office of Vocational Rehabilitation have similar field staffs, also coordinated into the regional offices of the Federal Security Agency. Their representatives work with State officials, the Department of Health and the Crippled Children's Commission (in most States) being the agencies with which the Children's Bureau makes its contacts, while the Office of Vocational Rehabilitation works chiefly with a Department of Education, or Welfare, and a Commission for the Blind (in some States). Field offices of the agencies mentioned here are discussed more fully in a separate report.

EVALUATION OF RESULTS

A considerable sum of money has been expended by the Federal Government through grants-in-aid to States for health work (table VII, p. 159). How these expenditures have resulted in improving the health of the people and in decreased sickness and death rates is impossible to measure accurately.

There are, however, certain indices which give a good picture of the health process of a population. One of the most reliable of these is the infant mortality rate—the number of deaths during a year of children under 1 year of age per 1,000 live births during that year. It is generally agreed that the infant mortality rate is a more sensitive index of the state of health of a community than any other. The rates for the United States registration area provide evidence of the worth of one of the grant-in-aid programs, namely the Maternal and Child Health Services (Social Security Act). Two periods of 11 years are presented in table VIII, page 160, one prior to the effective operation of the program and one subsequent.

These same data are presented graphically in chart V, page 158, which shows that on the average the infant mortality rate dropped faster subsequent to the effective beginnings of the program. The projection line (C) represents a theoretical trend which would have prevailed had the "old" rates persisted. It can be argued that these

CHART V—Trends in Infant Mortality and the Social Security Act

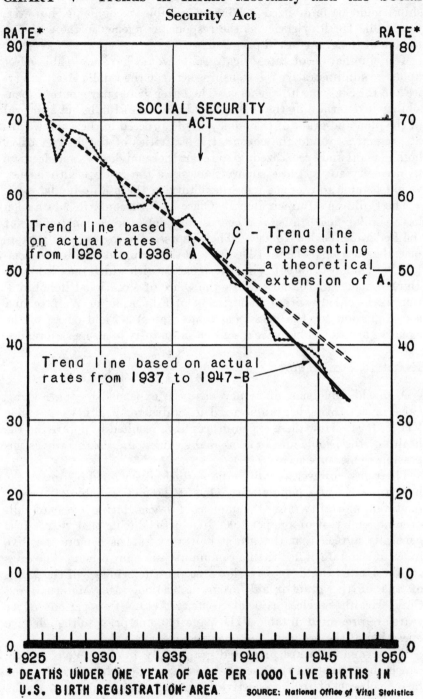

RATE*

SOCIAL SECURITY ACT

Trend line based on actual rates from 1926 to 1936 A

C - Trend line representing a theoretical extension of A.

Trend line based on actual rates from 1937 to 1947-B

* DEATHS UNDER ONE YEAR OF AGE PER 1000 LIVE BIRTHS IN U.S. BIRTH REGISTRATION AREA

SOURCE: National Office of Vital Statistics

158

TABLE VII.—Federal grants-in-aid to States for health—U. S. Public Health Service

[In thousands of dollars]

Year	Total	Rural sanitation	Venereal disease control	General public health	Tuberculosis control	Cancer control	Hospital survey and construction	Mental health	Children's Bureau		EMIC	Office of Special Services, Vocational Rehabilitation
									Maternal and child health	Crippled children		
1916	25	[1]25										
1917	25	[1]25										
1918	150	[1]150										
1919	1,062	[1]150										
1920	1,036	[2]45	[2]912									
1921	305	[2]31	[2]991									
1922	274	[2]45	[2]274									
1923	971	[2]46	[2]229						[1]716			
1924	1,014	[2]44	[2]209						[1]877			
1925	1,026	[2]68	[2]93						[1]933			
1926	1,026	[2]78	[2]25						[1]948			
1927	1,023	[2]66							[1]957			
1928	1,036	[2]79							[1]957			
1929	1,111	[2]334							[1]777			
1930	332	[2]332										
1931	286	[2]286										
1932	319	[2]319										
1933	265	[2]265										
1934												
1935												
1936	4,435			[2]2,451					[2]1,252	[2]732		
1937	13,881			8,882					[2]2,990	[2]2,009		
1938	15,534			9,117					[2]3,722	[2]2,695		
1939	17,330		[2]2,400	8,208					[2]3,724	[2]2,998		
1940	22,304		4,379	9,723					[2]4,823	[2]3,379		
1941	26,282		5,672	11,500					[2]5,468	[2]3,920		
1942	29,353		7,817	11,222					[2]5,983	[2]4,053		
1943	32,000		10,170	11,027					[2]5,740	[2]3,863	[2]1,200	
1944	61,828		10,276	11,454	1,370				[2]5,946	[2]3,782	[2]29,700	[2]670
1945	80,855		12,247	11,614	5,200				[2]5,553	[2]3,874	[2]45,000	[2]1,197
1946	78,557		12,522	11,000	6,880				[2]5,935	[2]4,059	[2]38,050	[2]1,791
1947	68,842		15,446	11,750	6,790	2,500	371		[2]10,672	[2]7,413	[2]10,953	[2]2,857
1948	68,252		13,954	11,217		2,500	6,396	3,000	[2]10,564	[2]7,423	[2]2,067	[2]4,341
Total	530,739	2,388	97,616	129,165	20,240	5,000	6,767	3,000	78,537	50,200	126,970	10,856

[1] Appropriated.   [2] Payments to States.

159

TABLE VIII.—*Deaths of children under 1 year of age per 1,000 live births (infant mortality rates) United States registration area*

Year	Rate	Year	Rate
1926	73.3	1937	54.4
1927	64.6	1938	51.0
1928	68.7	1939	48.0
1929	67.6	1940	47.0
1930	64.6	1941	45.3
1931	61.6	1942	40.4
1932	57.6	1943	40.4
1933	58.1	1944	39.8
1934	60.1	1945	38.3
1935	55.7	1946	33.8
1936	57.1	1947 [1]	32.6

[1] Rate for 1947 is provisional.

"savings" in human lives may be due in part to the great extension of maternal and child health services which took place in 1937 and thereafter. This may be considered a beneficial result of the grant-in-aid program.

A comparison of death rates from several causes in 1935 and 1945 is presented in table IX, below. The changes herein observed are unquestionably influenced to a certain degree by the fact that more well-trained public health workers were located in communities where their services were utilized in the latter year than in the former. In table X, below, is a comparison of the number of people residing in areas in which the standard milk and restaurant ordinances were in effect (in two selected years). These increases undoubtedly represent progress in the health protection of the people.

Another, and perhaps more pertinent, measure of the effect of the grant-in-aid programs is a study of the numbers of local health units established throughout the country before and since the money became available. Such data are presented in table XI, page 162, and chart VI, page 161, and, though not representing the number of lives saved, they do indicate the extent of the health services brought to the people.

TABLE IX.—*Deaths per 100,000 population from selected diseases in 1935 and 1945 (United States registration area)*

	Mortality rates	
	1935	1945
Typhoid fever	2.8	0.4
Diphtheria	3.1	1.2
Scarlet fever	2.1	.2
Measles	3.1	.2

TABLE X.—*Population residing in communities in which standard ordinances were in effect (1937 and 1946)*

	1937	1946
Standard milk ordinance	17,000,000	27,000,000
Standard restaurant ordinance	43,000	40,000,000

160

CHART VI

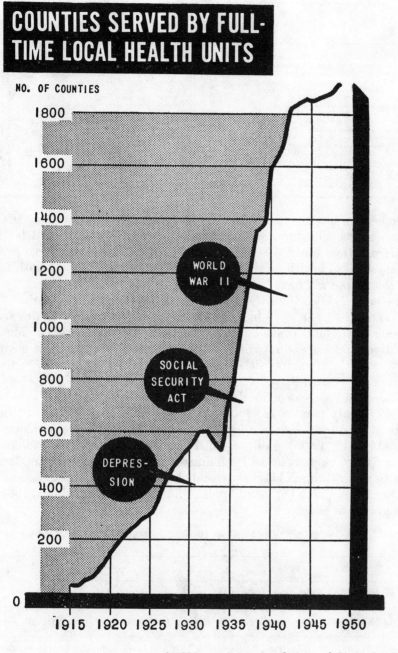

COUNTIES SERVED BY FULL-TIME LOCAL HEALTH UNITS

NO. OF COUNTIES

SOURCE: U.S.P.H.S.   Bureau of State Services

161

TABLE XI.—*Number of local health units (full-time) in operation in the United States: by years*

Year	Number of counties served	Year	Number of counties served
1915	14	1932	610
1916	17	1933	569
1917	30	1934	542
1918	44	1935	762
1919	76	1936	946
1920	138	1937	1,164
1921	186	1938	1,371
1922	211	1939	1,381
1923	237	1940	1,577
1924	278	1941	1,668
1925	316	1942	1,828
1926	347	1943	1,845
1927	426	1944	1,849
1928	476	1945	1,841
1929	519	1946	1,851
1930	553	1947	1,874
1931	610	1948	1,958

The local unit is the ultimate health service agency and without it all our ever-growing knowledge about health and disease would be of little practical use. When our entire population has available to it adequate local health services, then the framework of good health for all the people will have been established.

In table XII, below, are shown the percentages of population, in 1935 and 1946 who lived in areas served by full-time local health services. Grants-in-aid are largely responsible for this increase. Many relatively poor areas have been helped to achieve at least basic health services. Other communities required stimulation to help them mobilize their resources.

The establishment of local health units through the use of Federal funds is only part of the picture. The grants have stimulated improved quality of work and the development of new programs on a sound basis. Training of personnel has helped to raise the standards of program content and of administration in both State and local health units (table XIII, below, and chart VII, p. 163. Considerable research, also, both basic and applied, has been made possible through the grants-in-aid.

TABLE XII.—*Percentage of population residing in areas served by full-time local health units*

	1935	1946
Percent of total United States population	37	72

TABLE XIII.—*Full-time personnel in county health units for 4 selected years*

	Total	Physicians	Nurses	Sanitary	Clerical	Other
1930	2,955	575	1,066	518	534	262
1935	3,435	601	1,339	593	621	281
1937	6,154	862	2,763	1,073	1,111	345
1947	11,092	780	3,974	2,193	2,535	1,610

CHART VII—Full-Time Workers in Local Health Units

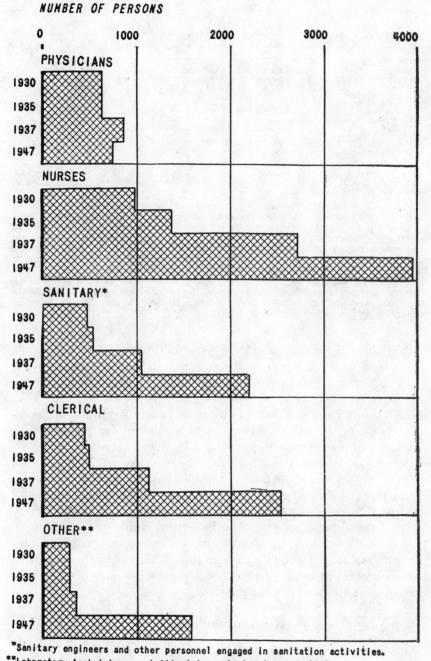

NUMBER OF PERSONS

PHYSICIANS
1930
1935
1937
1947

NURSES
1930
1935
1937
1947

SANITARY*
1930
1935
1937
1947

CLERICAL
1930
1935
1937
1947

OTHER**
1930
1935
1937
1947

*Sanitary engineers and other personnel engaged in sanitation activities.
**Laboratory technicians, nutritionists, veterinarians, dentists,
  health educators, etc.

163

TABLE XIV.—*Expenditures from all sources by State and local health departments exclusive of operating costs of hospitals and sanitoria as reported to Public Health Service for fiscal years 1937, 1940, and 1946*

Source of funds	Amount			Percentage		
	1937	1940	1946	1937	1940	1946
All sources	$25,633,213	$52,077,268	$110,461,634	100.0	100.0	100.0
State government	7,536,031	15,471,813	28,964,335	29.4 } 54.3	29.7 } 60.2	26.2 } 71.3
Local government	6,370,208	15,904,304	49,885,242	24.9	30.5	45.1
Federal grants-in-aid:						
Public Health Service:						
General health	6,727,912	8,727,319	10,576,857	26.2	16.8	9.6
VD control	-----	3,771,639	8,060,306	-----	7.2	7.3
TB control	-----	-----	2,981,138	----- } 45.7	----- } 39.8	2.7 } 28.7
Children's Bureau:						
Maternal and child health	2,990,262	4,823,207	5,934,539	11.7	9.3	5.4
Crippled children	2,008,800	3,378,986	4,059,217	7.8	6.5	3.7

SOURCE.—1. Manuscript, "Ten Years of Grants in Aid for Public Health," Mountin, J. W.; Hankla, E. K., Druzina, G. B., U. S. Public Health Service. 2. Children's Bureau, Personal Communication, Katherine F. Lenroot, July 27, 1948.

NOTE.—The complete picture of health department expenditures cannot be precisely determined. In some instances, especially in earlier years, reports upon which the totals were based failed to include jurisdictions of activities unless expenditures involved funds allocated to the States from Federal sources. Figures given exclude the Territories and District of Columbia. Also excluded are some funds contributed by foundations and spent by health departments. Because of liquidation of encumbrances and encumbrances incurred and not liquidated, the figures do not entirely agree with those given elsewhere as Federal "payments to States." Children's Bureau figures represent "payments to States" and are as given by the Children's Bureau rather than as reported to the U. S. Public Health Service by States.

Participation by State and local communities with their own funds has helped promote understanding of public health in many parts of the country. The State and local financial participation has increased enormously between 1937 and 1946 (as shown in Table XIV, above), rising from less than 14 million to nearly 79 million in the respective years. Total governmental expenditures for public health (exclusive of medical care) at State and local levels rose from approximately 25 millions to 110 millions for the same years. The proportion of Federal funds in these totals dropped from 46 to 29 percent, indicating that the Federal grant program has served to increase State and local participation, both absolutely and relatively.

The grant-in-aid program has been responsible for progress in public health work. The quantity of services to the people has increased markedly, the quality of programs has definitely improved, human benefits in terms of better health have been achieved. There is reason to anticipate further progress.

Recommendations

Grants-in-aid have been in existence almost as long as our Government, but the first important grant for health work appeared as part of the Social Security Act of 1935. Subsequently, a number of others were enacted and about a dozen are now in operation.

1. The laws setting up the several grants-in-aid are not uniform in their underlying philosophy as to the Federal-State relationship in public health administration. Some specifically state their purpose to be an "enabling" one, while others tend to emphasize operation by a Federal agency. Economy and efficiency call for clarification of this point. It is recommended that the Congress reexamine the laws which have set up grants-in-aid with a view toward codifying and unifying them. This would require a determination as to the role of the Federal health agency in the administration of public health; whether it is to be a supervisory agency with powers to control practices in the various States, or whether, at the other extreme, it is to be merely a dispensing agent with no authority to set even minimum standards. The best stand would be at an intermediate point instructing the Federal health agency to permit as much administrative autonomy in the States as possible, so that the latter may use the funds most effectively. The Federal agency on the other hand must be satisfied that the State has a plan for a program in which the funds are to be used, and that this plan is sound from the point of view of local needs, effectiveness of proposed procedures, and judicious use of the funds. Beyond this, the State health authority should be the determining factor in the administration of the program, so long as the approved plan is carried out.

2. The grants may be classified chiefly as pertaining either to a group of persons or to a disease. The trend in recent years has been to add categories as interest was aroused, and the continuation of this trend indefinitely will result in a further accumulation of heterogeneous laws, varied administrative practices, and deleterious effects on grantees and public. Each State has its own health problems with considerable variation from one State to another, and emphasis of attack must differ. Categorical grants tend to be too restrictive as regards determination of use by the State health authority. The granting of "block" funds to a State for all purposes combined, such as health, welfare, education, etc., is condemned as tending to foster political juggling of use of these funds. Any consolidation of categories should not go beyond a classification of grants for general health purposes as an extreme.

It is recommended that Congress reconsider the categorical versus the general approach in the promulgation of grant-in-aid programs. Fewer categories would increase the determinative powers of the State health authority, allowing him to concentrate more upon the public health problems which exist in that locality.

3. The responsibility for carrying out the provision of each act having to do with grants-in-aid is definitely placed, but with no uniformity. The Public Health Service carries most of the current programs and three categories are now outside of it. Though consolida-

tion is not now indicated, the three agencies involved should coordinate their grants-in-aid programs.

With several new acts, additional advisory councils have been set up, seemingly a top-heavy organization. Either with or without the categorical system, a general advisory council (with specialized consultant committees) would facilitate the administration of these programs. The use of the same council by the Children's Bureau and the Office of Vocational Rehabilitation would bring the programs of all three agencies closer together.

It is recommended that the Congress codify the laws which provide funds for grants-in-aid with a view towards unifying their provisions and their placing of administrative responsibility. The present categorical councils should be transferred into consultant committees to the National Advisory Health Council.

4. The funds in most of the programs are apportioned through the use of a formula which weighs: (*a*) Population, (*b*) financial need, and (*c*) extent of the problem. Others consider one or more of these factors, but not all of them. In one instance (dental) the entire matter is left up to a recommendation of the advisory council. Unification in this respect, whether or not the categorical system is retained, would clarify many issues.

It is recommended that the Congress review the modes of apportionment as written into the present acts and codify these provisions so that there is unification. Mode of apportionment on the basis of (*a*) population, (*b*) extent of the problem, (*c*) financial needs of a particular State, (*d*) such other factors as the advisory council may recommend, would be equitable and reasonable. Financial needs should receive more relative weight, in accordance with the basic philosophy of grants-in-aid.

5. The conditions that the recipient must meet in order to qualify for a grant vary from one act to another. Especially confusing is the requirement in some that the State match the funds, in others that they pay one-third, in others there is no mention of the proportion, Here, too, more rational provisions in the legislation are indicated.

It is recommended that Congress revise the acts with respect to the conditions that the recipients of grants must meet, in order to rationalize the requirements. It is recommended that these requirements be general rather than specific, and that the Surgeon General be required to consult with the State and Territorial health officers and with the National Advisory Health Council before he promulgates any regulations which govern the conditions which should be met by the States, and that the administrators of other programs consult analagous bodies.

6. Some acts specify that the State health authority shall administer a grant-in-aid program, some specify a State agency, others make no

specific requirement. In order that the standards of public health work be maintained, and even advanced, health work must be the responsibility of a group professionally qualified to do the job. The State health authority is the agency best qualified for this purpose, and the Federal Government, in the interest of raising standards, should foster the channeling of health grants-in-aid through it insofar as is possible.

It is recommended that all grants-in-aid relating to health work be administered within a State by the constituted health authority of that State. Merit system requirement should be a legal provision and not a regulatory one.

7. Within the Public Health Service, grants are administered by five divisions within the Bureau of State Services and by three divisions in other bureaus. In addition, two other grants operate within the Children's Bureau and one other in the Office of Special Services. Obviously this situation requires reorganization.

It is recommended that the Public Health Service reorganize its grant-in-aid functions in order to place the administration of these funds in one unit of the service, namely a grants division to be established in the Bureau of State Service, with the technical divisions acting in an advisory capacity. The Children's Bureau and Office of Vocational Rehabilitation should coordinate their grant-in-aid programs with those of the Public Health Service.

8. Rules and regulations define and interpret the terms used in the legislative acts. There is some diffusion here, but codification of the acts would lead to simplification of the regulations. The extent to which specific requirements are made of the recipients is nicely balanced and places most of the responsibility for planning and execution upon the State, where it belongs.

It is recommended that new rules and regulations be written in accordance with the content of any codification of existing laws on grants-in-aid or any consolidation of the responsibilities pertaining thereto. These new regulations should keep the same balance of responsibility between the Federal agency and the respective States.

9. District officers of the Public Health Service (and of the other two Federal agencies herein mentioned) act in an advisory and consultative capacity to State health (and other) agencies. There are, in their relationships, some aspects of the supervisory function, but this could and should be minimized as much as possible.

It is recommended that, with relation to the States, the consultative and advisory functions of the district offices should be emphasized and their supervisory functions minimized.

10. Grants-in-aid have been responsible for (a) an increase in the number of local health units; (b) coverage of a greater proportion of

the population with local health services; (*c*) the promotion of training and placing of larger numbers of well-qualified public health workers in positions where they could best serve the public; (*d*) the stimulation of interest in public health and the participation of State and local funds; (*e*) research, both basic and applied; etc.

In short, grants-in-aid have made possible the extension of more and better health services to the people. Further progress is anticipated.

It is recommended that grants-in-aid be considered to have evolved through the experimental phase, and recognized as a reasonable and just function of the Federal Government.

FEDERAL FIELD OFFICES FOR PUBLIC HEALTH

Administration of grant-in-aid programs, technical consultation with State and local health departments, domestic interstate and foreign quarantine and other activities involving Federal-State relations and direct service demand decentralization in large operation such as those of the Federal Government. No attempt will be made at this point to describe the field organization of Federal agencies with secondary health activities, only those with primary public health responsibilities (all within the Federal Security Agency).

PRESENT ORGANIZATION

The Public Health Service has maintained nine district offices located in New York, Richmond, Chicago, New Orleans, San Francisco, San Juan, Kansas City, Denver, and Dallas. Each of these offices has a district director representing the Surgeon General and various divisions and offices in carrying out the programs and policies of the Service in the States covered by the several districts; administering field activities of Federal-State cooperative programs and inspecting and facilitating work of field stations of the Service specialists representing divisional categorical programs (tuberculosis, venereal disease, hospital construction, cancer control, etc.) have been assigned to districts. All grant-in-aid requests channel through the districts, and other relationships with States are handled likewise.

The Children's Bureau field offices were amalgamated with those of the Social Security Administration July 16, 1946, at the time the Bureau was transferred from the Department of Labor. Offices were located in New York, Chicago, Kansas City, Denver, San Francisco, Dallas, Atlanta, and Washington. Responsibility is largely decentralized to the field staff in cooperative programs with States. The Division of Health Service endeavors to maintain a team in each region consisting of medical director, and consultants in nursing medical social work, nutrition, and administrative methods. There is a strong feeling in the Bureau that the "team approach" is of great importance and unceasing effort is made to represent the points of view of the various "disciplines" (professional groups) in all planning and relationships. The bureau representative in welfare has coordinate authority and responsibility with the regional medical director.

For the past year or two the Federal Security Administrator has recognized that coordination between field units of the Agency was lacking and a committee has studied various plans. When Congress

169

precipitated reorganization of the Social Security Administration in 1948, the time seemed ripe to overhaul the entire regional activities of the Agency.

The Association of State and Territorial Health Officers had also found great difficulty in working with the field offices of the Children's Bureau and the Public Health Service because of their different districts and separated offices, and on December 5, 1946, recommended that districts be made the same and offices be located in the same building wherever possible.

In July 1948 the Federal Security Administrator ordered the organization of 10 regional offices with headquarters in Boston, New York, Washington (may be moved to Richmond), Cleveland, Chicago, Atlanta, Kansas City, Dallas, Denver, and San Francisco. The regional directors are under civil service (CAF–15) except for one who is a commissioned officer in the Public Health Service. Their duties will be:

1. To represent the Federal Security Administrator in the region:
   a. Carry out policies applicable to the Agency as a whole.
   b. Direct broad public relations of the Agency in the region.
   c. Provide appropriate management service to facilitate work and promote economy, including supervision of:
      (1) Personnel practices.
      (2) Provision and operation of office space. As soon as practicable under existing leases nearly all field offices of the Agency will be consolidated in each region.
      (3) Purchasing.
      (4) Staff assigned to him.
   d. Maintain liaison with officials of public and private agencies in the region.

2. To exercise general administrative supervision over the principal representatives of the constituent organization of the Federal Security Agency stationed in or detailed to the region, including among other things:
   a. Development of program priorities for the region.
   b. Official staff contacts with representatives of States and other Federal agencies.
   c. Travel.
   d. Exercise leadership in developing integrated regional programs involving two or more constitutent units.
   e. Resolve differences between units in cases where reference to Washington is not required.

It is understood that principal representatives of Federal Security Agency constituent organizations retain responsibility for program operations and the technical services of bureau staff assigned them, and that there is to be interposed no barrier to communication with technical bureaus in Washington. However, copies of correspondence even of technical nature will doubtless be submitted to the regional director and the degree of supervision over technical matters which he exercises will depend somewhat upon his own personality.

3. To maintain a general review of activities of the Agency not operating out of the regional office, especially in the field of public and intergovernmental relations.

The following constituent organization of the Federal Security Agency with operations involving important Federal-State relations will operate regionally with identical regional boundaries and as parts of the consolidated regional office: Children's Bureau; Bureau of State Services, Public Health Service (representatives will be assigned to Boston and Cleveland, not formerly established as district offices of the Public Health Service); Office of Vocational Rehabilitation; Bureau of Employment Security; and Bureau of Public Assistance.

The Office of Education with no regular field staff; the Bureau of Employees Compensation with activities concentrated in port cities; the Food and Drug Administration with three districts presently but which must coordinate its field work very closely with Washington, plus other FSA organizations will not be included in the regional office.

As yet, no director of field operations for the FSA has been provided, though coordination of routine operations will be handled by the field division (July 23, 1948 organization chart of FSA). The assistant administrator is taking responsibility for field operations at present.

On May 18, 1948, the Surgeon General of the Public Health Service appointed a committee on organization representing the various bureaus, and in a preliminary report certain recommendations are made regarding district office organization. The districts would become administratively responsible to the Bureau of State Services rather than the Surgeon General, since practically all the activities are in the Federal-States relations field. The staff would be composed primarily of general public health administrators rather than the specialized consultants in various fields. The latter would be assigned to demonstration projects, research and investigation centers, regional laboratories and training centers, hospitals, professional schools or detailed to the States. Thus the specialists would become specialists in fact rather than "by declaration" as has been the case not infrequently up to now, and would be available for consultation as needed, and prepared to give really useful technical assistance.

Under the proposed reorganization plan, grants-in-aid to States would be centralized under a grants division in the Bureau of State Services, quite comparable to the Division of Research Grants and Fellowships in the National Institute of Health, with administrative responsibility for all categorical grants as well as general health grants to States. Technical problems would be the province of the various technical divisions. The grants program would be the principal responsibility of the district offices; and close coordination with the Children's Bureau health grant program would be sought. This recommended reorganization is sound and should be carried out.

Closely connected with field services are the matters of fiscal and merit system audits of State grant-in-aid programs which have been conducted separately by the various constituent units of the FSA. The State and Territorial health officers have objected to the separate audits of the Children's Bureau and the Public Health Service and proposed that they be coordinated. Some action toward this end had been taken prior to June 21, 1948, when the Federal Security Administrator ordered that fiscal and merit system audits for the Agency be centralized under the Office of Federal-State Relations. This includes audits of the Public Health Service, Children's Bureau, Office of Education, Office of Vocational Rehabilitation, and the Bureaus of Public Assistance and Employment Security. In implementing this order, steps apparently are being taken to retain for the program bureaus sufficient voice in the audits to avoid interference in technical problems, which is important.

Financial savings will be made under his new audit plan, and State and local governments should find the consolidated scheme a great improvement over the previous system.

RECOMMENDATIONS

Proper organization of Federal field services is highly important in public health where a major Federal function is that of providing technical assistance and stimulation to State and local health departments. Decentralized authority and simple, clear-cut lines of communication are essential. It is quite possible to separate scientific competence from responsibility for the "housekeeping" aspects of office management, which the new FSA regional plan is intended to accomplish. It should also be possible to separate the work of specialist consultants from that of grant-in-aid administration, thereby broadening the vision of the administrator and sharpening the competence of the specialist; this is an objective of the Public Health Service Committee on Organization.

Probably the outstanding function of the Children's Bureau is that of presenting everlastingly and persistently the needs of the whole child in the field of health, welfare, and education. The "team" approach has been useful though representation of the field of education in the Bureau has been minimal. If individual persons could be found or trained who would be able to represent the whole child in the regional offices as do the chief and associate chief of the Bureau in Washington, it should be possible for the Bureau to do an even more effective job than at present. The "team" has certain obvious disadvantages when it comes to dealing with State and local people, which would not be true of an individual.

If field offices are to function effectively, sufficient travel funds must be provided to allow headquarters and field to maintain close liaison, and to permit field personnel to actually work with State and local governments. If travel money is adequate, the district office tends to operate behind an iron curtain with only the mail "air lift" as a channel for communication.

1. Decentralization of authority and simple lines of communication with the field should be constant objectives. The regional office plan of the FSA now being set up is generally sound and implements these aims.

2. Separation of "housekeeping" administrative responsibility and scientific activities is desirable in the regional offices. It should be possible under the new FSA plan.

3. Channels of communication between program bureaus in Washington and their representatives in the regional offices must be clear without the interposition of administrative checks by regional directors. This does not mean that the regional director should be frustrated in well-considered attempts to coordinate Agency programs and to integrate the health, welfare, and educational work of the Agency.

4. Specialists consultants in the health field should be available to regional offices, but assigned to duties enabling them to pursue their specialized work actively most of the time, rather than being stationed directly in the regional office. Recommendation of the Public Health Service Committee on Organization regarding district offices should be carried out; it should also be applied to the Children's Bureau.

5. Field representatives of the Children's Bureau should embody in the highest possible degree the coordinated approach to all the problems of children. A policy should be followed by placing a single individual conversant with the broadest possible range of childhood problems to represent the Children's Bureau in regional offices.

6. Centralization of fiscal and merit system audits by the FSA is thoroughly justifiable, but it is highly important that bureaus responsible for program operations retain opportunities to determine policy within their particular fields in matters involving professional judgment.

7. Adequate travel funds are essential to the efficient operation of field offices.

THE VALUE OF PREVENTIVE MEDICINE

Activities within the field of health encompass a very broad range of services which include the promotion of health; prevention of disease and injury; diagnosis and alleviation of disease and injury once they have developed; and the rehabilitation of those with handicaps which could not be prevented by proper treatment. The field was a much narrower one before research made new techniques available, and before, through knowledge and action, the professional groups and the public were supplied with the fruits of research which could be translated into programs for action.

With medical care alone available a certain proportion of those seeking treatment could be cured, but the remainder continued round and round in a vicious circle. But in a balanced program, research at the center contributes constantly to knowledge and makes action possible. Numbers of potential patients are spared the effects of disease and injury through measures to promote health and prevent disease. Those who develop disease in spite of this can expect a higher percentage of cures than ever before. And a quite considerable proportion of those not cured may be rehabilitated and enabled to return to work. Only a relatively small proportion of the whole group fails to receive benefit from any of the health measures available and continues in the vicious circle.

Only with proper emphasis on all phases of the health program will it be possible to obtain the best results. It is essential that medical care programs and medical research conducted by the Federal Government be related closely to public health and preventive medicine activities. As research (basic, developmental, and administrative) makes new procedures available, they must be incorporated into the practice of public health and preventive medicine. The people must have knowledge of what is available and must be induced to take action necessary to secure for themselves the benefits of modern medical science. Thus an increasing part of their heavy burden may be taken from the members of the health team engaged in diagnosis and treatment of disease. As time goes on we may expect that more and more disease will become regarded as a result of failure to apply the knowledge we have, rather than the result of bad luck.

Savings Through Prevention

It is extremely difficult at the moment to estimate accurately the amount of possible saving in the costs of illness that might be brought about by full use of all present knowledge of disease prevention. However, it is profitable to consider the question provided one realizes the difficulties and fallacies involved.

One cannot assign money value to health and productivity since there are intangible values which spur us to seek health even after age has made productivity unlikely. It is also unprofitable to attempt a complete separation of prevention and treatment since the one merges more or less imperceptibly into the other. The treatment of a case of syphilis in the communicable stage prevents transmission of the disease to others and at the same time reduces greatly the chances of late complications in the patient treated. The actual statistics necessary to study the problem adequately are also deficient, particularly the statistics of illness rates which are much less complete than those regarding deaths. We also do not have completely reliable figures on the actual costs of controlling disease to the irreducible minimum or even to any specified proportion of its present prevalence.

Certain of the costs of illness may be computed with reasonable accuracy, but others are found to be indefinite. There are the direct costs of doctors' bills, medicines and hospitalization, plus the loss of wages during illness and the loss of potential earning power through premature death. Then there are costs more difficult to compute such as the loss to industry of having machines idle and the reduced productivity of other workers hampered by absence of the man who is ill.

Various measures to reduce the losses are available. Immunization can be used to actually prevent cases of certain diseases such as diphtheria. Useful treatment measures will reduce deaths (penicillin in pneumonia) even though cases cannot be prevented. In other diseases (diabetes-insulin; pernicious anemia-liver, etc.) it is possible to reduce greatly the disability even though the disease itself continues. In other situations diagnosis in the early stages (tuberculosis, cancer) enormously improves the value of treatment. In still other cases the chain of disease spread from one individual to another may be broken by measures affecting the environment such as purification of water, proper disposal of sewage, pasteurization of milk, control of certain air-borne infections through measures to "sterilize" the air, and the control of insects which spread malaria, typhus, etc., by the use of D. D. T.

Current expenditures for medical care are estimated roughly as follows:

Expenditures for medical care of civilians, United States, 1948, by billions of dollars.[1]

	Billion dollars
Private individuals and organizations	6.5
Government:	
Federal	.6
State and Local	.9
Total	8.0

[1] Division of Public Health Methods, USPHS, personal communication.

The loss in output caused by disease and injury has been estimated as follows:

Loss in output caused by disease and injury, United States, 1948, by billions of dollars [1]

Loss in output due to:	
Temporary disability	5
Extended or permanent disability	11
Partial disability	11
	27

[1] Division of Public Health Methods, USPHS, personal communication.

There are additional costs due to loss of output not included in the estimate above, such as that of those not in the regular labor force, including housewives, and of those over 65 years of age.

Added together, the two sets of figures above give a total cost due to illness and injury of some 35 billion dollars. No attempt will be made to indicate how much of this amount could be saved if all known preventive measures were applied to the fullest possible extent, and if research were supported at the optimum level to make available new methods of prevention, health promotion, medical care and rehabilitation as rapidly as possible. Unquestionably the results would be astounding. Examples of what might be accomplished in specific fields will be given, and they may serve as a sort of index of the possibilities.

Employers who set up a good department of industrial medicine and safety can save its operating cost through improvement in operating efficiency of their plants due to reduced absenteeism from sickness and accidents. In addition, there is the clear gain to employees of the medical service received for sickness and injury occurring at the plant, plus the extra wages received due to their being able to spend more time on the job.[28]

Recently the National Association of Manufacturers asked about 2,000 plant operators what their savings were due to establishment of

[28] Brundage, D. K., an estimate of the monetary value to industry of plant medical and safety services, Pub. H. Re. 51 : 1145–59 Aug. 21, 1936.

medical and safety departments. Essentially all reported that the project was a paying proposition, and the following average percentage reductions were reported: [29]

Reduction in occupational disease	62. 8
Reduction in absenteeism	29. 7
Reduction in compensation costs	28. 8
Reduction in labor turnover	27. 3

Preventive medicine for executives also pays dividends as shown by the experience of General Motors,[30] which instituted an annual diagnostic examination for its "key" men because of concern over the high toll of illness and death among this group. Thirty percent of those examined had medical conditions urgently in need of treatment.

These are but a few examples of what may be accomplished by an aggressive industrial health program. The strength of America lies to a great degree in its extraordinary productive power. Obviously, the Federal Government has a great interest in maintaining this power at its maximum, and is thoroughly justified in providing technical assistance necessary to help build up industrial health and safety programs.

Programs by Diseases

CANCER

A very recent study from Connecticut shows much hope for reducing cancer deaths if cases are discovered and treated early, which is the basis of the cancer control program at present. (See Table XV, page 178.) In Connecticut, the educational program is showing results, for whereas only 16 percent of breast cancers in 1938 were treated without delay, this percentage rose to 46 percent in 1946.

As shown by the following table, a large proportion of cancers are fairly accessible for doctor's examination, and in this group—skin, mouth, breast, genitalia, etc.—the proportion of cases that may be cured is quite high if treatment is given before the cancer has spread. The outlook for females is even more optimistic than for males, more than a third of females being cured by early treatment, whereas a fourth of males may be saved. Were the very best methods now available used in all cancer cases, we might even anticipate an average cure rate of 55 percent for males and 64 percent for females.

If we apply these figures to the Nation's estimated population of 143,300,060 for 1948, the following simple table results:

---

[29] National Association of Manufacturers of the United States of America—Health on the production front, January 1944, and Industrial Health Practices, May 1941.

[30] Quoted from text of a radio talk prepared by the Statistical Bureau of the Metropolitan Life Insurance Co. and supplied through the courtesy of that organization.

Results of various treatments for cancer (theoretical)—Number of five-year cures depending on type of treatment, and state of disease when treated

	New cancer cases annually	Optimum care for all cases	Average type of care		
			Early	Moderate spread	Wide spread
Females	176,260	112,806	63,453	33,489	7,050
Males	157,630	86,697	39,408	14,187	1,576
Total	333,890	199,503	102,861	47,676	8,626

TABLE XV.—*Cancer, new cases annually and survival rate by site and sex, Connecticut*

Site of cancer	New cases annually per 100,000 population, 7-year average		Percent of new cases		Percentage of cases surviving five years by stage of disease on admission					
					Localized		Moderate spread		Wide spread	
	Male	Female	Male	Female	Male	Female	Male	Female	Male	Female
Skin	23.5	17.3	12.1	7.8	39	48	21	29	3	0
Lip, mouth, larynx	20.7	3.7	10.7	1.7	31	28	13	18	1	0
Breast		62.6		28.3		45		22		3
Lungs and esophagus	18.7	4.2	9.6	1.9	4	4	2	0	0	0
Stomach, intestines, rectum	64.0	51.1	32.9	23.1	16	21	5	12	1	3
Genitalia	22.6	53.4	11.6	24.1	19	34	17	19	4	6
Other	44.9	28.9	23.1	13.1						
Total	[1] 194.4	[1] 221.2	100.0	100.0	[2] 25	[2] 36	9	19	1	4

[1] Dorn, H. F., Illness from Cancer in the United States, Reprint No. 2537, Public Health Reports, gives a cancer incidence rate of 246 for females and 220 for males.

[2] The same author (Dorn) in a recent personal communication estimates that if "the best known skills and techniques at present are made generally available and that cases are discovered at an early age so that the maximum benefits from treatment are available" we might expect "an average cure rate of 55 percent for males and 64 percent for females."

Source: MacDonald, E. J., The Present Incidence and Survival Picture in Cancer and the Promise of Improved Prognosis, Bull. Am. Coll. Surg., June 1948.

Thus employing the best possible care with full use of modern knowledge of the importance of reporting to the doctor early, skillful diagnosis and the best treatment, will expect to save the difference between the 199,503 survivors of this type of treatment and 102,861 survivors from average treatment in the early stages of cancer. There is a difference of 96,642 lives that might be saved if all had the best care now known (without waiting for results of research now under way or that we may be undertaking later). Contrasting the 102,861 survivors with early average treatment with the 8,626 that may be expected to survive with late treatment, we find a theoretical saving of 94,235; or if the two widest extremes of optimum treatment and late treatment are contrasted, there would be a saving of 190,877 lives each year!

While many cancers occur in older people, the percentage of cases under 50 years old in the Connecticut series was 20.1 for males and 33.8 for females.[31] The group under 60 years old made up 44.5 percent

[31] There are minor fallacies in applying the figures from Connecticut to the whole country because of difference in age distribution of population in the various States and certain other factors.

of the male cases and 59.7 percent of the females. One may conclude quite fairly that a very considerable number of productive years may be saved by the widespread application of known cancer-control methods. As research improves the results of treatment, the outlook will undoubtedly improve further.

TUBERCULOSIS

The National Planning Association [32] has estimated the annual direct and indirect cost of tuberculosis to the Nation at 355.6 million dollars at 1943 standards. If we were willing to spend 387 million dollars each year (only 31.4 millons more than the amount we are already spending) for a 10-year period, it is estimated that the disease could be reduced to such a degree that only 37 million dollars a year would be needed thereafter to keep it well under control, contrasted with the actual annual direct cost of 174 million dollars. Thus, the annual saving which might be brought about by temporarily increasing expenditures for control would be 137 million dollars, plus some 181.6 million dollars which is the computed indirect cost due to loss of wages because of tuberculosis.

Some authorities question the possibility of eradicating tuberculosis, but there is general agreement that it could be reduced to a very low level through an active control campaign.

SYPHILIS

Effects of the relatively intensive efforts to control syphilis which have been made in recent years (very largely due to stimulation and financial assistance provided by the Public Health Service) are already discernible in lowered death rates from the disease. This reduction is all the more significant because there has been a tendency to report more syphilis deaths as due to their real cause in recent years than formerly.

The reduction in total deaths amounts to about 27 percent, and in infant deaths due to syphilis there has been a 65-percent reduction.

The age at which syphilis deaths occur has become greater, which

Syphilis mortality rate, United States, 1933–46 [1]

	Deaths per 100,000 population			Infant deaths per 1,000 live births
	Total	White	Nonwhite	
Average of 1943–45, inclusive	11. 4	8. 0	39. 5	0. 26
Average of 1933–35, inclusive	15. 5	11. 1	54. 3	. 74

[1] Kahn, H. A. and Iskrant, A. P., Syphilis Mortality Analysis, Jour. Venereal Dis. Inf. 29:193–200 July 1948.

[32] National Planning Association, Joint Subcommittee on Health, Good health is good business, February 1948.

means that even though death from syphilis may not be avoided in all cases, the life expectation of a person with syphilis is increasing. By combining the effect of the lowered syphilis death rate and the increased age at death, comparing 1933 with 1944 and using life tables of 1930 and 1945, and computing figures only up to age 65, there was an increased life expectancy of 91,600 years in 1944.

Median age of white syphilis deaths, United States, 1935–1944 [1]

	Median age of persons dying from syphilis	
	Male	Female
1944	57. 2	54. 4
1935	52. 8	49. 0
Increase	4. 4	5. 4

[1] Kahn, H. A., and Iskrant, A. P., Syphilis Mortality Analysis, Jour. Venereal Dis. Inf. 29:193–200, July 1948.

MALARIA

It is estimated [33] that there are at least 2 million cases of malaria annually in the United States, and that the disease costs the country 500 million dollars a year. During the last war intensive malaria control activities were carried on in areas around military camps at a cost of some 10 million dollars a year. The results were brilliant as shown in the accompanying chart, with a very much lower malaria rate among troops in the continental United States than was true during World War I. It is estimated that with 7 years of intensive effort, costing a total of 53 million, the disease could be virtually eradicated, and only about $250,000 a year would be required thereafter to keep it under control.[34]

There would doubtless be valuable byproducts also from such malaria control. Recent experience with DDT control in Ceylon [35] has shown that, as the cases of malaria are reduced, there is a coincident drop in infant mortality. In one area over a 3-year period there was a drop from 818 to 158 malaria deaths per 100,000 population, accompanied by a fall in infant deaths from 239 to 145 per 1,000 live births.

MATERNAL AND CHILD HEALTH

There seems no biologic reason why the maternal and infant mortality rates in the States with the best records could not prevail in the other States of this country as well. If proper public health and

[33] Williams, L. L., Jr., Economic importance of malaria control. Proc. 25th Annual Meeting, New Jersey Mosquito Extermination Association, pp. 148–151.
[34] Personal communication, Division Public Health Methods, USPHS.
[35] Abhayaratne, O. E. R., Infant mortality in Ceylon. Unpublished thesis for doctorate of public health, Harvard School of Public Health, 1948.

180

medical care were available; if housing, sanitation, nutrition, and general economic factors were favorable, such a situation would doubtless prevail. On the assumption that the infant mortality rate in Utah of 27.2 deaths per 1,000 live births in 1946 had prevailed elsewhere in the United States, 21,611 infant lives might have been saved. Had the maternal mortality rate of 0.9 per 1,000 live births in Connecticut and Minnesota in 1946 been that for the country as a whole, 2,127 mothers' lives would have been saved.

Preventative Medicine in the Armed Forces

Probably no other large group has employed preventive measures appropriate to age and environmental conditions more effectively than the armed forces. A few examples will illustrate this fact.

1. Typhoid Fever Control

The increasing effectiveness of vaccine and sanitation in controlling typhoid and paratyphoid fevers is one of the most striking examples of what preventive medicine can accomplish. With no vaccination available during the Spanish-American War the typhoid-paratyphoid rate was approximately 300 times as great as during World War I. With constant improvement, the World War II rate was reduced to about one-seventh that experienced in World War I.

Typhoid-paratyphoid and dysentery in U. S. Army, World War I and World War II

[Rates per 1,000 men per year]

	Typhoid		Paratyphoid		Diarrhea and dysentery[1]	
	World War I	World War II	World War I	World War II	World War I	World War II
United States	0.24	0.007	0.01	0.006	17.8	9.1
Overseas	.53	.05	.09	.07	28.9	40
Total	.37	.03	.05	.03	22.4	21.4

[1] No vaccination applicable to this group. Diarrhea and dysentery rate was actually higher in the second world war than in the first, for overseas troops, many more of whom were in the tropics than during the first world war.

2. Tetanus Prevention

During World War II tetanus toxoid was used routinely, and the reduction in tetanus cases as compared with the first world war was nothing short of dramatic.

3. Smallpox—Effectiveness of Vaccination

Vaccination against smallpox was compulsory during the second world war, but this was not universal during World War I; the contrast is striking.

181

Tetanus, U. S. Army, World War I and World War II

	Admission for wounds and injuries	Cases of tetanus	Cases of tetanus per 100,000 wounds and injuries
World War I	523,158	70	13.4
1920–1941 inclusive	580,283	14	2.4
World War II	2,734,819	12	.44

Smallpox cases, U. S. Army, World War I and World War II

	Number of cases	
	World War I	World War II
United States	780	10
Overseas	73	106
Total	853	116

4. Typhus (*Epidemic Louse-Borne*)

Typhus was prevalent among civilians at one time or another in areas of Europe, Africa, and the Middle East in which troops were operating. However, less than 100 cases (all mild with no deaths) occurred in American troops due to vaccination against typhus and the use of DDT.

5. Cholera

This disease was present in epidemic form in many areas where troops were stationed, such as China, India, and Burma. Yet only 14 cases occurred in troops, 13 of these in China. Vaccination plus protection of food and water accounted for the saving of many lives.

6. Plague

Outbreaks of plague occurred among civilians in the Azores, New Caledonia, Egypt, Senegal, China, and India where troops were stationed. Due to control measures including vaccination, no cases occurred among American troops.

7. Yellow Fever

The effectiveness of yellow fever vaccination was well demonstrated prior to adoption by the Army. No cases occurred among American troops. There was no great exposure to this disease, however.

8. Meningitis

In addition to a very greatly reduced case fatality rate from meningitis, it proved possible to actually prevent the spread of the disease

182

among units of troops by giving sulfa drugs to reduce the carriers of meningococci. One report showed only two cases among 15,000 men, giving sulfadiazine as a preventive measure, while among 18,800 controls not receiving sulfa there were 40 cases during the same period. Both the treated and the control groups had essentially the same percentage of carriers in their group at the outset of the experiment.

9. Malaria

Navy and Marine Corps.—During 1941 the average monthly case rate per 1,000 per year was 1.2. In the first 9 months of 1942 the average was 3.7, but between November 1942 and June 1943 the range was from 31.2–49.4. Repressive drugs were available during this period, but enforcement of recommendations that they be used regularly were lax. As soon as enforcement became strict and general, the malaria rate dropped, running between 10.7–17.2 during October 1943–March 1944 and falling thereafter to a very much lower rate. The figures quoted are for Navy and Marine Corps as a whole; were they restricted to personnel actually in malarial areas they would be even more striking.

Army.—The Army figures on malaria within the continental United States during World War II are even more striking when compared with the World War I incidence of malaria.

10. Tuberculosis

Except in the early stages of World War II, candidates for induction into the armed forces were screened by X-rays to detect tuberculosis and nearly 150,000 cases eliminated at induction centers alone. Already this procedure has proved extremely profitable to the Federal Government in reducing the number of tuberculosis cases both in the armed forces and among veterans.

In testimony before a Senate committee in 1944, the Deputy Surgeon General of the Army stated that only 3 percent of wounded died of their wounds (tetanus toxoid, blood transfusions, sulfonamides, and penicillin, "preventive" surgical management). The over-all death rate from disease was given as 0.6 per 1,000 per year, which is much lower than the civilian rate for the same age group. Com-

Tuberculosis in armed forces, World Wars I and II

	Peak strength	Average admission rate for tuberculosis in forces (per 1,000)	Average annual mortality rate (Army) (per 100,000)	Average annual mortality rate—civilian corresponding age (per 100,000)	Tuberculosis—percent of all awards for disability
World War I	4,200,000	11.8	66	150	15.2 (1923)
World War II	14,361,000	1.0	7	48	1.5 (1947)

municable diseases such as smallpox, the typhoid fevers, typhus, yellow fever, etc., which are largely preventable by vaccination, were essentially unknown. Meningitis which had a case fatality rate of 38 percent in World War I showed a reduction to 4.2 percent with sulfonamides, and this was even lower with penicillin.

Expectation of Life

Life-expectancy tables throw much light on public-health programs of the past and on future problems. Figures for the United States before 1900 not being available, comparable figures for Massachusetts beginning in 1850 are used to supplement those for the United States in table XVI, below. For the sake of simplicity consideration is restricted to white females. Other groups show similar trends.

At Birth

During the 40-year period 1850–90 life expectation at birth increased from 40.5 at an average rate of only 0.1 year per year to 44.5. In the next 20 years the rate of increase quadrupled to 0.43 year per year rising to 53.1 in 1910. In the 36-year period 1910–46 the rate of increase was about the same, being 0.46 year per year with an expectation of 70.3 years attained in 1946. The greater part of this remarkable increase during the last 50 years has been due to bringing most of the acute communicable diseases under control and to reduction in infant mortality (the Massachusetts infant-mortality rate in 1890 was 166.6; in 1946 it was 31.6).

A great deal of work remains to be done before it can be said that acute communicable diseases have been controlled even as well as we know how to control them at present, not to mention the future possibilities research may disclose. And there is still much room for reduction of infant deaths. In both of these fields, the law of diminishing

TABLE XVI.—*Expectation of life at birth and at age 50, by years—White females*

Massachusetts 1850–1910

	1850 [1]	1878–82 [1]	1890 [1]	1893–1897 [1]	1901 [1]	1910 [1]
Birth	40.5	43.5	44.5	46.6	49.4	53.1
Age 50		23.5	22.1	22.1	21.6	21.6

U. S. 1900–1946 (death registration area)

	1900–1902 [2]	1909–11 [2]	1919–21 [2]	1929–31 [2]	1939–41 [2]	1946 [3]
Birth	51.1	53.6	58.5	62.7	67.3	70.3
Age 50	21.9	21.7	23.1	23.4	24.7	26.0

[1] Metropolitan Life Insurance Co., Statistical Bulletin, December 1927.
[2] Greville, T. N. E., U. S. Tables and Actuarial Tables 1939–41, U. S. Government Printing Office, Washington, D. C.: 1946.
[3] National Office of Vital Statistics, news release, July 26, 1948.

returns will become operable, however, as soon as control measures are more uniformly applied in all areas of the country, especially the rural ones not now properly covered.

At Age of 50

Between 1880 and 1900 there was actually a slight reduction (1.9 years) in expectation at age 50. But from 1900–1946 life expectation for the woman of 50 has slowly increased at an average rate of 0.09 years per year—interestingly enough, about the same rate of increase as was taking place for infants at birth prior to 1890.

This slight degree of improvement indicates that progress in controlling diseases characteristic of later life, such as most cases of heart and kidney disease, diabetes, cancer, etc., has been much slower than has been the case with "childhood" diseases. Obviously, there is a definite limit to how long life may be extended, but based on the experience of other countries three or four additional years expectation at age 50 is not unreasonable.

The need for research to provide better methods of controlling these "degenerative" diseases is enormous. Even so, we are by no means applying all our present knowledge and there is an enormous field for studies to develop the best administrative techniques for doing this.

CAUSES OF DEATH

There is value in examining the major causes of death during the productive period of life (age 20–65) to learn what might be achieved if deaths from these causes could by some means be eliminated completely. While this is obviously impossible, we may nevertheless gain an idea of the relative importance of these causes which can serve as a guide in planning public health control measures as well as research. Table XVII, page 186, indicates that during 1945, 4,369,000 years of working life were lost from the 15 major causes of death at ages 20–64. If these causes were all eliminated 178,500,000 years of productive life up to age 65 would be added for white males alone in the United States; and the life expectancy at age 20 would rise from the 1945 figure of 39.85 years to 43.8.

Some of the most important causes of death during this age period are very definitely amenable to preventive measures now available. Certainly accidents may be prevented in large part; tuberculosis and syphilis may be controlled to a large extent. It is quite legitimate to assume that early treatment of the best quality now available would very materially reduce the deaths from cancer, diabetes, pneumonia, appendicitis, hernia, and intestinal obstruction. It is perhaps uncertain how much reduction in suicides and in peptic ulcers may be anticipated from applied mental hygiene, but it would doubtless be con-

185

TABLE XVII.—*Effects of eliminating important causes of deaths on life expectancy and increase in productive working years—White males, age 20–65*

15 major causes of death at ages 20–65	Lost years of working life, ages 20–64, on account of deaths in 1945 from specific causes	Increased years of working life, age 20 to age 65 based on 1945 experience and as increased through elimination of deaths from specific causes	Increased expectation of life to age 65 at age 20 based on 1945 experience and as increased through elimination of deaths from specific causes
Heart disease	1,033,000	58,000,000	1.20
Accidents	1,251,000	33,500,000	.81
Cancer	401,000	21,500,000	.45
Tuberculosis	373,000	17,000,000	.44
Nephritis	176,000	8,500,000	.19
Intracranial lesions	160,000	9,000,000	.18
Pneumonia and influenza	472,000	7,500,000	.17
Suicide	142,000	7,000,000	.17
Cirrhosis of liver	64,000	3,500,000	.07
Ulcers, stomach and duodenum	58,000	3,000,000	.07
Syphilis	61,000	3,000,000	.06
Diabetes	60,000	3,000,000	.06
Appendicitis	62,000	2,000,000	.04
Hernia and intestinal obstruction	44,000	1,500,000	.03
Biliary calculi, etc	12,000	500,000	.01
Total	4,369,000	178,500,000	3.95

Source: Lew, Edw. A., Metropolitan Life Insurance Co., personal communication.

Possible increases in life expectancy through elimination of major causes of death at ages 20–65

	Expectation factor	Possible increase
Diseases largely preventable (80 percent):		
Accidents	0.81	
Tuberculosis	.44	
Syphilis	.06	
Total	1.31	1.05
Material reduction possible (40 percent)		
Cancer	.45	
Pneumonia and influenza	.17	
Appendicitis	.04	
Hernia and obstruction	.03	
Diabetes	.06	
Total	.75	.3
Questionable reduction (25 percent):		
Suicide	.17	
Ulcer	.07	
Biliary calculi	.01	
Cirrhosis liver	.07	
Total	.32	.08
Little reduction possible (10 percent):		
Heart disease	1.2	
Nephritis	.19	
Intracranial lesions	.18	
	1.57	.16
Total	3.95	1.59

siderable. Not a great deal could be promised in diminishing deaths from heart disease, intracranial disease, and nephritis with our present knowledge, though it is quite reasonable to suppose that early diagnosis and careful treatment would produce measurable reductions.

It is then evident that with full use of modern knowledge and facilities we might confidently expect that the life expectation at age 20 up to age 65 could be increased by 1.59 years, and that 68.2 million years of working life would be added to the white male population in this age group.

Preventive medicine as applied to the individual and his family and public health as applied to the community are integral parts of a balanced health program. Other activities included are health promotion, medical care, and rehabilitation. All are supported by research and education. Only by support of all phases can the best and most economical results be achieved.

Recommendations

1. Generous support of preventive measures and those which promote health will reduce the costs of medical care for disease and injury.

2. As the wards of the Federal Government comprise one-seventh of the total population, expenditure of Federal funds for general health promotion and disease prevention among the population as a whole will produce more than general health benefits for the Nation. Very considerable savings will result in the Federal Government's obligations to its own wards for medical care.

3. Very intensive preventive measures are financially justifiable for Federal wards. There is every reason to expect that expenditures for such measures will be repaid many times over by savings in medical care costs.

Chapter III

EXISTING FEDERAL HEALTH ACTIVITIES
BY AGENCIES

Federal Security Agency

The Federal Security Agency came into existence July 1, 1939, in accordance with the provisions of the Reorganization Acts of the same year (53 Stat. 561; 5 U. S. C. 133).[1] As set forth in its authorization, its purpose is to produce "social and economic security, educational opportunity, and the health of the citizens of the Nation." To carry out this broad purpose, the Federal Security Agency brought together and coordinated into the present framework four main operating branches: (1) Education; (2) Social Security Administration; (3) Office of Special Services; and (4) Health and Medical Care. All of these branches have some activities which are directly related to health and health protection as will appear in the body of the text.

The activities of the Federal Security Agency are under the direction and supervision of a Federal Security Administrator. The five agencies principally concerned with health in this agency are (1) Public Health Service, (2) Children's Bureau, (3) Division of Research and Statistics in the Office of the Commissioner of Social Security, (4) Office of Vocational Rehabilitation, and (5) Food and Drug Administration.

THE PUBLIC HEALTH SERVICE

The Public Health Service had its origin in an act of Congress, July 16, 1798, establishing the Marine Hospital Service for sick and disabled American seamen. Its broad powers and duties as now constituted are authorized in Public Health Service Act of 1944 and its amendments.[2] The principal function of the Public Health Service

---

[1] Additional groupings of Federal agencies operating in the field of health were accomplished in 1940 (reorganization plans 2 and 4). Again under the Reorganization Act of 1945 (59 Stat. 613; 5 U. S. C. 133 Y) plan 2, effective July 16, 1946, the Children's Bureau from the Department of Labor and the Division of Vital Statistics from the Bureau of Census were transferred to the Social Security Agency.

[2] Public Law 410 (58 Stat. 682) and amended by the National Mental Health Act of July 3, 1946 (60 Stat. 421; 42 U. S. C. 201), Public Law 487; Federal Hospital Survey and Construction Act of Aug. 13, 1946, Public Law 725; and Government Employees' Health Program, Public Law 658; etc.

is to safeguard the health of the people through its four services as established by Public Law 410: (*a*) The Office of Surgeon General; (*b*) National Institute of Health; (*c*) Bureau of Medical Services; and (*d*) Bureau of States Services, which are administered by the Surgeon General under the general direction and supervision of the Federal Security Administrator. In time of national emergency, the Surgeon General heads the Division of Commissioned Officers with the same title and provisions as the Surgeon General of the Army.

The principal functions and activities of the Public Health Service may be stated as follows:

1. *Communicable disease control—quarantine.*—Both maritime and interstate. This service is to protect the country from the importation of quarantinable diseases from abroad and to prevent the spread of diseases by means of interstate quarantine.

2. *Research.*—To find the causes of and means for the control and prevention of diseases.

3. *Regulatory functions.*—The control and supervision of biologic products.

4. *Medical care.*—The provision of general medical and dental services for those beneficiaries of the Government who are legally provided for in the act.

5. *Vital statistics.*—The collection and tabulation and trends in health statistics in the United States and territories.

6. *Dissemination of public health information.*

7. *Grants-in-aid* to assist State and local health agencies.

8. *International health.*

9. *Cooperation with other Federal, State, and local health agencies* in the discharge of their health duties through the assignment of public health personnel as advisors, etc.

10. *Hospital construction* in the fulfillment of the Hill-Burton Act.

11. *Commissioned officers* of Public Health Service constitute a mobile corps for special service in times of disaster.

12. *Environmental sanitation.*

Office of Surgeon General

The primary function of the Office of the Surgeon General is the administration of the "internal affairs of the Public Health Service as contrasted with the administration of services to the public by other bureaus." [3] The Office is under the direct supervision of the Surgeon General, who, with the Deputy Surgeon General and execu-

---

[3] Compilation of Public Health Service Regulations, September 16, 1947.

tive officers with the "advice and assistance" of the general staff, directs and supervises the broad functions of the Public Health Service. This Office is principally concerned with the formulation of policies and the planning of health programs of national significance. Aside from its administrative functions, the Office conducts surveys and makes important analyses of fact-finding groups pertinent to the administrative activities of the Office. Here, the National Office of Vital Statistics (formerly of the Bureau of the Census) has the responsibility of collecting, tabulating, and analyzing the vital statistics of the United States and its territories and island possessions.

One of its important functions is the maintenance of cooperative relationships in the field of public health between the various agencies of the Government, Federal, State and local, and between the divisions of the Service. Furthermore, this Office includes the international health activities of the Office of International Health Relations as they are related to our Federal public health program. (See section on International Health, p. 100.)

The Sanitary Engineering Division of the Office develops definite patterns of cooperation with other Federal agencies doing sanitary work. It advises the Office of the Surgeon General regarding plans of environmental sanitation and formulates uniform policies for other agencies of the Public Health Service and for the Federal and State governments. The Division's operating program is chiefly concerned with (1) the technical supervision and consultant services that are given to Federal, State, and local health agencies, and (2) the establishment of standards and uniform sanitary engineering policies and programs. These functions are administered through six sections covering the sanitation problems of land, air, and water; transportation facilities; milk and foods; and a general sanitation section dealing with housing sanitation, bathing beaches, and garbage refuse disposal. See Environmental Sanitation, page 122.

The Dental Division, the Divisions of Nursing and of Public Health Methods likewise assist and advise the Surgeon General's Office on matters of policy and in the formation of public health programs. The Divisions of Dentistry and Nursing exercise general supervision over professional standards while the Division of Public Health Methods, through its specific activities of collecting and tabulating current statistics relating to problems of health and medical care, evaluates current procedure, and develops methods for meeting health needs.

The Division of Commissioned Officers.—Not a few Federal agencies operate health programs more or less incidental to their major activity. These health programs are concerned either with medical care or with public health. A mechanism has been devised and made effective (by law or by agreement) to provide the necessary technical personnel to carry on these services. Officers from the Commissioned

Corps of the Public Health Service are assigned on a lend-lease basis to other Federal agencies which in most cases reimburse the Public Health Service for their salaries. The following table shows their assignments as of August 31, 1948. (See table XVIII below.)

This procedure centralizes recruiting of medical personnel in the Public Health Service and makes rotation of duty possible. It also provides individuals with public health experience who are able to utilize the broad facilities of the Public Health Service to better advantage than individuals who have not had this background.

During and after the past war, officers were assigned to the Army and to the Health Division of the United Nations Relief and Rehabilitation Administration in various parts of the world. This arrangement worked admirably.

Personnel assigned by the PHS should be chosen for assignment ᴖo other Federal agencies on the basis of their training, experience, and personal qualifications for this particular assignment, so that their special knowledge and techniques of public health methods may apply more effectively to this assignment.

TABLE XVIII.—*Federal Security Agency, Public Health Service, Public Health Service commissioned officers detailed to other agencies, Aug. 31, 1948*

	Total	Medical	Dental	Sanitary engineer	Nurse officer	Scientist
Details from Public Health Service	208	122	59	3	23	1
Details from Office of Surgeon General	13	10		3		
State Department	4	3		1		
Pan American Sanitary Bureau	6	5		1		
National Security Resources Board	2	1		1		
FSA regional director	1	1				
Details from Bureau of Medical Services	192	109	59		23	1
U. S. Coast Guard	71	29	34		7	1
U. S. Maritime Commission	18	9	8		1	
Bureau of Prisons	77	47	16		14	
Bureau of Indian Affairs	12	10	1		1	
Bureau of Employees' Compensation	5	5				
Office of Vocational Rehabilitation	4	4				
Agriculture Department (Animal Industry)	1	1				
State Department (Foreign Service)	1	1				
Coast and Geodetic Survey	2	2				
Bureau of Old Age and Survivors' Insurance	1	1				
Details from Bureau of State Services	3	3				
Farmers Home Administration	1	1				
Philippine Government	2	2				

In the past the uncertain tenure of service, frequently short, has prevented these officers from becoming an integral part of the agency to which they have been assigned. Their knowledge and skills have not had an opportunity to be given full play, nor have they had the personal satisfaction of planning and developing a program. They

192

should remain in an agency long enough to permit them to become an integral part of the agency.

Office of Personnel, PHS.—The Office of Personnel in the Surgeon General's Office is concerned with the recruitment, classification, placement, and training of the civilian employees and commissioned officers of the Public Health Service. Table XIX, below, shows the total personnel for the Public Health Service broken down by agencies.

TABLE **XIX.**—*Civilian personnel employed by Public Health Service by organization as of June 30, 1947*

	Total	Civilian	Commissioned
Public Health Service, grand total	[1] 16,818	[2] 14,964	1,854
Office of the Surgeon General, total	1,298	1,189	109
Immediate Office of the Surgeon General	23	18	5
Office of Personnel	104	104	0
Office of the Chief Clerk	89	89	0
Office of Purchase and Supply	70	68	2
Budget and Fiscal Office	188	188	0
Division of Commissioned Officers	63	54	9
Dental Division	12	9	3
Division of Nursing	109	95	14
Division of Public Health Methods	185	180	5
Sanitary Engineering Division	155	100	55
Office of International Health Relations	39	23	16
National Office of Vital Statistics	261	261	0
Bureau of Medical Services, total	9,791	8,769	1,022
Office of the Chief	15	13	2
Foreign Quarantine Division	695	642	53
Mental Hygiene Division	996	908	88
Federal Employee Health Division	39	9	30
Hospital Division	6,960	6,268	692
Freedmen's Hospital	501	501	0
Federal Penal Service	420	345	75
Coast Guard	149	83	66
U. S. Maritime Commission	16	0	16
Bureau of State Services, total	4,381	3,881	500
Office of the Chief	103	102	1
Office of Health Education	9	9	0
Division of Hospital Facilities	182	167	15
Industrial Hygiene Division	70	34	36
States Relations Division	2,095	1,853	242
Tuberculosis Control Division	327	236	91
Venereal Disease Division	767	663	104
USPHS District Offices	196	187	9
Philippine Rehabilitation	632	630	2
National Institutes of Health, total	1,235	1,125	110
Office of the Chief	340	337	3
Division of Infectious Diseases	228	201	27
Division of Physiology	112	92	20
Biologics Control Laboratory	24	18	6
Chemistry Laboratory	16	16	0
Pathology Laboratory	33	24	9
Division of Tropical Diseases	61	46	15
Industrial Hygiene Research Laboratory	108	93	15
Research Grants Division	62	59	3
National Cancer Institute	251	239	12
Details to other Government Agencies, total	113	0	113
From Office of Surgeon General	54	0	54
From Bureau of Medical Services	23	0	23
From Bureau of State Services	35	0	35
From NIH	1	0	1

[1] Includes 906 part-time employees, many of whom were not on duty June 30, but who worked at least 1 day during the month.
[2] Does not include 4,588 "WOC's" who worked intermittently without compensation.

193

Recommendations.—In our earlier attempts to assign the public health activities of the Federal Government to a single agency the functions of the Public Health Service were related solely to sanitation and the prevention of disease. Public health problems were attacked in the belief that the absence of disease and infirmity connoted health. Little was known about the social and mental factors involved in the health of the individual and his community. Today we define health as "a state of physical, mental, and social well-being." This concept of health has been developed on the basis of our expanding knowledge in such fields as psychosomatic medicine, nutrition, etc.

Various agencies of the Federal Government have implemented their services with those directly or indirectly related to health. These health activities were started independently of the Public Health Service. They operate in agencies of government where they are related to the basic functions of the agency, such as in Agriculture, Education, Indian Affairs, etc. To isolate these health activities from their parent agency would rob them of their effectiveness. They serve health better where they are now placed.

In accordance with this modern concept of positive health, the activities of the Public Health Service are closely related to the activities of the other bureaus of the Federal Security Agency which operate in the broad social and educational fields of welfare.

If the Government decides to depend primarily on departmentalization to achieve coordination of the programs of these several agencies, the Public Health Service is properly placed in the Federal Security Agency. Proposals for an independent department of health should be considered only in the event that the Government establishes an effective central agency of overhead administration directly under the President to obtain coordination of programs that extend across departmental lines.

The National Institutes of Health

The National Institutes of Health are the research divisions of the Public Health Service. Their broad programs of research in all aspects of the medical and public health problems are related to the causes, spread, diagnosis, treatment, and prevention of disease. The Divisions of Infectious Diseases and Tropical Diseases are chiefly concerned with research in these fields. In the Division of Physiology, the fundamental problems of cell functions and the biochemical processes in diseases are studied. In the Pathology Laboratories, diagnostic services are given to the various hospitals of the Public Health Service as well as to the Coast Guard, Bureau of Mines, Office of Indian Affairs, Maritime Training Stations, and other Government agencies. The laboratories also conduct fundamental research in human pathol-

194

ogy and in the use of radioactive isotopes as tracers in its studies on the mechanism of immunity and cellular physiology.

The National Cancer Institute conducts and sponsors studies related to the causes, treatment, and prevention of cancer. It also provides fellowships for research, administers a special program of grants-in-aid for field studies, and finances assistance for physicians desiring special preparation in the treatment and control of cancer.

Through the Biologics Control Laboratory, the Public Health Service insures safe and standard biologic products such as serums, toxins, vaccines, and arsenicals. The regulatory functions of Public Health Service rest with the National Institute of Health for the enforcement of the National Biologics Law. Licenses for the manufacture of biological products are issued by the Federal Security Administrator under regulations made jointly by the Public Health Service and the Army and Navy.

The National Institute of Health administers through its Research Grant Division grants-in-aid for research in medical sciences. (See section on grants-in-aid in public health, p. 148.) Through this provision the Institute provides financial assistance to public and private institutions and individual investgators. The National Advisory Councils on Health, Cancer, Mental Health, and Heart recommend and certify applications for aid. The National Institute of Health also provides for fellowships for medical research investigation. During 1947, 333 grants were made representing a total of $3,027,012.33 paid to research investigators in 81 different institutions located in 26 States and the District of Columbia.[4]

Two additional research divisions, that of chemistry and that of physical biology—formerly the Industrial Hygiene Research Laboratory—contribute scientific knowledge for the promotion of public health. The Division of Chemistry is primarily concerned in the field of organic and biochemistry as applied to public health. In the Laboratory of Physical Biology, basic research problems as applied to health hazards in industry are investigated. The research of this laboratory has application to the "effects of radiation on normal cell structure and metabolism as well as fundamental research in biological chemistry and physics."

A complete statement of the research activities of the National Institute of Health with specific recommendations are given elsewhere in this report.

The Bureau of Medical Services

The Bureau of Medical Services is divided into seven subdivisions, six of which are definitely concerned with medical facilities and

---

[4] Annual report, U. S. P. H. S. (1947), p. 319.

medical care. They are: Hospital Division; Freedmen's Hospital; Mental Hygiene Division, which operates hospitals for the mentally ill of Federal employees, Federal prisons, and hospitals for drug addicts; Federal Employees' Health Division; medical care for Federal Security Agency personnel; and medical care in other agencies. These services are reviewed by the Committee on Medical Services. Aside from the medical services conducted by the Mental Hygiene Division, a program of research on the causes, prevention, and treatment of mental and nervous diseases is carried forward. The division allots grants-in-aid for research to public and private institutions and to individual investigators. It also gives financial assistance to institutions for training of personnel and grants-in-aid to States for community mental health services. These provisions were made possible by the National Health Act, Public Law 487, approved July 3 ,1946. (See section on mental hygiene, p. 135.)

The Foreign Quarantine Division, Bureau of Medical Services, operates under the following act:

The Quarantine Act of February 15, 1893 (27 Stat. L 449) is still in force. It gives authority for all domestic and marine quarantine regulations. (Now Public Health Law 410, pt. 8, sec. 361–369.) This law states that "it shall be unlawful for any merchant ship or other vessel from any foreign port or place to enter any port of the United States except in accordance with the provisions of this act and with such rules and regulations of State and municipal authorities as may be made in pursuance of or consistent with this act."

For details see section on quarantine under International Health, page 106.

Bureau of State Services

Administration of the Federal-State cooperative health program and operation of Public Health Service activities which complement and strengthen that program, are the major responsibilities of the Bureau of State Services. Grants-in-aid to States for general public health work, venereal disease control, tuberculosis control, industrial hygiene, and hospital and health center construction are handled entirely by the Bureau. Grants for cancer control and mental health are joint responsibilities with the National Cancer Institute and the Mental Hygiene Division, Bureau of Medical Services. Plans for grants for dental health and for the heart program are just getting under way and will likely be organized as joint responsibilities with the Office of Dentistry, (Office of the Surgeon General) and the National Heart Institute. (See recommendations of this report regarding grant-in-aid administration and reorganization of the Bureau of State Services, pages 52 and 148.)

Interstate quarantine and certain emergency health and sanitation activities (Philippine Rehabilitation, Alaska Sanitation and Health Program) are also Bureau activities.

The Bureau carries on developmental and administrative research which is designed to strengthen and improve the Nation's public health practice. Some training, especially of technicians, is done directly at the Communicable Disease Center, Atlanta; and the whole field training of public health workers of all types is an important interest.

The component divisions of the Bureau are:

1. Office of Administrative Management.
2. States Relations Division.
3. Venereal Disease Division.
4. Tuberculosis Control Division.
5. Industrial Hygiene Division.
6. Hospital Facilities Division.
7. Office of Health Education.
8. Office of Public Health Nursing.
9. Communicable Disease Center.

Much of the Federal-State program administration is decentralized to the district offices where specialists in hospitals, tuberculosis, venereal disease, cancer control, health education, and the like are assigned to provide consultation service to States and to actually administer major aspects of the work for their respective divisions. Real criticism of these specialists has been made, and some of it is justified, that they are not all sufficiently trained and qualified to consult with men who have worked for years in these special fields. They are rather specialists by declaration. Only qualified specialists should be so employed.

Office of Administrative Management.—This office directs and coordinates business activities of the Bureau and its constituent divisions and offices, including budget and finance, grants-in-aid, personnel, contracts, procurement, organization, and administrative procedures.

With the recent transfer of fiscal and merit system audit of grant-in-aid program to the Federal-State Relations Office of the FSA, the Bureau of State Services is no longer responsible for this function.

States Relations Division.—This division, the general public health practitioner of the Bureau, administers the general health grants-in-aid and supervises the technical training of public-health personnel employed by State and local agencies.

Demonstration programs are carried on in cooperation with selected health departments and other agencies to explore and perfect new disease-control techniques, and to train health workers. Current demonstrations are conducted to determine the best methods of applying fluoride to prevent dental caries; evaluating heart-disease diagnostic apparatus and developing a public-health heart-disease control program; developing similar diagnostic and control plans for diabetes; studing the nutritional status of population groups and for record keeping in health departments.

The development of full-time, well-balanced local health units is promoted. Public-health surveys are planned. Annual conference of State and Territorial health officers, which is advisory to the Surgeon General, is set up in this Division.

Funds for general health, Public Health Service

[In thousands of dollars]

Year	Total	Grants-in-aid	Direct expenditure by PHS for research, demonstrations, administration, etc., complementary to grants-in-aid
1948	$21, 405	$11, 217	[1] $10, 180
1947	22, 260	11, 750	[1] 10, 510
1946	13, 478	11, 000	2, 478
1945	12, 640	11, 614	1, 026
1944	12, 426	11, 454	972
1943	11, 479	11, 027	452
1942	12, 005	11, 500	505
1941	11, 764	11, 222	542
1940	10, 166	9, 723	443
1939	8, 602	8, 208	394
1938	9, 510	9, 117	393
1937	9, 276	8, 882	394
1936	3, 711	3, 333	378

[1] Includes funds for operation of Communicable Disease Center.

Venereal Disease Control Division.—From the period following World War I to 1939 when the venereal disease grant program was reestablished, this Division was relatively inactive. Since 1939 an extensive program has been fostered, with particular emphasis during the recent war when cooperation with the armed forces was quite close. The director represents the Federal Security Agency on the Interdepartmental Committee on Venereal Disease, with representatives from the Veterans' Administration, the Navy, Army, Air Force, State Department, and the American Social Hygiene Association. This committee is responsible for an 8-point agreement which helped to clarify responsibility of agencies concerned with the venereal-disease problem.

State grants-in-aid for venereal-disease control and the Rapid Treatment Center program are administered by the Division. A strong developmental research program is carried on.

Unlike the other Divisions, this one until recently conducted its own health-education program rather than using services of the Office of Health Education. The reason was given that the field was a new one which required special experimentation; the reasons, however, seem rather inadequate.

Funds for venereal disease control (including rapid treatment centers)

(In thousands of dollars)

Year	Total	Grants-in-aid	Direct expenditure by PHS. for research, demonstrations, administration, etc., complementary to grants-in-aid
1948	$16, 217	$13, 954	$2, 263
1947	17, 508	15, 446	2, 062
1946	15, 525	12, 522	2, 003
1945	14, 983	12, 247	2, 736
1944	12, 735	10, 276	2, 459
1943	12, 497	10, 170	2, 327
1942	8, 750	7, 817	933
1941	6, 200	5, 672	528
1940	5, 046	4, 379	667
1939	3, 157	2, 400	757
1938	168		168
1937	142		142

Tuberculosis Control Division.—The diagnosis, prognosis, treatment, control, and prevention of tuberculosis are the concern of this Division, particularly as they are related to State and local programs. Operations are conducted through four offices:

1. Office of administration: Responsible for administrative policies and procedures, budgets, personnel, scientific publications and information, statistical and other reporting.

2. Office of State aid: Provides medical, public health nursing, and medical social service consultation and personnel to State and local health departments. Reviews State plans for grants-in-aid for tuberculosis work, and recommends approval or modification.

3. Office of radiology: Investigates problems related to X-ray equipment and materials, trains technicians, and works with communities in conducting mass X-ray case finding surveys.

4. Office of field studies: Conducts and subsidizes field research concerned with immunization against tuberculosis, diagnosis in early stages of the disease, new methods of treatment, fungus infections related to tuberculosis, and related problems.

Close liaison is maintained between this Division and the armed forces, Veterans' Administration, Office of Indian Affairs, Bureau of Prisons, the National Tuberculosis Association, and other voluntary agencies and professional societies.

The tuberculosis grant-in-aid program began in 1944 and has expanded rapidly with major emphasis on case finding. There has been

199

some criticism of this very great emphasis, in that demonstrations of a general program of tuberculosis control might have been more effective in the long run. One must admit, however, that large numbers of people have been reached by the case-finding program within a comparatively brief period. No funds are available for medical care of patients. This is an expensive portion of the total control program, and one which may well be left largely to State and local communities for the present except for legal beneficiaries of the Federal Government.

Funds for tuberculosis control, Public Health Service

[In thousands of dollars]

	1944	1945	1946	1947	1948
Total	$231	$2,347	$6,486	$8,441	$8,342
Grants-in-aid		1,370	5,200	6,880	6,790
Direct expenditure by PHS for research demonstrations, administration, etc., complementary to grants-in-aid	231	977	1,286	1,561	1,553

The Industrial Hygiene Division.—Under the general provisions of Public Health Law 410 (78th Cong. sec. 314), Grants and Services to States, the Division of Industrial Hygiene functions as follows:

This Division supervises the industrial hygiene phases of the total Federal-State cooperative health program, with special reference to the control of occupational diseases and the promotion of health among industrial workers. It provides consultant services and technical aid to the States, especially to State industrial hygiene units, as well as to industrial establishments and labor organizations. It sponsors and promotes the establishment and maintenance of industrial hygiene service in State governments.

Thirty-two Public Health Service surgeons, engineers, sanitarians, and nurses are assigned to this Division from the Office of the Surgeon General. Its services includes:

Surveys of industrial hygiene problems within particular areas or industries; laboratory analysis of substances believed to be hazardous; investigation of occupational disease outbreaks, especially of occupational dermatose to determine the causes and to recommend methods for the elimination of control of the hazards, collection, analysis, and publication of occupational morbidity and mortality statistics. The several units of the Division deal with, and offer technical assistance in, the various elements of an industrial hygiene program, as: medical, engineering, and chemical control of hazards; industrial dentistry and nursing; morbidity records and reports.

The activities of this Division are discussed under the section on industrial hygiene, page 85.

200

Hospital Facilities Division.—This Division was established to implement the Hill-Burton Hospital Survey and Construction Act, 1946. Provision was made for each State to survey its needs for hospitals of various types and for health centers, and to develop a coordinated plan for future construction and for regional integration of the facilities.

The job involves complicated studies of community medical care needs, resources and the development of standards to insure full utilization of best modern practices in the design and construction of the buildings. The communities themselves actually make the contracts, so that Federal participation involves paying one-third of the cost and seeing that standards are followed. Since the program is not one of Federal construction, the Federal Works Agency was not brought in.

Operations are carried on through five offices:

1. Office of Administrative Management: Responsible for fiscal, personnel and general administrative services.

2. Office of Special Services: Long-range planning and educational activities.

3. Office of Program Operations: Handles project applications, legal work, expediting, etc.

4. Office of Technical Services: Staff of architects and engineers which reviews plans and specifications and studies problems of hospital construction.

5. Office of Hospital Services: Studies problems related to construction and efficient operation, the standpoints of professional care of patients and the business administration of hospitals.

In the district offices of the Public Health Service, the Division assigns a physician, a "hospital representative," an architect, and engineer. In areas where private hospital architects are few or nonexistent, it has been necessary to provide a more elaborate district organization than in other sections.

Funds for hospital facilities, Public Health Service

[In thousands of dollars]

	1947	1948
Total	1,079	7,324
Grants	371	6,396
Direct expenditure by Public Health Service for research, demonstrations, administration, etc., complementary to grants-in-aid	708	928

The program provides no Federal funds for hospital operation. These must come from the community. Much of the new construction fortunately is at present in rural areas and smaller towns where the

201

need is greatest. Many places are able to secure funds for hospital operations during boom times which may not be available in periods of financial stringency. This is something which the Federal Government may have to face in the future.

The States' interest in the hospital program is well envisaged by the fact that to date all, or 53, States and Territories have conducted surveys, and all of except 3 have applied for planning funds. A total of 6 hospitals have been completed under the plan and 92 are now in the process of construction. These additional hospitals will provide 5,666 beds at a cost of $41,097,000. Of the 92 hospitals, 58 are general hospitals with 2,807 beds; 7 mental hospitals with 859 beds; 2 tuberculosis hospitals with 900 beds, including the 800-bed hospital in Puerto Rico; 15 public health centers; and 10 adjunct services such as laboratories, etc.

As of September 9, 1948, 369 applications, including the 92 above, have been approved at a total cost of $200,132,000 of which approximately 31 percent will be met by the Federal Government.

Office of Health Education.—The office assists States and local communities in carrying out their health education programs. Recruitment and training of personnel is provided for. In addition, health education personnel is assigned to operating divisions of the Public Health Service, as the Tuberculosis Division, Diabetes Control Demonstration, and Heart Disease Demonstrations. This personnel advises the directors of these divisions on the educational aspects of their activities and assists in carrying out the communities' health program. The health education specialist of the United States Office of Educaton is appointed to the staff of the Office of Health Education in the Public Health Service and, in turn, the director of this Office has a similar appointment in the Office of Education, in order to assure coordination of their health education activities and to avoid overlapping of services. The Office of Health Education also assists foreign countries in the promotion of health educational programs.

The Department of Agriculture is also developing health specialists to work with rural people. Close working relationships are maintained between the two agencies in the training program.

For detailed statement, see special report on health education, page 126.

Office of Public Health Nursing.—The activities of this office are chiefly given over to the general supervision of public health nurses of the Bureau of State Services and to the recruitment, selection, and assignment of nursing personnel. The Office conducts the annual census of public health nursing, determines the number of vacancies in nursing positions available and advises, as far as practicable, the placement of nurses within the public health services and in other health agencies.

Communicable Disease Center.—Assists State and local health authorities in their communicable disease control problems, especially those spread by animals and insects. Practical control methods are evaluated, such as the uses of DDT; control equipment is studied and developed. Teams of experts with mobile equipment are available to investigate disease outbreaks when requests for such assistance come from the States.

Field training is provided for public health personnel. Audio-visual aids are produced for training purposes at the Center and in other educational programs. As an example, film strips are now being produced for use in preventive medicine courses.

Obligations

The total obligations of the Public Health Service are given for the years 1940, 1947, and 1948 in tables XX, XXI, and XXII, pages 204, 205, and 206.

The total obligations reported for the fiscal years 1940, 1947, and 1948 agree with obligations shown in the printed Budget (1942 Budget for 1940 data, 1949 Budget for 1947 and 1948 data), with certain adjustments in 1948 for reserves, estimated savings, and deferred obligations. The detailed break-down of obligations by division and function is based on estimates in those cases, in which obligations data are not maintained on this basis.

The break-downs are shown under the nine major categories important in carrying on the health activities of the Public Health Service. The comparison of 1940 obligations with those for 1947 and 1948 is difficult to evaluate:

Because of changes in organization and organizational responsibility which have taken place since 1940. Where a division in existence in 1940 has continued with a change in name during the years intervening between 1940 and 1947, obligations for 1940 have been reported under the new name. An example is the States Relations Division, which was formerly known as the Division of Domestic Quarantine. Where a division has been newly created since 1940 and the functions assigned to it were performed elsewhere in 1940, the obligations for that year have been reported under the division which at that time was responsible for those functions. An example is the function of medical care in penal institutions, for which the Division of Mental Hygiene was responsible in 1940 but which came under the general supervision of the Bureau of Medical Services when that Bureau was created and is there reported for 1947 and 1948. In most cases, data which would show the 1940 obligations for such transferred functions are not available as they are merged with remaining obligations of the responsible division. Another difficulty in comparing the detail of 1940 obligations with those for 1947 and 1948 results from the unavailability of separate obligations in 1940 for the various divisions of the National Institute of Health.[5]

---

[5] Statement from Bureau of the Budget.

TABLE XX.—*Obligations of Public Health Service, Federal Security Agency, 1940*

| Bureau and Division | Total obligations, 1940 | State-aid (including administrative costs) | | Research | | | | Regulatory | Medical care (including administration hospitals, clinics) | | | All others (inclusive over-all administration) |
		State grants	Direct operations	Direct activities	Grants to institutions and individuals	Fellowships	Training		Narcotic	Marine	All others	
Office of Surgeon General	$842,449											$842,449
Sanitary Engineering	[1]											
Public Health Methods	420,193											420,193
National Office of Vital Statistics	[2] 634,612											[2] 634,612
Office International Relations	[1]											
National Institute of Health	1,413,737		$25,495	$1,413,737								
National Cancer Institute	558,500			343,898	$61,380	$69,850	$57,877					
Division Infectious Diseases	[3]											
Division of Physiology	[3]											
Division of Tropical Diseases	[3]											
Division of Research Grants and Fellowships	[3]											
Biologics Control Laboratory	52,850							$52,850				
Chemistry	[3]											
Laboratory of Physical Biology	[3]											
Pathology Research Laboratory	[3]											
Bureau of Medical Services												
Foreign Quarantine Division	1,546,865										$1,546,865	
Hospital Division	9,514,659								$2,387,097	$9,514,659		
Mental Hygiene Division	2,405,573			18,476								
Federal Employees Health Division	[1]											
Bureau of State Services	167,668		167,668									
Industrial Hygiene Division			883,721									
States Relations	10,884,427	$9,500,706	644,145									
Venereal Disease	4,956,709	4,188,399		98,518			25,647					
Hospital Facilities	[1]											
Tuberculosis Control	[1]											
Communicable Disease Center	[1]											
Total, Public Health Service	32,898,242	13,689,105	1,721,029	1,874,629	61,380	69,850	83,524	52,850	2,387,097	9,514,659	1,546,865	1,897,254

[1] Division or Bureau nonexistent in 1940 under this or any predecessor title.
[2] In Department of Commerce in 1940.
[3] Break-down not available; 1940 amounts reported under National Institute of Health.

TABLE XXI.—*Obligations of Public Health Service, Federal Security Agency, 1947*

By Bureau and Division	Total obligations, 1947	State-aid (including administrative cost)		Research			Training	Regulatory	Medical care (including administration hospitals, clinics)			All others (including over-all administration)
		State grants	Direct operations	Direct activities	Grants to institutions and individuals	Fellowships			Narcotic	Marine	All others	
Office of Surgeon General	$16,089,882						$12,746,549					$3,343,333
Sanitary Engineering	1,173,701		$294,250	$181,467								697,984
Public Health Methods	561,783											561,783
National Office of Vital Statistics	970,886											970,886
Office of International Health Relations	369,134											369,134
National Institute of Health	1,167,422			1,167,422								
National Cancer Institute	4,118,359	$2,305,359	51,632	1,090,005	$480,234	$56,013	135,116					
Division of Infectious Diseases	758,543			758,543								
Division of Physiology	411,163			411,163								
Division of Tropical Diseases	473,571			473,571								
Research Grants and Fellowships	3,415,379			270,410	3,044,329	100,640						
Biologics Control Laboratory	113,442							$113,442				
Chemistry Laboratory	69,804			69,804								
Laboratory of Physical Biology	315,484			315,484								
Pathology Research Laboratory	125,284			125,284								
Bureau of Medical Services	1,391,662						100,189				$1,291,473	
Foreign Quarantine Division	2,438,496										2,438,496	
Hospital Division	24,678,635									$23,520,375	1,158,260	
Mental Hygiene Division	3,120,932			46,603					$2,935,360		138,969	
Federal Employee Health	448,573										448,573	
Bureau of State Services	1,707,040		218,040				137,213				196,622	1,155,165
Industrial Hygiene Division	1,658,557	1,000,000	658,557									
States Relations	12,122,369	10,716,797	1,320,517				85,055					
Venereal Diseases	17,270,244	12,977,802	3,680,552	490,180			25,170				96,540	
Hospital Facilities	1,061,865	357,622	704,243									
Tuberculosis Control	8,397,866	6,872,646	1,173,853	351,367								
Communicable Disease Center	8,106,367		7,906,367				200,000					
Total, Public Health Service	112,536,443	34,230,226	16,008,011	5,751,303	3,524,563	156,653	13,429,292	113,442	2,935,360	23,520,375	5,768,933	7,098,285

TABLE XXII.—*Obligations of Public Health Service, Federal Security Agency, 1948*

Bureau and Division	Total obligations, 1948	State-aid (including administrative costs)		Research				Regulatory	Medical care (including administration hospitals, clinics)			All others (including over-all administration)
		State grants	Direct operations	Direct activities	Grants to institutions and individuals	Fellowships	Training		Narcotic	Marine	All others	
Office of Surgeon General	$7,582,661						$3,995,197					$3,587,464
Sanitary Engineering	1,062,210		$330,899	$245,384								485,927
Public Health Methods	535,925											535,925
National Office of Vital Statistics	1,011,740											1,011,740
Office of International Health Relations	352,920											352,920
National Institute of Health	1,535,890			1,525,890								10,000
National Cancer Institute	13,634,116	$2,500,000	474,406	2,806,710	$4,778,711	$300,000	2,774,289					
Division Infectious Diseases	929,413			929,413								
Division of Physiology	784,969			784,969								
Division of Tropical Diseases	620,751			620,751								
Division of Research Grants and Fellowships	6,661,526			266,526	6,245,000	150,000						
Biologics Control Laboratory	128,406							$128,406				
Chemistry Laboratory	96,262			96,262								
Laboratory of Physical Biology	432,005			432,005								
Pathology Research Laboratory	167,392			167,392								
Bureau of Medical Services	1,394,432						82,900				$1,311,532	
Foreign Quarantine Division	2,688,725										2,688,725	
Hospital Division	25,974,608									$24,733,328	1,241,280	
Mental Hygiene Division	8,007,343	2,250,000	355,687	218,916	400,000	70,000	1,164,416		$3,391,475		156,849	
Federal Employee Health Division	552,575										552,575	
Bureau of State Services	2,199,206		299,206				213,345				300,000	1,386,655
Industrial Hygiene	1,628,445	964,666	663,779									
State Relations Division	11,657,163	10,252,373	1,311,433				93,357					
Venereal Disease Division	17,722,514	13,636,692	3,376,052	566,993			25,170				117,607	
Hospital Facilities Division	6,123,703	5,230,107	893,596									
Tuberculosis Control Division	8,204,903	6,690,000	1,152,437	362,466								
Communicable Disease Center	7,753,660		7,553,660				200,000					
Total, Public Health Service	129,443,463	41,523,838	16,411,155	9,023,677	11,423,711	520,000	8,548,674	128,406	3,391,475	24,733,328	6,368,568	7,370,631

The total obligation for 1940 amounted to $32,898,242 as compared to $112,536,443 for 1947, and $129,443,463 for 1948. This is an increase of 293 percent in about 9 years.

The largest obligation listed in the tables for the 3 years is for State aid; in 1940, $15,410,134 was obligated compared with $40,238,-237 for 1947, and $57,934,993 for 1948. This is an increase of 276 percent or almost three times that of 1940. For research grants to institutions and individuals in 1940 the total sum was $61,380, by 1947 it had increased to $3,524,563, and in 1948 the total obligation for grants to institutions and individuals increased to $11,423,711. This is about 186 times the obligation of 1940. In 1940, the total obligation for the training program was $83,524 and in 1947 it was $13,429,292 or 85 times that of 1940. The total obligation for training in 1948 had dropped to $4,880,618. The total obligation for research, including direct activities of the Public Health Service, grants to institutions and individuals, and fellowships for the years 1940, 1947, and 1948 was $2,005,859, $9,432,519, and $20,967,388, respectively. For a complete break-down of obligations for the Public Health Service for the years 1940–47 and 1948 see tables XX, XXI, and XXII, pages 204, 205, and 206.

Definitions of Terms

1. State-aid programs include those carried on in cooperation with State health authorities or other appropriate State agencies, as Federal-State programs. The term does not include research grants or other examples of Federal programs not requiring an over-all State plan.

State grants are monetary grants-in-aid allotted to States for use by State or local governments.

Direct operations include such activities as consultative services; demonstrations; detail of personnel; the Federal share of cooperative programs such as mass X-ray, malaria control, and special cooperative projects; and headquarters and field administrative expenses of State-aid programs such as approval of budgets, program review, and financial audit.

2. Research includes the work of organizational units principally devoted to the development of new knowledge, basic or applied, in medical and related fields of science. The term does not include such research as is performed as an incidental part of program operations.

Direct activities include research carried on at Federal stations, and research performed by Federal personnel by arrangement at non-Federal establishments.

Grants mean monetary grants-in-aid for projects approved after application has been made, whether the recipient be public or private, institutional or individual.

Fellowships mean monetary subsidies to individuals to permit them to engage in research work, either at Federal research stations or at non-Federal institutions.

3. Training includes the work of organizational units principally devoted to the giving of training courses and conferences for health personnel, whether Federal employees or otherwise; and includes monetary grants to non-Federal

institutions and agencies for student or professional training, including stipends and scholarships. The term does not include such training as is performed as an incidental part of the operations of an organizational unit.

4. Regulatory includes activities carried on pursuant to legislative responsibility to enforce standards, regulations, or licensing provisions, and work incidental thereto.

5. Medical care includes activities primarily requiring medical attention to individuals, such as care of the sick or medical examination for quarantine or employment purposes.

Narcotic includes operating costs of Public Health Service narcotic hospitals.

Marine includes operating costs of Public Health Service marine hospitals and relief stations.

All other includes foreign quarantine service and miscellaneous hospital and clinic operations not primarily research or part of a State-aid program.

6. All other includes all-over administration and such matters as public works, vital statistics, miscellaneous studies, surveys, international activities, and special short-term activities, not included in any of the above categories; and general administration not directly chargeable to such categories.

SOCIAL SECURITY ADMINISTRATION

The Administration was created under the Reorganization Act of 1945 (59 Stat. 613; Suppl. 5, title 5, U. S. C. 133y), Reorganization Plan II, effective July 16, 1946. This act abolished the original three-member Social Security Board and transferred its functions to the Federal Security Administrator under the supervision of a commissioner.

The health activities of the Administrator are carried on through the health and welfare services of the Children's Bureau and indirectly through the Division of Research and Statistics.

Children's Bureau

The Children's Bureau has responsibility under two laws:

1. The Act of 1912, which created the Bureau, and which directs the Bureau to "investigate and report . . . upon all matters pertaining to the welfare of children and child life among all classes of our people . . . . especially . . . the questions of infant mortality, the birth rate, orphanage, juvenile courts, desertion, dangerous occupations, accidents and diseases of children, employment, legislation affecting children in the several States and Territories." [6]

2. Title V of the Social Security Act, which makes funds available for grants to the States.

a. For the purpose of enabling each State to extend and improve, so far as practicable under the conditions in such State, services for promoting the health of mothers and children, especially in rural areas and in areas suffering from severe economic distress, . . . the sum of $11,000,000.[7]

---

[6] 37 Stat. 79.
[7] Pt. 1, sec. 501.

208

b. For the purpose of enabling each State to extend and improve (especially in rural areas and in areas suffering from severe economic distress), as far as practicable under the conditions in such State, services for locating crippled children, and for providing medical, surgical, corrective, and other services and care, and facilities for diagnosis, hospitalization, and after-care, for children who are crippled or who are suffering from conditions which lead to crippling . . . the sum of $7,500,000.[8]

c. For the purpose of enabling the United States, . . . to cooperate with State public-welfare agencies in establishing, extending, and strengthening, especially in predominantly rural areas, public-welfare services (hereinafter in this section referred to as "child-welfare services") for the protection and care of homeless, dependent, and neglected children, and children in danger of becoming delinquent, . . . the sum of $3,500,000.[9]

The Children's Bureau has carried on a wide variety of activities. It has made and participated in basic research. Its studies of methods of providing services have been made for the purpose of formulating statements of what is the "best practice" within current knowledge. It has developed material to be used by parents about various aspects of child life, for example, "Infant Care," "Your Child From One to Six," and others. It has published its findings and made them freely available to citizens and to committees of Congress.

Because of the broad scope of the act of 1912 it has been possible for the Children's Bureau to initiate as well as participate in many different kinds of activities which affect the welfare of children. The Bureau has worked closely with other agencies of the Federal Government concerned with health, education, and welfare in carrying out these broad responsibilities.

The grant-in-aid funds available under title V have been administered in the light of its enunciated purpose—to extend and improve health and welfare services for children. The effort has been made to give advice and consultation in all areas of these programs with respect to the States which ask for help.

The number of different fields in which the Children's Bureau is directed to act makes it a multifunctional agency of Government. It does not conform to the prevailing Government pattern, which is to have an agency deal with services on a single functional basis. The Bureau's experience has demonstrated a positive value in the combination of services for which the Children's Bureau is now responsible.

Functions of Division of Health Services.—In general, the functions of the Division of Health Services of the Children's Bureau are (1) to improve health services for children in the United States, and (2) to keep the standards of these services abreast of the research and scientific knowledge available in these fields today.

---

[8] Pt. 2, sec. 511.
[9] Pt. 3, sec. 521.

The professional staff of the Division, under the leadership of the Director, operates in both the areas of program planning and field operation, and is organized to give help to consultants in the regional offices and to State and other agencies concerned with providing health services and medical care to mothers and children, and crippled children.

The program of the Health Services Division is developed by its Program Planning Section with a professional staff under the direction of a physician as chief. This staff consists of units of specialists in nursing, nutrition, medicine, dentistry, medical-social work, and administrative methods, who work together as a team. Each unit brings its professional knowledge and skills to the evaluation, development and improvement of services for mothers and children, and for crippled children, and the extension of training opportunities in all professional fields contributing to health services for children. This division evaluates the special needs of children throughout the country.

Each unit is responsible for providing leadership needed for improving the health and welfare of mothers and children and crippled children in this country and in other countries within the scope of the Bureau's international relationships. It gives technical supervision to the work of its regional consultants and the maintenance of consistent standards of service through conferences, individual consultation, and joint field visits.

The Program Development Section arranges for conferences of advisory groups of lay people and experts on the special health needs of children. Standards are developed for maternal and child health services and for services to children who are the victims of crippling conditions, of cerebral palsy and rheumatic fever. Special consultation is given State agencies on their medical programs, on maternal, pediatric, and orthopedic nursing, on medical-social procedures, nutrition, and physical therapy, and on hospital administration and accounting. Its physicians assist medical schools to develop curricula and graduate courses designed to train physicians in the most effective methods of care of mothers and children. Staff members cooperate with schools of public health, nursing, social work, and nutrition, in developing courses in maternal and child health and in promoting improved training in child health for professional workers in other fields.

In order to develop an integrated service for children, the professional staff of the Health Services Division cooperates closely with the other divisions of the Bureau. Under the Bureau's mandate to "investigate and report" this division cooperates with the Division of Research and Child Development in planning research projects as a basis for more efficient program planning. The Statistical Research Division cooperates in the analysis of data, especially in the field of infant mortality statistics and in statistical data whch are part of State and regional reports, in the development of reporting systems, etc.

In cooperation with the Division of Reports, both technical and popular material has been developed for distribution. The Division of Reports also gives consultation to States on health information problems.

Bringing the Health and Welfare Services for Children together within the same organizational unit has facilitated their administrative and program coordination. Many problem areas require the combined services of both the health and welfare divisions in order to meet the wide variety of needs of children. These include day care facilities, programs for unmarried mothers, and programs developed for children with personality difficulties. The coordination of the Health Services for Children with other health service programs, and of the welfare service for children with other welfare service programs, has been brought about by continual intraagency planning. Specifically in relation to the health programs, the Children's Bureau health service staff meets regularly with the staff of the Bureau of State Services of the Public Health Service. There is consistent analysis and planning in relation to categorical health programs administered by the Public Health Service, that is, venereal disease, tuberculosis, mental health, cancer, etc.

An advisory committee for this Division meets semiannually to assist the Division in formulating its general policies focused on the health needs of children. This committee represents nationwide professional and lay interests in child development through the following groups: One-fourth of members chosen by American Medical and Dental Association, one-fourth of members representing medical, dental, and other specialists chosen by the Children's Bureau, one-fourth of members representing citizens' groups interested in child development (as parent-teachers association, labor organizations, etc.), one-fourth of members representing citizens at large, chosen by Bureau on same basis.

The use of such committees by the Children's Bureau since its development has been one of the distinct contributions the Bureau has made in the field of Government planning. These committees consisting of cross sections of both professional and lay groups have not only shared in program planning, but they also have been intelligent interpreters of the Bureau to the general public.

Field Operation Section.—The professional staff of the Division coordinates and integrates its field operations. It reviews States' plans and budgets; apportions the funds allocated to States on the basis of need, and facilitates, through regional offices, consultative services to State agencies.

At the present time, the services of the specialists in health are channeled through the 10 regional offices, the Federal Security Agency regional offices, where they are fully coordinated with the regional offices of the other constituent agencies of the Federal Security Agency. Each regional unit of the Children's Bureau when fully staffed consists of a medical director, a nurse, nutrition consultant, a medical-social worker, and an administrative-methods consultant. Individually or as a "team" regional consultants visit each State health agency and crippled children's agency conferring with directors and staff members and advising on the operation of State programs, standards of service, and ways of extending and improving health services for mothers and children.

Grant-in-aid program.—To enable the States to extend and improve health services for mothers and children, Congress has allocated annually to this Division funds for administering two grants programs as follows:

	Funds for 1948
1. Maternal and child health grants	$11,000,000
2. Crippled children's	7,000,000
Total	18,000,000

By the provision of the act, the total funds appropriated are allocated to States to assist the State and local operations of this program. One-half of all the funds available is matched by the States, dollar for dollar.

This program is in operation in all the States, the District of Columbia, Alaska, Hawaii, Puerto Rico, and the Virgin Islands. State plans for each of these health services are reevaluated annually on the basis of joint Federal and State cooperative planning, and in relationship to both Federal and State expenditures needed and available to develop the programs. These plans are approved by the Chief of the Division. Federal and State funds are allocated by the State's agency in accordance with its plan to county and local health departments for maternal and child health services.

Maternal and child health services.—In general the maternal and child health grant is used in individual States in the following ways:

1. To develop in accordance with the need in individual States services such as maternity clinics; child health conferences; health services for school children; dental care for children; nutrition education; inspecting and licensing of hospital maternity services. The pattern of each State's program is tailored to fit its need. Quality of service is given particular emphasis. There is no national pattern. No State is meeting its total needs. There are many areas which have not been reached.

2. To give further training to staff personnel who are employed full-time, part-time, or on a fee-for-service basis. Postgraduate

courses in obstetrics and pediatrics are held for practicing physicians and institutes and training courses are held for public health nurses and other health workers. Stipends are provided for staff workers in State and local health departments, to enable them to take additional professional training. Money from these grants has been used for initiating or improving courses of graduate study in these fields. In Arkansas, which lacked pediatricians, for example, graduate courses in pediatrics, entirely financed from these funds, were set up in the State medical school. Three schools of public health have contracts with States for the improvement of graduate education in matters related to child and maternal health. Two schools now receive funds for improving graduate work in children's dentistry.

3. To share with State departments of health the cost of a child health division within the framework of the State health department, in order to extend and improve maternal and child health services, especially in rural areas and in areas suffering from serious economic distress.

Locally, the maternal and child health program is carried on by the county or city health department. Physicians provide medical supervision to mothers in prenatal clinics and to children in child-health conferences. Clinics provide dental care for children in many States. In addition to clinic service, the public-health nurse conducts classes and makes home visits. Health services for school children are conducted in cooperation with the schools.

In a limited number of areas home-delivery nursing service is provided at the request of the attending physician. Supervision is given midwives, and in some counties nurse-midwives are provided to train and supervise midwives and to a limited extent to give midwifery service. In a few areas in the States, medical care for mothers at delivery and care for sick children, with hospitalization if necessary, are provided.

Reports from State health agencies indicate that during 1946 about 129,000 mothers received prenatal medical care under maternal and child health programs financed in part with Federal funds. About 456,000 infants and preschool children attended medical child-health conferences; about 952,000 infants and preschool children received public-health nursing service; and health supervision for some 1,587,000 school children was provided under State health departments in cooperation with school authorities. Additional funds and more trained professional workers are urgent needs to extend these services.

Crippled children's services.—The services for crippled children in each State follow the same general pattern as the program for maternal and child health in order to extend and improve services for crippled children and for children with crippling conditions.

The State agencies responsible for administering services for crippled children are as follows: Health departments, 30; public welfare departments, 10; crippled children's commissions, 5; departments of education, 4; State university medical schools or hospitals, 3. The State staffs usually include physicians, specialists in orthopedic and plastic surgery, orthopedic nurses, medical-social workers, and physical therapists. Local health departments, welfare departments, and school authorities cooperate with the State agencies.

State agencies may include within their crippled children's programs all services needed to alleviate the handicapping conditions of childhood. There has never been a Nation-wide analysis taken of children with crippling conditions under whatever definition. It is believed, however, that the ratio of children with crippling conditions to population is fairly uniform throughout the United States. However, the registry of crippled children maintained by all the State crippled children's agencies, showed over 442,000 registered on December 31, 1946. It is estimated that 500,000 children are estimated to have rheumatic fever, 160,000 cerebral palsy, 200,000 epilepsy, in addition to those with hearing and visual defects.

The grants are used for organized programs of medical, surgical, corrective, and other services and care for children who are crippled or who are suffering from conditions that lead to crippling, and to provide facilities for diagnosis, hospitalization, and aftercare for such children. Twenty-two States, for example, now have organized programs for the care of children suffering from rheumatic fever or heart disease.

Diagnosis and some treatment is provided in clinics held for crippled children in permanent clinic centers, or at intervals in itinerant clinics. The State agency assumes responsibility for arranging for hospitalization, medical and surgical care; the subsequent care of a crippled child in a convalescent home or in his own home; and for medical and public-health-nursing supervision and physical therapy to complete his physical restoration. Medical social service also aids the children in adjusting at home, at school, and in neighborhood activities. Children for whom such opportunities are appropriate are referred to the Vocational Rehabilitation Service for vocational training when they reach 16 years of age.

There are long waiting lists for admission to hospitals for crippled children.

Division of Statistical Research.—The Division of Statistical Research is responsible for the reporting services for the crippled children's as well as the maternal and infancy programs. Data on the cost of hospital care are contained in requests from hospitals for reimbursement for hospital care provided under the Federal-State programs.

214

In general this Division collects and analyzes, for administrative use and public information, statistics of the Bureau's programs in the fields of maternal and child health and welfare. In addition, the Division promotes the development and use of statistics by State and local agencies concerned with the welfare of children.

A major activity of this Division is statistical research into the trends and conditions of maternal, infant, and childhood mortality. Continuing analyses are made of registered vital statistics and of data derived from administrative records and special studies. (See table XXIII below.)

Mental health unit.—Recently the Bureau has developed a small mental health unit to be concerned with the question as to how mental and emotional health may be developed in children, as well as the preventative and curative aspects. The mental health unit fosters wider understanding of mental health by doctors, dentists, social workers, nurses, and others who work with children, stimulates development and improvement of mental-health services for children in child health and welfare programs supported by public or private funds, promotes development of diagnostic and treatment resources for children with personality and behavior problems and for mentally retarded children, and provides consultative service. This unit has been placed outside of both the Social Services Division and the Division of Health Services for the purpose of making it possible to work coordinately with both.

Division of Research in Child Development.—The Children's Bureau was primarily a research, fact-gathering, standard-setting, informa-

TABLE XXIII.—*The impetus given to the development of specialized services on State and local levels by the health services' grant-in-aid program of the Children's Bureau*

Children's Bureau programs in State departments of health	Budgeted positions when the grant-in-aid program started		Positions at present		Remarks
	Number of States	Number of positions	Number of States	Number of positions	
Nutrition	3	9	50	170	As of December 1947. (1) For the fiscal year 1945–46, 63 percent of these nutrition positions were charged to Children's Bureau funds, 9 percent to Public Health Service funds, and 28 percent to State and local funds.
Medical social workers	2	6 or 7	51	250	
Nursing service; nurses trained to give consultation services in—					
(a) hospitals, on child and maternal care.	0	0	19	25	As of July 1, 1948.
(b) pediatric care	0	0	38	81	Do.
(c) orthopedic care	0	0	45	115	Do.

tional agency.   In its first decade the Children's Bureau, in line with its mandate to investigate and report, concentrated its small resources on studies of conditions surrounding the lives of children.   The series of community studies on infant mortality revealed the social and economic factors associated with a high mortality rate.   These studies have influenced the development of services both within and without the Federal Government that have helped in reducing deaths in infancy.

As a result of the knowledge gained from such studies, the Bureau published a pamphlet for parents, Infant Care.   This pamphlet has been rewritten from time to time to keep it abreast of the development of newer knowledge in infant care.   Last year 1 million copies of this pamphlet were given away; more than a million were sold.   It has been translated into four languages.   Seventy percent of the budget of the Division of Reports, or $129,965, has been used during the last year for the publication of a series of monthly letters to parents on prenatal and infant care.   These monthly letters are based on the results of current research.   They have a voluminous circulation. This budget also includes answering letters from parents who ask specific questions growing out of their own problems.   These reports are based on the results of current research in these subjects.

Following its broad legislative mandate, research carried on by the Bureau has been characterized by the diversity of its subject matter. The greatest portion of the Children's Bureau research effort has gone into the fields of child health, child labor, and child welfare.   Children's Bureau studies have characteristically related to two or more of these fields, including considerations of the general social and economic factors relating to children.

The purposes of Children's Bureau research, broadly speaking, have been to survey and analyze the nature and extent of problems affecting children; to review and evaluate community facilities and programs designed to treat and prevent these problems; to develop techniques and procedures for improving child care and services to children.

From the viewpoint of methodology the predominant type of study has been the field survey, employing schedules to collect data susceptible of statistical treatment.   The Bureau has also undertaken legal research, chiefly in State statutes, relating to children.   Some research has consisted entirely or in large part of case studies.   Much of the recent research activity in the Bureau has consisted of statistical analysis of data collected by the Bureau or by other governmental agencies.

In the general curtailment of all work not directly related to the war, the research program was greatly reduced.   Since the war the Children's Bureau has been giving serious consideration to renewing its emphasis on its research program, in an attempt to learn what research is needed in the total field of child life.

216

Major advances have been made in research in child life by research agencies and individuals outside government. The movement for research in child growth and development, stimulated by the Rockefeller Foundation 20 years ago, through grants to child-research stations, has produced significant results. Important developments are occurring in research in the biological, physical, and social sciences, bearing on problems of child development. Gains are being made in the provision of health and welfare services for children which both utilize the results of research and bring to light new research problems.

These and other developments call for a basic review of the present status and future direction of research in child life. The scope of research needed has received little focused attention. National interest in research during and since the war has centered principally on the physical and biological sciences.

During the period of 1947–48 the Children's Bureau appropriations for direct research amounted to $31,000.

The Children's Bureau has no authority nor funds for grants-in-aid for research. The present funds of the Children's Bureau for research purposes are on an extremely restricted basis. While it has the responsibility under its basic act of 1912 for child research the financial support for this allows only limited activities. Under the Social Security Act it has funds which go to the States for the extension and development of underlying services for children. These funds can be used for investigative purposes only when the investigation is directly connected with services for children and then in a limited way only. The Children's Bureau at present has no authority to make grants to anyone for research unconnected with operating services in the States. But cooperative arrangements have approved a useful technique for assisting research in which the Bureau has a special interest but for which its finances are insufficient.

The Bureau, in cooperation with a group of distinguished leaders in research in child life, have been (1) examining the need for research in child life and exploring the directions it should take; (2) reappraising the role of the Children's Bureau as the Federal Government's principal research agency in the field of child life; and (3) considering research in relation to training and service.

As a result of these deliberations the Children's Bureau has already established an information center of research-in-progress in the Division of Research and Child Development as a clearinghouse on research in child life. This clearinghouse will ascertain currently what research is going on, both inside and outside the Federal Government, and will coordinate the Bureau's research program with those undertaken otherwise.

The Committee on Child Development of the National Research

Council, a committee of long standing, has been reorganized to serve as part of a permanent Research Advisory Committee of the Bureau.

Liaison has been established with the National Institute of Health and with other Federal agencies doing research which touches child life, as the Office of Education and Bureau of Home Economics and Nutrition in the Department of Agriculture, in order to exchange ideas and advise on these research programs in order to prevent duplication. (See the following table.)

Health activities of the Children's Bureau

Items	1940	1947	1948
A. State aid, including administrative costs:			
1. State grants	$8, 202, 193	$29, 038, 195	$20, 054, 965
2. Direct cooperation	276, 000	571, 000	547, 000
B. Research: 1. Direct activities	39, 000	32, 000	31, 000
C. All other including all-over administrative costs	124, 000	226, 000	237, 000
Total obligations	8, 641, 193	29, 867, 195	20, 869, 965

Recommendations.—During its 37 years of operation, the Children's Bureau has developed services in those areas in which the rights of children need protection, such as: Children living under improper home conditions, juvenile delinquents, crippled children, children working in industry. It has been responsible for legislation to protect children. It has a research program, but is not allowed to make research grants. It operates, under title V of the Social Security Act, three grant-in-aid programs: (1) For maternal and child care, (2) for crippled children, and (3) for child welfare services.

When the Children's Bureau was in the Department of Labor it enjoyed a remarkable degree of autonomy, with the Chief being directly appointed by the President. At present the Bureau is administratively under the Social Security Administration and the Chief does not have direct access to the Federal Security Administrator. This arrangement makes it administratively difficult for the Bureau to perform its assigned functions of concerning itself with all the problems of children; of developing plans to meet these problems; and, in general, making sure that children are considered in all the planning of the FSA. It is therefore recommended that, in order to perform this broad function properly, the Bureau should be placed in the organization of the proposed Department of Health, Education, and Security in a general staff capacity where it can advise the Secretary of the new Department as well as the Directors General of Health, Education, and Security. It is also recommended that the scope of the Bureau be broadened somewhat beyond its present fields so that it may be equipped to deal more adequately with problems in the educational field.

The grant-in-aid programs for which the Children's Bureau is responsible have been administered admirably. Tremendous strides have been made in making maternal and child health available to people, though much remains to be done. Nevertheless, there is no unanswerable reason for leaving the grant-in-aid programs indefinitely with the Children's Bureau. Its primary functions should be those of research, planning, and promotion. A large administrative responsibility is inconsistent with the maximum performance of the Bureau's proper functions. Unquestionably, funds should be available for demonstrations, for training personnel, and for research conducted on a direct and a grant basis.

It is therefore recommended that as soon as the Public Health Service develops a more unified approach to the administration of its own grant-in-aid programs, and as soon as the promotional phase is passed in the grant-in-aid programs now operated by the Children's Bureau, the health grant-in-aid programs should be transferred to the Public Health Service.

Division of Research and Statistics

The Division of Research and Statistics reviews and analyzes problems related to social security "that are beyond the immediate scope of any other bureau." Its work in the field of health activities is limited, as only one professional staff member is set aside for this work.

The Division makes occasional special studies on health aspects of social security, and compiles information, answers inquiries, advises on program or legislative matters. Occasionally, it compiles new information on existing social security (health) provisions, public or voluntary.

The Division also collects and analyzes information on health aspects of broader social security programs (e. g., "health and welfare" provisions established by employers or under collective-bargaining agreements; foreign social security programs).

Obligations.—The total budget for the Division (1948–49) is $125,000. On the basis of present outlook, about $15,000 will probably be expended on all "health activities." [10]

UNITED STATES OFFICE OF EDUCATION

The Department of Education [11] (1) collects statistical and other information on the programs of instruction and administration in

---

[10] Communicated from Division of Research and Statistics, September 24, 1948.

[11] The U. S. Department of Education was created March 2, 1867, by an act of Congress (14 Stat. 434; 20 U. S. C. 1). It was transferred under the President's Reorganization Plan No. 1 from the Department of the Interior to the Federal Security Agency on July 1, 1939.

schools, colleges, and universities, and other educational institutions; (2) gives advisory and consultative services to State and local school authorities; (3) administers grants-in-aid to educational and special programs; (4) conducts research on educational practices. Its educational activities include school public-health education. As a part of its physical education program it encourages medical examinations for school children and teachers, and studies the effect of these examinations upon child health. Through its grants-in-aid programs for vocational education it assists in the training of health teachers and practical nurses. The department is responsible for the direction of the activities of the Columbia Institution for the Deaf, Howard University, and the American Printing House for the Blind.

The school health activities of the United States Office of Education have grown up as a contributory program to the field of education rather than a program designed for health itself. In this connection the school hygiene program of State and local education departments had the direct interest and support of the United States Office of Education rather than the United States Department of Public Health. However, the United States Office of Education conducts school health educational conferences in cooperation with State departments of health, recreational associations, and nongovernmental health agencies. For a discussion on health education, see page 126 of this report and the report on Federal Policy and Organization for Education (Brookings Institution, Hollis P. Allen), which discusses the school health education program fully.

OFFICE OF VOCATIONAL REHABILITATION

The Vocational Rehabilitation Act of July 6, 1943 (Public Law 113, 78th Cong.) provides "for the promotion of vocational rehabilitation of persons disabled in industry or otherwise and their return to civil employment." The Federal Security Administrator is responsible for carrying out the provisions of this act through the granting of money to States whose plans he approves and through seeing to it that these plans are followed.

The law specifically provides for a State board of vocational education as the sole agency for the administration, supervision, and control of the State plan, with a commission for the blind caring for the blind if such a body exists in that State. The State agency must have a merit system of personnel administration and must make required reports. Maximum fee schedules must be set by the State agency and the Federal Security Administrator is required to specify the classes of individuals eligible to receive benefits under this act. The extent of State financial participation is specified, differing for several categories of persons (such as one-half for all eligibles, except war-disabled civilians or civil employees of the United States, for whom the Federal Government pays all the expenses).

The Federal Security Administrator (or his representative) promulgates regulations after consultation with the executive committees of both the States Rehabilitation Council and the National Rehabilitation Association. These regulations are based on the act, and contain the more specific provisions under which the program is administered.

Administration of the act is delegated by the Federal Security Administrator to the Office of Vocational Rehabilitation (a section of the Office of Special Services). The medical aspects of the program are handled by a staff of Public Health Service officers assigned for duty with this Office. Consultative and advisory work with the States is carried on through representatives in the regional offices of the Federal Security Agency, medical officers too being assigned from the Public Health Service.

The Office of Vocational Rehabilitation works through two functional divisions: (1) Administrative Standards, and (2) Rehabilitation Standards. Within the latter, the section on advisement, training, and placement is concerned with staff development and promotion of sound professional performance. State agencies send their rehabilitation workers to federally sponsored training institutes, and development of acceptable standards is an important function of this section.

The section on physical restoration is concerned with the development of standards, policies, and techniques governing the provision of physical and mental restoration services. Mental (or emotional) disabilities are considered to be conditions subject to correction or alleviation, and a psychiatric social worker in this Office is consultant to State agencies.

Services to the blind are centered in another section of this Division. Consultation to States on problems associated with employment of the blind is an important function, as well as preparation of training materials, job descriptions, etc.

The sections on information services and research and statistics operate along lines implied in their titles.

To summarize, the Office of Vocational Rehabilitation provides funds which assist States in training, treating (medically), and placing into employment those individuals who are of employable age and otherwise competent to work. The appropriations for the past 2 years have been 18 million dollars per year, and in the 1947 annual report the amount of $400 was estimated as the average cost per restoration. It was calculated, too, that the annual income of those who were returned to employment increased from 14 million to 68 million dollars, resulting in an increase in the national annual earned income of 54 million dollars. From a cold statistical viewpoint, this would seem to justify the program, but the increased happiness and psychological self-sufficiency which result from the return of a disabled person to gainful employment cannot be expressed in money values. They are perhaps incalculable.

The percentage of the total appropriation to States which is expended for medical services, though increasing, is not large: 1944—4.97 percent; 1948—12.06 percent. "A wide range of services are available under the Vocational Rehabilitation Act. Training, maintenance, medical services, occupational tools and equipment, and transportation are the principal services which are purchased for eligible clients. Guidance, counseling and placement activities are rendered by the staff of the State rehabilitation agencies." It is apparent that medical service is but a small part, financially, of the total rehabilitation cost. For this reason, it would be unwise to suggest separation of the medical service program from the other aspects of vocational rehabilitation at the Federal level, especially since the Federal activities involve grants rather than direct service. At the State level, strong arguments could be made for administration of the medical services by the agency administering the program for crippled children.

Extent of Federal financial support to State programs

| Fiscal year | Total appropriation for payments to States | Federal share of services purchased for clients | Federal share of expenditures for medical services | | | | Percentage of "total appropriations" for medical services |
			Medical and surgical treatment	Hospitalization	Prosthetic appliances	Total	
1944	6, 730, 000	1, 700, 340	19, 998	13, 244	301, 493	334, 735	4. 97
1945	8, 000, 000	2, 674, 424	108, 365	136, 373	353, 733	598, 471	7. 48
1946	11, 705, 400	3, 749, 853	234, 171	304, 776	356, 547	895, 494	7. 65
1947	12, 359, 800	5, 131, 073	421, 027	470, 678	536, 806	1, 428, 511	11. 56
1948	18, 000, 000	6, 875, 808	609, 437	688, 236	872, 975	2, 170, 648	12. 06
1949	18, 000, 000						

Recommendations.—1. The medical services aspect of vocational rehabilitation should be retained as part of the over-all program of the Office of Vocational Rehabilitation, though at the State level there are strong arguments for administration of medical aspects by the agency responsible for crippled children's work.

2. Assignment of medical officers from the Public Health Service to the Office of Vocational Rehabilitation to advise on the medical service activities is a wise procedure and should be continued.

FOOD AND DRUG ADMINISTRATION

The Food and Drug Administration was created by an Act of Congress in 1906 (34 Stat. 3915; 21 U. S. C. 1, secs. 1–5), and an Agricultural Appropriation Act of 1931 (46 Stat. 392). It was transferred to the Federal Security Agency by the President's Reorganization Plan No. 4, effective June 3, 1940. Its Commissioner acts under the direction of the Administrator of the Federal Security Agency.

Organization and functions.—The Commissioners, in carrying out the functions of the Administration, are assisted in their duties by heads of 11 divisions. These divisions are chiefly concerned with the technical work of their division and the coordinating and regulatory activities of the Administration. The Divisions of Pharmacology, Microbiology, and Vitamine Bacteriology are concerned with research as it is related to their respective divisions. The Divisions of Food, of Drugs, and of Cosmetics, likewise confine their activities to scientific methods of their specific problems of enforcement. The Divisions of Interstate, Import, and State Corporations are administrative offices specifically planned and directed for the enforcement of laws and the coordination of the Administration's activities. The Medical Division is responsible for the medical policy of the Administration with respect to the chemical studies, and the efficacy and safety of food and drugs for man and animal.

As the activities of the Administration are Nation-wide, regional offices located in strategic cities, fully equipped with analytical facilities, are maintained. The country as a whole is divided into 16 inspection "station territories." These stations are under the supervision of a "station chief" who is responsible for the enforcement of the law within his area and who reports directly to the Washington office. The responsible area officials are commissioned by the Federal Security Administrator as agents for the Federal Security Agency in the control and enforcement of the Federal Food, Drug, and Cosmetic Act.

Collaborations.—The Administration controls and maintains close cooperation with the Division of Customs in the Department of the Treasury. It also cooperates with the Post Office Department and the Federal Trade Commission in the analysis and investigations of medical and other related products. It gives technical assistance to the Departments of the Interior, War, Justice, Veterans' Administration, and other Government and private agencies requesting technical services.

Health activities, regulatory.[12]—The Food and Drug Administration protects the consuming public against misbranded or adulterated foods, insecticides and fungicides and the enforcement of the Food, Drug, and Cosmetic Act (21 U. S. C. 301 et seq.), the Federal Tea Transportation Act (21 U. S. C. 41), the Federal Caustic Poisons

---

[12] For a complete discussion of the legal aspects of the activities of the Food and Drug Administration and the Federal Trade Commission, see Legal Aspects under Federal Trade Commission, page 228.

Act (15 U. S. C. 401), the Federal Import Milk Act (21 U. S. C. 141), and the Federal Filled Milk Act (21 U. S. C. 61).

The Administration advises manufacturers on keeping within the requirements of the act. Violations are reported to the Department of Justice with recommendations for seizure, criminal prosecution, or injunction actions within the Federal court.

Research.—It also conducts research that has regulatory objectives. Pure research as a distinct activity is not undertaken by the Administration. Many research studies are planned and carried out with the sole objective of adequate and efficient enforcement of the law. To make its regulatory objectives work, the Administration must conduct studies that will give the technical knowledge necessary for law enforcement; to detect fraud in terms of proof that will sustain court action, as well as serve to detect new types of adulteration and new processes. For Government agencies that do not have laboratory facilities and technical personnel, the Food and Drug Administration assists in conducting studies essential to their program. In order to maintain the standards set by the United States Pharmacopoeia, or the National Formulary, and to determine the safety and the efficacy of medicines, the laboratories of the Administration make vitamin assays, bacteriological analysis, and investigations into the toxicity of ingredients used in the manufacture of foods and drugs, and in related fields which protect health. For example, in the field of bacteriology, investigations are made on food poisoning and the identification of contaminating organisms. Studies are being made to detect the prevalence of brucella in the manufacture of cheese from raw milk. This study does overlap the brucellosis research made in the Bacteriological Division of the National Institute of Health. The Food and Drug Administration conducts research on poultry diseases in an effort to determine worthless preparations in the control and prevention of diseases which are similar to the studies made by the Bureau of Animal Industry on various anthelmintics and methods of control of animal and poultry diseases.

Recent publications exemplifying such research as Metabolism and Permeability of Normal Skin (Physiol. Rev. 24: 495, 1946); The Treatment of Gonorrhea With Streptomycin (American Journal, Syphilis, Gonorrhea, and Venereal Diseases 31: 268, 1947); Observation On the In Vivo and In Vitro Development of Bacterial Resistance to Streptovyvin (Journal Bact. 53: 481, 1947) might appear offhand to be out of the field of regulatory research. However, such researches are made to secure technological knowledge necessary to detect fraud and to enforce the law. They therefore fall well within the regulatory research activities of the Administration.

These researches appear to be overlapping. However, since they are solely made for the detection of adulterations, they do not require the high degree of competence required in PHS researches, and can, therefore, best be undertaken in connection with the regulatory powers of the Food and Drug Administration.

The Biologic Control Laboratory, National Institute of Health, Public Health Service, has enforcement provisions for the control and sale of any therapeutic viruses, serums, toxins, vaccines, or analogous products, including arsphenamine or its derivatives used in the prevention, treatment, or cure of diseases or injuries of man. This control is enforced under section 351, Public Health Service Act (Public Law 410, 78th Cong.), formerly the act of July 1, 1902 (32 Stat. L. 728, ch. 1378). Provision is made for annual inspection of licensed and nonlicensed laboratories, under its standards of minimum requirements for licensed products as to their potency, purity, and safety. Although the purpose of this act is to assure the consumer that those biologics are potent and free from contaminants, it gives no authority to control the sale of biologics. That obligation belongs to the States. The act also provides for the conduct of research on the development of new biologics and the new methods for their control.

The work carried on by the National Institute of Health in the administration of the control and development of biologics is such that it does not involve unnecessary duplication. It is chiefly concerned with the therapeutic value of the products, their purity, and their potency. This service done chiefly for the medical profession is essentially scientific and technical in character.

The Bureau of Animal Industry, Department of Agriculture, also has powers to control the interstate shipment, the importation and exporting of viruses, toxins, and medicines used in the prevention and treatment of animal diseases. The Food and Drug Administration apparently carries a part of the same function in making veterinary tests and reporting on the sale of these veterinary products.

Obligations.—The total obligation for health activities in the Food and Drug Administration is used for the protection of health through law enforcement. In 1940 the obligations were $2,572,466, $4,620,053 in 1947, and $4,815,700 in 1948, respectively.

Recommendations.—As the Food and Drug Administration is essentially an agency designed by law for the protection of health, it should be transferred to the Public Health Service in the proposed Section of Health Standards and Inspection where its techniques for law enforcement would be strengthened. Furthermore, to strengthen its regulatory functions for the protection of health, regulatory powers except meat inspection which is after all concerned with the grading of meat for commercial purposes, as well as health, within the Department of Agriculture related to health should be consoli-

225

dated under the Food and Drug Administration. Research facilities are established by law in the Food and Drug Administration because research is vital in obtaining the knowledge necessary for law enforcement. The facilities for law enforcement and research are, therefore, well combined in one agency.

With respect to the National Biologics Act, Public Health Service, and the Virus, Serum, Toxin Act of the Bureau of Animal Industry, Department of Agriculture, they could well remain where they are now. Both are regulatory activities, one affecting man and the other animal. The control of animal biologics should be retained in the Bureau of Animal Industry, Department of Agriculture. The control of biologics dealing with man should be transferred from the Biologics Control Laboratory, National Institute of Health, to Food and Drug Administration. The control of both human and animal biologics has been sustained through professional channels of both the physician and veterinarian.

Federal Trade Commission

The activities of the Federal Trade Commission which may be interpreted as public health services are based on its regulatory acts to prevent unfair or deceptive practices in the handling of foods, drugs, cosmetics and medical devices. The Commission's policy has been to "proceed only when the resulting dangers may be suspicious or the public health may be impaired and in such cases to require that appropriate disclosure of the facts be made in the advertising." [13]

Creation, Functions, and Organization

The Commission was created by an act of Congress, September 26, 1914 (38 Stat. 717; 15 U. S. C. 41–51). It was originally enacted to prohibit the "unfair methods of competition," the restraint of trade, and the practices of price fixing. The phrase "unfair methods of competition" was purposely not defined in the act; it was left to the Commission and to judicial reviews to determine the meaning of the phrase with respect to individual cases. One of the methods of competition early proceeded against by the Commission as unfair was the misbranding and misrepresentation of goods. Subsequent court action involved false and misleading advertising, misbranding of such commodities as food, drugs, cosmetics, medical devices, and poisons.

The law was amended by the Wheeler Act of March 21, 1938 (52 Stat. 111–117; 15 U. S. Code, sec. 41–58), in several important respects, one of which was to make unlawful "unfair or deceptive acts or practices" as well as "unfair methods of competition." Under the amended act it was not necessary for the Commission to prove injury to competition where an act or practice can be shown to be unfair or deceptive and [where] there is substantial public interest in its prevention.[14] The Commission, furthermore, is empowered and directed to prevent persons, partnerships or corporations, except banks and common carriers subject to the act to regulate commerce, from using unfair methods of competition in commerce. The Commission under these acts also has the power to control false advertising of food, drugs, cosmetics, etc., over the radio and to control medical and health broadcasts of public-health significance. Section 12 of the same act makes it unlawful to use the United States mails for the dissemination of unfair and deceptive practices of false advertising.

[13] Rules, Policy, Organization, and Acts, November 20, 1937, p. 42.

[14] Federal Trade Commission personal communication. Report on Public Health Activities for the Commission on Organization of the Executive Branch of the Government.

The Federal Trade Commission carries out the functions under its acts through 8 bureaus and 20 or more divisions.

The Bureau of Medical Opinions (formerly Medical Advisory Division) furnishes the Commission with professional opinions in matters involving health, medical, and technical questions insofar as they are related to legal aspects of law enforcement. Its scientific personnel consists of a director, a chemist, and a medical officer. In cases where specialized testimony is required, appropriate expert witnesses are employed.

The Bureau of Medical Opinions maintains contacts with governmental and nongovernmental scientists and agencies, who serve as the Commission's liaison officers.

The Commission has no technical laboratories of its own. Analyses are made in the laboratories of the Food and Drug Administrator, furnishing scientific information for its enforcements. The larger proportion of the total appropriation of the Bureau of Medical Opinion is spent for advisory and regulatory services. For 1948 the total appropriation amounted to $35,100.

Obligations

The total cost for 1940 is estimated at $22,640, which represents about 1 percent of the total appropriation. In 1947, $29,754 was spent, and for 1948, $35,100, of which 90 percent is for advisory services.

RECOMMENDATIONS

Bureau of Medical Opinions.—The control of advertising is quite as important as proper labeling in regulatory activities relating to food and drugs and the two functions are intimately related. Both should be administered by the Food and Drug Administration with transfer of duties relating to misleading advertising from the Federal Trade Commission.

Tennessee Valley Authority, Division of Health and Safety

The TVA was created by an act of Congress approved May 18, 1933 (48 Stat. 58; 16 U. S. C. 831–831dd). By Executive Order 6161 of June 8, 1933, there was conferred upon the Valley Authorities the right to conduct investigations to aid in the proper conservation, development, and use of the resources of the region. Authority was also given to TVA to cooperate with State and local agencies and institutions in the valley in order to make possible the fullest effectiveness of its work. In view of this authority TVA has extended its cooperation to the State and local health departments in the Tennessee Valley in the control and prevention of malaria, stream pollution, and in supporting public-health activities by contracts for services to counties of certain Valley States in which potential hazards incident to TVA activities are recognized.

TVA's Public Health Responsibility

The activities of TVA have brought about environmental changes which directly affect public health. For instance, many acres were flooded. In consequence, health hazards, peculiar to this condition, developed. These changes in the environment obligated TVA to provide health protection for the people of the Valley States from this adverse condition. In certain instances direct responsibility is assumed by TVA. Otherwise, TVA gives financial assistance to State and local health agencies in order to strengthen their present health services to cope with problems created by operations of TVA. The professional staff of the Health and Safety Department plans and administers its health activities in cooperation with State and local health agencies in (a) public health engineering which includes stream and environmental sanitation and industrial hygiene engineering; (b) malaria control and research in malariology; (c) vital statistics and health education; (d) medical care services and hospitalization; and (e) special research projects as, for example, the effects of phosphorus on individuals exposed to elemental phosphorus and its compounds in the fertilizer plants, and nutritional studies of plants and domestic animals conducted by the land-grant colleges of the region in cooperation with the Agricultural Relations Division. For employees' health, prevention is stressed. This includes immunization, periodic health examinations, and health guidance for permanent employees, mental hygiene, and maintenance of health records for every

229

employee.   Medical service is maintained for the diagnosis, treatment, and care of diseases and injury related to employment.   In the early years of its preventive health program, TVA aided the PHS in extensive studies on the incidence of tuberculosis, using the assistance of local and State health authorities.   The high incidence of this controllable disease has been a barrier to an effective application of TVA's functions and toward the improvement of the general welfare of the valley people.

Malaria

The TVA's program of regional development has converted the Tennessee River into a series of slack-water lakes, where the breeding of malaria-carrying mosquitoes has created health hazards.   As the control of malaria has become the responsibility of TVA within flight range of its reservoirs, it has established cooperative and research facilities for study and prevention of the disease.   In this connection TVA has established malaria laboratories at Wilson Dam, Ala., for acquiring new knowledge applicable to field control operation and in developing more efficient and economical work methods for the prevention of mosquito breeding and the transmission of malaria.   Within the College of Medicine, University of Tennessee, it aids in an integrated research program concerning that part of the life cycle of the parasite spent in man, projects of which have ranged from the management of clinical malaria and the testing of new antimalaria drugs during the war years to present studies of the parasite itself.   From a small beginning made in 1937, the university now provides support for the major proportion of the total research project.   Other sources of support and cooperation have included the Office of Scientific Research and Development, the Mary Markle Foundation, and the Public Health Service.   Support from TVA is now but a small fraction of the total for the project as a whole.[15]

In Alabama a malaria educational program is supervised by a health coordinator with the assistance of the faculty of Florence State Teachers College, and a small amount available from TVA.

In Kentucky, prior to impoundage of Kentucky Reservoir, funds available through TVA contracts with the State health department were used to assist teachers, nurses, and sanitarians to study and teach facts about malaria and its control.   Murray State Teachers College provided the educational facilities for this work.

In Tennessee, the Austin Peay State College has also assisted in this special type of educational program.

---

[15] Tennessee Valley Resources, Their Development and Use, Tennessee Valley Authority, Knoxville, Tenn., December 1, 1947.

The Authority takes the responsibility for mosquito control. This project implies an extensive control of mosquito breeding in reservoirs of the Valley and in areas a mile or so beyond the shore lines. It is estimated that more than 10,000 miles of shore line is controlled against mosquito breeding in areas where actually or potentially malaria constitutes a serious public-health problem. The Valley Authority, in order to reinforce control operations on its own shore line, has from time to time set up cooperative projects with the State sanitary engineers and given financial assistance for planning and developmental work.

The effectiveness of the TVA malaria control program is shown in the reduction of incidence of disease and the widely accepted use of its methods. In the last four years, 1943–47, the incidence shown by surveys has been less than 1 percent as compared with 10 percent found in the first survey of 1938. Well-planned preparation of the reservoirs prior to impoundage, shore line maintenance, water-level management, and extensive DDT aerosol application by airplane have been effective. The Health Education and Information Service of TVA has developed literature on malaria and its control which has been widely used by the armed forces and teaching institutions at home and abroad.

Stream Pollution and Sanitation

TVA's work in the control of stream pollution and its approach to public health problems of communicable diseases is another example of its health activity. Through its construction program of impounding streams, changes in the character of stream tolerance to pollution occur, thus creating health problems which are also complicated by an expanding industrial development. This situation created for the Valley Authority new opportunities in the field of public health that could not be met all at once by the local and State governments. TVA and the Valley States, in cooperation, are developing effective measures for the control of stream pollution. Instrumental in the controlling of communicable diseases was the enactment of laws in three of the Valley States to control pollution and to conserve the water resources of the area.

One of TVA's fundamental objectives is the development of the Tennessee River as a basic physical resource of the region. In this connection stream sanitation is an important factor. Use of streams in the Tennessee Valley to receive domestic and industrial wastes is a reasonable use as long as limits of stream tolerance are not exceeded. When excessive pollution loads are discharged into these streams, conflicts with other interests arise—for example, fish and wildlife, source of water supply, and recreation. TVA's approach to the pollution problem is based upon cooperation with industrial organizations, municipalities, and State and Federal agencies in the furtherance of stream sanitation so that all interests may be served.

By the end of 1947, 63 percent [16] of the sewered population within the valley area of Tennessee, Georgia, North Carolina, and Virginia had sewage-treatment plants either planned or in operation. Because of its position as a Federal agency, TVA reviews and approves all plans prepared for water supplies, disposal of sewage and garbage, and the establishment of food and milk standards for TVA villages and construction areas, and also the operation of all such activities, in relation to standards established by State and local agencies. TVA has also provided in part the chemical analyses and other technical services relating to sewage and waste disposal in the Tennessee Valley.

The whole stream sanitation program of the Authority is a cooperative enterprise with the Valley States. For example, consultation is continuously available from the Public Health Service, which also cooperates in certain of the laboratory research and more fundamental problems. The State health department laboratories undertake certain definitive studies as they are able to develop their facilities, and the TVA, as a regional agency, fits in as a component in the program, complementing, but not duplicating, other resources.

Other Activities

TVA, in cooperation with the Department of Agriculture and the seven land-grant colleges of the Valley States, is conducting a program in the field of agriculture and power utilization. At its Muscle Shoals laboratories the Authority conducts research for improving and cheapening fertilizers, particularly phosphates. In encouraging the widespread use of these materials to build up the fertility of the soil, the program has done much to build up the mineral deficiencies in food. It encourages increased production of livestock and dairy products in the system of diversified agriculture. Likewise, through the use of its electrical power, better methods of preparation, preservation, and storage of foods have increased the year-round supply of foods and made an adequate diet possible.

The nature of TVA's construction activities has made the development of industrial hygiene important; the problems are connected with the potential health hazards of welding fumes, radiant heat, phosphorus and its compound poisons. The Division of Industrial Hygiene of the Public Health Service has cooperated in the planning and evaluation of TVA services, and has supported and encouraged studies related to the control of the environment and safety conditions of the employees.

The application of public health methods to the conservation of

---

[16] Annual Report of the Tennessee Valley Authority, 1947.

human resources in the valley is just as dependent upon the availability of trained personnel as upon the existence of basic technical knowledge. To this end, the Authority has cooperated with health agencies and educational institutions of the valley to assist in making possible training programs in the field of health.

In addition to its direct health services, TVA assists both Government and non-Government institutions financially on contractual basis for a specific type of work or investigation related to the problems and responsibilities of TVA. With this help, State and local departments have been able to expand and improve their health services with technical assistance from TVA, and have usually maintained the expansion after withdrawal of TVA support.

TVA has made every effort to stress cooperation with States and local agencies in order to achieve a more unified and effective development of health services. It has supported the idea of State legislation for full-time health department personnel and the consolidation of areas for effective control and for the economic operations of public health activities. TVA's health activities have gone far beyond county and municipal boundary lines in setting up an efficient health service, which is a commendable approach to the national health problems since it provides for utilization of regional experience in the solution of problems which also have national significance.

Obligations.

The total obligation for the health activities and medical care for 1940, 1947, and 1948 are given in the following table:

Total obligations of health activities and medical care of TVA

Items	1940	1947	1948
State aid (including administrative costs): Direct cooperation_	$38, 443	$22, 170	$16, 393
Research: Contractual agreements with institutions and individuals_	31, 309	20, 533	17, 586
Medical care_	250, 554	435, 019	392, 082
All other (including all-over administrative costs)_	42, 335	112, 300	117, 352
Total_	362, 631	590, 022	543, 413

The total TVA payments to health departments of Valley States for health services rendered through contractual agreements represent amounts given to the Valley States, as follows:

	Fiscal years—		
	1940	1947	1948
Tennessee_	$13, 989. 96	$3, 207. 97	$2, 070. 69
Alabama_	17, 303. 08	8, 089. 12	8, 247. 08
North Carolina_	2, 500. 00	3, 038. 50	2, 015. 74
Mississippi_		1, 000. 00	1, 000. 00
Kentucky_	4, 650. 68	6, 834. 56	3, 060. 00
Total_	38, 443. 72	22, 170. 15	16, 393. 51

These obligations are not considered as total monetary grants-in-aid as the term is ordinarily defined. The cooperative health program as envisaged by TVA is "one in which it secures services from States and local health agencies in the discharge of TVA responsibility to its employees, and in recognition of temporary aggravation of local health problems resulting from TVA programs." [17]

The contractual agreement between TVA and institutions and individuals for research has been a decreasing item since 1940. For all health-research activities only $17,586 was obligated for 1948.

Personnel.

The Division of Health and Safety has about 200 employees; of this number about 20 are doctors. Included among the 200 are those engaged in the public health aspects of the program as well as those who provided medical services. In addition to the employees of the Division of Health and Safety, selected member of the work crews are trained to give emergency first aid.

Comments.

In areas where TVA operates, it has assumed health obligations similar to those of both local and State agencies but always cooperatively with such agencies. This was necessary in the beginning of TVA's construction work as the impounding of streams and the shifting of population groups created health problems beyond the control of local health authorities. Thus it became necessary for TVA to provide health protection for people living in the Valley States who were exposed to the hazards of its construction and operational programs. Through the cooperation of Federal, State, and local health agencies working with TVA, great advantages in the technical developments of the Valley States' health program have accrued. However, as the local and State health agencies are able to extend their services to meet the usual functions of State health needs of this area, the health activities of TVA should then be responsible for only those health conditions which its activities have created and which are beyond the normal control and responsibility of the local and State governments. All usual types of local health activities should be carried out on a local and State level with complete responsibility resting with the authorities of State and local governments. To meet this end, TVA has consistently withdrawn its support as rapidly as other agencies could assume the burden. Moreover, it has sought and is still seeking the development of methods and relationships by which problems concerned with its own responsibilities can be dealt with under the administrative management of cooperating health agencies of the valley.

---

[17] Personal communication from TVA.

234

TVA has unique opportunities to stimulate and initiate the development of projects in special fields related to public-health problems of the valley. For example, in nutrition its studies and developmental work stop short of human nutrition, yet this is related to plant and animal nutrition.

RECOMMENDATIONS

It is recommended (1) that TVA should continue those activities which prevent adverse effects created by its activities on the region and its people, and (2) that it should continue to operate in the development of those health activities which will enable the region to realize complete health protection, and (2a) that insofar as it is possible within the framework of its cooperative relations with health agencies of the area, it should consider the desirability of appropriate activity in this and other fields when opportunities for constructive collaboration in useful projects occur.

References: Personal communication of June 9, 1948, with attached mimeographed reports. Annual reports, 1947. County Government and Administration in the TVA, July 1940. Cooperative Health Program of the TVA by O. Merton Derryberry, M. A., August 17, 1943. The TVA Lessons for International Application by Herman Finer, International Labor Office, Montreal, 1944. Personal communication of August 20, 1948, from E. L. Bishop, M. D.

Federal Works Agency

The Federal Works Agency was established by the President's Reorganization Plan No. 1, of April 25, 1939, under the provisions of the Reorganization Act of 1939. It was created to consolidate the various agencies of the Federal Government whose functions dealt with the engineering and the construction of public works "not incidental to the normal functions of other departments." The Federal Works Agency consists of the Office of the Administrator and a Commissioner for each of the offices of Public Roads, Public Buildings, Community Facilities, and staff officers. The Bureau of Community Facilities plans programs that are concerned with health activities under two separate authorizations: (a) The activities that were provided for under the Lanham Act,[18] and (b) under the Advance Planning Program as authorized by title V of the War Mobilization and Reconversion Act.[19] Under titles II and IV of the Lanham Act and as amended provision was made for the Bureau to provide both physical facilities and general assistance to States and localities in aiding them in their problems of water supply, sanitation and recreation facilities, hospitals and health centers, and in other health activities for the common good.

The résumé of the activities of the Federal Works Agency authorized under titles II and IV of the Lanham Act give some idea of its public services related in part to the field of public health.

As of June 30, 1946, 874 projects for construction of hospital facilities under this program had been approved. Such facilities were estimated to cost $120,987,093, of which amount Federal funds equaled $93,813,891. Closely allied with the hospital construction were 90 projects for construction of child-care facilities estimated to cost $3,080,340, of which amount Federal funds totaled $2,992,595. Four hundred and fifty-nine projects for provision or extension of water supply were approved. These projects were estimated to cost $103,934,841, of which amount Federal allotments totaled $79,263,694. Four hundred and forty-six projects for construction or extension of sewage collection and treatment facilities were approved. These projects were estimated to cost $65,509,678, of which amount Federal allotments totaled $53,914,413. Seven hundred and twenty-six projects for construction of recreational facilities were approved. Estimated total cost of such construction equaled $31,847,458. The Federal allotment toward such construction equaled $30,819,742.

In addition to the construction of physical facilities, the Bureau provided essential service for hospital operation at 99 locations. Such service included

---

[18] The Federal Works Activities of the Lanham Act are now in the process of liquidation.
[19] The provisions of the War Mobilization and Reconversion Act of 1944 terminated on June 30, 1947, insofar as advances to local Government agencies were concerned.

a large venereal disease rapid treatment program. The estimated total cost of these services amounted to $25,515,626; the Federal allotment equaled $16,-304,142. In addition, service for 828 child-care projects were approved at an estimated total cost of $76,177,742, toward which amount the Federal Government provided $51,131,872. No services were given in the maintenance or operation of the water or sewer facilities furnished. However, 273 projects for recreational services were approved at an estimated total cost of $12,788,425. Federal allotments toward this cost equal $7,387,968. Most of the service projects were closed by June 30, 1946. All such projects were closed prior to December 31, 1946.[20]

Under the provisions of title V of the War Mobilization and Reconversion Act, Public Law 453, the Agency, acting through the Bureau of Community Facilities, provided additional wartime health services which are as follows:

A total of 7,144 applications were approved under this program covering advances in the amount of $59,433,644. Of this total, 221 projects were for the design of hospitals and health facilities. Advances on these 221 projects totaled $3,865,030. The estimated construction cost of the facilities for which such advances were made totaled $111,362,714. When costs of land and right-of-way, equipment, plan preparation, and other costs are added to the construction costs, the total estimated cost of facilities to be provided equals $137,638,078. Three thousand four hundred and seven advances for planning of sewer, water and sanitation facilities were approved in the amount of $23,060,399. Such advances were for the planning of work whose estimated construction cost equaled $902,-301,182. When other necessary costs are added to this amount, the total estimated cost of the proposed facilities equals $1,050,063,567. Two hundred and forty applications for the planning of parks and other recreational facilities were approved in the amount of $1,755,338 to plan work whose construction costs were estimated to equal $59,037,911, and the total cost of which was estimated to equal $68,583,022.

Prior to the approval of any application for an advance under the advance planning program, the financial ability of the applicant to construct such facilities was reviewed and reasonable assurance obtained that the applicant not only would be able to finance the proposed construction but intended to do so as soon as materials and manpower became available. As of April 30, 1948, none of the projects for planning of hospitals and health facilities had resulted in the award of contracts or start of construction and repayments in the amount of $60,371 made to the Federal Government. The total estimated cost of the facilities placed under construction equaled approximately $2,600,000. Three hundred seventy-one of the sewer, water, and sanitation facility projects have been started, and repayments of $1,212,823 made to the Government. Estimated total cost involved in this category equaled $76,728,000. Sixteen of the park and other recreational facility projects had been placed in operation and repayments of $29,944 made to the Government. Estimated total cost of the facilities being provided equaled $1,375,000.[21]

Along with the activities as outlined above, the Federal Works Agency in administering the Lanham Act provided funds for a

---

[20] Personal communication of May 27, 1948.
[21] Personal communication of May 27, 1948.

child-care program at a total cost of $77,931,366 of which the Federal Government provided 66.62 percent of the total.[22]

The wartime health activities of the Federal Works Agency extended also for (*a*) construction of recreational services for both civilian and servicemen, (*b*) hospitals and venereal disease rapid treatment centers in cooperation with the over-all venereal disease program of the Venereal Disease Division, Public Health Service.

While most of the Federal Works Agency wartime health activities have ceased, the favorable results of these activities have suggested programs for the continuation of its services in cooperation with the Public Health Service.

Of primary interest is the passage of the Hospital Survey and Construction Act, bill 191, otherwise known as the Hill-Burton Act, approved August 12, 1946. This bill provides for hospital planning and construction along the general pattern laid down by the Lanham Act. (For details of this bill 191, see Public Health Service, Division of Hospital Facilities, p. 201.)

Of third importance is the passage of the Water Pollution Control Act (S. 418), which recognizes the primary rights of States (1) to control pollution; (2) to support research and to devise methods of treatment; (3) to provide Federal technical services to States, interstate bodies, and industry; and (4) to provide financial aid in the exercise of the abatement program. This act provides furthermore for cooperation of the Public Health Service with the Federal Works Agency. The act sets up the following division of responsibilities between the Surgeon General of the Public Health Service and the Administrator of the Federal Works Agency.[23]

Surgeon General	*Federal Works Agency*
1. Prepare comprehensive programs for pollution elimination.	1. Make loans to States or municipality for construction of works, and for preparation of plans.
	1a. Project must be on PHS program.
	1b. Limited to 33⅓ percent of cost or $250,000 (smaller).
2. Make joint investigation (joint with other Federal or State agencies) of sewage discharge.	2. FWA and PHS shall review all reports of examination, research, investigations, plans, studies, and surveys; also loan applications.
3. Encourage action by States for elimination of pollution; collect and disseminate information on pollution; support and aid research in treatment methods; report results of surveys and investigations.	3. Consideration to be given to: (In considering desirability of works) public benefits, propriety of Federal aid, relation of cost and maintenance necessity, adequacy of provision to maintain and operate.

---

[22] Personal communication (Mimeo. Rept., pt. 3, May 27, 1948). For Report of Maintenance and Operation in Child Care Facilities under the Lanham Act, under Report on the Development and Scope of War Public Services.

[23] Source: Office of Federal Works Agency.

Surgeon General	Federal Works Agency
4. Advise States and offender of public nuisance created by discharge of pollution. Ultimately, bring suit; to abate if State fails to.	4. Authority to appropriate to FWA $1,000,000 per year 1949–53 (⅓ or $20,000) for grants for plans, etc., preliminary to construction.
5. Conduct investigations and surveys upon request of State.	5. Authority to appropriate to FWA $500,000 per year administration.
6. Water Pollution Control Advisory Board.	6. Authority to make request of FSA for transfer of appropriation made for loans.
7. Authority to appropriate to Federal Security Agency: 22,500,000 annually 1949–53—5 years, for loans for construction: 5×22,500,000= $112,500,000×3=$337,000,000 total cost. Also $1,000,000 annually (5 years) for allotment to States for their investigations, surveys, studies of pollution caused by industrial waste.	7. Administer bonds.
8. Authority to appropriate $2,000,000 per year to FSA for administration.	8. Prescribe regulations.

The sum of $75,000 has been appropriated for the administration of this act for 1949.

The act authorizes the Surgeon General of the Public Health Service to prepare programs for the elimination of stream pollution and improving sanitary conditions of surface and ground water, and, furthermore, grants authority to the Federal Works Agency to extend Federal aid in the form of loans to States, localities, or other public bodies for the construction of necessary sewage treatment plants and for the preparation of engineering reports, plans, and specifications. In making loans, the Federal Works Administrator shall adhere to the order of projects or their priority as determined by the Surgeon General and that the engineering plans and details of construction conform to the project as approved by the Surgeon General. Under this bill, the Public Health Service functions as the controlling and operating power with the Federal Works Agency acting as its banker.

What appears to be at cross-purposes and quite distinct in its philosophy of government is the difference between the above act and the Hospital Construction Act, in which the Division of Hospital Facilities of the Public Health Service has the responsibility of administering the law and the allotment of funds to States for surveys of hospital needs, and for the planning and construction of hospitals and health centers. To meet these requirements the Public Health Service prepares architectural standards and maintains a specific staff of architects to provide blueprints and construction details to applicants for construction funds. While much of the construction is, no doubt, done on a State level, duplication of architectural and construction services is most evident.

As a matter for comparison of Government operation, the Committee on Public Buildings and Grounds of the Seventy-ninth Congress, dealing with similar problems of duplicating of services between the Office of Education and the Federal Works Agency, decided that the Office of Education should determine its needs and then certify these needs to the Federal Works Agency, which would then be responsible for the engineering and construction program within the limits of the needs as certified. The Committee was confident that the two agencies working together could do better work than either alone. It would also add efficiency and save money in eliminating the duplication of services. This view was endorsed by the Federal Security Agency, by the Federal Works Agency, and finally was accepted by the Seventy-ninth Congress and by the President.

In conclusion, there is no useful purpose to be served by assigning engineering and construction functions to a public health agency when such facilities have already been established by law and provided for within the Federal Works Agency. The adjustment of the working conditions between Education and Federal Works Agency is logical and the principle of specific responsibility should be applied in all cases. The Public Health Service should be responsible for its health aspects, including the planning of hospitals, and the Federal Works Agency should be responsible for the engineering and construction aspects of the public health program.

Obligations

The only funds obligated for 1947 and 1948 for health activities by any bureau of the Federal Works Agency were the amounts for construction of Marine hospitals and for repair of these hospitals by the Public Buildings Administration. The amounts obligated for this purpose for each of the specified years are as follows:

Item	Fiscal year [1]		
	1940	1947	1948 [2]
Total	$3,013,584	$446,364	$893,270
Construction	2,850,636	1,774	3,206
Repair	162,948	444,590	890,064

[1] SOURCE.—Federal Works Agency, Aug. 31, 1948.
[2] Reports from all division offices.

RECOMMENDATIONS

1. Actual construction of hospitals should be the function of the Federal Works Agency.

2. Public Health Service may well be responsible for studying needs, indicating hospital standards, and types of construction in the field of health.

3. Agencies such as the Public Health Service should not operate such facilities as the Federal Government maintains in other agencies for direct services, as in the field of construction.

4. Cooperative construction programs when the Federal Government participates on the grant-in-aid basis or as a lending agency and where the actual construction is carried on by the State and locality are in a somewhat different category from Federal construction per se. Under such circumstances the administrative rules of the Federal Works Agency or the Public Health Service should be determined by decision as to whether the major role of the Federal Government is that of construction or assistance with the determination of needs and priority and the fixing of standards.

Atomic Energy Commission

Aside from the Commission's "paramount objective of assuring the common defense and security" of the Nation, the Atomic Energy Act of 1946 (60 Stat. 756; 42 U. S. C. 1802) provides for the "improving of public welfare and increasing the standards of living" in so far as it is practicable in the utilization of atomic energy. Its work in the field of disease control has a direct bearing upon the individual health. The most striking advances are being made through the use of radioactive materials in medicobiology alone, holding promise more effective perhaps than atomic power itself. The tracer elements are now used as tools for the study of disease and in determining the actions of biologics and drugs upon the diseased cells of the body. In these studies the work of the Commission is concerned with health and the problems of disease control and prevention.

The act provides for a general manager, whose appointment is subject to Senate confirmation, and a General Advisory Committee appointed by the President. By provision of the act, a Military Liaison Committee, representing the Army, Navy, and Air Force, is detailed by their respective Secretaries for consultation on all matters related to military application. A Congressional Joint Committee on Atomic Energy, composed of 9 members of the Senate and 9 members of the House of Representatives, has jurisdiction over all bills and other matters in the Congress concerning the work of the Commission on Atomic Energy. In order to carry out the health and medical care program of the Commission, a Division of Biology and Medicine is provided.

Health Activities—Research

The commissioner's medical and biological research program divides itself into four parts. Medical and biological research is conducted on a major scale at the Commission's own installations, particularly in the national laboratories at Clinton (Oak Ridge), Brookhaven (Long Island) and Argonne (Chicago). Second, a fellowship training program involving 175 fellowships in biology, medicine and health physics has been set up under the administration of the National Research Council. Third, support is given to selected research projects at nongovernmental institutions. About five such projects are administered by the Commission itself and about 60 others by the Office of Naval Research for the Commission. Finally, the Commission has

242

developed a broad cancer research program which includes distribution of radioisotopes for cancer research, support of cancer research at civilian institutions, establishment of cancer research facilities at the Commission's laboratories, and support of the National Research Council's Committee on Atomic Casualties.

The activities of the Division of Biology and Medicine are chiefly concerned with research insofar as it related to improving public welfare and increasing the standards of living. In helping to provide the professional personnel necessary to carry out a research and medical care program, the Commission supports research fellowships in the Biological Sciences administered by the National Research Council. The purpose of the Commission in granting these fellowships is to provide two types of training: (a) To obtain additional graduate training, and (b) to encourage research for the doctorate in some field commensurate to the trainee's ability in the field of atomic research and development. Any field in the biological sciences in which atomic fission can be applied is open to applicants for these fellowships. The annual basic stipend is from $1,500 to $3,000 per year, depending upon the training of the fellow and the progress he has made toward his doctorate. The Oak Ridge Institute of Nuclear Studies offers 1-month training courses for physicians and other scientists. The Atomic Energy Commission has budgeted about $1,000,000 for the training program in medicine and biology.

The Commission's health and medical program provides laboratories (with a staff of 88 persons) at Oak Ridge, Tenn., where basic studies are made on the effects of radiation, including the genetic and physiological aspect. In the Health Physics Division, detection of radiation in its various emanations is studied. This laboratory has a staff of 40 people. There is also research contact with the University of Tennessee. There is also a public health unit in Oak Ridge, a town of about 30,000 people. A 300-bed hospital provides medical care and hospitalization to the employees of the community.

The Brookhaven National Laboratory at Palchogue, Long Island, with 35 professional personnel, is concerned in the broad biological field of research as it is related to plant and animal ecology and biosynthesis of "labeled" compounds. This laboratory operates a 40-bed clinical reasearch hospital for the application of atomic energy as applied to medical research. Here it is expected cancer research will be carried on.

At the Argonne National Laboratory, staffed with 90 persons, closely affiliated with the University of Chicago School of Medicine, special studies are carried out on radiation sickness and the abnormal body growth reaction to radioactive material. This laboratory will in the near future operate a clinical cancer research unit.

At Hanford, Wash., there is a 100-bed hospital. No research is carried on.

At Los Alamos, N. Mex., there is also a 100-bed hospital which serves the community and conducts research on the prevention of radio-sickness and methods of detecting overexposure. This laboratory has a staff of about 20 persons.

Research is also carried on at various universities and colleges over the country. These research activities extend from the practical to the highly theoretical aspect of the effect of radiation; such as cancer research, air-borne infectious disease, metabolism of the nervous system, atomic energy and the blood cells, and the physiologic and pathologic effects of radioactive elements. In 1948, some 40 colleges and universities conducted research in the medical and health fields cooperating with the Division of Biology and Medicine, at a cost of $1,422,434.20.

The Commission supports and encourages research in other agencies of the Federal Government. In the National Institutes of Health of the Public Health Service, laboratories have been set up for studies of the effect of radiation on mammalian tissue fractions and the effect of various radioactive elements on the mechanism of the protection against disease.

The Department of Agriculture conducts investigation on the stimulating effect of organic compounds as they can be applied to plant growth.

The Army and Navy medical research program is greatly augmented by the Atomic Energy Commission. In cooperation with the Commission, the Navy conducts research on cancer with radioisotopes. In addition, the Commission has made contracts with private industry in carrying forward research programs on atomic power.

In developing these programs, the Commission has had support from the United States Public Health Service, National Research Council, Army and Navy, as well as other governmental and nongovernmental institutions.

Obligations

The United States Atomic Energy Commission's medical and biological program for the years 1947 and 1948 cost the Federal Government approximately $6,249,000 and $16,595,000, respectively. These amounts are broken down into four major categories: (*a*) Research; (*b*) training; (*c*) medical care, and (*d*) all-over administrative costs. In general, the obligations, as shown in table XXIV, page 245, incurred in 1 year relate to expenditures made in the following year.

TABLE XXIV.—*U. S. Atomic Energy Commission—medical and biological programs obligations* [1] *for fiscal year 1947 and 1948* [2]

	Fiscal year 1947	Fiscal year 1948
A. Research:		
1. Direct activities:[3]		
Brookhaven National Laboratory	$0	$1,550
Argonne National Laboratory	[4] 1,500	2,411
Oak Ridge National Laboratory	[4] 1,500	2,572
Hanford Works		335
Cancer research units at National Laboratories	0	300
Betatrons		800
Total	3,000	7,968
2. Contracts to institutions and individuals:		
Columbia University	0	323
Harvard University	0	2
Kettering Research Foundation	0	20
New York University	0	50
Trudeau Foundation	0	20
University of Rochester	1,452	950
Western Reserve University	141	155
Radiation Laboratory, University of California	5	350
University of California at Los Angeles	340	700
University of Washington	160	25
Office of Naval Research and others	0	1,895
Atomic Casualty Commission	0	750
Total	2,098	5,240
B. Training: Fellowships, through National Research Council	0	1,100
C. Medical care (net):		
1. Hospitals and clinics:		
Oak Ridge Hospital	508	775
Los Alamos Hospital	370	426
Hanford Hospital	193	286
Total	1,071	1,887
D. Administrative costs (estimated)	80	400
Grand total	6,249	16,595

[1] In general, obligations incurred in 1 year relate to expenditures made in the following year.
[2] Neither AEC nor its predecessor agency was in existence in fiscal year 1940.
[3] AEC does not operate any of its laboratories with civil-service employees. The installations listed are operated by contract with various univerisities and industrial concerns.
[4] Obligations applicable to medicine and biology equal to 60 percent of 1948 (estimated figure).

REFERENCES.—A. E. C. Research Contracts Administered by O. N. R. in Biology and Medicine. U. S. Atomic Energy Commission, Report to the Congress, July 22, 1947, 2d Semi-Annual, 1947. Personal communications, May 2, 1948, and July 16, 1948.

Housing and Home Finance Agency

The National Housing Agency, now called the Housing and Home Finance Agency, was created by Executive Order 9070 in an attempt to consolidate the agencies of the Government interested in housing functions and activities which were formerly supervised by the 17 or more agencies and administrative units. At present this agency is composed of two major administrations, the Federal Housing Administration and the Public Housing Administration, which conducts projects that are related to health.

The Federal Housing Administration, established by the National Housing Act (48 Stat. 1246; 12 U. S. C. 1702) approved June 27, 1934, and as amended, develops (1) model uniform plumbing code, (2) conducts investigations through a joint project with the Public Health Service of design problems in connection with individual sewage-disposal systems, and (3) consults with the Public Health Service with respect to sanitary engineering aspects of the Veterans' Emergency Housing programs. It also establishes standards in connection with health, safety, and sanitation applicable to the construction and operation of federally owned or aided housing projects. These standards are made the basis of eligibility for credit aid to private residential construction through mortgage insurance.

In the case of the Public Housing Administration, the primary concern is financial aid for the development of low-rent houses and slum-clearance projects. The primary interest of the Housing Agency in health is to see that all homes under their jurisdiction have proper sanitary facilities.

Obligations

The office of the Administrator has spent for technical studies and testing programs bearing directly on the field of public health, safety, and sanitation, the following amounts: [24]

	1947	1948	Total
Uniform plumbing code	$13, 450	$43, 000	$56, 450
Individual sewage-disposal systems	30, 000	70, 000	100, 000
Consultation—sanitary engineering	57, 039	3, 000	60, 039
	100, 489	116, 000	216, 489

The total number of employees of the Housing and Home Finance Agency is 11,574, of which approximately 4,747 are in the Federal Housing Administration.

[24] Communication from Housing and Home Finance Agency, September 17, 1948.

Department of Agriculture

In brief, the Agriculture Department arrived at its present organization by an orderly evolution in response to many acts of Congress. It had its small beginning in the Patent Office, then in the State Department during the year 1830. By 1839, the first provision was made to expend $1,000 out of its current income for agricultural purposes. The bill establishing the Department was approved by Congress on May 15, 1862 (12 Stat. 387; 28 U. S. C. 392; 5 U. S. C. 511, 514, 516, 519, 557), but not until February 9, 1889 (25 Stat. 659; U. S. C. titles 5, 21, 26, 39) were the duties of the Department enlarged. Agriculture was made an executive department of Government and the commissioner became the Secretary of Agriculture. Public Health significance was first enjoined in the Bureau of Animal Industry "to prevent the spread of contagious diseases among domestic animals."

The Secretary of Agriculture has two under secretaries and staff officers, who act as a cabinet for the Bureau of Agricultural Economics, and the Directors of Agricultural Economics, Finance, Foreign Agricultural Relations, Information, Personnel, Office of Plant and Operations, the Solicitor and the Chief Hearing Examiner in policy making and program planning.

In Agriculture there are 18 agencies (bureaus and services) which are sufficiently concerned with health to designate financial support, and which merit some description of their health activities. In the Bureaus of Human Nutrition and Home Economics, of Animal Industry, of Agricultural and Industrial Chemistry, investigations related to health constitute a large part of their programs. In the other bureaus, health activities per se can be regarded as only incidental to their functional activities. For example, the activities of the Extension Service, which is principally educational in scope, are generally related to rural health problems, and for which the Service spent in 1948, $2,847,120. The regulatory functions and research projects in a few of the agencies bear upon health protection and the improvement of health. Through the Farm Credit Administration, which specializes in rural health cooperatives and other health programs, health activities are facilitated and directly promoted. In the Office of Personnel medical care is provided for the personnel of the Department.

247

Eight of the 22 services and divisions of Agricultural Research Administration conduct activities that have a direct bearing on health.

Bureau of Human Nutrition and Home Economics

The Department of Agriculture was authorized by Congress to develop research in the field of human nutrition as early as 1894. The first directive was to the Secretary of Agriculture to investigate and report upon the nutritive value of commodities used as human food, and to prevent waste and a more economical use of these commodities. Not until 1924 was the Bureau of Human Nutrition and Home Economics created by the Agriculture Appropriation Act.[25] See Nutrition Chapter II, page 74.

The National Institute of Health also conducts research in nutrition, particularly in relation to disease prevention. The Department of Defense faces nutritional problems in supplying and feeding personnel of the armed forces. Food industries also are concerned with the nutritive value of food products and their uses for human consumption.

Obligations.—For the support of the Bureau's health activities the sum of $155,040 was expended in 1940; by 1947 it was $487,960; and in 1948, $628,400 was appropriated.

Recommendations.—The Bureau of Human Nutrition and Home Economics is well placed in the Department of Agriculture. The overlapping in the nutritional studies of the Bureau with Public Health Service and other agencies of the Government, is small in comparison with the interrelationship of the Bureau's scientific cooperative work with the experiment station, Extension Service of the Department of Agriculture, and with land-grant colleges that work closely with this Bureau. The Bureau cooperates in a wide field of activities with Federal and State agencies as well as with nongovernmental agencies.

Bureau of Animal Industry

Many of the functional responsibilities of the Bureau of Animal Industry are directly and indirectly related in many aspects of its activities to health. The Bureau is chiefly concerned with the protection and development of the livestock industry in the United States; it conducts research on the etiology, control, treatment, and prevention of animal diseases, which in some cases directly affect the health of man. The Bureau has regulatory powers in animal quarantine and

---

[25] The bureau was created by an act, 43 Stat. 1289, and in accordance with Research Administration Memorandum 5, pursuant to an Executive Order 1069, and in conformity with Secretary's Memoranda 960 and 986.

the Virus-Serum-Toxin Act. Also in the Meat Inspection Act, the Imported Meat Act, Renovated Butter Act, all of which affect health protection. It has made outstanding discoveries in the transmission of diseases by insects, the effect of cattle tuberculosis on man, the use of tuberculin tests for tuberculosis, and the various studies on livestock diseases which are transmitted to man, as trichinosis and other parasitic diseases, and milk-borne diseases, as undulant fever.

The Tuberculosis Eradication Division.—The Tuberculosis Eradication Division of the Bureau directs its activities to livestock tuberculosis control and the eradication of brucellosis in cattle, commonly known as undulant fever in man. The effectiveness of the cattle tuberculosis control program can be recognized in the reduction of the disease—approximately 5 percent in 1918 to 0.2 of 1 percent in 1947.

Regulatory.—The regulatory functions of this Bureau designed to protect the public health include inspection of all meats intended for shipment in interstate commerce; the control of biologics used for the treatment of animal diseases; the examination of livestock entering this country; inspection and testing of animals and meats for export; and the inspection and disinfection of animal byproducts. See Foreign Quarantine chapter II, page 105.

The Meat Inspection Service implements its regulatory powers within the various diseases of animals as a health-protection measure, and in the causes of the spoilage and poor-keeping qualities of meat. The Division also investigates the toxicity of synthetic resins and other materials used in the wrapping of meat products; the chronic toxicity of chemicals used in animal fats to retard rancidity. In addition, to assure a wholesome meat supply to the consuming public, the Bureau conducts investigations on the effect of disease-producing bacteria, toxins, and parasites.

Obligations.—It is not possible to allocate with any degree of accuracy funds devoted to public health protection because the research work of the Division is concerned with the health of livestock. However, in the Meat Inspection Division some $5,433,000 was made available in 1940. In 1947, the actual cost of this function of the Bureau amounted to $10,400,000, and in 1948, an obligation of $11,200,000 was made for this service. A total of 6,914 persons are employed.

Cooperation.—As the work of the Bureau of Animal Industry is important in the promotion of public health, the Public Health Service cooperates with the Bureau in many of its activities, and also assists in conducting services to determine the transmissibility of animal diseases to man. Cooperative agreements are made with livestock sanitary officials of all States. Some activities of the Bureau are technical and specific in nature. There is very little overlapping or duplication of service.

Bureau of Agricultural and Industrial Chemistry

The Bureau of Agricultural and Industrial Chemistry was organized in 1942 and in conformity with Secretary's Memoranda 960 and 986 as a research organization. It conducts investigations in the field of chemistry, physics, and biology in relation to agricultural products and methods of finding new uses for them. A portion of its research activities is related to health.

Of those activities, the increased production of penicillin through the use of corn steep liquor has been of great importance. The Bureau's discovery of the antibiotic "tomatin," which has proved effective in the control of fungi in both plant and animal is of vital significance. The research in the development of subtilin, now experimentally used in the treatment of bovine mastitis and human tuberculosis is under way, and, in addition, the Bureau has developed rutin, a drug effective in the control of capillary fragility and in the treatment of radiation injuries, control of botulinum and Salmonella food poisoning organisms; and production of vitamins from agricultural products. The research as outlined above is carried on in the general course of the Bureau's research activities. The discoveries applicable to human health are only incidental to its functional activities. No information is currently available in Washington, as to what percent of the 1947 appropriation of $8,210,337 might be legitimately considered used for direct health purposes, nor is the time available to survey the individual projects in the various experiment stations which contribute to health protection.

Office of Experiment Stations

The Office of Experiment Stations, established on March 2, 1887 (by act, 24 Stat. L., 440) has supervision over Federal-grant and research contracts for agricultural research as provided for by the Hatch, Adams, Purnell, and supplementary acts and title I of the Bankhead-Jones Act. The Office reviews project proposals initiated at States' levels in regards to their conformity to these laws, to their provision for adequate personnel and for effective investigation, and to coordinate their research with that carried on within the Department of Agriculture. The responsibility for conducting the research rests entirely with the State experiment stations involved if it conforms to the condition of the act. All projects are reviewed annually in cooperation with the project leader.

At present, in the various State experiment stations over 45 research projects in the field of nutrition and rural health are under way.

Obligations.—In 1930 and in 1947, the sums of $29,008, and $37,790 were expended for the health activities of the Office of Experiment Stations, respectively. In 1948, the sum of $194,000 was appropriated for the same purpose. In the Hatch, Adams, and Purnell Act no matching of funds by States is required. The Bankhead-Jones Act required matching in full, while the Research and Marketing Act of 1946 required 72 percent of direct allotments to be matched in full.

Bureau of Dairy Industry [26]

Two divisions in this Bureau have activities related to public health protection: The Division of Nutrition and Physiology and the Dairy Products Research Laboratories Division. These divisions conduct chemical, bacteriological, nutritional, and technological investigations in the production and handling of milk. The investigations of the two divisions are related to (1) the practices and processes for the production of dairy products; (2) methods of producing milk for human nutritional purposes; (3) regulatory function in the manufacture or processing of renovated butter.

The Bureau cooperates with State agencies in the promotion and use of pasteurized milk.

In 1948, the sum of $570,096 was spent for activities related to health. On June 30, 1948, approximately 282 persons were employed.

Bureau of Entomology and Plant Quarantine [27]

The Bureau conducts researches that have direct bearing upon the control of insects, vectors of human diseases and of insect pests and plant diseases that constantly threaten our food production. The control of insects that transmit such diseases as malaria, dengue, typhus, filaria, plague, Rocky Mountain spotted fever, and intestinal diseases will eventually reduce the incidence of these diseases if not the elimination of them. Thus, the work done incidentally by the Bureau attacks fundamentally the problem of health protection.

The activities related to health protection are conducted by the Divisions of Insects Affecting Man and Animals and the Division of Control Investigation which conducts investigations in close cooperation with States, and other agencies and at the laboratories located in Georgia, Florida, Oregon, Texas, and Maryland; Divisions of Insecticides, Insect Identification and Bee Culture are conducting researches that are incidentally related to health. The Division of Bee Culture, in cooperation with the Public Health Service, have discovered promising antibiotic agents that may be utilized in combating diseases of man.

---

[26] The Bureau of Dairy Industry was established by the act of May 29, 1924 (43 Stat. 243; 7 U. S. C. 401).

[27] The Bureau was created by an organizational merger provided in the Agricultural Appropriation Act of 1935 (48 Stat. 467).

Regulatory.—The Bureau's regulatory functions enforce quarantine and restriction orders which prohibit or regulate the importation or interstate movements of injurious insects and plant diseases. It cooperates with Federal, State, and local agencies in its enforcement programs.

Obligations.—For health and related activities the sum of $63,000 was spent in 1940. In 1947, the sum of $48,100 was spent, and in 1948, a total of $44,300 was appropriated. For the research on antibiotics associated with honey bees, $18,500 was appropriated.

Bureau of Plant Industry, Soils, and Agricultural Engineering [28]

The investigations of this Bureau are essential to the improvement and promotion of the general health and welfare of the people. Through its work on methods to improve crop and soil management in order to supply a higher quality of food, feeds, and vegetable oils, and its investigation on the cultivation of medicinal plants, condiments, insecticides, etc., the bureau contributes to general health. It is not feasible to assign any definite portion of the funds available to this Bureau totaling $9,437,730 in 1948, for public health protection activities.

FARMERS HOME ADMINISTRATION

The primary function of the Farmers Home Administration is the extension of supervised credit through which loans are made to low-income farmers. These loans may be used for (1) the purchase, enlargement, or improvement of family type farms, (2) needed farm supplies, seeds, livestock, etc., and (3) defraying costs of family medical care, and helping the family to meet their general health problems including health education, health care, and sanitation. State and county offices recommend policies and procedures that will insure better living and health conditions for farm families. The only full-time health services are given by staff members attached to the Health Services Section of the Production Loan Division, under the direction of a chief medical officer assigned from the Public Health Service as a technical health adviser. State directors and county employees keep local health agencies informed about the health problems of borrowers and aid them in obtaining assistance. FHA cooperates with State Extension Services, Experimental Stations, State Colleges of Agriculture and PHS.

---

[28] The bureau was created through the coordination of the Bureau of Plant Industry and the Bureau of Chemistry and Soils. This change was reflected in the Agricultural Appropriations Act of 1940. U. S. Government Manual, 1947, p. 264.

The Farmers Home Administration has in the past provided the following health services incidental to making and servicing the loans, although at the present time this work has been largely curtailed.

Assistance in obtaining needed medical care.—Through the aid of the loan the borrower has the privilege of participating in a group prepayment plan which provides for medical and dental care and hospitalization at a nominal cost, or obtaining health and medical service on any other basis. As a matter of interest, 787 counties throughout the Nation, with a total of 38,408 families participating, had established group health associations in 1947.

Environmental sanitation.—Proper sanitation, an adequate and pure water supply and protection against insect pests are among the basic health measures that can be provided through the loan of the Administration. The borrowers are advised on how to make necessary improvements and are furnished with construction plans for making those improvements.

Assistance toward improved diets.—The Farmers Home Administration also encourages the production of an adequate food supply for family use. Supervisors from State and local offices advise on quantity of food crops, milk, meat, and eggs necessary for an adequate and well-balanced diet.

Referral to local agencies providing health services.—Supervisors of local Farmers Home Administration offices encourage borrowers to use local and State health agencies for their health services. This may include maternity and child health clinics, school health programs, and immunization against preventable diseases.

Referral of cases for vocational rehabilitation.—The services provided by the Farmers Home Administration with respect to the handicapped borrowers or members of their families are references to State institutions for corrective medical treatment. Some 1,900 such cases were referred to corrective institutions in 1947.

Obligations.—In 1940 the sum of $3,577,803 was spent for health activities under authority which existed under the Farm Security Administration. During this period, the FSA's health activities constituted an important phase of its rural rehabilitation program. This sum does not, however, include grants to individuals for health protection as no records were maintained showing distribution of grants by purposes. By 1947, a total of $230,723 was spent. In the meantime, the Farm Security Administration was liquidated. By 1948, only $8,413 was spent on health activities. It should be recognized that the FHA serves only a portion of the health needs of its borrowers who constitute only a small segment of the Nation's total farm population.

Farm Credit Administration

The health activities of the Farm Credit Administration are only incidental insofar as it "assembles information concerning specialized rural health cooperatives and other health programs in which farmers' cooperative associations participate. In this capacity it collects and analyzes such factors as costs, benefits, and general effectiveness of the prepaid service or insurance plans as they are used by rural cooperative groups." In 1947, the total expenditures which could be assigned to health promotion were $2,367, and in 1948 a total of $3,880 was spent for this work.

Production and Marketing Administration [29]

The Production and Marketing Administration has objectives that are not primarily health purposes; however, their importance in the protection of health is well recognized.

It operates through three branches, Dairy, Food Distribution, and Poultry, all of which administer services related to the wholesomeness and purity of foods.

Under the Food Distribution Program Branch, the school lunch program is administered under an appropriation for 1948 of $87,200,-000. This program is considered educational and is fully described under the educational report.[30] The report recommends:

That the responsibility for the administration of the National School Lunch Act should be placed in the Federal educational agency; except (2) the direct purchase and distribution of foods for price support and the listing of foods in abundance for priority purchase, when necessary, should be retained in the Department of Agriculture, (3) subsidy should be made available to State departments of education * * * [and] (4) the nutritional aspects of the program, although carried out by the Federal educational agency—should be done with advisement from the best informed agency of the Government in nutrition matters.

A fourth branch, the Livestock Branch, deals with regulatory powers concerning the manufacture of insecticides, fungicides, rodenticides, and disinfectants. For activities of this administration in nutrition program planning, see chapter II, page 78.

---

[29] The Production and Marketing Administration was created by Secretary's Memorandum 1118, August 18, 1945, under authority of section 22 of title 5 of the U. S. Code, Executive Order 9577, June 29, 1945, and related Executive orders.

[30] Federal Policy and Organization for Education, a report prepared for the Brookings Institution as a part of its larger studies concerning Federal welfare activities for the Commission on Organization of the Executive Branch of the Government, by Hollis P. Allen, August 25, 1948.

Total cash for activities related to health protection in the Production and Marketing Administration

	1948	1947	1940
Branches:			
Dairy—inspection service	$570,096	$575,681	$57,428
Nutrition program	30,000	40,000	
Livestock—insecticides, etc	368,500	293,500	193,180
Poultry—improving egg-processing facilities	18,600	1,500	
Total	987,196	910,681	250,608
School-lunch program	[1] 87,200,000	81,636,149	12,646,656

[1] Of which $54,000,000 were State grants, and $33,000,000 for direct operations.

The Administration employs 9,380 persons.

COOPERATIVE EXTENSION SERVICE [31]

The Cooperative Extension Service develops educational programs to improve the economic welfare, nutrition and health, family and community life of rural people. In principle, the Extension Service functions as a distributing agent for all technical knowledge developed in the other agencies of the Department of Agriculture. The activities of the Service functions in cooperation with health organizations and agencies and professional groups on the basis of State and county needs.

Activities

The activities of the Extension Service related to health are:

1. *Food and nutrition.*—This program includes new methods of food preparation and preserving, planning, and preparing meals to meet human needs, planning for the school lunch, and training of personnel.

2. *Home and environmental sanitation.*—Programs designed in this field have to do with modernizing plumbing, drainage, and general sanitary measures for the prevention of filth-born diseases.

3. *Rural health services.*—The Extension Service in 1946 began to develop a health educational program to bring the benefits of modern health measures to rural people. This program is developed in close cooperation with Federal and State agencies, voluntary health organizations, and local professional groups.

4. *Livestock disease control.*—The educational effort to interest rural people to control the spread of livestock disease, such as Bang's disease and tuberculosis, have an important relationship to public health protection.

---

[31] Provision for the Extension Service in the Department of Agriculture was made in the Agriculture Appropriation Act of 1924 (42 Stat. 1289), and Secretary's Memorandum 436, effective July 1, 1923.

The Extension Service feels that it has a "responsibility in aiding people to improve their health and medical services" and that the Extension Service specialists in rural health should . . .

develop, on the basis of the survey of needs, a plan of action with short-time and long-time goals which will lead to the realization of a comprehensive health service. To direct groups to resources, local, State, and national, to which they may turn for technical advice in planning this program, [and] to undertake specific projects, ranging from such simple measures as immunization clinics and better school health services, to the more complex programs of procuring medical personnel, expanding public health services, constructing hospitals and health centers, and organizing prepayment plans for medical care—all of which are important parts of a comprehensive health service for all rural people.[32]

Obligations

In 1940, through State aid (including administrative cost) the sum of $1,944,845 was spent for health activities. In 1947 and in 1948, expenditures for the same purposes were $2,956,990 and $2,847,120, respectively. Extension personnel cooperating with but not paid by the Department of Agriculture is 11,778 (as of June 30, 1947).

BUREAU OF AGRICULTURAL ECONOMICS [33]

This Bureau is primarily concerned with the collection and distribution of agricultural statistics. It is concerned with the number and type of farm accidents and their economic significance in relation to farm production. It also conducts statistical analysis of the available medical personnel and services and type available; and the incidence of disease, patterns of health care, and death rates that occur in rural areas. The Bureau cooperates with land grant colleges in determining the health needs of rural communities.

Obligations.—In direct health activities the bureau spent in 1947 for statistical analytical studies the sum of $24,200. In 1948, for the same studies and rural health needs, a total of $23,000 was appropriated.

OTHER AGENCIES OF THE DEPARTMENT OF AGRICULTURE

Certain other bureaus and services are remotely related to health activities per se, and on which no definite monetary valuation can be placed. Three of these agencies, Soil Conservation, Forest Service, and the Rural Electrification Administration, conduct activities that have significant protective health application. In soil improvement,

---

[32] The Extension Service's Responsibility in Aiding Rural People To Improve Their Health and Medical Services, U. S. Department of Agriculture, Extension Service, Washington, D. C., July 1947, p. 12. Statement approved by the USPHS.

[33] The bureau was established by the Agricultural Appropriation Act of 1923 (42 Stat. 532; 7 U. S. C. 411).

whereby more and better nutritional food crops are developed, health is the end result. The science of biodynamics has grown out of the belief that food grown on better soil produces better health.

The Forest Service is the safeguard of the health of those individuals who use the "great outdoors" as a source of recreation. Sanitation standards recommended by the Public Health Service and the Joint Committee on Rural Sanitation guide the engineers of the Forest Service in maintaining such safeguard as the disposal of garbage and sewage, and policing and enforcing sanitary laws. REA programs provide electric service which enables the farmer to make use of refrigeration and modern sanitation, etc., which contribute to health protection.

Obligations.—The compilation of the total health expenditures of the various agencies of the Department of Agriculture is significant only in showing the range and the estimate of the expenditures of the public health activities in the Department of Agriculture. Some of the agencies have functions that are only incidentally related to health and in others no accurate estimate of the cost could be made even though the activities have some relationship to the problem of health or health protection.

All figures and allocations have been supplied by the Bureau of the Budget for the years 1940, 1947, and 1948, and show as far as it is possible the actual expenditures of the various agencies for these specific years.

The expenditures do not reflect always the full extent of the activities as no direct appropriations were made. This is true in cooperative work between agencies and where health activities were formed and financed out of other funds for which no specific appropriations were provided.

Under the agency's school lunch program of the Food Distribution Branch, the sum for each of the 3 years is carried as a footnote on the financial tabulation since the school health program amounting to $87,000,000 in 1948 has been considered as an "educational project" [34] and no consideration of this expenditure is included in the total health estimates.

The largest expenditure for health protection in the Department of Agriculture is spent for meat inspection. This totaled $11,200,000 in 1948 as compared with $10,400,000 in 1947, and $5,433,000 in 1940.

The second largest expenditure is in the Extension Service. In 1948, the sum of $2,847,120 was spent as State grants. In 1947, expenditures were somewhat larger, totaling $2,956,990, and in 1940 only $1,944,845 were spent as State grants. Comparatively, the other health expenditures were small. The total expenditures for health and medical ac-

---

[34] See Report in Education, Hollis P. Allen, for a full account of this activity.

tivities as could be reasonably determined amount to $16,166,109 in 1948, compared to $15,264,863 in 1947, and $11,544,004 in 1940.

In the divisions of Soil Conservation, Forest Service, and Rural Electrification, a total of $12,087, $22,575, and 960 persons are employed, respectively.

OFFICE OF PERSONNEL

The Division of Employee Health of the Office of Personnel renders medical services in accordance with provisions of Public Law 658, Seventy-ninth Congress, second session. These include:

1. Preventive services relating to employee health.
2. Emergency treatment of on-the-job illnesses.
3. Preemployment and other physical examinations.
4. Cooperation with and referral to other health agencies and private practitioners in maintaining optimal employee health.

This service has recently been established. The sum of $45,000 is appropriated for 1948.

The health program as envisaged in Miscellaneous Publication No. 573 of October 1945 on "Better Health for Rural America," prepared by the Department of Agriculture Interbureau Committee on Postwar Programs,[35] suggests a health plan of five objectives, with one goal, for the American farmers. These objectives are: (1) Health, education, and preventive measures, (2) increase medical and health personnel for rural areas, (3) improve rural medical services comparable to that of the city, (4) rural health facilities, (5) find means of easing cost of medical care.

Just how far these objectives can be carried out is conjectural. However, since the Public Health Service has assumed leadership in all these areas the primary responsibility for initiating and developing these services should rest with the Public Health Service and not with Agriculture. The Department of Agriculture can cooperate with the Public Health Service by keeping the Public Health Service concurrently abreast of the rural health problems, and interpret to the farm families the availability of public-health facilities.

In addition to the suggested plans of action for better health facilities for rural areas, the Department of Agriculture has maintained for a number of years a committee on environmental sanitary engineering. Seven agencies and the Office of the Secretary are represented. It makes information available in the field of sanitary engineering that will set uniform standards for the development of better

---

[35] See also "The Experimental Health Program of the U. S. Department of Agriculture," subcommittee monograph No. 1, 79th Cong., 2d sess., January 1946.

rural sanitation. Through the work of this Committee on Rural Sanitation, the technical aspects of rural sanitation are coordinated.

RECOMMENDATIONS

1. That since the Public Health Service has assumed the responsibility and leadership in all areas of public-health activities, the initiative and direction should rest with the Public Health Service and not with Agriculture.

2. That insofar as possible the Department of Agriculture should work in cooperation with the Public Health Service and keep them informed on all rural health problems.

3. That the regulatory functions except meat inspection now in the Department of Agriculture regarding human health should be transferred to the Food and Drug Administration (for reasons, see Food and Drug).

4. That as the Biologics Act is concerned principally with the therapeutic value of serum, toxins, and viruses in the treatment and control of animal diseases, it should remain in the Bureau of Animal Industry, Department of Agriculture.

Department of the Interior

By a congressional act (9 Stat. 395; 5 U. S. C. 481) the Department of the Interior was established on March 3, 1849. Its purposes have substantially remained the same since it was created; to "advance the domestic interests of the people of the United States" and "promote domestic welfare" through the conservation of natural resources.

The Department of the Interior is administered by the Secretary of the Interior. All bureau chiefs are directly responsible to him. He has jurisdiction over the Division of Territories and Island Possessions, and the administration of mines, parks, and Indian services, fish and wildlife, geological survey, land management, fuels, and power development.

Health activities.—Only three of the bureaus, offices, and services of the Department conduct activities directly related to health. They are: (1) The Bureau of Mines in its Division of Health and Safety; (2) the Fish and Wildlife Service in connection with its research in vitamins, and, indirectly, in its wildlife disease program; and (3) the Office of Indian Affairs, which has supervision over the health of the Indians. The sanitation program of the National Park Service and the water resource program of the Bureau of Reclamation also influence the promotion of health.

BUREAU OF MINES, HEALTH AND SAFETY DIVISION

Creation and functions.—The special factors that were most effective in calling attention to the advisability of action by the Federal Government for a Bureau of Mines were disasters in coal mines and a growing realization of the waste of both life and resources in the varied mining and metallurgical interests of the country. As a result Congress passed the Organic Act of the Bureau of Mines, May 16, 1910 (36 Stat. 369).

The Bureau of Mines directs and coordinates the activities of the three branches which constitute the Health and Safety Division (health branch, safety branch, and coal mine inspection branch), comprising 500 persons (engineers, coal mine inspectors, chemists, physicists, safety instructors, clerks, etc.) working in or out of 22 offices or laboratories in 18 States and Alaska, and functioning to some extent in every State and in Alaska. Since the Health and Safety Division of the Bureau is an integral function of the total industrial hygiene problem of our Government, the activities of this Bureau are discussed under the general subject of industrial hygiene.   (See ch. II, Patterns of Industrial Hygiene in the Government, p. 86.)

FISH AND WILDLIFE SERVICE

This Service was established June 30, 1940, by the consolidation of the former Bureau of Fisheries and the Biological Survey in accordance with the President's Reorganization Plan 3, following the Reorganization Act approved April 3, 1939; both of which were transferred to the Department of the Interior.   The Bureau of Biological Survey, established in 1885, was transferred from the United States Department of Agriculture.   The Bureau of Fisheries was established in 1871, and transferred from the Department of Commerce.

The original research and investigation functions of these services were retained in the new agency of Fish and Wildlife Service.   Management, propagation, and restoration of these resources and their protection were added.   The functions of the Service are carried forward under the direction of a central headquarters (located in Chicago, Ill.), 4 divisions—1 each for administration, management, commercial fisheries, and research—and 6 regional offices with definitely prescribed geographical boundaries.   Within these areas some 400 field stations, laboratories, wildlife refuges, fish markets, and rodent-control districts are now maintained.   The major function is therefore concerned with the conservation of the country's natural resources of both land and water mammals, fish and shellfish, and birds.

The health activities, though incidental to the Service's major function, are included in such work as (1) fishing industry, (2) fish biology, (3) predator and rodent control, (4) stream and lake pollution, (5) wildlife and fishery research, and (6) public relations which disseminates information developed through research and to facilitate law enforcement by acquainting the public with needs for regulatory action.

Federal grants are made to the States on the basis of cooperative agreement between State fish and game commissions and the Washington office.   These State commissions must initiate all projects concerned with Fish and Wildlife Service.

Grants.—Federal aid to States' projects for wildlife restoration is given under the authority of the Pittman-Robertson Federal Aid to Wildlife Restoration program (September 2, 1937, 50 Stat. 917; August 18, 1941, 55 Stat. 632; 16 U. S. C. 669–69j and as amended July 24, 1946).   Under this provision the United States, by congressional action, may pay up to 75 percent of the cost of States' projects, the funds for which are obtained from a portion of the proceeds of an excise tax of 11 percent on firearms, shells, and cartridges used for sporting purposes.   The States contribute 25 percent of the cost of

261

each project. The amounts collected and appropriated each year since the program started are as follows:

Fiscal year	Amount collected	Amount appropriated
1939	$2, 976, 020	$1, 000, 000
1940	3, 707, 844	1, 500, 000
1941	5, 535, 773	2, 500, 000
1942	5, 072, 588	2, 750, 000
1943	1, 149, 333	1, 250, 000
1944	1, 061, 045	1, 000, 000
1945	3, 132, 402	900, 000
1946	5, 232, 465	1, 000, 000
1947	[1] 8, 423, 216	2, 500, 000
Total	36, 290, 688	14, 400, 000

[1] Amount collected from July 1, 1946, to May 31, 1947, inclusive.

Regulatory functions.—The Fish and Wildlife Service has control over the issuance of permits for importation of foreign wildlife, the responsibility for making importation regulations regarding disease-bearing birds and animals. The Public Health Service made the regulations concerning importation of parrots into the United States in order to combat the disease psittacosis. Formerly, enforcement for keeping undesirable wildlife out of the country rested with Fish and Wildlife Service with the cooperation of the Bureau of Customs. During the Eightieth Congress, an amendment to the Lacey Act of 1900 was passed which gives the Bureau of Customs the authority to honor the permits of the Fish and Wildlife Service to bring wildlife into the United States.   (See Foreign Quarantine, ch. II.)

Health Functions of the Branch of Commercial Fisheries and Wildlife Service.

The following research programs definitely related to the promotion of health and conservation of foods are carried forward.

Of first significance are the researches related to the nutritive value of fishery products.   These studies comprise (*a*) investigations of the wholesomeness of some algin compounds extracted from the seaweed kelp (this type of compound has properties of stabilizing food products such as salad dressings and dairy products); (*b*) protein determination of several cooked fishery products; (*c*) vitamin B analysis; and (*d*) biological tests to determine the nutritive effect in food with certain seaweed gums used as ingredients in food products.

In the protocols of vitamin A studies the objectives are (*a*) to determine improved methods of producing vitamin A in fish liver oils; (*b*) to attempt to find new sources of vitamin A in fishery products; (*c*) to ascertain the stability of vitamin A, and methods of increasing that stability; (*d*) preparation of vitamin A standard in collaboration with industries interested in the separation and manufacture of vitamin A, and (e) carry out animal assays of vitamin A content. These researches are important to health since nearly all of the vitamin A used in pharmaceuticals is derived from fishery products.

The Service likewise carries out research programs on the toxic properties of fish and shellfish, and the best methods of handling fishery products for public consumption. The present studies are designed to find methods to (a) check the variation in the toxicity of fishery products and (b) to develop methods to preserve the purity of fish and their products without destroying their nutritive value. In the handling of fishery finished products, the Service is indirectly concerned in assisting industry to comply with Federal and State sanitary standards now in effect, and to find new methods of food preservation. Some of the problems are: (a) Treatment of plants and waste materials with DDT sprays to eliminate flies and other insect pests; (b) determination of the incidence of enteric bacillary infections in groups of sea-food workers as indicated by cultural and serological methods; (c) determination of the value of detergents in eliminating the bacteria responsible for decomposition of various types of sea foods; and (d) studies of the effect of sewage pollution on the shellfish areas and development of methods for treatment to eliminate such contamination.

This Service also conducts a variety of investigations under the title "Wildlife Resource and Management Investigation," for which special funds are provided. Such studies include (a) disease problems affecting wildlife population; (b) control of diseased and injured birds and animals which are vectors of such diseases as tularemia, botulism, brucellosis, sylvatic plague, trichinosis, and the transmission of other diseases such as bubonic plague and typhus fever, and (c) cooperative research in 16 colleges and universities assigned to train technical assistants and managers of fish and wildlife preserves. The trainees are biological students. One-third of their stipend comes from the colleges, one-third from the States' fish and game commissions, and one-third from Federal appropriation.

Control of Predatory Animals and Injurious Rodents

The Service maintains wildlife disease research laboratories at Laurel, Md., and at Denver, Colo. It also maintains six technological laboratories and six biological research laboratories.

With funds provided in the Department of the Interior's appropriation bill, for control of predatory animals and injurious rodents, the Fish and Wildlife Service conducts cooperative programs for the control of injurious mammals. The programs as a whole are financed with approximately three dollars of cooperative funds for each dollar appropriated by the Congress. The program of predatory animal control includes the larger predatory animals such as wolves, mountain lions, coyotes, bobcats, predatory bears, and, at times, foxes. The public health relationship of this phase of the program has to do primarily with the fact that some of these animals, particularly coyotes and foxes, at times become infected with rabies. Such infections are a menace to humans and to livestock. The primary purpose of controlling predatory animals is economic but, at times, the health problem is of importance.

The program of injurious rodent control includes the suppression of prairie dogs, ground squirrels, jack rabbits, kangaroo rats, pocket gophers, field mice, common rats, and house mice as well as other species of field rodents. The primary purpose of this cooperative program is to prevent economic loss to foods, feeds, and forage in the field and storage. The control of rodents also has, at times, a public health significance in that they are carriers and disseminators of certain human and livestock diseases such as bubonic plague, typhus fever, trichinosis, etc. Since the rodent control activity of the Fish and Wildlife Service is basically cooperative, local programs to control any particular specie or species of destructive rodents require that the activities of all agencies and individuals concerned be correlated into a unified effort. Such correlation has been particularly effective in rodent control.[36]

Medical and Health Service on Pribilof Islands

The Service also provides medical care for the inhabitants of the Pribilof Islands. It maintains a year-round physician at each of the two stations on the islands St. Paul and St. George.

The physician on St. Paul Island is also the medical officer on both islands. In addition, a nurse and a dentist stationed on St. Paul Island give medical and health service to a population of 500 resident natives and 20 permanent employees. Hospital facilities are maintained at the village of St. Paul. At St. George, a small village, clinical services, including dental and X-ray facilities, are provided.

Missions visited the islands in 1944 and again in 1946 to review the health program and give surgical treatment if necessary. The Territorial Commissioner of Health under a working agreement with the Territorial Department of Health for Alaska acts in an advisory capacity on all health and welfare matters of the islands' population. The cost for medical service on the islands amounts to $28,738.70 for 1948.

Cooperation

Cooperative agreements, in which supervision of the actual operations is vested in the Fish and Wildlife Service, are drawn between the Service and its numerous cooperating agencies, Federal, State, and local, that are concerned with the problem of controlling injurious rodents and predatory animals. These agencies interpose no objection to such agreements because this work is done expeditiously and efficiently under the direction of trained men. Cooperative agreements with some public health significance are in force between various agencies of the Department of the Interior and several services in

---

[36] Personal communication of June 18, 1948.

the Department of Agriculture, and United States Public Health Service.

TVA, through the office of the chief conservation engineer, cooperates with Fish and Wildlife Service in conducting investigations essential to the development and utilization of its fish and wild game as a source of food supply in the Tennessee River valley system.

Cooperative agreements extend also to counties, State fish and game departments, livestock associations, farm organizations, and municipalities, predatory animal and rodent control.

Public health projects of the Fish and Wildlife Service are under a working fund supplied by the Surgeon General, Department of the Army, and a formal cooperative agreement. The project includes studies of diseases carried by wild animals susceptible to infection by the virus of infectious hepatitis, and the interference with infections in certain viral diseases, with special reference to influenza.

As this cursory survey indicates, the conservation and development of wildlife is not carried on in the Fish and Wildlife Service alone, but also in other bureaus and divisions of the Government whose functions are directly related to human welfare and the promotion of health.

The apparent overlapping of activities is partly due to the fact that the Federal bureaus and offices, cooperating with Fish and Wildlife Service, function on a wide range of necessary activities. For example, the Bureau of Indian Affairs administering large tracts of land is entrusted with the protection of wildlife as food resources for the Indians.

Both the Forest Service and the National Park Service are established on a geographical basis, and in areas entrusted to them they are responsible for carrying on certain functions of fish and game preservation, and the elimination of harmful species. Stream pollution and the planting of trees and shrubs which serve as food and shelter for wildlife affect their health and the health of people. Consequently, all agencies of the Government concerned with the administration of waterway, land, and forest are bound to have an effect upon wildlife, and the problem of overlapping activities will necessarily continue.

Obligations

The total obligation for direct research and medical care of the Fish and Wildlife Service amounted to $55,612.78 for 1940, as compared with $91,722.77 for 1947, and $89,318.70 for 1948. Of these amounts, $11,242.78, $16,277.77, and $28,738.70 were for hospitals and clinical work for each of the three respective years. Of the total amounts for research, the Division of Wildlife spent $31,270 in 1940, and $15,900 and $22,550 for 1947 and 1948, respectively. The Division of Commercial Fisheries spent for research projects related to health the sums of $13,100 for 1940, and $59,545 and $38,030 for 1947 and 1948, respectively.

Recommendations

The health and medical care activities accomplished through the Fish and Wildlife Service, though indirect, are of value and should be continued. Emphasis should, however, be placed upon cooperation with other Federal and State agencies directly interested in the protection and promotion of health.

References: Résumé of the Cooperative Predator and Rodent-Control Work of the Fish and Wildlife Service. Annual Reports, Fish and Wildlife Service, 1946–47.

BUREAU OF INDIAN AFFAIRS, DIVISION OF HEALTH

Care of the Indians was the responsibility of the War Department until 1849 when the Office of Indian Affairs was created in the Department of the Interior. It was not until 1873, however, that a Division of Medicine and Education was created to protect and improve the health of Indians. The Division was discontinued in 1877, but a certain amount of medical service in the field was continued by the Division of Education. In 1909 a rudimentary health section was created in the Division of Education. In 1924 it became the Health Division directly under the Commissioner of Indian Affairs. Since 1926 the Public Health Service has detailed personnel to this Health Division, which now operates a comprehensive medical and health program for Indians and for the Alaska Native Service.

A public Health Service officer is director of the Division. The associate director is a civil-service employee. The director of public health services (formerly titled hospital administrator), the dental supervisor, and the public health nurse consultant are, like the director, detailed from the Public Health Service.

In the two regional offices (Portland, Oreg. and Billings, Mont.) of the Indian Service, a regional medical officer (Public Health Service) and a nurse consultant (Indian Service) supervise the medical program in the area. Similar units exist at Phoenix and Oklahoma City, and in the headquarters of the Alaska Native Service at Juneau. Close cooperation is maintained with the district offices of the Public Health Service, particularly with the sanitary engineers on duty there.

Each reservation and independent unit has a health staff which varies according to the geographical area and population density of the jurisdiction. The larger agencies have a senior medical officer; he is administratively responsible to the reservation superintendent but professionally responsible to the regional medical officer.

Beneficiaries

The responsibility of the Secretary of the Interior for the care of Indians is not formally defined in general legislation. Obligations of the United States to the Indians are to be found in a plethora of treaties and scattered legislation. The closest thing to a general mandate is a provision in the act of November 2, 1921 (25 U. S. C. 13), providing that funds may be spent for the relief of distress, conservation of health, etc., among Indians. The act of April 16, 1934, provides that the Secretary may contract for education, medical attention, and other benefits for Indians. Annual appropriation statutes include funds for conservation of health.

There is no general statutory definition of the persons who may be considered Indians and entitled to medical benefits. The regulations of the Bureau of Indian Affairs define Indian beneficiaries as follows (25 U. S. C. 84.8) :

All persons of Indian descent who are members of any recognized Indian tribe now under Federal jurisdiction ; all persons who are descendants of such members and who reside within the present boundaries of any Indian reservation and all other persons of one-half or more Indian blood.

Intermarried white men are not entitled to medical treatment (25 U. S. C. 84.11). Preference is given in admission to hospitals to those of a higher degree of Indian blood. Nonresidents returning to a reservation to receive free care are admitted only as a matter of courtesy (25 U. S. C. 85.4). The white wife of an eligible Indian is herself eligible for hospitalization and medical services (25 U. S. C. 85.8), but the Indian dependents of a white man are eligible only if they maintain a permanent home on the reservation and participate in tribal affairs (25 U. S. C. 85.9). All beneficiaries who can afford to are expected to pay fees based on the cost of services rendered (25 U. S. C. 84.8), but in practice few collections are made.

The difficulties of ascertaining an individual's degree of blood and of taking the census on some nomadic reservations preclude an accurate count of those entitled to the benefits of the medical and health programs of the Indian Service. The total Indian population is estimated at about 400,000, of which about 250,000 reside on reservations and about 120,000 among the Five Civilized Tribes in Oklahoma on their own lands.

Health Services

The health services for Indians are now provided for under the Conservation of Health program, which is primarily designed to give complete public health and medical care for all age groups. In this regard, the Indian Service is unique among the Government agencies in that it provides health education, preventive and curative measures, and sanitation to individuals and communities from the cradle to the grave. The practices and methods used are applicable to any rural community. These consist of three general plans: (1) Health services concerned with the control and prevention of disease and the promotion of better health; (2) the use of field dispensaries and clinics for physical examinations, and means for health education, and (3) medical care program through the use of hospitals for treatment of general medical and surgical conditions, and the use of special hospitals as sanitoria for tuberculosis cases.

The public health services now carried forward by the Reservation Health Service of the Office of Indian Affairs are: (1) Public health field nursing, (2) health services to the Indian schools, (3) communicable disease control, (4) health education, (5) nutritional studies and health surveys, (6) community and home sanitation, and (7) special health activities that are closely related to the medical care program such as the control of trachoma, tuberculosis, and the maternal and child health clinics.

For the promotion of health services, examining rooms and dispensaries are established at key locations throughout the reservations and serve for public health promotion work as well as clinics for examinations and treatment centers. These centers are supplied by field visiting nurses, staff doctors, dentists, and other personnel. The doctors act as county health officers and family physicians, when available. Mobile dental units devote the larger part of their time to dental care of children in the schools. The senior physician consolidates health and medical care services of the reservation and is supposed to maintain close cooperation with State and county health departments. The effectiveness of these services is dependent upon the public health and medical personnel on the reservation, and where they are not available, the Indian Service employs on a contractual basis part-time physicians and other health personnel. These arrangements also make use of the provisions of the contractual services authorized by the Johnson-O'Malley Act (48 Stat. 596, Amend. 49.1458).

Where this has been accomplished, as in Minnesota, Wisconsin, and North Dakota, the cooperative efforts have proved to be satisfactory, and at the same time developed within the States a consciousness of health needs among the Indians.

The most important health problem of the Indians is the control and eradication of tuberculosis. Mobile X-ray units provide early diagnosis. The use of B. C. B. (Calmette Guerin) vaccination against tuberculosis has given the Indian Service a valuable tool in its work against the disease. Plans for its use on a "wide scale" are in progress.

Hospitals and sanitaria.—The medically indigent Indians of the reservation receive free medical care in hospitals and sanitaria. Health education is emphasized. A résumé of these services follows:

268

In the Indian Service there are 66 hospitals, including 8 "limited service units," with a total of 3,614 beds, of which 2,648 are for general medicine and surgery and 966 for tuberculosis. There are four sanitoria used exclusively for tuberculosis and four more with combined facilities for tuberculosis and general services. During the past fiscal year these hospitals furnished 806,958 in-patient days' treatment to a daily average of 2,229.2 patients—only 61.7 percent of capacity, and 350,604 out-patient treatments. In addition, physicians gave 428,260 out-patient treatments in field clinics, homes, and schools.

These hospitals are equipped to give general diagnostic facilities and staffed to treat general illnesses and other conditions found among the Indians. Otherwise, treatment is given in a nearby Service hospital or through a contractual basis with public private hospitals.

Obligations

The total health expenditure, including over-all administrative cost and medical and health services, for 1940 was $5,088,170. No accurate break-down of this amount could be obtained. For the years 1947 and 1948 the expenditures vary little, the sums of $7,131,400 for 1947 and $7,315,300 for 1948 include the cost of tuberculosis control; field health and private physicians; hospital and clinic expenses. The total expenditures for 1948 also include approximately $500,000 for the care of patients in non-Federal hospitals and St. Elizabeths Hospital in Washington. For comparison, Congress has appropriated for the fiscal year 1949, $6,714,500 for "expenses necessary for the conservation of health among Indians, transportation of patients and attendants to and from hospitals and sanitoria . . . clinical surveys and general medical research in connection with tuberculosis, trachoma, and venereal and other disease conditions among Indians . . ." A companion appropriation of $472,710 is for Welfare of Indians. Conservation of health in Alaska is financed from a $4,118,962 appropriation to the Alaska Native Service. The appropriation of over $5,000,000 to the Navajo and Hopi Service includes about $1,500,000 for health.

The basic appropriation of $6,714,500 is about $600,000 less than the appropriation for fiscal year 1948. It is over $2,000,000 less than the amount recommended in the President's budget, but the actual decrease is about $1,000,000 since about $1,235,000 was transferred to the appropriation to the Navajo and Hopi Service.

The report of the House Appropriations Committee included the following paragraphs on the health program of the Bureau of Indian Affairs:

There is still some need for continuation of the Indian hospitals. But in many cases, we have found that the Indian is as well treated in the public and charitable hospitals as any other patient. In fact, in many instances, he perhaps would fare better than in an Indian hospital, for in the strictly Indian hospitals, in many instances, due to legal limitations of salary provisions for doctors and nurses, the services offered in these hospitals are inadequate and inferior.

In some instances, contract services are more practical than the construction and/or maintenance of separate hospitals, and where such conditions exist, the contract program should be followed on an economical basis, calculated to render the best possible service to the Indians.

Personnel

Aside from the few position filled by personnel detailed from the Public Health Service, the Bureau of Indian Affairs is dependent upon civil-service recruitment for its full-time personnel. During the war the general shortage of physicians in the Indian Service created a serious problem. This situation continues. The higher salaries offered by the Veterans' Administration and the rewards of private practice have added to the recruitment problems.

In all, there are about 2,200 employees in the medical program. This figure includes about 110 full-time and 85 part-time physicians, 13 full-time and 5 part-time dentists, and about 500 nurses (of whom about 50 are public health nurses).

The civil-service system is not providing professional personnel to fill authorized positions. In the case of doctors, for example, there are about 30 vacancies. The plight of the Indian Service is also evidenced by the fact that 8 percent of its physicians are under 36 and 20 percent are over 60 (in the Public Health Service 47 percent are under 36 and 3 percent over 60).

Recommendations

In comparison with the medical service of the Prison Bureau, for which the Public Health Service provides the complete medical staff and supervision, the system used in the Bureau of Indian Affairs of detailing Public Health Service personnel to a few key positions appears to be a hybrid of doubtful merit. There may be no specific evidence of friction between the civil-service personnel of the Indian Service and the Public Health Service personnel assigned. However, the situation is inherently difficult from both points of view: On the one hand, the Public Health Service has some responsibility but diluted authority; the civil-service personnel are aware of the greater advantages enjoyed by the commissioned officers by whom they are supervised.

On the assumption that no other changes are made in the organization of Federal medical services, there are positive reasons for giving to the Public Health Service more complete responsibility for the medical and health programs among the Indians.

Such a step would help solve the desperate problem of recruiting young and able doctors for the Indian program. The program would also be in a better position to secure funds commensurate with the size of the problem, particularly for preventive medicine. Moreover, experience in the comprehensive medical and health problems of an Indian community would provide unequalled training for Public Health Service officers. The Public Health Service, finally, might with its great prestige more easily withstand the pressures, chiefly political, which are exerted on the Indian Service.

In an integration of the medical services to the Indians the same arguments would obtain. The operation of the Indian hospitals could be continued on a sounder financial basis and with improved services if directly conducted or at least supervised and staffed by an agency equipped to obtain the necessary personnel. The policy of gradual liquidation of the hospitals and the absorption of Indian patients in other Federal or non-Federal systems could be accelerated. If the Public Health Service were left outside the central agency but confined to purely public health activity of the Indian Service, it could push the Indian health program with greater vigor, and greater integration with national and State programs than is now possible.

The Public Health Service itself is evidently reluctant to take on the responsibility for care of the Indians. The inherent difficulties of the tasks in themselves are a deterrent to an agency which takes pride in a clean record in relatively uncontroversial fields.

Moreover, it is said that the function of medical care of the Indians cannot feasibly be separated from other aspects of the Government's guardianship. The Brookings Report of 1937, for example, noted that it was "highly questionable whether the property work and welfare work could be successfully divided." Considerations which did not apply in 1937—chiefly, the shortage of personnel—might well dictate a different conclusion today. At the very least, it is difficult to see why the use of the Public Health Service could not be put on the same basis that exists in the Prison Bureau.

In this connection, a bill (S. 787) was introduced on March 5, 1947, by Senator Langer to transfer to the Public Health Service responsibility for the maintenance and operation of hospitals on Indian reservations and the conservation of the health of Indians. No action was taken on the bill.

The fate of our health and medical care program among the Indians should follow the purposes of our Federal-aid program for the Indian peoples. This program of financial support and other services has been to enable them to earn their own livelihoods in harmony with their own aims and ideals as American citizens with all rights of citizenship guaranteed. These rights assure the Indian of the privilege to earn his own living and to provide for himself the necessities of life and protection. Under this policy the present health and medical care program should be incorporated into whatever health and medical care program is in effect in the State where he resides. What now is apparently needed is an increased effort to carry out the intended purposes of the Government in order to hasten a self-supporting health program as a part of the State and local governments.

During this transitional period the following program should be carried out:

1. The Federal Government should utilize the facilities of State health departments or other health agencies within the States to provide health services for the Indians, the Federal Government undertaking to provide the necessary subsidies.

2. The present program of direct operations by the Federal Government could be improved materially if the entire operation of health services were the responsibility of the Public Health Service on a basis similar to that in effect with the Bureau of Prisons, Department of Justice.

Other Departments

DEPARTMENT OF LABOR

The Congressional Act of March 4, 1913, creating a Department of Labor in the Federal Government, charged it to "foster, promote, and develop the welfare of wage earners. To promote their working conditions. . . ."

Since the health and safety activities of the Department of Labor are an integral function of the total industrial problems of our Government, these activities are discussed under the general subject of Industrial Hygiene. (See Industrial Hygiene, ch. II, p. 85.)

DEPARTMENT OF TREASURY

Bureau of Narcotics

By the Act of Congress approved June 14, 1930 (46 Stat. 585; U. S. C. 282-824), the Bureau of Narcotics was established, to be directed by the Commissioner of Narcotics, and to be charged with the duty of regulating, supervising, and controlling the traffic in opium and other narcotic drugs; that of preventing and combatting, in cooperation with the United States Public Health Service, the spread of drug addiction; and that of suppressing the illicit traffic in narcotic drugs, in connection with which the bureau enjoys the cooperation of the Bureau of Customs. The Bureau of Narcotics is vested by law with the requisite authority in these premises.

The national control of habit-forming and habit-sustaining drugs is an integral part of an international control, and for its effectiveness depends in no small measure on its relationship to the controls set up by the United Nations, through the United Nations Economic and Social Council in its Commission on Narcotic Drugs (United Nations Document 2/20, Feb. 15, 1946, pp. 9–10). The control of narcotics is considered in the section on narcotic drugs on International Health program, chapter II, page 100.

DEPARTMENT OF STATE

The principal responsibility for the determination of the policy of the Government in relation to international problems devolves upon the Department of State.

The cooperation of the State Department in international health is developed in chapter II, page 100.

Part Three

FEDERAL POLICY AND ORGANIZATION
FOR EDUCATION

Chapter I

INTRODUCTION

The American people have evolved a system of schools which make educational opportunities available on a scale unknown elsewhere in the world. This system is testimony to our belief in the worth of the individual, and the priority of the individual over the State. It is founded on the view that the development of individual intellect and understanding is essential to the health and development of our democracy. Historically this program has been largely initiated and developed through energy and vision in local communities and the several States, by public and private enterprise. Because of our national cultural homogeneity we have developed a national type of education without the rigidity imposed by a uniform national system.

Our tradition of local control of education, an outgrowth of the isolation of the pioneer community, still exists, supported by the Tenth Amendment to the Constitution and by our basic belief that the local community and State must be the cornerstone for all matters concerning the welfare of the individual and his participation in democratic society. This tradition has been strengthened by our zeal for freedom and individual liberty. We have a compelling desire to keep power decentralized in all matters which concern influence over the thinking of the individual; we abhor deeply anything savoring of centralized or totalitarian control of thinking through education. Among the varied and numerous activities of government, there is none closer guarded from excessive Federal control than education. The decentralization of administration and control of public education should be maintained.

Despite this tradition, our Federal Government has played a long and important role in the development of our national educational system, in collaboration with the States. This role long antedates the creation of any Federal agency specifically designed to deal with educational matters. Land grants for the support of education in newly formed States preceded by 80 years the establishment of our Office of Education.

This Office has traditionally been small and its role confined to research, dissemination of facts, and collaboration with other authorities. Other Federal agencies, acting in pursuit of particular functions and interests, have far overshadowed the Office in the size of programs, amounts of perquisites or money distributed, and influence over the educational institutions throughout the Nation. Certain Federal agencies, such as the Army and Navy, have set up their own specialized educational institutions, as well as collaborating with those of other agencies within and without the Government. Others have had to make provision for such educational responsibilities as the education of Indians, native populations, or other special groups. The impact of these latter programs on the educational system of the Nation has been, on balance, greater than that of the information disseminated and leadership exercised by the Office of Education. Finally, such multiple-purpose projects as the school lunch program, which combines the utilization of surplus commodities and the support of agricultural prices, improvements in public health through reduction of malnutrition, and such specifically educational aspects as the dissemination of dietary information and improvement of dietary habits, introduce special elements of complexity. It is impossible fully to judge such programs on their educational aspects alone, although it is imperative that their educational elements be made clear.

Brief Review of the Evolution of Federal Concern for and Participation in Education

The Federal Government from its inception has evidenced an interest in and a support of public education in all States. Most of the States were first organized as Territories, in all of which Congress provided for public school systems. Starting with grants of Federal land for public education in the Northwest Territory, the land-grant program has since then aided all levels of education in the States and Alaska by Federal grants of probably over 165,000,000 acres.

These early land grants were for the general support of education. The first move toward Federal control appeared in the Morrill Act of 1862. This law, in granting land for State agricultural and mechanical colleges, specified broad areas of curricula, thus introducing a mild type of control.

Since 1862 the increasing Federal concern for and support of education, in cooperation with the States, is evidenced by Federal subsidies for such activities as agricultural experiment stations (1887); resident instruction in land-grant colleges (1890); agricultural extension service (1914); vocational education in secondary schools (1917); vocational rehabilitation (1920); and the school-lunch program (regularized in 1946). Subsequent added subsidies for these projects have been made from time to time.

278

It will be noted that each of these cooperative projects is in a very specific area of education. There are those who believe that, both because of their specificity and the Federal controls which in varying degree accompany them, these constitute a threat to State and local autonomy. Suffice it to state that, for the most part, these specific educational projects carried out by the States with Federal encouragement have been in response to defensible needs in areas of education not adequately cared for by local initiative. Some, with modest Federal subsidies, have produced excellent participation in States. An added question may be raised, aside from the question of control, concerning the wisdom of Federal support of specific types of educational service to the States which may tend to place education in a state of imbalance and without regard to priority of local needs.

It would be improper to conclude that the Federal interest in education stops at cooperation with the States. In fact, by far the greater part of the Federal budgetary items concerning education are in other areas, or through other than State channels. Assuming a rather broad definition of education, but limiting it to matters involving schools and higher educational institutions and students therein, during each of the last few years the Federal Government has expended several billions of dollars through these channels, with participation by practically every major governmental department and independent agency.

Federal activities which directly relate to public and private educational institutions, particularly colleges and universities, are assuming increasing importance. Projects in this area include such activities as military scholarships, Reserve office training programs, the veteran programs under the GI bill of rights (Public Law 346),[1] and Public Law 16 [2] providing for vocational rehabilitation for World War II disabled veterans. Closely related to these are Federal research projects by contract with institutions of higher education through such agencies as the Army, Air Force, Navy, Atomic Energy Commission, and Public Health Service (Federal Security Agency). There is a marked and increasing use of schools and colleges in the Federal interest.

Several agencies of the Government promote or prepare materials for instruction in schools such as the Civil Aeronautics Administration (Department of Commerce) in the field of aviation education or the Immigration and Naturalization Service (Department of Justice) in the field of citizenship eduction.

The education and training of pre- or in-service Government personnel is of itself a major enterprise, including extensive activities in regular colleges and universities, educational institutions operated by various governmental agencies, and less formal activities in practically every division of the Government.

---

[1] 58 Stat. 284.
[2] 57 Stat. 43.

More difficult to classify are such Federal ventures in education as the Graduate School of the United States Department of Agriculture, and Graduate School of the National Bureau of Standards, institutions which, although in the Government, enroll some students who are not in Government service.

There are distinct, special, and direct Federal responsibilities or activities for education, such as for natives on Guam, American Indians, children on approximately 1,100 Federal reservations and special projects, children of federally employed American nationals in occupied areas, exchange of persons for international and intercultural benefit through education, the schools of the District of Columbia, schools in Territories, or education in Federal penal institutions.

Even with such a brief listing of Federal activities in education it becomes evident that this is a major governmental enterprise. For a full inventory, see the appendix. The items of overlapping jurisdictions and services, the multiplicity of agencies conducting these activities, the varied methods of making contact with educational institutions in the States, the variety of fiscal and administrative policies involved, and the piecemeal manner in which much of the legislation has been enacted are but a few of the complicating factors.

The problem is further complicated by the fact that no agency now exists in the Government with adequate status or resources to assume leadership in respect to the situation. The United States Office of Education, in the Federal Security Agency, has neither sufficient authority nor status among governmental agencies to do so. There are several agencies of the Government which have larger educational staffs, preferred status, and greater educational resources than the Office of Education. Although this Office has performed well the functions which Congress has given to it, and has a good record of service to and coordination with other Federal agencies dealing with education, it has not been an effective integrating force in the total Federal educational picture. Its administrative budget is less than those of several other Federal agencies or subagencies dealing with education in the States. Its total budget, including some $32,000,000 in subsidies which it is distributing to the States in fiscal 1949, is approximately 1 percent of the Federal expenditure through or for educational institutions and students therein.

This subordinate position of the Office of Education is not a matter of mere chance. It is a reflection through Congress of the concern of the States and of the people that the control and administration of education not be nationalized. It has been assumed that control follows money and that status precedes centralization. Whether or not this claim is valid as applied to education will be analyzed in later chapters.

It is neither desirable nor feasibly to centralize all Federal educational activities. However, there should be an orderly distribution of these activities among appropriate agencies and much desirable coordination and integration can be effected.

Current Status of Education in the United States

How does the status of our population reflect the effectiveness of our educational program?

Each generation has been receiving progressively more education. In 1947 half of the 25- to 29-year-olds had completed 12 or more years of schooling, while one-sixth of the persons 65 or over in age had received that amount of education. While the achievement over the years is commendable, we are still faced with the fact that among those recently completing their education (25 to 29 years of age) half have not completed high school.

Illiteracy is being reduced, although 10 percent of our population 25 years old and over in 1947 had completed fewer than 5 years of elementary school. For the 25-to-29-age group, however, this figure was 4 percent.

Marked differences in education by racial groups persist. In 1947, of all white persons [3] 25 years old and over, about 35 percent had completed 4 years of high school or more, while only about 13 percent of nonwhites in this age group had received this amount of education. While 1 white person in every 10 has less than 5 years of schooling, among nonwhites 3 in every 10 have not reached this minimal standard. Although the median white person age 25 to 29 has completed 4 years of high school, the median nonwhite in this age group has only completed elementary school. The lag in education of the nonwhite is also indicated by the fact that among whites who completed most of their education more than a generation ago (65 years old and over) the proportion completing less than 5 years of elementary school is approximately the same as for nonwhites recently educated (25 to 29 years old).

In 1947, 81.2 percent of youth 14 to 17 years of age were in school, an all-time high. By contrast, in 1910, 58.9 percent of children of this age were in school. Of 18- and 19-year-olds in 1947, 27.7 percent were in school. Between 1900 and 1947 the resident enrollment in higher institutions increased tenfold. During the period from 1890 to 1940, secondary-school enrollments increased about nine times as fast as the general population and more than twenty times as fast as the popu-

---

[3] Most persons of Mexican birth are classified as white. "Nonwhite" consists of Negroes, Indians, Chinese, Japanese, and other nonwhite races.

lation group 14 to 17 years of age. Practically all the 6-to-13-age group are now in school.

The rapid increase in child population during the war years is yet another complicating factor in the matter of providing educational facilities, teachers, and programs for an increasingly large school population. Between 1945 and 1950 the elementary schools of the country will be forced to accommodate some 2,000,000 more children although estimates of this increase vary. The increased birth rate and migrations of peoples will make it necessary to double the school plant and staff within the next few years in some areas of the country. The growth will soon reflect itself in the secondary schools. A solution of the problems involved will demand planning and leadership at local, State, and Federal levels.

In the early 1940's, within the continental United States, there were over 180,000 elementary schools, of which all but approximately 10,300 were public. Of about 32,000 secondary schools, over 90 percent were public. Of the 1,749 higher institutions, slightly more than one-third were public institutions. These educational institutions had an enrollment of pupils and resident students of some 29,000,000 individuals in 1947. Of these, approximately 20,000,000 were in elementary schools, 6,200,000 in secondary schools, and 2,354,000 resident in colleges and universities.

Issues

We have entered this study with the belief that the basic responsibility for education lies in States and in local educational institutions. With this in mind our major concern is for the regularly constituted schools and higher educational institutions in States, and this concern is mirrored in our major issues. Is there undue direct or indirect Federal control of education in States? Is it possible to have Federal educational activities reaching into States without undue control? Has the Federal Government done all in its power to administer its activities which have an impact on education in States in such a manner that self-reliance and self-sufficiency have been encouraged at the State or institutional level? Have these Federal activities strengthened education in States in a balanced manner? Historically have Federal educational activities been beneficial to education throughout the country? Have Federal activities overlapped, duplicated, or worked at cross purposes with other Federal activities or with State or local educational activities? What are the individual and total effects of Federal educational activities on schools and higher educational institutions in States? What should be the role of the Federal Government as related to education in States? These questions indicate the areas in which we believe the major issues of this report are located.

Education and educational institutions are a powerful and useful force and means for accomplishing Federal purposes. How far can the regularly constituted schools and colleges of the country be used for these Federal purposes in the national interest? When does the breaking point come as it concerns the best interests of the schools and higher institutions? How can the specialized interests of the various departments and independent agencies of the Government be furthered while at the same time giving full protection to the need for well-rounded education in the States? How can we develop an integrated and coordinated total program of activities through the educational institutions of the land and still recognize the close association of many of the activities with the specialized and sometimes competing interests of the various governmental agencies?

Unless the Federal Government directly assumes responsibility for certain educational activities, many individuals will be denied equal opportunity for education as in the case of dependent children on reservations or Indians or other native peoples. What is the responsibility of the Federal Government to these individuals? Can an over-all policy be developed or will it be necessary to continue piecemeal and unequal programs operated by the many governmental agencies involved? To what extent can the regular schools in the States or Territories be used for these individuals?

It is assumed that we will continue to need a Federal educational agency. How can such an agency be set up to give maximum assurance against bureaucratic Federal control of education? How can it be protected from partisan influence? How can it best serve the interests of education in States? How far should the various Federal educational activities be centralized in this agency? For dispersed Federal educational activities should it serve as an integrating and service force? Where should the Federal educational agency be located in the Government?

With such questions in mind, it is the broad task of this report to survey the present distribution of functions and responsibilities relating to education in the Federal Government; to make clear their interrelations and impact on the Nation's educational system and resources; to state the main elements of a national policy for education; and finally, to propose certain over-all administrative arrangements compatible with our national traditions which will assure more orderly, effective, and fruitful Federal contributions to the Nation's schools. These recommendations will fit in with our current Government structure and patterns of fiscal relations with the States. If these matters are significantly changed, educational recommendations may require reexamination.

283

Chapter II

THE EDUCATIONAL ACTIVITIES OF THE FEDERAL GOVERNMENT

Public education, broadly conceived, is concerned with individual and social competency, benefit, and growth. Yet the Federal Government has used education and the schools of the country for ends which do not always aim primarily at general individual and social competency. With few exceptions, the Federal interest in education centers on special groups of individuals, special programs in promtion of causes sponsored by Federal departments or agencies, or on research and training to promote some Federal concern such as national defense or competence in Federal work. Hence it would be wrong to assume that the large sums for the programs and activities described in this chapter necessarily reflect an equivalent contribution to general education. For instance, better than 90 percent of the money obligated by the Federal Government for education in fiscal year 1947 went for war or defense-connected items such as education or educational facilities for veterans, schools in defense areas, pre- or in-service military education, military research through universities, or raising the educational level of the armed forces. The percent rises higher if such items are included as in-service training in military service schools, educational activities of the Atomic Energy Commission, and the value of surplus war property given or sold at a discount to educational institutions. It is obviously difficult to discriminate between programs or elements of programs which are primarily an aid to education as contrasted with those which use education as a tool to further some noneducational interest.

The full range of Federal educational activities is indicated by the material in the appendix, which describes briefly 200 separate educational programs conducted by the various departments and agencies giving summary figures of money obligated by or available to each activity for the fiscal years 1940, 1947, 1948, and 1949.

This chapter describes Federal educational activities as they are related to various levels of phases of education. At the elementary and secondary levels, the promotion of curricula, the school-lunch program, general educational assistance to specific geographical areas, education for dependent children of Federal employees, and the education of Indians or other native peoples, Federal research and leadership, and miscellaneous problems are considered in turn. At the level of higher education, the topics of research, higher education of special groups of individuals or of individuals in special fields, relations with special types of State higher institutions, general service and research, education and training for Government service, the administration of international educational programs, and federally operated higher institutions are treated. The next section covers Federal activities not specialized as to level, such as education of special groups of individuals, institutional on-farm training, and civilian education for members of the National Military Establishment. The following section discusses Federal activities not connected with established educational institutions, such as in-service training for Government service, or programs for non-Federal employees. The final sections deal with nonbudgetary Federal assistance, Federal activities tangential to education, and a sketch of noncontinuing emergency Federal activities in education from 1933 to 1946, such as the National Youth Administration or Lanham Act operations.

Federal Activities Clearly Concerning Elementary and Secondary Education

Promotion of Curricula

Traditionally the development of a curriculum has been considered a function for State or local jurisdiction. Notwithstanding this fact, the Federal Government has had five readily identifiable programs (four of which are currently active) in promotion of special curricular fields which are generally available to the regularly constituted elementary and secondary schools of the country. These programs, which call for an expenditure in fiscal 1949 of over $28,000,000, are: (1) Citizenship education, under the Immigration and Naturalization Service of the Department of Justice; (2) aviation education, under the Civil Aeronautics Administration of the Department of Commerce; (3) school savings, under the Savings Bonds Division of the Treasury Department; (4) vocational education, under the Office of Education, Federal Security Agency; and (5) food conservation education, under the Office of Education, Federal Security Agency (discontinued after 1947).

The manner in which the agencies involved promote these special curricular fields should be considered. If they develop specific textbooks and teaching materials, they infringe upon the rights of the States in this respect. A possible exception is noted in the citizenship education program of the Department of Justice for which the development of specific and curricular textbook materials in anticipa-

286

tion of United States citizenship is a matter of Federal concern. However, the actual development of texts for classroom use, such as has sometimes been done in the promotion of aviation education and the school savings programs, is a direct violation of our tradition of State curricular responsibility.

The grants to States for vocational education and for education in food conservation, insofar as they leave the primary initiative for the details of internal administration, supervision, and curricular content to the States, are justifiable activities of the Federal Government. Yet entire responsibility for these programs should not be given to the States without assurance on the part of the Federal Government that the purposes for which funds are appropriated are carried out by the States. Thus it is necessary to maintain such Federal controls as may be needed to ensure that the Federal purpose is attained.

More serious than the criticisms indicated above is the criticism that the Federal Government has been interested only in the promotion of highly specialized fields within the curriculum. Is it appropriate that the Federal Government should extend its substantial influence on curriculum only in the promotion of these few highly specialized areas? Can the Government afford to be placed in the position of lending its prestige to these few areas while neglecting the total curricular need of the country? Can we as a Nation allow more and more agencies of the Government to develop uncoordinated specialized curricula? We believe these questions must be answered in the negative.

We have overlapping and independent curricular promotion on the Federal level. It has no semblance of the over-all curricular coordination considered essential at State and local educational levels. As other agencies of the Government realize the potency of the public schools of the country in promoting their individual causes, this situation could easily become chaotic.

To centralize all curriculum promotion activities in the Federal educational agency would deny the wealth of technical knowledge in the noneducational Federal agencies. A more appropriate solution would involve over-all Federal coordination of the work of various governmental agencies. All present Federal activities in promotion of elementary or secondary curricula should be transferred to the Federal educational agency, and this agency in turn should be a coordinating and clearinghouse body for the specialties of the non-educational agencies. The Federal Government, through its various departments and agencies, has some of the most competent specialists available in this country in practically every area of human interest and concern. These areas constitute those which, to a large extent, make up the curricula in our schools and areas from which a curriculum more vital to individuals and our society can be developed. Avenues should be opened whereby these Federal resources may be coordinated and made available to the schools of our country when services are requested by States.

The School Lunch Program

A special section is devoted to the school lunch program because of its magnitude, significance, and the fact that it is the only program of its type conducted by the Federal Government. This activity, administered by the Production and Marketing Administration of the Department of Agriculture, devotes $92,000,000 to the schools of the Nation in 1949. This includes subsidies to States and purchased food for distribution to schools. It was initiated on a more modest basis during the depression period of the 1930's as a proper use of surplus agricultural commodities and to furnish work to unemployed. Three major groups in American life have stimulated its development: The agricultural groups, the educational group, and others interested in the physical well-being of children. Much of the confusion and lack of clarity of this program may be due to this threefold interest therein. It is not appropriate that the study in the field of education should arrive at a conclusion as to whether it is necessary to support prices of farm commodities through this program, particularly in times of high economic return. Suffice it to say that, if the Federal Government purchases surplus food, this program is an extremely worthy outlet for such commodities. It is better to furnish nutritious food to children than to destroy food crops. However, to the extent that this program utilizes only those foods which are surplus or in abundance, it runs the risk of violating basic principles of a well-rounded diet.

There are those groups who are quite insistent that the school lunch program is not an educational activity. Some of this insistence may have been prompted by the fact that assistance under this program is extended to private and parochial schools. By calling the program noneducational, we avoid the dilemma of Federal educational assistance to nonprofit private including parochial schools. No good can come from an extended and academic discussion of this question in this connection. The fact is that thus far in our national history we have maintained a rigid policy of no Federal aid to parochial schools. This problem, within limits, up to now has been left to the States to decide. The school lunch program furnishes assistance to nonprofit private and parochial schools through State channels in States which permit this, and the United States Department of Agriculture deals directly with such schools in States which prohibit this.

Actually, whether or not this program is called educational, it oper-

288

ates in public, private, and parochial schools. Because in the large majority of cases its operations are through public schools and through State departments of education, it is believed desirable regardless of name that its general administration and grant-in-aid activities be moved to the Federal educational agency. State and local school officials need redress from their complaint that they are forced to deal with too many Federal agencies in the conduct of their programs. Unless evidence is clear-cut to the contrary, all Federal activities involved with the regular elementary and secondary schools of the country should be administered by the Federal educational agency. The Office of Education has always followed the practice of placing as much initiative and responsibility for administration of Federal programs as is possible on State departments of education. Noneducational Federal agencies, many of which have been involved in direct action within States, often have underestimated the advantages of maximum centralization of educational responsibility and initiative at the State level. If dietary needs of children are given priority over need for disposal of surplus foods or foods in abundance, this can be better assured if the program is administered by an educational agency. This would not preclude the utilization of surplus foods or foods in abundance as determined by the Department of Agriculture, when and if such utilization is desirable. The schools of the country have always risen to emergencies in the national interest. The listing of foods in abundance for preferential purchase by schools and the purchase, warehousing, and distribution of foods in abundance should be retained by the Department of Agriculture. The Federal educational agency should utilize the best resources available in the government in developing the nutrition and dietary aspects of the program. By proper coordination with the Federal educational agency, this program can be made more effective than at present, in the interests of all parties concerned.

The school lunch program should be thought of as a part of the total effective experience of the children in the schools. It should be correlated with proper instruction in dietary habits and nutrition. By placing its administration in the normal educational channels from the Federal to the State and local levels, the school lunch program can become a part of a valuable educational and instructional program. With the transfer of the grant-in-aid aspects of the program to the Federal educational agency, the prohibition specifically contained in the present act against any influence to the instruction or curricular program should be rescinded. Historically the Office of Education has for many years furnished assistance and encouragement to the States and the schools therein in respect to nutrition, dietary needs of children, and proper school lunches. Many publications had been issued long before the Federal school lunch program was developed. The Office of Education for many years has been the Federal source to which schools have looked for assistance in respect to school lunch programs. In addition to the thousands of schools which now share the Federal subsidy for school lunches, there are other thousands of schools which operate school lunch programs without Federal support. The United States Office of Education is expected to render advisory assistance to both groups and does so to a considerable measure. It is an unnecessary duplication that both the Office of Education and the Department of Agriculture should be called upon for similar services. The Office of Education is constantly being consulted by States for advisory assistance in the planning of school buildings, most of which include school lunch facilities. There is needless overlapping between the school lunch program of the Department of Agriculture and this activity of the Office of Education.

Many of the States with the current unprecedented fiscal demands upon them have found it extremely difficult to enable their State departments of education to include the necessary administrative personnel to give proper administration and supervision to the school lunch program. This has sometimes resulted in necessity for the Department of Agriculture to make an undue number of local audits and render services which might better be left to State and local initiative. It is thus recommended that a small amount of school lunch subsidy be dedicated for State administration of the program. This would take the Federal Government out of some operations which might better be left to State jurisdiction and place more incentive for proper conduct of the program on the States where it belongs.

In summarizing, four recommendations are made: (1) The responsibility for the administration of the National School Lunch Act should be placed in the Federal educational agency; except (2) the direct purchase and distribution of food for price support and the listing of foods in abundance for priority purchase, when necessary, should be retained in the Department of Agriculture; (3) a small subsidy should be available to State departments of education to insure proper State administration and supervision of the act (unless other means are available for adequate support of State departments of education) ; (4) the nutrition aspects of the program, although carried out by the Federal educational agency, should be done with the advice from the best informed agency of the Government in nutrition matters. There is little reason why, if the current manner of caring for the school lunch program in nonprofit private schools is satisfactory in the Department of Agriculture, the same plan may not be operated just as effectively by the Federal educational agency.

There are four readily identifiable activities of the Federal Government concerned with giving general assistance for elementary or secondary schools, or both, in special geographic areas. These are: (1) The payments to New Mexico and Arizona to defray partially the loss in State revenues resulting from the high proportion of tax-exempt Federal lands in those States, (2) support of the local government expenses of the District of Columbia, (3) assistance to the territories and other areas under special Federal jurisdiction, and (4) the emergency aid to communities provided under the Lanham Act. The total cost of these programs in fiscal 1949 will be almost 5 million dollars, 3 million of which is for Lanham Act aid.

DEPENDENT CHILDREN OF FEDERAL EMPLOYEES

Between 1935 and 1947 the number of school-age children of Federal employees on federally owned properties increased from 24,000 to 56,000, and is estimated at almost 60,000 in 1948. Because of the failure of the Federal Government to establish a comprehensive policy in respect to these children and the prevalent lack of State recognition of responsibility for their education, they often do not have the opportunity to a free public education which is guaranteed to other children as a part of their birthright. Type situations to which we refer are: Communities under the jurisdiction of the Atomic Energy Commission; military installations in the continental United States or abroad; the National Parks; Federal construction projects; the Tennessee Valley Authority, and the foreign installations of the Department of State. Suffice it to say that there are marked disparities in educational opportunity in these and comparable situations.

The States, similarly, have varying policies relative to children living on Federal reservations and properties. Only 10 States have provided any legislation to solve the problem, and in these the scope is limited. It is clear that even beyond those children for whom States pay all educational expenses by specific State provision, those which may have been admitted to public schools by the benevolence of other States, and those covered by emergency Lanham Act support, a substantial number of children living on such reservations are educated at the expense of their parents. Of those children living on federally owned properties in the several States, Hawaii, Alaska, and the Canal Zone, approximately 73 percent are on reservations where in general the local authority assumed no responsibility. It has been felt by many individuals and groups cognizant of the problem that the education of these children should not be contingent upon the generosity of State and local taxpayers or a burden on the parents.

In brief summary, the education of many children on reservations, federally owned properties, and special Federal jurisdictions either at home or abroad, is a Federal responsibility if we accept the tenet that all of our children are to be given an opportunity for elementary and secondary education at public expense. The large diversity of situations—geographical, jurisdictional, and administrative—complicates the problem. Several governmental agencies have quite different policies and there is seldom consistency in policy within an agency. There is some cause for having called these children "educational orphans." The recent increased tendency of Congress to enact piecemeal legislation in reference to individual situations or agencies without regard to any well-established over-all policy is not satisfactory.

There is a very apparent need of a Federal policy to cover all situations treated in this section. It is recommended that comprehensive Federal legislation be initiated which will recognize this responsibility. It is believed that the Federal educational agency should be the major administering and coordinating force in the Government for this activity. Only in the most exceptional cases should it be expected to operate schools. Federal funds should normally be channeled through the Federal educational agency to contracting agencies to care for these dependent children. Preference should be given to the regularly established schools in the States and Territories where possible. In some cases the Federal agency responsible for operations in a given jurisdiction might well be the contracting agency. For instance, the Navy may best be able to operate the program for education of Navy dependents on Guam. The important thing is that these children have an equal opportunity as compared with children on the Atomic Energy Commission projects or as compared with dependent children in Germany or Japan. The piecemeal legislation of the past should give way to a comprehensive over-all plan by which the Federal Government will step in when States and Territories are unwilling or unable so that many of these children cannot further be known as "educational orphans." The Federal Government should be first rather than last in recognizing its responsibility to children under its jurisdictions. In excess of $23,500,000 is budgeted for this purpose in fiscal 1949, through a variety of arrangements.

Such residue of the Lanham Act situations which may continue can also be brought into a general framework as suggested above.

EDUCATION OF INDIANS AND OTHER NATIVE PEOPLES

The Federal Government is engaged in furnishing elementary and secondary education to native peoples through several departments, at a total cost in fiscal 1949 of approximately $15,000,000. The Office of Indian Affairs in recent years has utilized the regular public schools

292

for the education of Indians to an increasing extent. It is believed that this policy should be encouraged.

The Fish and Wildlife Service of the Department of the Interior maintains schools for the inhabitants of the Pribilof Islands, the Navy for the children on Guam and certain other occupied islands, and the Department of the Interior has certain responsibilities for education in Puerto Rico, the Virgin Islands, and Hawaii. Thus, several agencies of the Government conduct schools for indigenous peoples or are basically responsible for such education. Under the present set-up there is little possibility that there can be a common policy for such education. Although it is realized that there should be much variation in educational programs for such peoples in terms of their local problems, special cultures, and other circumstances, it is assumed that one of the purposes of education is to bring them into accord with certain of the broader fundamentals of American tradition and civic responsibility. Hence there should be some policy common to these programs even though administration, particularly for the smaller groups, might be decentralized to the Federal agency concerned with more general operations in the areas involved.

It would be appropriate to establish an interdepartmental council, headed in the Federal educational agency, for this purpose. This agency should also be responsible for conducting periodic surveys and for the conduct of research in connection with these programs and activities. A satisfactory solution of all the educational problems of these peoples, with the great variation in circumstances which exist, cannot be immediately expected. It is believed essential, however, that there be coordination immediately and that infomation be made available periodically in order that we may develop even more effective programs for meeting our obligations to these peoples.

Federal Research and Leadership

The United States Office of Education is the only Federal agency which is concerned with the furnishing of general leadership and research service to the regular elementary and secondary schools in the States. The activities of the office exclusive of elementary and secondary education all fall under the classification of "administration" and may be considered as practically the only Federal activities which have concern for the general welfare, progress, and promotion of these schools generally throughout the country. Their support, in fiscal 1949 less than $500,000, constitutes a mere pittance in comparison with the total programs and cannot be expected to balance the large number of Federal activities which are involved with special phases of education, special groups of individuals, or special assistance to geographical areas. The moneys for these activities of the Office of Education are all expended on the Federal level for personal services, publications, travel, and so forth. Only 21 percent of the staff of the Office of Education is devoted to these three activities. If the Federal Government is to avoid being accused of favoritism to special interests and of encouraging imbalance in the elementary and secondary schools of the country, it is essential that it do more than is here evidenced to render general service for a balanced program of education and a balanced service in respect to educational problems to the schools generally throughout the country.

MISCELLANEOUS ACTIVITIES

Two Federal programs concerning elementary and secondary education are not readily identified with the classifications considered previously in this section. These are the support of American-sponsored schools in Latin America and the apprenticeship training program of the Department of Labor (cost in fiscal 1949: $2,615,000). While the former falls more appropriately into a report on the Department of State, it should be noted here that the 14 sponsored schools in Latin America which received over $170,000 in general support for elementary or secondary education in 1947 were given much more favorable fiscal treatment than the Federal Government has ever been willing to bestow generally for elementary and secondary schools in the United States. A private educational organization in this country, rather than the United States Office of Education, is responsible for the administration of this program. As for the apprenticeship training program, suffice it to say here that there should be much greater cooperation between this activity and the vocational education program, especially in terms of improving vocational guidance and instruction, developing a mutuality of interest, and insuring better coordination of these two programs at the State and local levels. Such coordination must be initiated at the Federal level.

One of the most startling educational phenomena of this decade is the tremendous growth of Federal utilization of the higher educational institutions of the land, public and private, for programs of research and specialized training both in the national interest and in the interest of special groups and special causes. It was only natural during the war that the rich technical and professional resources of these institutions should be devoted in large measure to war purposes. These resources, "discovered" during the emergency period, are being further exploited. This report analyzes the impact of these programs on higher education in the country at large.

Federal Activities Clearly Concerning Higher Education

RESEARCH

Nine departments or independent agencies of the Government through many more of their subagencies are making grants or entering into contracts for research through colleges and universities. Between 1947 and 1949 there was almost a doubling of Federal research funds through the colleges and universities of the country. Of the total of over $160,000,000 of Federal funds in 1949 for this type of activity, the major amount is expended on the college or university campuses and thus has to a considerable extent a definite effect on the programs of these institutions. Practically all this research is in technical or scientific areas.

Although there is no overt Federal effort to influence the course of higher education by these programs (indeed, many universities are probably acting more in the capacity of private contracting research organizations than as educational institutions), there is a definite lack of coordination between the colleges and the Federal agencies. In the interests of common policy and efficiency, measures to insure against unnecessary overlapping and duplication are essential. However, the national welfare justifies Federal participation in this kind of activity.

HIGHER EDUCATION OF SPECIAL GROUPS OF INDIVIDUALS AND INDIVIDUALS IN SPECIAL FIELDS OF STUDY

Federal programs for higher education of special groups and of individuals in special fields are increasing. Under this classification are placed the programs of assistance to such institutions as Howard University and St. Elizabeths Hospital, grants to States for public health training, support of certain resource development programs under the Tennessee Valley Authority, various fellowship grants, and most important, the extension services of the Department of Agriculture. That part of the total budget for these items which can be identified exceeds $56,000,000 in fiscal 1949. Of this, over $31,000,000 is allotted to the agricultural extension program. It is the preponderance of support granted to this last which causes concern. For many years the farm people of the country have been in a favored position in this respect. The current efforts of other groups, notably labor, to obtain support for similar programs leads to the conclusion that a dangerous tendency is in the making. Essentially the agricultural extension service is a program in the field of adult education. It would be unfortunate if the Federal Government were to build up, without integrating, several separate extension services, each for a special group in the population. Such a situation, aside from its relative unfairness to whatever sections of the population are omitted from consideration, would involve the dangers of partisanship, multiple administration, possibilities of overlapping, and kindred ills. Education, properly protected from partisanship, may be used as a unifying force in the development of our citizenry. Extension programs for specific groups in the population may have a place, but we also need programs which will enable our people to realize that there are important problems, aspirations, and understandings which concern the whole of our society. This problem goes to the roots of effective democratic life.

Special Types of State Higher Institutions

The Federal Government gives general support to two separate types of State higher educational institutions, the State maritime academies and the land-grant colleges, at an anticipated cost in fiscal 1949 of approximately $6,500,000. The duplication which results from the maintenance of Federal and State merchant marine academies may not be warranted. Perhaps State maritime academies have outlived their usefulness and should either be taken over by the Federal Government or the activities of the State maritime academies should be consolidated into the more general training programs of the United States Maritime Commission. The State contribution to these academies is relatively small as compared with the Federal contribution. Thus there is little for the Government to lose financially and there may be much to gain in unification.

The general support for resident instruction in the land-grant colleges administered by the Office of Education is sometimes referred to as the most effective grant-in-aid made by the Federal Government. This, coupled with the generous endowment of these colleges by grants of Federal lands, has developed 69 colleges and universities in the States and territories many of which rank among our strongest institutions. The expenditures by States for these institutions are many, many times greater than the amount of Federal support. The grants having been quite general in nature involve practically no administration on the Federal level. With minor exceptions the Federal grants have been well administered by the States. We have here an illustration that a rather general cause in the field of education can be supported by the Federal Government without undue Federal controls. A question may be raised as to whether this financial grant has outlived its usefulness. As an incentive this support is no longer needed. The majority of these institutions could carry on without it. In some of the more poverty-stricken States and territories, however, the income from this source is essential to the proper operations of the institutions. Also to withdraw such funds at this time would in effect be a penalty for good administration. Out of fairness to all concerned, these grants should be continued.

GENERAL SERVICE AND RESEARCH

The Federal Government expends many hundreds of millions of dollars each year through higher educational institutions for special types of research, education of special groups of individuals, fellowships in special phases of the curriculum, for the pre- or in-service training of Government personnel, and for exchange of students and professors in the international interest. Yet the only clear-cut case of Federal interest in the general and well-rounded development of the higher institutions of the land is limited in 1949 to the $167,000 which it has made available for the support of the Division of Higher Education in the United States Office of Education. That the support of this division of the office has more than doubled in the last 2 years is encouraging. That the amount is so small in relationship to the vast amount expended through these institutions for special causes and groups, raises the question as to whether it can be effective as a balancing force to the higher institutions of the land. The Federal Government having supported so many specialized activities in higher institutions owes them more regard for their general interest.

EDUCATION AND TRAINING FOR GOVERNMENT SERVICE

There are in operation 14 separate programs, under Federal auspices, designed to offer pre- or in-service training for Government service through the regular colleges and universities. There has been a very marked increase in the use of the colleges and universities for pre- or in-service education and training between the years 1940 and 1949; the cost of such programs has risen from a 1940 figure of over $4,500,000 to an expected outlay of just under $34,000,000 in fiscal 1949. The bulk of the funds used for this purpose are spent for the officer training programs of the armed services. Programs of this nature, particularly when implemented by highly selective recruitment methods and subsequent scholarships, point up the fact that there is a competition for the brains of America to an extent hitherto unknown. It is important for the well-rounded growth of America that no one individual group or calling be given too great an advantage in this competition. The Federal Government should reexamine its programs to make sure that it does not draw off unwarranted proportions of talent into specialized fields.

INTERNATIONAL INTEREST

Federal educational activities involving international elements and collaboration of colleges and universities consist in the main of the

297

program of cooperation with other governments in the exchange of students and professors, and the Fulbright program. Although the sums of money spent are relatively small (approximately $900,000 in fiscal 1949), these programs raise specialized and complex problems for the higher institutions of the country. Their complexity is increased by the fact that administrative responsibility is shared by several Federal agencies working through the private Institute for International Education.

FEDERALLY OPERATED HIGHER INSTITUTIONS

The Federal Government operates several higher educational institutions of its own, in addition to its work through those outside. These are: The Military, Naval, Coast Guard, and Merchant Marine Academies, the graduate schools of the National Bureau of Standards and the Department of Agriculture, and a postgraduate school for naval personnel. Institutions of this nature which confine themselves to in-service training pertinent to the work of the sponsoring institution raise no broad problem. This is not the case, however, with such an agency as the Graduate School of the Department of Agriculture, which serves a student body composed as follows: 14 percent from Agriculture; 74 percent from other Federal agencies, and the remainder from outside Government. The courses of study are not confined to agricultural subjects, but run the gamut of the humanities, the natural, and the social sciences.

Is this the beginning of a national university? Over the years when the matter has been discussed Congress has always thought it would be contrary to good public policy to have a national university. Are there regularly organized universities in the Washington area which can care for the in-service and general cultural needs of the clientele now served by the Graduate School of the Department of Agriculture? This report does not attempt an answer to these questions. Insofar as this Graduate School serves the in-service training needs of personnel of the Department of Agriculture it is to be commended. The fact that much of its work is beyond that which is specifically of the Department of Agriculture raises doubts regarding its function and place in the Federal structure.

It is suggested that consideration be given to a plan whereby the needs for in-service training of a graduate nature in fields related to the activities of the various departments of the government be centralized in the Civil Service Commission with coordination and assistance from the Division of Higher Education of the Office of Education. In such a plan, general cultural education and whatever areas of technical and scientific study are already well developed by regular higher institutions in the Washington area, may well be cared for by those institutions.

298

An evaluation of the academies of the Army and Navy, Coast Guard, and Maritime Commission is not undertaken in this section of the Commission report. It may be pointed out, however, that the general tendency throughout higher education in this country is to devote the first 4 years of college to more generalized and basic studies of the curriculum leaving professional training for graduate work or at least to the last 2 undergraduate years. There may be some merit in reviewing the programs of these academies in this respect with the possibility of unifying the earlier years of study. This might help to develop a national defense force better able to think in terms of the total defense needs rather than in terms of the separatist tradition of individual departments of the National Military Establishment.

In passing, the question is raised as to whether there may be unnecessary overlapping between certain basic training in seamanship offered by the Navy, the Coast Guard Academy, and the Merchant Marine Academies. Because of their close relationship particularly in time of national defense emergency, the possibility of unifying at least a portion of the program should be seriously reviewed.

Federal Activities Covering All Levels of Education

This section deals with a number of important Federal programs which affect all levels of education. These include education of veterans, institutional on-farm training, vocational and physical rehabilitation, and education in nonmilitary subjects within the military establishment.

EDUCATION OF SPECIAL GROUPS OF INDIVIDUALS

Activities in the category of the education of special groups of individuals at all levels of education through the regularly constituted educational institutions of the country, include the programs for the education of veterans under Public Laws 16 and 346 administered by the Veterans' Administration, and the program for the rehabilitation of disabled persons in educational institutions, administered by the Office of Vocational Rehabilitation in the Federal Security Agency.

Education of Veterans

The programs for education of veterans under Public Laws 346 and 16 are so well known that it is unnecessary to devote a detailed description to these activities. These programs are among the most significant ventures in education that the Federal Government has ever undertaken. Their commendable reception by the public at large, by educational institutions, and by veterans is testimony to their value.

299

A few features of these programs are noted, however: (*a*) the sums devoted to these purposes constitute the majority of the total Federal funds for all educational purposes, a figure of roughly 3 billion dollars in 1948; (*b*) the average enrollment of veterans for the months of February through April 1948 increased more than 600,000 over the average enrollment for 1947. Institutional on-farm enrollment increased 136 percent for the same period, enrollment in noncollegiate institutions rose 65 percent, schools of higher learning increased enrollments by 30 percent, while on-the-job training enrollment dropped by 9 percent; (*c*) almost 5.5 million veterans, approximately half of whom were in training on April 30, 1948, have taken advantage of these programs.

It is important to add that there has sometimes been a wide disparity between the purpose of Public Law 346 and the actual practice in this program, particularly with respect to much of the training given in school courses below the college level. For example, huge sums have been expended under the law for such things as sport flying, ballroom dancing, hobby photography, and other training in fields offering few vocational opportunities compared to the number of veterans enrolled. This situation was partially corrected by the 1949 Supplemental Independent Offices Appropriation Act which passed Congress in June of 1948. By this, expenditures are eliminated for courses determined by the Administrator of Veterans' Affairs to be avocational or recreational in character, except that flight courses elected for use in the veteran's occupation or contemplated occupation are not to be considered avocational or recreational. Also limitations were placed upon profit schools in which the majority of the enrollment consists of veterans.

In our effort to keep the Federal Government from exercising any control over the standards and purposes of education in States we have permitted abuses to arise. We are now attempting by a process of negation to eliminate the worst of these abuses. It would seem that the Federal Government has a greater right to demand minimal standards than has previously been evidenced in this program.

Institutional On-Farm Training

The institutional on-farm training program for veterans under Public Law 346, as amended, is deserving of special mention due to a number of its rather distinctive features. Certain planning for this program was made in coordination with the Division of Vocational Education of the United States Office of Education. Considerable responsibility is placed on States and in most cases the State boards for vocational education have assisted with the program. The Veterans' Administration reimburses the States, and through them the local areas, or reimburses local areas directly, for conducting the program at an agreed cost which is found to be fair and reasonable, including a fair and reasonable allowance for administrative costs. In 32 of the States, as of June 30, 1948, agreements were in existence between the Veterans' Administration and the State boards for vocational education (or other designated State agencies) for the operation of the program. In other States, the agreements were with local boards of education or individual schools. Such administration and supervision as is done by staff under the Federal program of vocational education is not reimbursable from Veterans' Administration funds.

In some instances the local high-school agriculture teachers assist with the program, but the more prevalent plan is to employ special vocational agriculture teachers for this purpose. Some 11,000 special teachers are currently employed by local boards of education throughout the country for this purpose. The usual ratio is 1 teacher for each 20 trainees. These teachers conduct the 200 hours of classroom instruction required of each trainee per year and the added and related 100 hours of on-the-farm instruction required for the self-employed veteran or 50 hours required for the employed enrollee. In some States each self-employed trainee must develop a plan for his farm, to be approved by a special council in each county. (In June 1948, 90 percent of veterans under this program were self-proprietors—that is, managers of farms they own or on which they are tenants.) On this council the various interests, including the county agricultural agent (U. S. Department of Agriculture extension program), representatives of the program for vocational education, and leading farmers, are represented. Here the assistance of the various local and Federal agencies dealing with related problems are enlisted and coordinated. This is an excellent example of coordination which might well be extended to other areas of Federal concern. The effort is not so much in the direction of defining areas of action and of defending those areas as it is in the direction of attempting to locate means and implementations for strong mutual support of a program. Rather than an overlapping of jurisdictions, there is coordinated and beneficial support.

General

The vocational rehabilitation program of the Federal Security Agency is involved with many activities outside of the field of education. Since 1943 its emphasis has changed from vocational reeducation to physical rehabilitation or restoration. Insofar as the programs of this section of our report have concerned or operated through the regularly constituted educational institutions of the country, they have been highly effective both in the interests of the institutions and in the national interest.

Except for a few matters mentioned above and which primarily involve profit institutions, these programs should continue much in their present form. There are those who have felt that the Veterans' Administration has curtailed States' rights in education by its procedure in dealing directly with educational institutions. Were this program primarily concerned with the secondary or elementary schools of the country, for which all States have a central control or operating staff, there would be merit in this objection. Very few States, however, have any over-all centralized State offices for dealing with higher educational institutions and even when such exist they have little or no control over private higher educational institutions. On the higher educational level particularly, these private institutions constitute a very definite part and parcel of the regularly constituted higher educational program of the land. Thus we know of no currently available means whereby the bulk of the program of veteran education and its administration could have been decentralized to the States. In fact, authority to approve schools which has been delegated to States has been the basic cause of the major difficulties which this program has encountered. The blame for this should not be placed upon the States, however, but rather on the Federal Government for not having previously set minimal standards for the selection of those educational institutions through which veterans might be educated.

"CIVILIAN" EDUCATION OF THE NATIONAL MILITARY ESTABLISHMENT

Among the many interesting and valuable educational contributions of World War II has been the growth of education similar to that offered in our regular institutions of the country by the armed forces. This has been motivated by several conditions. In the modern type of military training and procedure the general educational level and the competency of individuals is an important factor. The opportunity to gain general educational advancement is an added incentive to enlistment. And beyond this, credit should be given to our military leaders for their desire to raise the educational level of society at large. In the long run the effectiveness of the military forces is closely allied with the effectiveness of individuals throughout the country.

The Armed Forces Institute is operated for the benefit of the Army, Air Force, Navy, and Marine Corps. Available for this service in fiscal 1949 is well over $4,000,000. Its over-all educational policies are determined by a committee of leading civilian educators and Army and Navy officers. Its correspondence courses, many of them prepared by leading educational institutions in the country, cover a broad variety of subjects at all levels of education. These programs are to be commended. They are in line with good military policy as well as good general social policy. Their continued support is highly warranted.

While the Office of Education contains divisions concerned with particular levels or phases of education, a large part of its general administrative budget must be considered as applying to all levels. This Office is also involved in the intergovernmental exchange of students and teachers program at all levels. The Navy, responsible for the general education of the natives of Guam and other island areas, provides certain facilities for higher education as well. The Department of Justice is concerned with the academic and vocational education of Federal prisoners. In a few instances, the Federal Government contributes financial support to certain private educational corporations—that is, the Columbia Institute for the Deaf and the American Printing House for the Blind.

The unique place of these two last-mentioned institutions in American life and in meeting the needs of special groups therein warrant continued Federal support. Were this support withdrawn, definite curtailment of essential services would result. Each institution, to a considerable extent, serves people from all parts of the country.

There is no indication within the activities of this classification of overlapping jurisdictions or of other matters which should concern this report. One might raise the question as to whether the professional staff of the Office of Education and particularly the Division of Vocational Education could be of assistance in advisement in connection with the education of Federal prisoners. It is assumed that if such assistance is needed, the Department of Justice should initiate the request.

Federal Activities Not Concerning Regular Institutions

A number of Federal educational or training activities, concerned with in-service programs for Federal personnel and the education or training of non-Federal employees in specialized fields of study not normally in the curriculum of the regular schools of the country, clearly do not concern the regularly constituted schools and colleges. The close relationship of these to education and the fact that the methods and materials of education are used in these warrants their inclusion here.

IN-SERVICE EDUCATION AND TRAINING FOR GOVERNMENT SERVICE

A listing of the more formal in-service training activities of the Federal Government—activities which do not concern the regular schools of the country—would indicate 36 such programs currently in operation under 11 Government agencies. The 36 programs are distributed as follows: One each for the Department of State, Army (including 38 service schools, etc.), Veterans' Administration, Interstate Commerce Commission, Tennessee Valley Authority, and Railroad Retirement Board; 2 each for the Departments of Justice, Commerce, and Interior; 4 each for the Treasury Department and the Federal Security Agency; 6 under the Air Force; and 10 under the Navy.

We have already noted many programs of the pre- or in-service nature which utilized the higher institutions of the land. When is it more desirable to utilize these or other already existing institutions? When is it more desirable for the Government to operate its own programs for education and training? A comprehensive study to find the answers to these questions should be made. Similarly, answers are needed to such questions as: Is there needless overlapping at some points in these activities? Could consolidations, as for instance in certain common training areas of the Army, Navy, and Air Force, be effected to advantage? Is there a possibility that a Federal educational agency could furnish desirable professional services in planning these programs, thus increasing effectiveness and eliminating necessity for duplicating professional staff in education? For instance, is it necessary or desirable to have technical staff and facilities for the production of training films and other audio-visual aids in several agencies of the Government? The same question might apply to other fields, including that of subject matter and psychological tests and measurements for personnel and training uses. What might be the role of the agency having major over-all responsibility for Federal personnel policies and administration in these regards? It is believed that research on such questions as these may be of assistance in obtaining higher effectiveness in the Government service as well as in eliminating unnecessary overlapping of staff and services.

PROGRAMS PRIMARILY FOR NON-FEDERAL EMPLOYEES

Similarly, the Federal Government has embarked on a number of specialized programs primarily for the education and training of individuals for non-Federal service. Examples of this type of activity are the National Police Academy of the Department of Justice, the Yosemite Field School of Natural History in the National Park Service, and the coal mine safety program under the Department of the Interior's Bureau of Mines.

Practically all these programs train personnel in fields close to the national interest. The existence of a well-manned merchant fleet is a national concern at all times, and particularly so in times when national defense needs are paramount. A coal mine disaster is always a matter of grave national concern. The proper policing of the country, and the coordination of crime investigation activities between local, State, and Federal agencies is a concern of all. To have properly trained medical and public health personnel generally available is important to the welfare of the people of the country. Important as these are, why stop here? An adequate supply of individuals capable and skilled in the building of homes is currently important for the national welfare. The national welfare is also very close to our effectiveness in having capable and skilled individuals to teach in our schools, to man our railroads, to transmit our communications, to assess our taxable property, to sell us our food, to supply us with proper clothes, and to conduct a myriad of other activities and services which concern us as individuals or as a collective body of individuals. It is apparent that to carry this policy of Federal training of non-governmental employees to its logical conclusion would create a paternalistic state. The policy is correct that the Federal Government should train nongovernmental employees in fields not available in our regularly constituted institutions of the country which are closely allied with the national defense. Beyond this, we are less certain. A strong democratic nation must have strength in the grass roots of its individuals, communities, and States. Insofar as Federal activities help build strength and initiative here, they serve the cause of democracy. Insofar as they tend to develop a paternalistic federalism they antagonize our basic philosophy of government. While mindful of the welfare of individuals and of the varied interests in the Nation, we must guard against the paternalistic approach. The method by which these activities are carried out may be the crux of the situation. A maximum of responsibility must be placed on the individual, the community and the State.

Nonbudgetary Federal Assistance to Educational Institutions

In addition to the fiscal budget activities which are operated by and under the executive departments, the Federal Government has rendered considerable assistance to education in nonbudgetary items, particularly in the post-World War II years. For example, during approximately 2 years to May 1948, surplus property (land, equipment, etc.) initially valued at $646,663,358 was made available to educational institutions by the War Assets Administration, Army, Navy, and Air Force, with the cooperation of the United States Office of Education. Also, under the veterans' educational facilities program, there has been or will be made available to educational institutions where need has been certified by the United States Office of Education a total of 16,534,000 square feet of buildings, the title to which passes to the institutions. Veterans' housing at educational institutions has been provided by the Housing and Home Finance Agency (previously the National Housing Agency) in cooperation with local agencies which provide site, development of streets, sidewalks, trunk utilities, and management. The McGregor Act (Public Law 796), which passed the Eightieth Congress on June 20, 1948, generously made an outright gift to educational institutions of all veterans housing which had been built on land belonging to them. It is estimated that by this act some 129,000 housing units were given to colleges and universities, who were thereafter to receive all rentals therefrom.

Federal Activities Tangential to Education

In the study of Federal services to education, some mention should be made of Federal libraries and Federal library services.

Many of these services are beyond the scope of the Commission's work since they involve activities of the legislative branch of the Federal Government, but the executive branch does assist school, college, and public libraries in many ways and Federal libraries have a profound effect upon library programs throughout the Nation.

The bibliographic services of the Department of Agriculture, the Army Medical Library, the Department of Commerce, and the publications of the various departments are eagerly sought by libraries as educational tools. In turn, many Federal libraries and Federal research programs are strengthened through the cooperation of outside libraries. The primary need in this field is correlation of these services and the establishment of standard procedures.

It is quite possible that greater cooperative use of libraries as distributing agencies for Government publications would increase the publications' effectiveness and eliminate much waste in their use.

The Service to Libraries Section of the Office of Education should assume leadership in the solution of such problems. However, until it is able to establish itself more firmly both financially and in the esteem of officials, it is not likely to be able to do so.

The History of Noncontinuing Emergency Federal Activities in Education, 1933–46

During the emergency periods of the depression and World War II, the Federal Government undertook a number of temporary educational projects, several of which were in marked contrast with previous national policy in respect to education. Certain other of these Federal activities are significant in extending policy as previously developed. A few of these projects are described in this section in the belief that certain lessons may be gained therefrom which will serve as guides to future educational participation and organization by the Federal Government.

Educational Activities Originating as Relief Measures During the Depression Period.

The Civilian Conservation Corps

The first Federal agency to deal with the problem of aggravated youth unemployment was the Civilian Conservation Corps, established in 1933. This was strictly a Federal project with practically no State or local educational participation. Although initially conceived primarily as a relief and conservation measure, it soon became evident that its work must of necessity be educational. Within a matter of months after the initiation of the Corps, the assistance of the United States Office of Education was enlisted in the establishment of an educational program. With new legislation in 1937, more prominence was given to the educational aspects of the program.

The technical details of this program were formulated and recommended by the United States Commissioner of Education, who appointed area, district, and camp educational advisers responsible to the military commanders at each level. With the multitude of cooperating Federal agencies and the high degree of coordination necessary, it is noteworthy that relatively little operational criticism has been made of the CCC program. On July 1, 1939, the CCC was placed under the Federal Security Agency, and in 1942 Congress provided that the Corps should be liquidated not later than June 30, 1943.

The National Youth Administration

The NYA was established in 1935 and was liquidated by January 1, 1944. Its purpose was to provide work training for unemployed youth and part-time employment for needy students so that they might continue their education. The NYA was strictly a federally operated and administered program. Most of its activities were involved either with: (a) Out-of-school work projects, or (b) student work projects. As both the NYA and the Office of Education were conducting programs involved with national defense training, considerable conflict in jurisdiction developed, culminating in an agreement signed by the administrators of each program in July of 1940. This friction stemmed primarily from the fact that the NYA established federally operated schools in some cases paralleling local facilities, and without coordination through existing State educational agencies. This led to the claim that the program was an infringement on the prerogatives of the regularly constituted educational system, and that it developed a needless duplication of facilities.

Miscellaneous Federal Educational Activities During the Depression

It is difficult, and, furthermore, unnecessary, to enumerate all the emergency educational activities of the Federal Government which were initiated during the depression period. Two programs illustrative of policy and procedure, the Works Progress Administration and the Public Works Administration, should be mentioned. The administrative relationship, with the previously existing educational agencies, both on the Federal level and in States and communities, varied, but in general it may be said that these existing agencies were by-passed. Usually the projects were conducted by noneducational Federal agencies directly with communities or local school systems.

Educational Activities for National Defense and War

It became evident as early as 1938 that the educational resources of the Nation were essential to prepare for defense. During the next few years many emergency educational programs were initiated or expanded by Federal agencies, and the schools and colleges of the country went through a reconversion to equip men and women for adequate participation in the war effort. The Military Establishment developed the largest program of adult education this country had ever known.

Major Defense and War Activities of the United States Office of Education

1. *Vocational training of war production workers.*—In the interval between April 1939 and May 1940 the Office of Education and Army representatives made an inventory of the equipment and training capacity of the public vocational schools of the Nation, anticipating that these schools might be a major factor in training skilled workers for the defense industries. On June 27, 1940, $15,000,000 was appropriated for the purpose of operating the defense training program. Plans had been so well laid that by July 1, 1940, hundreds of vocational schools were in operation under this program, with enrollments of approximately 75,000 trainees during the month.

The program was administered by using the same channels and organization available for the Federal-State cooperative program of vocational education, with such expansions in personnel as needed. The Office of Education administered the Federal phases of this activity, dealing through the State boards for vocational education with the vocational schools in local school systems.

The Federal Government paid the cost of instruction, and equipment was to be purchased only after specific proposals were approved by the Office of Education. States contributed use of previously available buildings and equipment and services of certain types of personnel. During the 5 years during which the program operated, $296,703,- 139.34 of Federal money was distributed to the States for operation of the program. There was considerable evidence of close cooperation with industry and with other governmental agencies in the conduct of this program.

2. *Rural war production training program.*—This program was inaugurated in October 1940 by Public Law 812 of the Seventy-Sixth Congress, third session. Initially concerned with training of farm youth not needed on farms in elementary skills sufficient to enable them to secure employment in defense industries, the program soon changed emphasis to production of food crops. More than 8,000 local secondary schools, through their departments of vocational education, participated in the program.

The administration of this activity was by the Office of Education through the State boards for vocational education, as in the case of the defense training program described above. Federal sums appropriated were $63,000,000 for the slightly less than 5 years during which the program operated. The actual expenditure was well within this figure.

3. *Engineering, science, and management war training.*—This program, established in October of 1940, utilized the facilities of the colleges and universities of the country to train technical specialists for the defense and war effort just as the vocational schools were used in training workers. The activity was administered by the United States Office of Education, and, as far as possible, the responsibility was decentralized to participating colleges and universities. The Federal Government expended nearly $60,000,000 on the program between its initiation and its close on June 30, 1945.

4. *Student war loans program.*—In order to bolster the diminishing supply of available persons in various professions, the Congress in 1942 authorized $5,000,000 for loans to students engaged in professional preparation. The accelerated program in colleges and universities had demanded the full time of students, making it practically impossible for them to be employed while studying. Loan funds were allocated to approved institutions by formula, and much of the administration was delegated by the Office of Education to the institutions.

Selected Defense and War Activities of Noneducational Federal Agencies.

1. *Educational activities under the Lanham Act.*—Although activity under this program had not yet entirely ceased in fiscal 1949, the program is included here because it was war-incurred and is generally conceded to be nonpermanent.

The Lanham Act [1] of 1941 provided for financial aid to communities where the presence of a war-incurred Federal activity had created financial burdens which the community could not be expected to bear.

---

[1] 55 Stat. 361.

Under this authority, considerable educational aid has been given. The act was preceded by a study made by the United States Office of Education, through State departments of education, at the request of the War and Navy Departments. From 1941 to June 30, 1947, a total of more than $187,000,000 was spent on programs of: (1) School construction and equipment; (2) school maintenance and operation assistance; and (3) child care.

Administration of the act was vested in the Federal Works Agency. Responsibility for advising on all educational phases of the program was given to the United States Office of Education. The Federal Works Agency undertook to deal directly with local school districts rather than through State agencies. Shortly after the program started, State educational officials objected to this practice, claiming that distribution of assistance was not always in accord with priority of war-incurred need. As a result, an amending act of 1943 [2] specified that no funds for education should be expended without prior consultation with the United States Office of Education and the State department of education involved. The final determination of allocation of funds remained with the Federal Works Agency, however, and in many instances the recommendations of these educational agencies were not followed. With the end of the war, the United States Office of Education terminated its part in the program.

a. *School construction program.*—Federal funds were used to finance, in whole or in part, the construction of new school buildings. Those financed entirely by the Government were federally owned (and leased without cost to school districts), while those largely financed locally were turned over to the school districts.

b. *Maintenance and operation assistance.*—Funds were provided to compensate school districts for education of children living on nontaxable Federal reservations, and in temporary war housing when Federal payments in lieu of taxes were insufficient to meet costs. In other localities where the tax base was reduced by Federal purchase of land and facilities and where there had been an influx of war workers, funds were made available for the operation of schools. Nursery schools to provide for the children of mothers working in war industry were also operated with funds from this act.

c. *Child care program.*—The primary purpose of the child care program under the Lanham Act was the provision of facilities for the children of working mothers in order that more women workers might become available for war activity.

Since the war this activity under the Lanham and subsequent acts has been diminishing. However, in 1947, $6,688,722 was obligated in

---

[2] 57 Stat. 565.

aid to these schools.   Schools in Georgia were provided with $1,090,-585, while schools in 19 States and Territories received no funds.   In 1949, $3,000,000 is available for this program.

2. *Miscellaneous activities affecting colleges and universities.*— Space does not permit a detailed description of the numerous war activities of the Federal Government which were carried out through the colleges and universities of the country.   A few are only very briefly mentioned here.

Many colleges and universities throughout the country were under contract with the Civil Aeronautics Authority of the Department of Commerce to train pilots subsequent to the passing of the Civilian Pilot Training Act of 1939.[3]   The CAA reimbursed these institutions on a full cost-of-instruction basis for courses in ground school subjects and for flight training.   The purposes of this program were to provide a reservoir of pilots to supplement in time of emergency the trained personnel of the military forces and to stimulate private flying.   After June 1942 the trainees were limited to military personnel.

Early in the war the Army Specialized Training Program was established, utilizing the staffs and facilities of about 200 colleges and universities across the country.   Enlisted men were sent by the Army to these institutions to pursue studies in engineering, medicine, chemistry, linguistics, mathematics, physics, and other fields, in combination with other regular liberal studies of the curriculum.   The program was based on long-range social needs as well as upon immediate military needs.   Under the ASTP, the enlisted men received regular Army pay, food, clothes, books, and rooms, and the Army paid tuition to the colleges and universities.

Several other programs with certain similarities to the ASTP were in operation, including the Navy College Training Program, Army Air Forces College Training, and Navy Air Forces Program.   On October 1, 1943, these 4 programs enrolled 212,528 men in 628 colleges and universities.

Many higher institutions of the country were used directly by the military forces for training units in specialized fields such as military government.   Other institutions were under contract to furnish specialized instruction such as for Army Air Forces weather officers.

The Armed Forces Institute, a large correspondence school operated for both the Army and Navy, gave courses in supplemental military instruction and in regular high-school and college subjects.

Following 1943, a Public Health Service subsidized individuals to train as nurses.

Extensive and invaluable research projects were conducted with Federal support, a total of $82,255,493 of Federal moneys being spent

---

[3] 53 Stat. 855.

through universities and colleges for this purpose during the 18 months following March 1943.

Without further illustrations or elaboration, suffice it to state that all major higher institutions of the country, and many smaller ones, were deeply involved in the war enterprise. The Federal Government found the resources of the colleges and universities of the country invaluable in the war effort. Without detracting from the value of this entire program in its large contribution to the war, it must be stated that without these Federal projects many of these higher institutions would have been hard pressed to maintain their programs. A number of the projects, either openly or tacitly, were designed to make it possible, with Federal support, for the higher institutions of the country to survive the period of low enrollments of the war period. This became a matter of Federal concern.

Chapter III

THE UNITED STATES OFFICE OF EDUCATION

Although the Office of Education plays a relatively minor role in the total educational enterprise of the country, in terms of personnel, salaries, and operating responsibilities, yet it is of major importance as the sole Federal agency concerned with over-all problems of educational policy and administration. Its organization and role must be considered in any treatment of Federal educational policy or organization. The following brief description of its history, mission, and structure gives the essential background.

History

The mid-1800's saw a heightened interest in public education in the States which was greatly stimulated by the Civil War and its aftermath. The limitations on the effectiveness of the several States in building an adequate educational system when working independently became increasingly apparent to educators and statesmen alike. The desirability of a national educational headquarters, which would study educational problems and collect and disseminate educational information, became increasingly apparent.

As a result, early in 1866 Representative Garfield of Ohio introduced a bill to establish a department of education in the Federal Government. The congressional debates which followed clearly indicated the desire to refrain from any centralization of educational authority in the Federal Government which might infringe upon the basic responsibilities of States. The opinion was expressed that the Federal interest would be furthered, as better education in the States would be a factor in preventing a recurrence of such a disaster as the Civil War. It was felt that no educated people would be led into revolt.

The bill passed Congress by a narrow majority and was signed in March of 1867. It specified a Department of Education, without Cabinet rank, for the purpose of . . .

. . . collecting such statistics and facts as shall show the condition and progress of education in the several States and Territories, and of diffusing such information respecting the organization and management of schools and school systems, and methods of teaching, as shall aid the people of the United States in the establishment and maintenance of efficient school systems, and otherwise promote the cause of education throughout the country.[1]

It further specified that the President should appoint a commissioner of education to receive $4,000 per year and, among other things, that the commissioner should report to Congress each year "the results of his investigations and labors, together with a statement of such facts and recommendations as will, in his judgment, subserve the purpose for which this department is established."

In the following year, Congress changed the name of the new agency to Office of Education, and placed it in the Department of the Interior, where it remained until July 1, 1939. On that date it was transferred to the Federal Security Agency. In 1870 the agency was renamed the Bureau of Education, and was so known until the name Office of Education was restored in 1929.

It will be noted from the basic act establishing the Office of Education as quoted above, its initial purposes were to: (1) Collect statistics and facts to show the condition and progress of education; (2) diffuse information to aid in the establishment and maintenance of efficient school systems; and (3) otherwise promote the cause of education throughout the country. These are still considered to be the primary mission of the office. They are attained through research, service, and leadership, which should continue to be the major means by which the office accomplishes its mission.

The Congress from time to time, however, has placed administrative responsibility for new or expanding activities in the Office of Education. A few of these are worthy of mention: (1) Responsibility for the education of native children of Alaska, 1885 to 1931; (2) responsibility for the administration of the fiscal grants for resident instruction in land-grant colleges, 1890 to date; (3) administration and supervision of the program of aid to States for vocational education (Smith-Hughes Act of 1917), 1933 to date; (4) since 1933, the administration of certain phases of several programs, such as the CCC, the NYA, the training of war production workers, the disposition of surplus properties to educational institutions, the provision of facilities for the education of veterans, and in the international exchange of persons.

While these activities have demonstrated the flexibility of the Office in meeting continuing or emergency needs of the country, they have involved it in activities secondary to its historical mission. However, the Office has always been a champion of the rights of the States to develop their educational programs, and has insisted, whenever possible, that programs operate by placing initiative and responsibility on State school systems and on individual institutions of higher learning. The degree to which administrative detail can be carried on

---

[1] 14 Stat. 434.

without undue interference with the major responsibilities of research, service, and leadership is a matter of concern which will be treated later in this report.

The Office of Education is currently organized in accord with recommendations made by the Commissioner in 1944. These recommendations were made on the assumption that:

The United States Office of Education should be strengthened and reorganized in order that it may be prepared to do its indispensable part in giving national leadership and assistance to the educational systems and institutions of the several States and their local communities in meeting the long-term educational demands of the postwar period.[2]

SUMMARY OF BROAD FUNCTIONS OF A FEDERAL OFFICE OF EDUCATION

In sum, bearing clearly in mind that the control and administration of education are State and local functions, and assuming that a spirit of cooperation and mutual helpfulness continues to exist between the States and the Federal Government in the field of education, the broad functions which the United States Office of Education should be prepared to carry on will include:

1. The collection of information with respect to education in the States and in other countries so as to make possible intelligent comparisons and conclusions regarding the efficiency of educational programs.

2. The formulation and recommendation of minimum educational standards which ought to be made to prevail in the schools and colleges of all the States and the preparation of suggested proposals and plans for improving various educational practices, arrived at by cooperative planning among private and public educational organizations and lay groups, such recommendations and proposals to be influential only if their merit and appropriateness warrant voluntary acceptance by the States and institutions.

3. The provision of services of a national character that cannot well be undertaken by single States acting alone, e. g., the collection, interpretation, and dissemination of national statistics, the conduct of national and other important surveys, the convening of conferences of national significance.

4. Pointing out desirable educational ends and procedures, evaluating educational trends, and giving educational advice and discriminating praise.

5. The offering of consultative services to States, school systems, and higher educational institutions on problems of reorganization, finance, administration, and curriculum.

---

[2] Annual Report of the United States Office of Education for the Fiscal Year 1944, Federal Security Agency, Washington, D. C., 1945, p. 67.

6. The coordination of Government activities relating to education through schools and colleges.

In all such functions, it will be apparent that encouragement and stimulation rather than control are envisaged as the objectives of the Office of Education with respect to education in the States.[3]

Although the plan for reorganization was formally placed in effect, most divisions are still only partially staffed. In this connection, some criticism has been leveled at the Office for having too many top-flight specialists and administrators in proportion to individuals in lower positions. The Office has believed that, if it is to exercse real leadership and provide useful service to the schools of the Nation, it must have capable men and women on its staff. To this end, if only a few positions. The Office has believed that, if it is to exercise real leader-the case, an effort has been made to bring strong personnel to top positions. It is argued that to fill subordinate positions first would deny competent professional leadership and service to the States and unduly complicate personnel problems if more competent individuals were added at the top later. A tradition of relative incompetency, started early in the reorganization, would jeopardize the whole program. The Divisions of Secondary Education and of Higher Education are cases in point. The high-type individuals recently brought to leadership in these divisions, even though the subordinate staffs therein are as yet very small, have already demonstrated a degree of leadership and service to the schools of the country out of proportion to the size of these divisions. The Office has been generally justified in giving priority to the filling of top positions when its appropriations are insufficient to fill all positions which are encompassed in its long-range plans.

This reorganization places the activities of the Office in eight divisions. The Division of Elementary Education has for its purpose the development of a continuous program of service which will make for the improvement of the elementary-school programs throughout the country. The four subgroups of this division are devoted to elementary-school organization and supervision, teacher education, instructional problems, and exceptional children and youth. In May of 1948, no staff members were assigned to the subgroup for teacher education.

The Division of Secondary Education was created to serve the areas of secondary education not served by the Division of Vocational Education. This division, although still much smaller than the Division of Vocational Education, is making an effort to balance the services of the Office in respect to all aspects of secondary education. The three subgroups of the division are devoted to secondary-school organization and supervision, teacher education, and instructional problems.

---

[3]Annual Report of the United States Office of Education for the Fiscal Year 1944, Federal Security Agency, Washington, D. C., 1945, p. 75.

Again, by May of 1948 no staff members had been assigned to the subgroup for teacher education.

The Division of Higher Education is designed to serve the needs of colleges and universities. The three subgroups of the division are organization and administration, professional education, and arts and sciences education. This division is very sketchily staffed.

The Division of Vocational Education is by far the largest purely educational division of the Office as now constituted, employing some 80 individuals, over half of whom are professional personnel. This division is responsible for the administration of the Federal-State cooperative vocational educational program. Its subgroups are concerned with State-plans operations and program-planning operations, the latter being divided into agricultural education, trade and industrial education, home economics education, business education, and occupational information and guidance. In the spring of 1948 the function of auditing of Federal vocational funds in the States was transferred to the Federal Security Agency offices.

The Division of Central Services brings together in one division those services that are necessary to facilitate the operations of the Office of Education as a whole. Its subgroups are research and statistical service, information and publications, Office of Education library, and administrative management and services (internal "housekeeping" for the Office). In 1948, the Administrator of the Federal Security Agency moved the education library to the Federal Security Agency library and withdrew the information and publications section to the Agency over-all information and publications section.

The Division of International Educational Relations carries on activities designed to aid in interpreting United States life and culture through educational agencies abroad and to help our people understand and appreciate the life and civilization of other countries. Its subgroups are devoted to American Republics educational relations, European educational relations, British Empire educational relations, and Near and Far East educational relations. The last two have had no personnel.

The Division of Auxiliary Services brings together six units, representing somewhat diverse functions, as follows: Services to libraries; administration of school and college health services; school-community recreation; problems of school-lunch programs (which has no personnel); educational use of radio; and visual aids to education.

The Division of School Administration has for its purpose cooperation with the State and local educational authorities in formulating and carrying on essential studies and services in the field of school administration. Its subgroups, indicating something of its activities, are as follows: General administration; school finance; school legislation; school housing; and (educational) business administra-

317

tion. The last subgroup has no personnel and other subgroups are scantily staffed.

The Office of the Commissioner of Education has on its immediate staff one deputy commissioner, one associate commissioner, and five secretaries.

Possibly agreement on a more clear-cut role for the Office of Education would enhance its opportunities for better internal organization. If its historical role is to remain predominant, it is believed that a number of changes should be made. Actually, the child progresses by continuous growth throughout his school experience. Our most advanced school systems of the country have attempted to set up their administrative and supervisorial services to encourage rather than to impede consideration of this continuous-growth process. To this end they have organized their top administrative offices so that curriculum, for instance, is planned as a whole for both elementary and secondary schools. If we are to have articulation between levels of the school system, it is essential that research and advisement not be arbitrarily split. A form of organization based more on functional aspects might be preferable to one which duplicates and separates school organization and supervision, teacher education, and instructional problems into a Division of Elementary Education and a Division of Secondary Education.

A number of other questions should be raised relative to this organization, of which the following are illustrative. Is it desirable for the Division of Secondary Education to have separate specialists in organization and supervision for large high schools, and for small and rural high schools? Is it necessary, for instance, to have "reimbursable" home economics (with Federal vocational education assistance) problems referred to the Division of Vocational Education, while "nonreimbursable" (supported entirely from State and local sources) home economics problems are referred to the Division of Secondary Education? Why should the Division of School Administration deal with certain administrative problems, while others go to subgroups for School Organization and Supervision in the Division of Elementary and of Secondary Education? Is it necessary or desirable to have specialists in school health problems located in three divisions of the Office?

Three functions have recently been removed from the Office of Education to the central offices of the Administrator of the Federal Security Agency: Office of Education library, auditing of educational grants to States, and the information and publications service. If the results of this removal are to improve services to the schools of the land, such a move may have much to commend it. If, however, it is for the sole purpose of amassing more power for the sake of power in the office of the Administrator, it is to be condemned.

318

The Office of Education library is one of the outstanding libraries of this field. Its purpose is primarily to aid in the researches of the Office and to answer requests for assistance. Its librarians have been just as much research assistants and research bibliographers as they have been librarians. Its use as a research tool should be increased rather than diminished. Any sincere attempt to make library services more effective by centralization and amalgamation should be balanced against the possibility of interference with the primary function of this library.

In the auditing of educational grants to States, the primary one being that for vocational education, we believe that the major concern should be that the general and specific purposes for which the Federal moneys are granted be carried out by the States. Certainly the Government, in making grants, should ascertain that its moneys are being used for the purposes for which they were intended. The certified public accountant type of audit will not necessarily be satisfactory in this respect. By too great or limited focus on fiscal statements, it may easily overlook more fundamental considerations of the nature of the educational programs which are purchased by the funds. The Congress has been quite specific in defining the nature of the vocational educational program. If this policy is to continue, it is believed that the audit must be in terms of both fiscal and educational program factors. The Office of Education has responsibility for the administration of the vocational education program in cooperation with the States. It has a "know-how" in dealing with State educational agencies. It has the staff for evaluation of educational programs. It is doubtful whether administrative responsibility and audit responsibility for a professional program of this type can be separated at the Federal level. It is even more dubious whether the best educational interests of the Government and of the States would be favored by such a division of responsibility.

Much that has been said of the two previous activities could be restated for the information and publications service of the office. The diffusing of information about education is one of the major functions laid on the office by law. The degree to which the centralization of this function at the Federal Security Agency level increases or decreases the ability of the office to carry out its congressional mandate on a highly professional level will be the test as to whether this has been a wise move.

While discussing the Office of Education library it may be well to mention a related problem. Increasingly the Library of Congress, the Office of Education, and specialized agencies of the Government are being asked for educational information, bibliographical materials, and kindred services by educational institutions, other governmental agencies, specialized scholars, and other interested parties.

These inquiries cover the gamut of the specialized fields of the curriculum as well as professional education. Educational systems and approaches in foreign countries are of particular concern in recent years. The rich resources of the Federal Government in specialized staff and libraries should be available for this educational use.

The meager appropriations of the Office of Education library and the fact that the Library of Congress does not have an educational reference service, place limitations on each of these agencies in rendering the desired services to the educational institutions and scholars of the land. The spread of this specialized information throughout the Government complicates the matter. It is needless that specialized staff or specialized library be duplicated at one point in order to render such service. It is equally needless, in the best interests of educational institutions and scholars, to have uncoordinated and apparently hidden resources not available to them. This suggests that a central clearinghouse be established to which such educational inquiries may be directed, so that they can be directed to the best qualified agencies, libraries, and individuals in the Government. This function is well within the mission of the Office of Education to otherwise promote the cause of education throughout the country.

Services

The various researches, consultant services, responses to calls for assistance from local, State, and Federal agencies, and other activities of the Office of Education form an extensive array. To enumerate them, however, is not essential to this report which concerns itself more with over-all Federal policy and organization rather than that relatively small portion which is involved with the United States Office of Education. Our concern is more with the Federal educational agency as it should be within the total structure of Government than with it as it is and has been in its relatively submerged role. However, the range and extent of the services offered by the Office of Education are worth noting.

For the years 1945 to 1947, the office distributed some 400,000 copies of approximately 70 publications per year. Due to budgetary limitations there has been a proportionate decline in publications in recent years. The list of publications for 1947 and 1948 illustrates how inadequately this literature covers educational problems and developments.

Even though many publications on a large variety of educational subjects which have been printed in previous years are still in stock, the office reports the following as examples of subjects for which there is considerable demand but for which publications are not available;

History of education, crime prevention, safety and accident prevention, remedial reading, hobbies, music education, art education, research bibliographies (more recent than 1941), and school buildings.

Titles published during the past 2 years, although worth while, give the impression that the purpose to "otherwise promote the cause of education throughout the country" has been emphasized far more than collecting such statistics and facts as shall show the condition and progress of education in the several States and Territories. The promotion of the cause of education would be furthered more generally, and with less fear of Federal domination of education in the States, if more publications dealt with basic research. State and local school systems are now greatly concerned with such problems as the proper organization of State departments of education, State and local tax systems for the support of education, equitable methods of distributing State school funds, the teacher shortage, more democratic internal administration of schools, population trends as they concern education and schools, and the redistricting of school administrative areas. No recent comprehensive research publications are available from the office in these major and critical fields. Timely summaries of previous researches and current basic research on conditions in the various States in respect to these and kindred problems would prove invaluable to many of the States.

It is primarily through greater strength and more capable administration in education at the State and local level that we can avoid or reduce Federal controls in education. For instance, as long as there are States incapable of proper insight and organization in respect to their programs of vocational education, it is essential that rather tight Federal controls be maintained over that program if we are to have any assurance that Federal moneys in support of this program are to be utilized for the purpose for which intended by Congress. When States fail to provide adequate and essential educational programs and facilities, the natural tendency is to look to the Federal Government. More effort by the office to provide the research information and subsequent consultant service and leadership which will make education stronger and more effective at the State level is basic to our whole concept of the place of education in American life. The large and fundamental problems concerned with this consideration should be given more emphasis. In this case the Federal interest is served best by a greater concern for State and local strength.

Of the titles of publications during the past 2 years, five were devoted to education in other countries, while no publication generally gives facts regarding the condition and progress of education in the several States and Territories. Publications such as Cooperative Planning— A Key to Improved Organization of Small High Schools, Teaching as a Career, or FM in Education, although worthy, are more promotional than factual in their nature. We believe that it is more fundamental for the Office of Education to do comprehensive basic research in these areas. If the facts disclose definite needs which can be generally recognized as such by the States, the office may well enter the phase of promoting solutions. The office should be a rich reservoir of current and important factual data, collected from an impartial research point of view, pertaining to the very real problems which confront educational systems and institutions in the States. These then should be made available to the general public for major use in promotion of causes in education as individuals and groups outside the office may desire.

Requests have come to the office for unavailable publications in several curricular fields. While the final development of curriculum is not a proper Federal function, this does not preclude Federal service to the States, by publication of basic research or summaries of research concerning specific curriculum areas. For instance, textbooks or teachers' manuals relative to reading should not be developed by the office. There is, however, much research in this field which may not be generally available to State and local school authorities or to interested organizations or individuals. The office may well make these available. Actual classroom methods which by research standards indicate unusual progress of students in reading may be described. But any such materials should be to assist others in developing their own programs. Such influence as the office gives to the purpose and content of education should primarily be by impartial research, fact, and description.

The most effective ways by which the office can perform its research, leadership, and service functions are through publications and field contacts by members of its staff. In 1946, the appropriations for publications were practically the same as for 1925 although the purchasing power was much less in 1946. The amount for travel in 1930 was $79,534 and in 1948 was $91,500. Larger amounts for 1945, 1946, and 1947 were primarily due to war and immediate postwar special activities. Between 1935 and 1948 the professional staff of the office, that staff which should be turning out research for publication to diffuse information and be traveling throughout the country to otherwise promote the cause of education, was doubled. It would seem pennywise and pound-foolish to increase the professional personnel of the office, both in quantity and in quality, and at the same time deny the most potent means by which it can accomplish its mission.

A number of instances have been noted in which specialists of the office have been desired for consultant services on important educational projects or problems in the States, but such services were not available due to lack of travel funds, unless paid for from local sources. This is no loss to the wealthier localities, since the inevitable trend

322

is to utilize the services of specialists in the wealthier areas of the country and those closest to the national capital. Poorer areas and those further removed from Washington are in effect denied services which should be extended to all alike. The services then may be denied to those who need them most.

The effect of too small appropriations for publications and travel on the personnel of the office should also be considered. From time to time the complaint has been made that staff members of the office have been involved in too much busy work and administrative trivia. It is doubtful whether this complaint has a foundation in fact. However, this might well be the case when undue limitations are made upon the professional staff in respect to publications and field contacts. There is little incentive to do important research when its chances of subsequent publication and broad utilization are slight. There cannot be a wholehearted interest in the very real problems of education in the States unless one has a chance to work with these problems where they exist. There cannot be a zeal for leadership when the means for exerting that leadership are curtailed. If one had to make a choice between added staff and added wherewithal to make a more limited staff effective in accomplishing its major mission, the latter might seem to be the better choice. Of course, the obligation always rests upon an agency to assure that the limited funds available for its publications and travel are used to the very best advantage in the promotion of its mission. It is recommended that serious consideration be given to more budget for publications and travel for the Office of Education so that it may accomplish its mission more effectively, better serve the less wealthy and more removed schools of the country, and utilize its staff to better advantage.

In the first part of this chapter, a number of operational programs for which the office has responsibility were mentioned. To these should be added a number of other operational programs of assistance to agencies of the Federal Government in the conduct of their programs. Illustrative are three activities in 1948, and continuing for 2 years, whereby the educational "know-how" of the office is used by the Air Force, the Navy, and the Public Health Service. The Air Force has transferred $25,000 to the office for a survey of training personnel and instructional program of the air training command. The Navy has transferred $30,000 for an evaluation of audiovisual aids used in its training program. The office has received $40,000 from the Public Health Service to assist in the procurement of visual aids for mental-health activities of the service. Another case in point is the exchange-of-students program operated by the Office of Education with funds transferred from the Department of State.

It is entirely unnecessary and undesirable for each noneducational department or agency of the Government to duplicate professional educational staff and facilities. Thus there should be more utilization of the Office of Education by other Government agencies for services similar to those mentioned immediately above. While the noneducational agencies have the subject specialists, the office has the specialists in organization and methods of instruction, and devices which can make instruction effective. The office also should be the best informed agency in the Government on the potentialities of the schools and colleges of the country for various activities which other agencies may wish to undertake in connection with these schools and colleges. However, all too often noneducational agencies attempt to deal with educational programs or institutions in a manner which entirely sidetracks the United States Office of Education.

Actually, then, the Office of Education has been to some extent, and may become to a greater extent, a service department in professional education for the other agencies of the Government. This function is a far cry from the central mission of the office. Is this desirable? The answer to this question must be qualified. It would be undesirable if it were to diminish the zeal of the office for its primary historical mission. On the other hand, it is highly undesirable to spread professional educational functions, staff, and facilities broadly throughout the Government. Too prevalent failure in the past of noneducational agencies to utilize the office as a major source for professional service may have been a partial reason for the widespread dispersion of Federal educational functions as they concern elementary, secondary, and higher education.

In many cases it will be necessary and probably desirable for noneducational agencies to continue their direct contact with the higher institutions of the land. Certainly there should be one agency in the Government, however, where information about these institutions could be available and where there could be enlightened advice relative to methods of contact and means by which maximum protection may be given both to governmental agencies and higher institutions. In the past, the office has rendered some service of this type. The point is that a policy should be adopted within both the legislative and executive branches of the Government to insure that such will be general and consistent rather than sporadic. It is believed that proper internal organization of the office can make it possible for this type of service to exist without diminution of the primary historic function of service to education in and through the States.

Thus it will be noted that, in general, the services of the U. S. Office of Education may be grouped into three categories. First, there is the historical functions, specified by Congress when the office was initiated in 1867. This involves the collection of statistics and facts to show the condition and progress of education, the diffusing of information to aid in the establishment and maintenance of efficient school systems, and otherwise promoting the cause of education throughout the country. This must be maintained as the primary function of the office.

Second, the office has become an operating or administering agency of the Government through a number of programs for which the Congress has given it responsibility. If the Federal situation relative to education as it concerns the regularly constituted schools of the country is to become less chaotic it is essential that the Federal educational agency be given more rather than less responsibility for the administration of operational programs.

Third, the office has become to a small degree a professional servicing agency for other departments and agencies of the Government. For reasons presented above, this should continue and expand. The important thing is that this rather new function should be so organized and administered that it will not interfere with the office's historical function.

Properly guarded, these two newer functions can be used to add strength to its primary function of educational service to the States and the educational institutions therein. Operations can enhance leadership, service, and research. Professional educational service to other agencies of the Government should involve the well-being of the regularly constituted educational systems and institutions in the States. Over the years, the Office of Education has been more keenly aware that determination of educational purposes should be retained by States and higher institutions than have most other agencies of the Government. It is believed that its influence, both in operations and in professional assistance to other governmental agencies, will be a safeguard against unwarranted educational activities in the Federal Government. The encroachment on State and institutional initiative through a widespread, chaotic, and uncoordinated dispersion of educational activities operating through or affecting educational institutions in the States is considered much more dangerous than an orderly development which makes for greater utilization of the Federal agency which has traditionally championed the rights of States and institutions to determine their own educational programs. The development of balanced education, locally planned and administered, is of greater concern to the Office of Education than to any other Federal agency. It must be afforded a greater opportunity to exert its influence in this direction unless we would face an increasing tendency toward Federal domination of education.

Appraisal

The Office of Education, as currently organized, exhibits important shortcomings, and is further circumscribed by dilemmas arising out of our national traditions governing the Federal role in national education. The educational responsibilities of the Federal Government are widely dispersed through many of its agencies. Some of these are responsible for much larger programs than those administered through the Office of Education, and in some respects exert more impact on local educational conditions. The very fact of dispersal tends to create imbalance and to generate administrative complexities. The Office of Education occupies a minor place in the Federal structure. Although the Commissioner of Education, subject to the Federal Security Administrator, the President or Congress can act as an autocrat in the field allocated to him, this field is sharply limited. He does not, however, enjoy the advice, counsel, and support of lay boards so well proved useful at lower governmental levels. Because of our national fear that a powerful Office of Education would threaten partisan capture and control of the Nation's schools, we have hesitated to grant power or status to that office. Yet by dispersing educational programs we have created possibly more powerful influences over local education than would have arisen had we concentrated them in this office. The position of Commissioner of Education, already less attractive in pay than a great many educational posts in secondary or higher education, is made even less so by the fact that the Commissioner exercises so little comparative authority over the Federal educational program as a whole.

As a necessary preliminary to making constructive suggestions to remedy these matters, the next chapter sketches the effects of the educational activities of the Federal Government on the regularly constituted schools, colleges, and universities in the States.

Chapter IV

EFFECT OF FEDERAL EDUCATIONAL ACTIVITIES ON EDUCATION IN THE STATES

Since the control of education is a function of the States, the criterion of Federal policy and action is their impact on the effectiveness of education within the States. This chapter evaluates briefly Federal education activities according to this criterion.

Historical Approach

Most major moves of the Federal Government in the past to support or encourage some specific type of education have come at times when there was a country-wide lack of sensitiveness to an urgent educational need. Education easily falls into the habits of the past, though changing social and economic conditions demand an alertness to current conditions and changing trends in American life. In spite of the fact that education has always had certain leaders who have insisted that its major function was to convey the culture of the past to the current generation, it is essential, especially in our form of government and our dynamic society, that education conceive of culture as something we live today and project into tomorrow. In a sense, Federal participation in education throughout our history has been a healthy urge to make education meet essential needs in our society which have been resisted by the rank and file of those who control education and educational institutions. While there have often been justified differences of opinion relative to the means used, the purpose has usually been approved.

At the beginning of our national life publicly supported education was either meager or practically nonexistent in most States. Education was mainly available to select groups and through private schools, either church or proprietary. For effective participation in the democratic life of our new republic it was deemed essential that education be extended to the general populace—a concept that was relatively new in the world of that day. The insistence by the Federal Government on provisions for general education in the Territories and the subsequent generous endowment of education through land grants to the new

States were definite acts to promote a new and needed program to which the society of the day had been resistant. In effect, these provisions were a protest by the Federal Government against the all too prevalent notion and practice that basic education was to be available only to the select few.

Similarly, the Morrill Act of 1862 was a protest against the then too current practice of limiting higher education to a select few and in studies usually unrelated to the social and individual needs of a growing scientific, agricultural, and industrial nation. The encouragement of agricultural experiment stations in the land-grant colleges by the Hatch Act of 1887 and the inauguration of the agricultural extension service by the Smith-Lever Act of 1914 were responses to the unmet needs of the rapidly expanding agriculture of the Nation. These constituted a distinct move on the part of the Federal Government, in cooperation with the States, to become realistic in respect to the problem of agricultural education for the masses on the farms.

What has been said about the Morrill Act of 1862 as a protest against the too formal higher education of that day can similarly be said to a considerable extent of the Smith-Hughes Act of 1917 for the development of the Nation's secondary schools. These institutions were developed initially to prepare youth for entrance into colleges and universities. Originally attended by a select few, during the late nineteenth century and early part of the twentieth century it rapidly became a school for the masses. The phenomenal growth of this institution in American life and its subsequent need to change its program of studies and its methods has been one of the major concerns of educators of our day.

There is considerable evidence that the vocational education program sponsored by the Smith-Hughes Act was a protest against academic formalism in the secondary schools of the Nation. That the somewhat rigid nature of the prescribed vocational program makes it difficult to extend it to many of the secondary schools, particularly smaller schools, and that it sometimes tends to segregate the vocational from the academic pupils, thus not meeting a balanced need of the majority of pupils, is still a matter of concern to those interested in the proper balanced development of secondary education.

Programs of education recently initiated by the Federal Government are more difficult to interpret in terms of their purposive significance to education in the States. The school-lunch program initiated to furnish an outlet for surplus foods and to furnish work relief to the unemployed, has recently given more emphasis to the physical well-being of children. As such it has met a need which has not been properly cared for by State and local agencies in many places. Its brief history, however, leads one to doubt whether it has been motivated primarily by a Federal desire to overcome malnutrition among children.

The very recent extensive use of the higher institutions of the land for federally sponsored research projects might be interpreted as an encouragement to these institutions to meet the current and expanding scientific needs of the country in more effective manner. It is difficult to impute motive and purpose when much of this activity is involved with the national defense.

The schools of the country have sometimes been laggard in using the most modern techniques in teaching the usual subjects of the curriculum. Certainly the activities of the Civil Aeronautics Administration and of the Treasury Department in promoting the introduction of live and timely methods is a help to such schools as may have been slow in this regard. These, however, should be classified more as an effort to promote a cause than as Federal assistance to overcome inertia in the schools.

The land and money grants to land-grant colleges, the experiment stations, the agricultural extension service, and the Federal support for vocational education all injected, to a greater or lesser degree, a federally preconceived curricular or subject-area purpose into education in the States. The States did not have to accept these programs, though all of them did.

The initiative for program operation was given to the States. The land-grant colleges have been an outstanding example of Federal promotion of State leadership and initiative. The very large local support as compared with the relatively small present Federal assistance is witness to this fact. Although these programs have all advanced definite and specific purposes in education—purposes which under complete State and local initiative had too often been lacking—it cannot be said that it was either contrary to State interests or good Federal policy for the Government to undertake these projects. They have had an excellent over-all effect on education. We have demonstrated through these programs that the Federal Government can promote specific causes in the field of education in a manner which leaves initiative and responsibility to the States. In respect to these programs, our problem is one of balancing the Federal concern that funds be used for the purposes intended, with the objective maximum development of initiative and leadership on the State and local level. Too great stress on the former can negate the latter. The development of more initiative and leadership on the State and local level is the best long-range insurance that Federal funds will be used for the purposes for which they are intended.

The educational programs of the Civilian Conservation Corps and the National Youth Administration are in a different classification. In spite of long recognition of the growing gap between time of leaving formal education and of entering employment, and of much dis-

329

cussion of the need for work-related experiences in education and education-related experiences in work, the rank and file of schools and colleges of the country have preferred to remain in their rather narrow groove of formalized education for the more academically receptive youth. To be sure, some few schools and colleges have deviated from the usual pattern, but they are exceptions. So, with the coming of the depression, the Federal Government undertook its own program for these youth. The CCC, conceived to use unemployed youth in conservation of our natural resources, soon became an educational institution. The NYA ultimately established a Federal system of vocational schools paralleling the regular vocational schools of the country. We believe, as fine as these institutions were in meeting the problems involved in a very direct manner, that the total educational program of the country would be stronger if in the future the regularly constituted institutions of the country would be encouraged and challenged to meet such problems. The educational, social, and economic problems which brought the CCC and the NYA into being still exist, though somewhat more dormant in good economic times. Many schools still go their way of relative unawareness to the problem. Because the Federal Government undertook these programs by itself, there is little residue of leadership at the State and local levels by which the good features of these programs can be used to supplement or influence existing programs. The Federal Government has effectively promoted other almost revolutionary changes in education which have had lasting effect when it has encouraged the States to take initiative and responsibility. We believe the latter to be the best long-range approach.

Historically, then, we find that the Federal Government has promoted a number of worthy changes in State and higher institutional educational programs. To the degree that these have encouraged State and local initiative and leadership, they have been well within our concept of the place of the Federal Government in education. To as great a degree as is possible, consistent with the Federal necessity of ascertaining that funds are used for the purposes for which they have been designated, responsibility for federally promoted programs should be decentralized to State and local educational authorities. The more general the purpose of Federal funds, the greater the amount of leadership and initiative that can be given to the local educational agencies.

It becomes clear that the Federal educational interest is much concerned with strong educational leadership in States. As long as we have professionally weak State departments of education, maintenance of satisfactory local standards calls for more Federal supervision than is desirable. More Federal supervision means more tendency to use bureaucratic types of organization and control. We must search for more effective ways of eliminating this vicious circle. A higher type of Federal leadership and encouragement of States to assume more responsibility and leadership is needed to correct this situation.

Elementary and Secondary Schools

If each State had one strong over-all planning and administering agency for all of its schools, from kindergarten through graduate schools, such an organization would simplify the development of criteria for educational activities of the Federal Government as they affect the regularly constituted schools and colleges in the States. Many direct dealings with schools and higher institutions could be eliminated. Much of the now necessary specificity of present assistance to States could be removed. The number of educational agencies within States through which Federal agencies deal could be reduced. Planning with States regarding their total educational needs could be facilitated.

Although such a State educational organization may be a goal for future attainment, a realistic approach must recognize that, although all but nine of our States now have State boards of education directing the responsibilities of the public schools, seldom do these boards have any over-all responsibility for higher education as well. Due to this, it is necessary to treat the problem of elementary and secondary schools in a different manner than higher institutions. The latter will be discussed later in this chapter.

The status of State departments of education, responsible for public schools, may be noted from a few statistics. In 31 States members of the State board of education are appointed by the governor, sometimes with senate consent. Other boards are elected, ex officio, or a combination of these. Qualifications for board members are surprisingly low. All States have a chief State school officer either by constitution or by statute. College education is required for this official in 11 States. In 5 States he must hold the highest grade educational certificate required in the State. Educational experience is required in 9 States. No qualifications are mentioned in 13 States. The State board or the governor specifies the requirements in 6 States. In 31 States this official is elected, in 8 he is appointed by the State board, the governor appoints in 8 States, and in 1 State the governor and the State board jointly appoint this chief State school officer. His term of office varies from 1 year to 4 years or for an indefinite period. The median salary for this office is $5,000. In only 16 States do professional staff members in the department of education have tenure. Staffs vary in size from 1 employee to each 1,219 school-age children in Delaware to 22,523 in Kansas. There is often divided responsibility with other boards or with other State officials in matters which concern the conduct or administration of the public schools.

What is the effect of Federal educational activities on the regularly constituted elementary and secondary schools of the country?

BYPASSING OF STATE DEPARTMENTS OF EDUCATION

While it is recognized that a strong State department of education is essential, various Federal agencies have weakened this institution by dealing directly with public schools and school systems within States. In other cases Federal activities in education or closely related thereto have been directed through State groups other than the State boards of education. Although the United States Office of Education has traditionally carried on its activities through its counterpart in the States, the State boards or departments of education, it is only natural when noneducational Federal agencies are involved they tend to operate through their noneducational counterparts on the State level. The dispersion of educational activities in the Federal Government has tended to encourage similar and even more undesirable dispersion at the State operational level. In those cases where coordination is desirable, as for instance between State educational and health agencies in developing a school program in health, certainly that coordination should start on the Federal level.

The bypassing of the State educational agencies in direct dealings between Federal agencies and local schools and communities on educational matters became rife during the depression. The WPA established nursery schools with little or no prior clearance with State educational agencies. Instead of making funds available to the States for establishment and operation, the nursery schools were operated directly by the Federal agency. Similarly, WPA funds were used for various types of adult education, but seldom through State educational agencies. The NYA, as related above, similarly bypassed State departments of education. The PWA particularly in its earlier years of operation ignored State educational agencies in setting up school building construction projects. As a result, situations occurred where buildings were more elaborate than needed, and where buildings were not placed in locations of greatest need.

The Lanham Act assistance to schools for buildings, maintenance, and operation similarly bypassed State departments of education in dealing directly with local schools and communities particularly in its earlier years. No really satisfactory arrangement for coordination with the United States Office of Education or with State departments of education was ever worked out. Engineers in a noneducational Federal agency were all too often attempting to determine school needs and procedures. In reviewing the program in 1943 one writer con-

332

cluded that, "The entire situation could hardly have been more absurd."[1]

The Department of Agriculture concluded from experience that its school lunch program should operate through State departments of education. Its earlier direct dealings with school systems in local communities, and even with individual schools within school systems have given way more recently to primary dealings through State departments of education. Much damage had been done to the prestige and resultant strength of State departments of education in the meantime. Some State departments of education have subsequently found it difficult to assume the sudden increased load of administration, making it necessary for the Department of Agriculture to make many audits in local communities.

The citizenship training program of the Immigration Service, Department of Justice, has worked both with State and local school systems. Essentially this is a part of the adult education program which should be sponsored and planned at the State level. The CAA program for promotion of aviation education and the Treasury Department program for school savings and thrift education have usually worked through State departments of education.

In the numerous programs for education of children on special Federal properties and reservations we find a large variety of situations extending from complete arrangement with the State department of education as in the Atomic Energy Commission, Hanford, Wash., project, to total neglect or bypassing of the State department of education in making arrangements or failing to make arrangements with local school districts. The failure of the Federal Government to have a comprehensive policy in respect to this problem has been an embarrassment to many State departments of education. What has been said of this problem applies to some extent to the Indian Service of the Department of the Interior. However, the recent policy of this agency to make an increasing number of contracts with State departments of education is significant. It should be noted, however, that the Indian Service made contracts with over 1,100 individual school districts in 1947. Similarly, all parties concerned with the labor apprenticeship program of the Department of Labor would be benefited if this program were geared so that it could not completely bypass the State departments of education.

Noneducational agencies of the Federal Government, when given educational responsibilities which concern the regular elementary and secondary schools of the country, almost always tend to bypass State educational agencies. Some of the most unwarranted Federal controls of education in the States have crept in by this means. These

---

[1] Edgar L. Morphet, We Have Federal Control of Education, American School Board Journal, July 1943, Bruce Publishing Co., Milwaukee.

activities have raised fears of Federal domination in education. But, most important, they have discouraged rather than encouraged the assumption of educational leadership and initiative by State educational agencies.

The Federal Government is not necessarily the culprit in the matter. In many States the departments of education have been so inadequately set up either in administrative relationships, staffs, or support that they have been unable to assume desired responsibilities. If a few States are unable to operate a federally sponsored educational program effectively, Federal administrators may tend to bypass all State departments in the interest of uniformity. This tends to reduce State educational initiative and responsibility. It is a vicious circle which can be broken only if the States take the initiative in developing educational leadership and initiative.

OVERLAPPING OF FUNCTIONS

In a sense, every situation cited in the subsection above reveals overlapping since each involves a contact with schools on an educational matter. Also a number of the Federal agencies are taking on functions which would better be left to State departments of education. Many of these State departments are equipped to handle the matters involved. Those which are not should be so equipped.

At least 14 departments or independent agencies of the Government are currently operating programs which impinge upon State or local school systems in matters concerned with elementary or secondary education. Some of these departments or agencies have several subagencies each dealing with school matters. No wonder that the National Council of Chief State School Officers has complained of piecemeal Federal encroachment, lack of Federal policy in education and the consequent confusion in dealing with so many educational agencies.

Functional overlapping exists as well as administrative duplication. Long before the United States Department of Agriculture started its school lunch program the Office of Education was equipped with staff and had put out a number of publications for assistance to schools in developing the school lunch and nutrition activities. While thousands of schools now participate in the United States Department of Agriculture school lunch program, other thousands do not and naturally look to the United States Office of Education for assistance and advice. Both offices are interested in proper facilities for school lunch programs. Both are interested in proper diet and in school lunch administration. Even Congressmen, who had a part in placing the school lunch program in the United States Department of Agriculture, refer many of their requests for information concerning school lunches to the United States Office of Education. The confusion which results is not good.

There is an increasing tendency for the program of the USDA Extension Service and that of the vocational education programs in agriculture and home economics sponsored by the Office of Education to overlap. Each has a youth program. Each is in the field of adult education. In 1928 a memorandum of understanding was developed which defined the areas of operation of each program and recommended joint committees at Federal and State levels "to meet from time to time as may be necessary to promote mutual understanding." [2] As far as can be determined, no such meetings were ever held by the Federal committee, although an effort was made to convene in 1948. We believe, however, that the approach of this memorandum has been wrong. Rather than attempt to build fences between the two programs, it is our belief that each has much to contribute to the other. It would be better policy to locate means of making the two programs mutually supporting.

The 4–H Club program, sponsored by the USDA through its Extension Service and extending to the local communities by way of the land-grants colleges, enrolls some 1,600,000 boys and girls. The club work of the Office of Education is closely associated with its vocational education programs in high schools. It operates at the State level through the State boards for vocational education. Its four clubs, enrolling over 500,000 youth, are Future Farmers of America (boys), Future Homemakers of America (girls), New Future Farmers of America (Negro boys), and New Future Homemakers of America (Negro girls). On the adult level, the Extension Service operates through the county agents and home demonstrators, dealing with individuals or groups largely through demonstrations or more informal meetings. The vocational education program is more involved with formal class situations and associated individual farm or home projects in its program for adults. The vocational education program in agriculture operates in over 8,000 high schools and the Extension Service is in over 3,000 counties of the country.

In many localities there is harmonious and well-correlated relationship between these two federally supported programs in cooperation with States. In others there are repeated claims that rural youth enrolled in vocational classes are denied the privilege of joining 4–H Clubs even though different projects would be used in the supervised training under each program; that some county extension workers discourage 4–H Club members from enrolling in vocational classes; that vocational teachers sometimes sponsor and direct activities in their

---

[2] Memorandum of Understanding Relative to Smith-Hughes and Smith-Lever Relationships in Agriculture, signed by representatives of U. S. Department of Agriculture and Federal Board for Vocational Education, Washington, D. C., December 20, 1928, page 7.

communities which are not definite parts of systematic classroom work, thus overlapping with extension workers; or that county extension workers conduct training schools for adults on an organized basis comparable to vocational training classes. All too often individuals responsible for these two closely related programs are not acquainted with each other and have never discussed their mutual problems. Although the agents, demonstrators, and teachers of these programs are largely the products of the land-grant colleges, these two federally supported programs often compete for their services.

There are those who believe that the solution is to transfer the program in vocational agriculture from the United States Office of Education to the Department of Agriculture. With these we cannot agree, although it must be admitted that the Department of Agriculture seems to have been more successful in getting adequate Federal support for its activities than has the Office of Education. If we were to make this transfer, we should then have to be consistent by transferring the trade and industrial vocational education to the Department of Labor, the vocational education in distributive occupations to the Department of Commerce, the vocational guidance program might go to the United States Employment Service, and probably the vocational education in homemaking would be transferred to another division of the Department of Agriculture. Such action would multiply rather than diminish the number of noneducational agencies dealing with the schools in the States; eliminate any semblance of over-all Federal-State development in the promotion of vocational education, and create more overlapping in Federal staff and services. This proposal fails to recognize that basically these two programs have different philosophies and modes of operation. It might lose considerable of the drive and zeal developed through the loyalties to these separate programs. It would further complicate administrative matters at the State level, as the USDA operates through the land-grant colleges in its extension program and would probably prefer to operate vocational agriculture through the same State agency. It would thus withdraw the program from the State departments of education, aggravating the Federal dereliction in weakening this State agency. The alternative of having the USDA deal through the State departments of education for this program multiplies the difficulties involved. We believe that the removal of the program in vocational agriculture from the Federal educational agency would be detrimental to the best interests of education in the States. A similar suggestion that the Agricultural Extension Service be transferred to the Office of Education has little to commend it for similar and other reasons.

Chapter II outlines the plan of present coordination of the institutional on-farm program for veterans, wherein the same agencies that are involved with this problem appear to be working harmoniously. There is no reason why schools with their facilities in staff and equipment and Extension Service personnel with their excellent understanding of rural and farm problems could not collaborate for the mutual advantage of all. Certainly the rural high school, sometimes referred to as the most neglected unit in the American school system, could draw much from the problems of community and farm life to revitalize its educational experiences by such a move. Kindred advantages should accrue to the Extension Service. From the Federal level there has been little incentive for it. Coordinated planning at the Federal, State, and local levels will do much to solve these problems.

There is overlapping between Federal agencies in programs to promote curriculum in the elementary and secondary schools of the States. The slight overlapping between the apprentice training program of the Department of Labor and the vocational education program of the Office of Education has been discussed in chapter II, together with suggestions for improvement of their relationship. The CAA program to promote aviation education overlaps to some degree with the promotion of vocational education through the United States Office of Education. Although the Office of Education through its divisions of elementary and secondary education has an interest in serving schools in the States in general matters of curriculum and has a small staff to accomplish this purpose, programs in thrift education, aviation education, and citizenship education are promoted independently by the Treasury, Commerce, and Justice Departments respectively. Should it be necessary for schools in States to seek curricular service in these three special fields from noneducational agencies of the Government, while dealing with the United States Office of Education in respect to curricular assistance in general? Is this a good procedure in encouraging the States to develop a well-rounded curriculum, with overall planning to meet the needs of their youth? Does it strengthen initiative and responsibility in the States to have four Federal agencies operating in the field of curriculum?

The answer to these questions in the long run must be in the negative. The Federal Government should place basic responsibility in the Federal educational agency for matters involving curriculum in the elementary and secondary schools of the country.

The overlapping between various educational functions of different agencies of the Federal Government has created a number of situations which are not in the best interests of education in the States. Divided authority on the Federal level has sometimes been mirrored in similar divided authority on the State level. Failure to coordinate adequately at all levels has resulted in some confusion and failure to reap all of the advantages at the operational level which might have been evident. We believe that these situations should be corrected both in the Federal interest and in the State and local interest.

While we agree that the Federal Government, particularly in historical retrospect, has been effective in the promotion of important special aspects of education which had often been neglected by States, we would also caution that the promotion of special aspects only may over the years have an undesirable effect upon balance of curricular emphasis. Education in the States must be based on our great need for a high and effective general and civic literacy. In 1949 we have $28,039,000 of Federal money available to promote special aspects of curriculum in the elementary and secondary schools of the country at large, of which $27,128,000 is in grants to States for vocational education. During this same year the only Federal activities which have specific concern for the general welfare and promotion of curriculum in the elementary and secondary schools of the land are the programs of the divisions of elementary and secondary education in the United States Office of Education. For these two divisions there is $363,000 available in 1949, and this is all to be expended on the Federal level. Our generosity with Federal vocational funds has generally built the State divisions of vocational education into the largest components of State departments of education. The United States Chamber of Commerce reports 14 States in which the number of employees devoting full time to vocational education in State departments of education either equals or exceeds the number of full-time employees in all other aspects of education within these departments. In 19 added States, at least one-half as many employees of State departments of education are in the vocational field as in the other fields combined.

The divisions of the United States Office of Education devoted to general curricular service or promotion are disproportionately small as compared with the Division of Vocational Education. The latter has available the sum of $511,000 for its operations in 1949, as compared with the $363,000 for general activities in elementary and secondary education as indicated above. The Division of Vocational Education has over two and a half times more funds available to administer one specific phase of secondary education than the Division of Secondary Education has in promotion of general aspects of secondary education. It is natural that this same situation should be reflected in States. Such administrative imbalance both at Federal and State levels is a matter of concern to those who desire curricular balance in our schools.

This is not an argument against Federal participation in the field of vocational education. It merely points up the fact that the Federal Government, by its lack of concern for the totality of education, has been a potential factor in developing a state of curricular imbalance in the States. Realistically we must admit that the promotion of special causes or specialized aspects of education has been of greater concern to the Congress than have the interests of a well-rounded program to meet the basic educational needs of the youth of the Nation. We have implemented State development in one field without sufficient concern for general educational leadership in States.

Emphatically it must be said that curricular balance involves an adequate program of vocational education. Inquiry has been made at a number of points as to whether a relaxation of some of the specific requirements of the Federal vocational education program would be in the best public interest. There is a considerable belief among those responsible for this program at the State level that the time is not ripe for a dimunition of Federal controls. These individuals in general feel that much that is valuable has come with Federal controls and that these gains might be wiped out in States where general leadership is not sufficiently broad to realize the importance of this program. They fear that the high standards of vocational proficiency training would be jeopardized; that a fusion with the program of general education might result which would diminish the effectiveness of this specific program; that vocational education might thus be made impotent to serve the needs of youth in equipping them to make a livelihood. They fear that the normal academically trained school administrator may not appreciate the significance of vocational education in our national life. In other cases they fear that politically selected State educational authorities might dissipate funds to less worthy causes or less worthy enterprises in the field of vocational education if Federal requirements were relaxed. If these individuals are correct, our program of education would then be in an opposite position of imbalance.

We again come back to the problem of adequate development of leadership and initiative at the State level. Should Federal vocational funds relinquish their detailed controls, but continue as grants for the general support of vocational education, a number of States could now take full responsibility for their vocational education programs with probably even more effective results than those carried on under the present Federal program. In other States, however, this would probably not be the case.

Another aspect of the problem must be mentioned. As there is considerable specificity in the program, derived both from Federal requirements and requirements which States write into their federally approved plans, it naturally takes a considerable staff at both Federal and State levels to administer and supervise the activity. In a sense this staff may become a vested interest which at least potentially may desire to perpetuate unnecessary detail in order to preserve positions. The administration and supervision of detail also is often not conducive to the best interests of desirable leadership, initiative, and fruitful experimentation. In these respects again we have a potential vicious circle.

What are the possible solutions of these problems as they concern vocational education? Several may be mentioned: (1) Eliminate all controls and make grants to States only for the general support of education; (2) eliminate detailed controls and make grants to States for the general support of vocational education; (3) attempt to build more effective ability in States to assume real professional leadership and initiative in all phases of their educational programs, including vocational education; (4) eliminate all Federal support of education.

The first has much to commend it. However, until the third is accomplished, the program of vocational education would be very likely to suffer great losses. This is a goal toward which we might well work, with the assumption that it might take a score of years to accomplish. For the present it must be discarded.

The second is more feasible, but still inappropriate until the third is accomplished. However, this might be attainable in a shorter period of time.

The third is essential if we would correct this and many other situations noted in this study.

The fourth is contrary to the national and State interest. Moreover, it is a denial of our extensive and beneficial historical tradition of Federal concern for education. It fails to recognize the rather startling differences in the fiscal abilities of States to support their own educational programs. It would perpetuate educational inequality and hinder the advancement of those poorer States which now are making above average effort in the support of their educational programs.

Thus we come to the conclusion that a combination of the second and third solutions offers our best chance of success. A federally sponsored program to strengthen State departments of education so that they may be able to assume more rather than less initiative and responsibility in the conduct of their educational programs, including those programs supported by Federal funds, is essential if we would care for the immediate situation under discussion as well as many other situations of concern to this report. It would probably be money in the Federal pocketbook in the long run if a relatively small Federal subsidy were granted to State departments of education for their general support. Rewards other than monetary should far exceed any Federal saving involved. To insure that this grant is used for appropriate purposes it may be advisable to make it contingent upon the Federal approval of a State organizational and functional plan. Such a plan should have considerable latitude within general minimal standards as specified by the Federal educational agency.

The United States Office of Education should embark upon a major program of research, service, and leadership to give assistance to States in planning more effective State administration of education. The total educational enterprise of the Federal Government as it concerns elementary and secondary education in the States should be revised to strengthen rather than weaken State departments of education. More funds should be given to the Office of Education so that it can render a balanced service to the States in educational matters.

A Case Study

In connection with this report a few members of the staff of the State Department of Education in New York were asked by the State Commissioner of Education to submit their reactions regarding the Federal activities which concern the operations of their programs within the State. These comments are so pertinent in review of the Federal activities as they concern the regular elementary and secondary schools of the country that excerpts are quoted therefrom. It will be noted that there is not complete agreement between these individuals on a number of points.

INDIVIDUAL A: To an increasing extent the Federal Government, through the United States Office of Education and various other agencies, is being interjected into the State and local picture, and current prospects for a program of Federal aid to education makes studies of this kind all the more necessary and important. . . . It is difficult in a brief memorandum to outline adequately certain of the problems involved. . . . For the purposes you have requested, I shall limit myself in this memo to little more than a bare enumeration of the various problems as follows:

1. *The lack of balance in Federal emphasis on education.*—The concern and participation of the Federal Government in education have developed on the basis of isolating certain phases of education for particular attention and assistance, depending upon the current popularity of these areas and the pressures exerted in their behalf, as, for example, in the fields of vocational education, vocational rehabilitation, and school-lunch programs. The effect of this policy has been to seriously unbalance the administrative and supervisory structures of State and Federal education agencies with distinctly unfavorable results. Examples of the extent to which this lack of balance exists can be seen in the organization of this or any other State department. For example, we have a bureau chief and four supervisors for the field of agricultural education for a program serving approximately 20,500 students. On the other hand, we have one supervisor of English in the Division of Secondary Education, despite the fact that approximately 1,000,-000 students study this key subject in the schools of New York.

2. *Arbitrary Federal control stultifies development of State and local programs of education.*—The best evidence of this problem can be seen in the lack of development of trade and industrial education in the small cities, villages, and rural areas of this country. This is largely due to Federal regulations which make it impractical, if not impossible, to develop sound programs of training in these fields in other than large urban areas. Attempts of the Federal Government to insure the proper expenditure of Federal moneys frequently make it impossible to adapt programs to the needs of particular communities. As a result, for example, it

has never been possible to develop industrial education in small cities and towns to the extent that employment opportunities in these areas warrant.

3. *Control of educational functions by noneducational Federal agencies.*—The history of the school-lunch program under the administration of the United States Department of Agriculture, and school construction in war-production communities under PWA, are glaring examples of how Federal authority can be used to bypass State departments of education, thus interfering seriously with State-wide plans and programs for the development of education in the various communities.

4. *Failure of Federal Government to consider over-all needs of education.*— This problem is somewhat related to No. 1 above but differs in its application and effects. While there have been attempts in the past to plan a program of Federal aid to education sufficiently broad in its aspects so as to permit each State and area to concentrate on its particular educational needs, no such program has yet received much consideration. Latest efforts (the Taft bill, for example) are directed toward meeting the problem of teacher salaries. While this is probably the No. 1 financial problem of education in most States, the fact remains that other needs, though becoming increasingly serious, are more or less ignored. If we are to have Federal aid for education, and that aid is to be used with maximum efficiency, every State and community should not be required to use that aid, say for teacher salaries, when, as in the case of New York State, for example, school construction, not teacher salaries, may be the most urgent problem. Another example of this difficulty has to do with the limitations placed on vocational subsidies. These subsidies are allocated to individual States with the provision, however, that they may be used only for salaries and teacher-training activities. This policy assumes that all the States and communities already possess, or are in a position to acquire, the necessary facilities in which to offer programs of vocational education. This is simply not the case, with the result that considerable amounts of these funds are forfeited each year by certain States lacking vocational facilities to those communities which, because of their superior ability to finance education, already possess the facilities for these programs. I do not have the information to substantiate this, but I am convinced that studies would show that a large portion of Federal aid for vocational education is now going to communities and States best equipped to finance such programs on their own.

There are other less fundamental problems involved and many ramifications to those mentioned above. Because of the effect which Federal policies have on this particular branch of the Department, I shall be extremely interested in the progress of studies contemplated. ...

INDIVIDUAL B: During the years of the depression, as well as during the wartime period, numerous Federal agencies used Federal funds for so-called educational projects and services. These agencies, as you know, include WPA, NYA, Federal Housing Authority, the Department of Agriculture in the distribution of surplus foods, later the [same Department] . . . in the allocation of funds for the use of schools in maintaining school lunches, the allocation of funds by the Federal Security Agency for the education of physically handicapped children and the numerous Federal agencies that have been involved in the allocation of excess and surplus Federal properties and the preparation of plans and specifications for school buildings. The situation is extremely complex even to those officials in State offices who are supposed to be reasonably familiar with Federal administrative practices. I am quite sure that a large part of our administrative difficulties in dealing with these agencies is due to the lack of [placing of authority in] . . . the United States Office of Education. A perfect example of this lack . . . was demonstrated when the administration of the Federal Rehabilitation Service was taken away from the Office of Education and made a separate department in the Federal Security Agency.

342

I have been rather intimately associated with the administration of the Smith-Hughes Act and subsequent acts providing Federal aid for vocational education. The purpose of the original Smith-Hughes Act was to promote vocational education and vocational teacher training through the allocation of Federal funds for these purposes to the various States. At the time of the enactment of the original Smith-Hughes law, vocational education was in its infancy and only a few States, including New York, New Jersey, Pennsylvania, Massachusetts, Connecticut, Indiana, and Wisconsin, had developed vocational training programs and very little attention was being paid in those States to the preparation of vocational teachers with the exception of those trained in the field of agriculture. I realize that many people complain about the standards imposed by the Federal Government in the administration of the vocational education acts. It is true, however, that all of those standards were based upon the experience of the States referred to above at the time of the enactment of the original Smith-Hughes law. The standards imposed by the Federal Government under the old Federal Board for Vocational Education were those recommended by the States that had made a beginning in the development of vocational education.

Outside of the time requirements in the day vocational schools, I am sure there has been little criticism of the administration of these vocational acts. The Federal laws are so flexible that the States are in a position to use the money in a way that will most effectively promote the further development of vocational education. Some of the more progressive States have encountered difficulties in persuading the United States Office of Education to interpret its policies so as to make it possible to undertake new and desirable types of vocational education. In our own State this was particularly true in the field of technical education, beginning in the early days of the development of our technical education, offering specialized technical courses, until a later date in the development of postsecondary technical training programs. All of these technical programs trained young men, and some women, for entrance into technical occupations which did not require the old type of craft skills. In general, however, I am convinced that the original Federal Vocational Education Act which required: (1) The establishment of teacher training programs 1 year prior to the establishment of vocational programs in the public schools; (2) the setting up of administrative and supervisory staffs in the State departments of education; and (3) the flexibility in the use of Federal funds; was fundamentally sound and did more than any single bit of Federal legislation to promote a sound program of vocational education. I realize that many of the weak States bitterly resented being required to provide central office administrative and supervisory personnel. This was absolutely essential in the development of any reasonably uniform and fundamentally sound program of vocational education. These same States would have welcomed Federal funds for the development of similar central office personnel in the fields of elementary and secondary education.

There is one other feature in the Federal Vocational Education Acts that is worthy of mention. All of the Federal money apportioned to the States is in accordance with certain population ratios established in the Federal acts. In other words, every State is guaranteed a given amount of money subject to the fluctuations which occur in population distribution in the States. As a result, the States can plan on a definite amount of Federal aid for every 10-year period. The slight changes in the allocation of Federal funds occur after each Federal census of population. From the standpoint of good State administration this is a fundamentally sound plan. It enables the States to promise to the public schools a definite amount of money for work carried on under the Federal acts. It also enables the State departments of education to request State appropriations with reasonable assurance that the Federal funds for the matching of State appropriations will be available.

I mention this basis of apportioning Federal funds because of the changed policy in Washington in regard to the allocation of Federal grants. Since the early thirties most Federal grants, and this statement does not particularly apply to education, are based upon evidence of need. As a result someone in Washington can determine from year to year the needs of a given State and allocate the funds on the basis of evidence of need. This has resulted in a control of the use of Federal funds far in excess of anything that has been provided by the Federal Vocational Education Acts.

The Federal Vocational Education Acts have been in operation for approximately 30 years and I am reasonably sure that the small amount of Federal money made available to the States has resulted in the development of a very comprehensive program of vocational education, including for the first time in the history of this country, vocational education opportunities ranging from courses in agriculture in a small rural high school to specialized technical training in large urban schools adapted to the interests and aptitudes of hundreds of thousands of youth. The funds have also made it possible to develop through continuation, part-time schools and evening schools, continued educational opportunities for hundreds of thousands of young people and adults whose chances for success in their chosen field of employment were greatly enhanced because of the special educational opportunities made available, in part at least, through the allocation of Federal funds. It is quite possible through the experience of the past years, the Federal Vocational Acts need to be amended to more adequately meet the present day vocational education needs of the country. For example, in the funds available for trade and industrial education, it is no longer necessary to ear-mark one-third of this money for part-time or continuation schools. Chonged social and economic conditions, plus laws requiring boys and girls to remain in school until they are 16 years of age, have eliminated the need for the continuation schools of 20 or 25 years ago. These proposed changes, however, represent minor refinements of legislation that is basically sound.

INDIVIDUAL C: From 1920, when our program (for vocational rehabilitation) was first initiated, until 1943 all expenditures were on a dollar for dollar matching basis. Fifty percent of the cost of administration, services and all other expenses were provided by the Federal Government and 50 percent by the State. Since 1943, following enactment of the Barden-Lafollette amendments to the Federal rehabilitation law, the Federal Government has been furnishing funds to cover all administrative costs plus 50 percent of the cost of case services. Under this financial arrangement the Federal Government has been providing 70 percent or more of the funds used by the respective States. Naturally, this has resulted in more Federal control, particularly with respect to the use of Federal funds, and a set of rules and regulations have been issued by the Federal office for the guidance of the States.

However, the Federal Government has not interfered seriously with the administration of the programs in the States. They have not duplicated personnel as in some other programs, but instead they have adhered to the policy that the States should operate their programs in accordance with their own policies and procedures. Each operates in accordance with an approved plan of administration, and as long as the State has administered the program in accordance with the provisions of its individual plan no serious objections have been raised by the Federal Government.

Those of us connected with the State programs have felt that the original rules and regulations, issued by the Federal office in 1943, were rather complicated,

344

somewhat difficult of interpretation and included statements of policy and certain recommended procedures as a part of the regulations. It was our opinion that the rules and regulations, being based on provisions of the law should include only regulations actually mandated by law. Our criticisms of the rules and regulations have resulted in the issuance of revised rules and regulations, which are easier of interpretation, less restrictive, and are confined to matters of interpretation of the law rather than to matters of policy. . . .

There is one matter with regard to this Federal and State relationship which I think should be borne in mind, and that is that the budget estimates, financial reports, statistical reports, and other information required by the Federal Government necessitates the hiring of additional personnel, which would not be needed if it were not for the information which has to be prepared for the Federal Government.

There is one other point which may be of interest although it may not apply to any other type of program. It is a matter which has been brought about by the difference in the provisions of the State rehabilitation laws compared with the Federal law. As an example, in our State law there is no provision which requires us to determine financial need for the provision of any rehabilitation service. On the other hand the Federal law requires that financial need be determined before certain services can be provided, and makes it necessary for the States to establish need in accordance with the Federal law before Federal funds can be used to cover the costs of the service. There have been times when this difference has raised some problems in the administration of our program. However, our State law includes a provision accepting any law enacted by Congress and for this reason we have felt that it was necessary for us to adopt the Federal policy of establishing need for certain services.

[I hope the above] . . . will point up certain questions which may arise in any program where Federal-State relationship is involved. . . .

Individual D: . . . The only activity in which I have direct responsibility relates to the fiscal affairs of the school-lunch program under the United States Department of Agriculture. Considering the fact that this is a new program and one operated by other than the Office of Education, I feel that we have been unusually successful in arriving at a smooth running relationship. Of course, we have had problems to work out with representatives of the Federal Government but these have all been eminently satisfactory up to date. Some matters are still pending but we have no reason for concern or complaint since they seem to be moving as rapidly as we have any right to expect.

[Reference has been made to] . . . "dumping" of surplus food. There have been numerous cases of this sort of thing but it creates no hardship on either the State or local community, since no cost to either the State or local communities is involved. It is a little disturbing sometimes to have too many sweetpotatoes to use or nut meats or any other commodity that is in surplus. I have no constructive suggestion as to better management of surplus foods.

Individual E: My comments relative to the impact of the Smith-Hughes and George-Deen vocational acts on New York State's program of vocational education are as follows:

1. During the past 30 years, there have been many instances when Federal funds have served a useful purpose. Vocational education is one of our most expensive subject areas. A Federal subsidy has often served to encourage small communities to establish appropriate types of vocational training. I am sure that a number of them would not have taken such action without Federal assistance.

2. I cannot recall a single instance of United States Office of Education interference with New York State's vocational education program in a manner contrary to our best interests. As a matter of fact, the existence of the Federal pattern of vocational school organization has often served to help us establish and maintain sound standards.

State Matching of Federal Funds—Effect on Equalization of Educational Opportunity

In economically poor States high taxes for schools often can pay for only mediocre educational programs while in wealthy States relatively low taxes can, potentially at least, provide much better education. When the Federal Government requires straight matching of its grants-in-aid, the tendency is to force the poorer States to dig relatively further into their tax pockets than the richer States, thus requiring the poorer States to make a proportionately greater fiscal effort or to curtail other desired educational or governmental functions. Neither of these is in the interests of equalizing educational opportunity in its broader aspects or of equalizing the tax burden for education. The matching plan, except as a temporary expediency to encourage all States to undertake desired educational activities in the hope that they will ultimately develop their own initiative, is not wholly desirable. The Federal Government may well introduce the factor of State fiscal ability to support education more generally into its grants. The effect of such a plan on the poorer States would be highly beneficial. One of the major concerns of the Federal Government should be to equalize educational opportunity in the Nation.

Higher Educational Institutions

The problem of Federal relations to higher institutions in the country is quite different from that of Federal relations to elementary and secondary schools, primarily due to four factors. First, privately supported institutions of learning are more definitely a part of our regularly constituted educational system on the higher level that on the level of elementary and secondary schools. Second, because of this, and due to the traditional independence of higher institutions whether publicly or privately supported, there is seldom an over-all State planning or administrative agency for these institutions. Third, because of the advanced and specialized nature of studies and researches in higher educational institutions there is often a specialized agency of the Government closely associated with or somewhat in the position of a Federal counterpart to the specialized interests within the colleges and universities. Fourth, and somewhat related to the third,

346

the higher educational institutions of the land have been found to be an excellent avenue for the promotion and extension of many matters in the national interest.

These factors complicate the relations between the Government and these institutions. Direct dealings between many hundreds of colleges and universities by scores of Federal departments, independent agencies, and subagencies naturally result. The large volume of activities and moneys involved in these varied relationships usually have not been subject to objective formulas, often resulting in competition between institutions for Federal activities or competition between Federal agencies to have their activities introduced into certain institutions. The varied nature of the projects makes it difficult to establish any comprehensive over-all Federal policy in these relationships.

It is not within the purpose of the report, devoted to education, to attempt an evaluation of these activities as they concern the promotion or operation of the various specialties of the noneducational governmental agencies involved. In this connection, however, it may be repeated that much unnecessary Federal duplication of facilities in specialized staff, buildings, and equipment is avoided by utilizing the rich resources of the higher educational institutions of the land. Our purpose is to answer two questions: First, what is the effect of this total of Federal activities on the higher institutions of the country; and, second, what policy and organizational changes are needed, if any, on the Federal level? Much more exhaustive studies than have been possible in connection with this report are needed. Only the barest outline, of necessity all too casual, can be included.

The President's Commission on Higher Education indicated a Federal expenditure of $1,772,000,000 in 1946–47 in connection with post-high-school education.[3] After considerable study we prefer not to present a total figure for Federal activities which involve higher education. As has been pointed out earlier in this report, it is practically impossible to obtain comparable figures for the various Federal activities in education. In other cases, as with the education of veterans, it is often impossible to arrive at even a crude estimate of that portion of total funds for an activity or group of activities which eventually reaches higher institutions. Rather than deal with an over-all total we believe it essential that the programs which involve higher education be reviewed individually or by groups. Suffice it to say that there has been a tremendous increase in Federal activities which involve higher educational institutions.

---

[3] A Report of the President's Commission on Higher Education, Higher Education for American Democracy, vol. III, Organizing Higher Education, Washington, December 1947, p. 38.

Practically all of these programs have concerned some special Federal interest in a special cause or a special group of individuals. A review of a few examples will be to the point:

Nine Federal departments or independent agencies through many more of their subagencies are sponsoring research in the regular colleges and universities of the country. Between 1947 and 1949 the sums of money for this purpose increased from almost $89,000,000 to over $160,000,000. The most significant activities in this classification are those of the three departments of the National Military Establishment which have over $53,000,000 available for research and development through higher institutions during 1949, the Atomic Energy Commission with 1949 research funds through colleges and universities of over $81,400,000 (of which over half is for research construction, the majority of which is "off-campus"), and the Department of Agriculture, which has available over $18,600,000 ($7,558,000 of which is for grants to States for agricultural experiment stations) for such purposes in 1949.

Federal activities which clearly concern higher education through the regular colleges and universities of the land for special groups of individuals or for special fields of study are operated by eight departments or independent agencies, with several more subagencies involved. With the reduction of certain war-incurred activities, Federal funds available for these types of activity settled down at over $56,600,000 in 1949. Most significant are the Agricultural Extension Service (increasing from $19,000,000 to almost $31,500,000 between 1940 and 1949); public health fellowships, teaching grants, and construction (increasing from $70,000 to $10,579,000 between 1940 and 1949); and the fellowship program of the Atomic Energy Commission initiated in fiscal 1948 with $2,600,000 available, increasing to $3,400,000 in 1949.

For general support of two special types of higher educational institutions, the State maritime academies and the land-grant colleges, the sum of $6,518,000 is available in 1949, the amount having been kept fairly constant since 1940.

For pre- or in-service training of Government personnel through colleges and universities the Federal Government obligated $25,300,000 in 1947 as compared with over $33,700,000 available in 1949. The ROTC and NROTC accounted for a major portion of these funds.

Several departments and agencies are responsible for activities in the international interest which operate through colleges and universities. For 1947, 1948, and 1949 funds for this purpose average about $1,000,000 per year.

The tremendous program for education of veterans under Public

Law 346 and Public Law 16 (well over $2,800,000,000 in 1948, as in 1949) [4] has devoted a considerable share of its funds to education and subsistence to students in higher institutions.

As contrasted with the varied and rather large programs which concern special phases of collegiate life, special types of research, or special groups of individuals, the only Federal activity which is solely concerned with the general welfare and promotion of higher education in the colleges and universities of the country is that of the Division of Higher Education of the Office of Education, which has $167,000 available in 1949.

Mention should also be made of the many hundreds of millions of dollars' worth of surplus property donated to or sold at discount to higher educational institutions, the over 16,000,000 square feet of floor space in buildings made available to educational institutions under the Veterans Educational Facilities program, and the well over 147,000 housing units made available for veterans attending educational institutions. No equitable value can be placed on these, nor can it be readily determined what proportion of these facilities went to colleges and universities. These institutions have been major recipients from these activities, however. Several other activities for which funds are not segregated by educational level will have been noted.

In all, 19 Federal departments and independent agencies have organized activities which are carried on in the regular colleges and universities of the country. Some of these activities reach all institutions, while others concern only a few. Scores of subagencies of these 19 Federal agencies deal independently with colleges and universities. It would be more simple to name the departments or independent agencies of the Government which do not deal with colleges and universities, but in the interest of a positive approach the list of these agencies which do have programs which operate in colleges and universities is given: Department of State, Department of the Army, Department of the Navy, Department of the Air Force, Department of Justice, Department of Commerce, Department of the Treasury, Department of Agriculture, Department of the Interior, United States Maritime Commission, Federal Works Agency, Veterans' Administration, Federal Security Agency, Tennessee Valley Authority, Housing and Home Finance Agency, National Advisory Committee for Aeronautics, Atomic Energy Commission, War Assets Administration, and the Institute of Inter-American Affairs (a Government corporation). In addition, a number of other Federal agencies have less formal activities or activities related to their more general regulatory operations which involve colleges and universities, such as the licensing of educational broadcast stations by the Federal Communications Commission.

---

[4] Revised unofficial estimates, as of June 1948.

To gain an idea of the dispersion of these various Federal programs to the individual colleges and universities and to learn something of the effect on these institutions, 40 letters were addressed to presidents of representative colleges and universities of the country. Thirty-one replies were received during May, June, and July of 1948.

Extent of Federal Activities in Individual Colleges and Universities

All these institutions had the usual educational activities with veterans, and most maintained ROTC or NROTC units. We submit the reports from two midwestern universities as representing fairly accurately the general picture of Federal activity on the higher educational level.

A midwest land-grant university estimates its 1947–48 receips from the Federal Government to be $211,000 for the agricultural experiment station; $611,000 for its agricultural extension service; $157,000 for training of vocational teachers and general support; and well over $500,000 for contract research and development from nine Federal agencies or subagencies. The Veterans' Administration pays tuition and fees for 8,500 veterans, for which the Government provided temporary living accommodations in 590 family apartments and dormitories for approximately 1,500 individuals at a cost to the university of $1,100,000. Temporary classrooms and storage facilities of approximately 110,000 square feet plus 15 quonset huts were federally provided, with the university share of cost being $550,000.

Added contracts for student instruction included fees for 3 officers from Army Corps of Engineers, 2 officers from Army Service Forces, 5 officers from the United States Military Academy, 1 officer from Army Quartermaster Corps, 23 officers from Air Corps Air Matériel Command, 150 naval officer students under NROTC and NACP (through Navy Bureau of Supplies and Accounts), 14 postgraduate officers from the United States Naval Academy, and 2 students under United States Public Health Service.

In respect to equipment, this institution dealt with the Air Corps, Navy, Army (Ordnance, Signal Corps, and Engineers), War Assets Administration, United States Office of Education, and the Federal Works Agency. Equipment included machine tools, hand tools, shop equipment and supplies, laboratory equipment, scientific equipment, electronic equipment and supplies, office and classroom furniture, office and dormitory equipment. Miscellaneous contracts with the Federal Government included counseling service to veterans at $38,300, including lease of space and telephone; $5,800 from the Navy for medical services, lease of space, and construction of facilities; $100 from the Department of Agriculture for lease of space; and $2 from the CAA for lease of space for weather bureau and beacon site. The Federal Communications Commission issues a 3-year contract and makes periodic inspections of the university radio stations. ROTC and NROTC units are maintained, with the university furnishing buildings and maintenance for the academic program.

A Great Lakes area State university, in addition to ROTC and NROTC, reports:

Vocational education	$31,310
Veterans Administration rent for consultation service	2,250
U. S. Public Health Service grants	232,151
Instructional contracts	94,252
Veterans Administration GI benefits to students	4,456,700
62 research contracts, largely science	6,099,496
Total Federal funds	10,916,159

Added activities include the following: United States Forest Service makes forest lands available for experimental work; Bureau of Entomology and Plant Quarantine (USDA) makes a truck available for work in forest entomology; a professor collaborates with the Bureau of Plant Industry, USDA; Federal funds for crippled children come indirectly to the university hospital; two professors are paid a small annual fee as consultants with the Public Health Service; a staff member is consultant in medical matters to the Navy which pays $1,000 annually to the Serological Service; office space is given to an officer and one other from the United States Public Health Service and the officer serves as a lecturer without compensation; the rapid-treatment center of the hospital, directed by the State department of health, is financed by the United States Public Health Service, pays rent, and so forth, to the university, and is used for teaching purposes; the Fish and Wildlife Service (Department of the Interior) has quarters for five individuals, two of whom serve on the graduate faculty of the university, and furnishes materials for biological research and access to its specialized library; housing is furnished to a district office of the United States Geological Survey and the officer in charge cooperates with departmental staff, serves on doctoral committees, and this activity "tends to bring oil people to the campus and makes for good public relations of the Department"; departmental members who manage the weather station are unpaid observers of the United States Weather Bureau; housing is furnished for staff of the Veterans' Administration who deal both with local students and veterans of the surrounding area.

EFFECT OF FEDERAL ACTIVITIES ON COLLEGES AND UNIVERSITIES

The officials of the institutions to whom the letter was addressed were asked for reactions to these Federal programs which operate through their institutions on such matters as improvement of staff, Federal controls, variability in Federal policy, curricular balance, impact on students, and long-range social and educational significance. Because of the extensive discussion of the problems involved over the years, we have taken the liberty of summarizing these replies rather extensively.

Near unanimity is to be found in the opinions expressed regarding the various contract research programs. A large majority of the reports describes the effect of these activities as "stimulating"—in terms of their impact upon faculty, students, and the academic community. An occasional demurrer appears, questioning the desirability of emphasizing the physical or "practical" sciences exclusively, or warning against the possibility that colleges and universities may become overly dependent upon Federal subsidy for their research activities. Similar consensus is evident with regard to the matter of Federal controls in this and other areas—again the majority expression evidences rather complete satisfaction with the restraint and respect for local independence which has characterized Federal operations. The reports express decided approval of the spirit governing university-government cooperation.

Likewise, the program of veterans' education meets with universal approbation. Some reports note with obvious pleasure the "lift" which the presence of the more mature, serious veteran student has brought to the campus, while others applaud the democratizing influences of the GI bill. Recognizing these to be desirable accretions, a few responses indicate some concern for the stability of colleges after the veteran load has subsided and note that their presence has created something of a problem of "integration" which "has not been sufficiently emphasized."

While a small minority of the replies indicates that Federal activities have had "little or no effect" upon regular collegiate pursuits it is clear that the great majority gives evidence of satisfaction with and approval of the various Federal programs now operative on university campuses. Indeed, a few find in this policy the means to more varied and extensive university offerings and at least one respondent hopes that certain of the services under Federal auspices will be extended. In the words of one college president:

I have no hesitancy in stating that in my opinion the social and educational significance of these Federal activities is beneficial from every standpoint, and I believe they have a favorable effect on higher education in general.

Suggestions for Improvement of Federal Relationships With Higher Institutions

Many suggestions have been given by these representative college and university officials, either directly or implied, for the improvement of Federal relationships with higher educational institutions. A summary of these follows:

The responses are nearly unanimous, and most rather vehement, in calling for simplification of the policies and procedures by which research contracts are negotiated. The necessity of utilizing a great variety of forms and accounting techniques, all of considerable complexity, the absence of any set of standards regarding contract provisions, the extended negotiations prolonged by needless red tape, these and similar complaints produce a pronounced demand for uniformity in contract procedures and mechanics. Although many are led to suggest a single contracting agency, and especially a single auditing agency, an equal number as vigorously denounce any tendency to consolidate all such activities in any one Government bureau. It is felt by some that a coordinating officer in the Office of the President or the projected National Science Foundation might be the logical locus of such an authority, but others point to the flexibility and freedom of choice which accrue to the colleges under a multi-agency arrangement and consider that the healthy element of competition . . . would not be present if all contracts were under a single Federal agency. Little disagreement is apparent, however, over the desirability of coordinating all Federal agencies which are engaged in essentially the same specific programs, such as the various housing authorities or those concerned with agricultural experimentation and extension service. It is obvious, to quote one report, that "there exists no pattern (of Federal-State relationships) that is common to all departments and agencies in their contacts with State institutions." Recognition of the need for such a pattern underlies all the reports.

Some sentiment is expressed in favor of the coordination of all Federal activities on the individual campuses but others voice the fear of "too much power centralized" in the grasp of any office so constituted. There is considerable criticism leveled at the inability of local and regional representatives of Federal agencies to make final decisions. Several university officials report in substantial agreement with the following: "We have been handicapped by the inability of our local or regional office to render prompt decisions on which we can rely. . . . This sort of centralization, in our opinion, is one of the greatest handicaps to an efficient and effective relationship between the Federal Government and educational institutions."

Several suggestions are made relative to the type of grant which is most desirable. There seems little objection to the policy of subsidizing worthy students and lines of research. As before, the absence of grants in the social sciences is decried and a plea is made for grants in such areas as community service as well as for "general grants for the support of basic research." Many indicate their favor toward grants for longer periods than the customary one or two years, noting the difficulty of securing capable personnel for temporary assignments. At least one official, however, feels that the specific grants provide an independence from Federal control which general subsidies would undermine. In general, the consensus seems to indicate great satisfaction with the spirit which motivates Federal activities in these areas—the main criticisms lie in the realm of procedure and mechanics.

GEOGRAPHICAL DISTRIBUTION OF PUBLIC HEALTH FELLOWSHIPS AND RESEARCH GRANTS

No effort has been made in this report to trace all Federal funds for fellowships and research to the higher institutions by geographical location except in the case of public health. Certain of those research activities in the field of national defense logically should be done through the institutions most capably equipped and staffed for such research. In the field of public health, however, a good case may be made for more consideration of general geographical spread of activities, particularly in areas of the country in greatest need of public health services.

As of April 1948, 186 public health fellows were on duty in educational institutions in the States, and 1,266 public health research grants totaling $13,589,456 had been approved for payment. A comparison of the percent of population and the percent of public health fellowships in the various geographical areas of the country will disclose that proportionately the Northeast and the Pacific Southwest States have had the larger number of fellowships. Of 39 added fellows who were on duty with other than educational institutions, 35 were in the Northeast. Fifty-six percent of the 181 additional fellows who were not on duty or had terminated programs prior to April 1948 had been studying in the Northeastern States. In contrast, while the Southeastern States have over 20 percent of the population, they had under 5 percent of the fellows on duty, and the Southwestern States, with over 7 percent of the population, had no fellows studying therein. To be sure, individuals from these areas may have studied in other parts of the country.

However, there has always been a tendency for students from a distance to locate subsequently in the vicinity of institutions where they do their graduate study and for educational institutions to draw a considerable portion of students from their immediate environs, leading to the conclusion that this geographical distribution of fellows may not be in the best interests of the total public health needs of the country. Of course, students should be encouraged to study at institutions which offer the best instruction. In the best interests of public health in regions of the country where health needs may be greatest, strong institutions in this field should be encouraged in those areas. The spread of fellowships may be a factor in increasing the strength of

354

a few good institutions at the expense of institutions which need to be made strong. Certainly the Southeastern and Southwestern States need individuals well trained in public health.

Similarly, but to a somewhat lesser extent, the amounts of money in public health research grants through educational institutions has favored the Northeast, while the Pacific Northwest, the Southwest, and the Southeast are in the least favorable positions. While research needs to be done in strong institutions, a secondary purpose of public health research is to train adequate public health personnel to serve the various areas of the country. Research grants tend to help make strong institutions stronger, which is good. However, this very process widens the differential between the strong and the weak institutions, thus making the less favored institutions proportionately weaker. Naturally, the Government wants to get the most for its public health research expenditures, which leads to the practice of using the stronger institutions. Yet in the long run and in the interests of strong programs in public health in all areas of the country, more should be done to encourage and strengthen the public health research programs of higher institutions in all areas of the country.

DISCUSSION

Letters of college and university officials of the country show their belief that the general effect of the various Federal programs is highly beneficial to their institutions. Their comments are usually directed to federally sponsored research activities. Only occasionally do they mention the long-range social and educational implications of these activities. Institutions which only a few years ago were concerned that any Federal moneys coming to them, or even to their students as in NYA, would eventually lead to Federal control are now receiving relatively large sums of Federal money for a variety of specialized activities and like it. They testify that they have seen little evidence of Federal control and that no Federal program has been thrust upon them against their will. Most of them report that they see little danger in upsetting their curricular balance by the added emphasis on the natural sciences which Federal research funds have given, although a few state that they must make added effort to gain funds from other sources to insure a balanced program. Others believe it would be unfortunate if they were to become too dependent upon any single source of funds for support of research or other general activities.

In the program for the education of veterans there has been little Federal influence on the curriculum or purposes of higher educational institutions. The primary Federal contact here has been with the individual veteran, who has had a very free choice in selecting the institution which he desired to attend and the course he desired to

355

take. Veterans have enrolled in all types of higher institutions, publicly and privately supported, church and secular, small and large, city and rural, rich and poor. They have undertaken studies in all areas of the curriculum. Thus the general cause of higher education in all types of institutions and in all areas of the curriculum has been served. Though no objective formula was used to spread the gains proportionately between institutions, geographical areas, or fields of study, the nature of the program was such that no formula was needed. Although this program has taxed the resources of many institutions, basically it has led to a well-balanced general benefit to higher education. The major Federal goal that veterans be well prepared to reassume their places in civilian life is being accomplished. The higher institutions of the nation are being benefited while being used to achieve a Federal service.

The Federal contract research program has been a vital and stimulating force in the higher institutions where it has operated. It has made it possible for these colleges and universities to improve and retain staff. It has produced much research essential to the physical well-being of individuals as well as for our general technical advancement. It works to increase our backlog of scientists essential to our general internal welfare as well as to our needs for national defense. It has rejuvenated the laboratories of many of our higher institutions.

It is doubtful whether the Federal program of contract research, largely in the natural sciences, is as generally wholesome for higher education in this country as the veteran program. Insofar as such research is deemed necessary by the Federal Government it may well be done through educational institutions. All higher institutions should be willing to undertake Federal research even to the extent of damage to their other programs when national defense is imperative. Moreover, support of pure research is in line with the aims and traditions of higher education. Although very little of specific controls go with the individual Federal research programs, the sum total of Federal research devoted largely to the medical, physical, and biological sciences cannot help affecting educational emphasis.

We as a society are already behind in adapting our social and economic organization in an age of rapid technological change. It is widely believed that the social and economic fields of study lag behind the natural sciences. Suffice it to say that the Federal Government should not increase this gap. Our strength as a nation requires continued fundamental research in all areas of study as they affect all phases of our lives, our associations, and the environment about us. We should not, however, curtail natural science to permit our understanding of human relations and other socio-economic matters to catch up; we should establish balance in our emphasis by strengthening work in other fields. Over the years, if the present Federal

356

emphasis on research only in the natural sciences is continued, the determination of the colleges and universities to retain balance may wane.

While the educational program for veterans spreads well over all higher institutions, this is not the case with contract research, nor should it be expected to be so in fields of immediate and vital national concern. With each of many Government agencies and subagencies involved in these matters working directly with institutions of their own choice it is conceivable that we could strengthen certain institutions, or concentrate aid in certain geographical areas to the comparative detriment of higher education elsewhere. Although some of this may be necessary in the interests of Federal economy, the question should be raised and an appraisal made. We have previously discussed this problem as it applies to the field of public health.

There is urgent need for over-all Federal understanding of the problems involved. As now operated, there is no assurance that there will be effective coordination, even between separate departments which are dealing in the same areas of research. There needs to be more uniformity concerning standards for research. It is not good business either for the colleges and universities or for the Federal Government to permit a situation whereby a project turned down by one Federal agency as being unworthy can be resubmitted to another agency and approved without knowledge of the prior refusal. The college and university presidents in their testimony give ample evidence of lack of uniformity of Federal policy in respect to such matters as contracts, payments, and audits.

Government research through colleges and universities is only a portion of the total Federal research. A considerable part is done through industrial laboratories or by the agencies of the Government in their own facilities. Thus the development of a comprehensive policy to assure coordination, over-all understanding, and absence of duplication and overlapping, is outside the scope of this report devoted to education. The well-being of the higher educational institutions of the land is involved in the development of such a comprehensive program.

A review of other Federal activities as they operate through the regular colleges and universities of the country, discloses that these institutions are utilized extensively for pre- and in-service training of Government personnel and in the international interest. This type of Federal activity has increased very rapidly in recent years. There is considerable evidence from the university and college presidents who were consulted in connection with this report that they consider the various programs in training of military officers to be desirable. Although they seldom mentioned the other programs in these classifications, there are no particular difficulties involved therewith, except that of the multiplicity of educational agencies and consequent varying Federal policies. For instance, inquiry should be made into the reasons why the NROTC varies from the ROTC and Air ROTC in the matter of payment of tuitions and fees.

Is it essential that the United States Office of Education care for international exchange of certain classes of educational personnel, while exchange of other types of educational personnel is cared for by the Department of State? The Office of Education should be the best-informed agency of the Government as to the educational resources of this country. It should be in a much better position than the Department of State to work out educational plans for visiting educators. It, through collection of materials over the years, is familiar with educational systems in foreign lands and consequently should be able to correlate the assignments of educators to educational institutions within this country with an undestanding of their foreign educational backgrounds. It has an extensive personal and professional relationship with our educational institutions. The United States Office of Education, in coordination with the Department of State, should be given more responsibilities in dealing with the international exchange of persons when educators or educational institutions are involved.

This discussion, thus far, has not dealt with the need of over-all Federal policy in matters which involve the colleges and universities of the country. Piecemeal Federal legislation and the independent determination of policy by a multitude of Federal agencies in programs which concern the higher institutions of the Nation may, in the long run, constitute a less conspicuous and more dangerous type of Federal control than would be evident in a more obvious and comprehensively developed approach. We do not want a dominating Federal department of education where all educational matters are controlled. But to go to the opposite extreme of decentralization, coupled with the strong tendency to increase rather than decrease Federal activities in higher education, certainly is not the appropriate solution. There is much need for the development of comprehensive Federal policies and effective coordination as related to the Federal activities which involve our colleges and universities.

After reviewing some of the problems involved, the President's Commission on Higher Education in 1948 came to the conclusion that it was . . .

. . . strongly of the opinion that, except for direct contract relationships, the activities of the Federal Government in relation to education should be coordinated through the United States Office of Education. It fully appreciates, however, that this is impossible in the immediate future, and urges, as an interim step, the appointment of an interagency committee within the Government, the Commissioner of Education to be chairman of such a committee.[5]

Although interagency coordinating committees are weak unless the agency responsible for the coordination holds at least a portion of the purse strings, this is the best solution which is immediately available. Coordination of specific functions or purposes is more effective than generalized coordination. An avenue must be opened for coordination and mutual appraisal of the problems involved. In addition, it is recommended that the United States Office of Education be required to collect and publish statistical and other objective descriptive data on all educational activities of the Federal Government as they concern the regularly constituted school systems, colleges, and universities of the country. This should be done at least biennially. An informed public will eventually find solutions to its problems. By lack of information of diversified educational activities tucked away hither and yon over the Government, we may unknowingly permit practices to grow which may hinder the development of strong and independent educational institutions in the States. The Office of Education is already under congressional mandate to . . .

collect such statistics and facts as shall show the condition and progress of education in the several States and Territories, and of diffusing such information . . . as shall aid the people of the United States in the establishment and maintenance of efficient school systems, and otherwise promote the cause of education throughout the country.

To insure that there will be no question about it, the mandate should be extended to include research and dissemination of information about the educational activities of the Federal Government as they concern the educational institutions of the country.

Eventually, if the type of Federal educational agency recommended here is established it can be a vital correlating and service force in connection with the problems treated in this chapter.

Should the Government in the future plan any new activities or extended expansion of present programs which support given areas of collegiate service or curriculum, we would strongly recommend that instead there be substituted a program designed somewhat along the lines of the present education of veterans. For reasons stated earlier in this chapter, this program seems to hold the best promise of any activity yet devised by the Government for strengthening higher education without undue control, either obvious or obscure. The selection of worthy and able students from all parts of the country who have considerable latitude in choosing institution courses of study relieves the Federal Government of any complaint that it is showing favorit-

---

[5] Francis J. Brown, President's Commission on Higher Education, "Higher Education," published by U. S. Office of Education, vol. IV, No. 13, March 1, 1948, Washington, D. C. (a digest of the report of the Commission).

ism to individual institutions, geographical areas, or to special phases of the curriculum. In such a plan Federal funds should be granted to States by an equitable objective formula, but choice of institutions by students should not be limited by State lines. Within general standards as determined by Congress, States should be given responsibility for the administration of the program as it concerns selection of able and worthy students, certification of educational institutions where studies could be pursued, and general administration of the program. If such a program were undertaken, a considerable part of the Federal funds now going directly to individual institutions for research, fellowships, and other purposes might better be channeled through it.

We have previously discussed the need for greater strength in over-all State educational agencies. What has been said applies with equal force at this point. Not only for the sake of benefit to the States, but for the sake of decentralization of Federal educational operations and the reduction of numerous Federal direct dealings with individual institutions, there is need for immediate Federal encouragement of more educational responsibility, initiative, and leadership at the State level.

Chapter V

CONCLUSIONS—FEDERAL POLICY AND STRUCTURE FOR EDUCATION

Background

Of the vast array of public functions carried on at the various governmental levels none is basically more important to the well-being of the individual citizen or life in a democracy than education. The opportunity for an adequate education, geared to realistic needs of individuals and of our type of society, is fundamental to our concept of the value of the individual citizen and of his place and participation in democracy. Although education is a basic responsibility of States and should remain so, the Federal Government has a justifiable concern that educational programs within States be realistic, effective, and compatible with broad national needs and standards. Whether we think nationally in terms of civic or general literacy, defense needs, welfare of individuals, industrial effectiveness, or a host of other important considerations, we come to the conclusion that an adequate education in the States is essential. Quantitative and qualitative changes in this education are imperative from time to time in order to meet the needs of the changing conditions in our dynamic life.

Historically the Federal Government has done much to encourage States to make such changes. This is evidenced by a number of activities such as the early land grants which were the basis for the development of public-school systems in new States, the encouragement of land-grant colleges to meet the needs of a growing agricultural and industrial nation and to further democratize the opportunity for higher education, or the Federal-State cooperative program for vocational education to encourage high schools to be realistic in meeting the needs of new hordes of pupils who were flocking to them.

Decentralization of the basic responsibility for education to the States should be continued and Federal activities in education need to be reviewed in the light of this principle. In the long run educational strength in initiative and leadership at the State level brings greater national strength in our form of government. It is our protection against using education as a force toward national partisan ends. In too many other countries we have recently observed the effects of nationalized educational systems used as a means to pervert democratic government and destroy individual and social freedoms. We do not want a Federal educational system with set uniformity which stultifies experimentation and subsequent progress.

However, if we assume that the Federal Government has no place in education we close our eyes to the history of Federal participation in encouragement and support of education in the States. By and large these Federal activities have been highly beneficial both from a State and a national point of view. If, in the future, education in the States is generally unresponsive to some very pertinent need of individuals in our type of society, certainly the Federal Government should retain the right to fill the gap by encouraging the States to undertake appropriate action. Or if certain poorer States after making a reasonable maximum effort are still unable to provide a minimum of education considered essential for general or civic literacy, the Federal Government may well offer assistance. Particularly in this day of mobile population and increasing importance of national civic participation the inability of a State to provide minimum educational essentials becomes a national interest. There is little historical support for the contention that we have had undue direct control in the Federal programs of education which have been conducted on a cooperative basis with States. Also many of the Federal programs which operate through States or institutions in States on other than a cooperative basis have no undue direct Federal control. Witness the Federal activities for the education of veterans, involving something over $2,800,-000,000 in 1949.[1] The major criticisms which are made concerning this program are leveled at too few Federal controls, a situation largely corrected by the Eightieth Congress. The college and university presidents have testified that they note practically no evidence of harmful control in the rapidly increasing Federal activities through their institutions. The argument of Federal control of education has often been used as a screen by those who oppose Federal assistance on other grounds.

The danger to education lies more in the uncontrolled spread of uncoordinated and specialized educational functions over the Government without regard to effective over-all educational development. Fearing a Federal centralization of activities which concern the educational institutions of the land, we have taken the alternate course of diffusing Federal activities in education among many of the departments and independent agencies of the Government. The United States Office of Education, the one agency of the Government which has traditionally championed the cause of general and balanced development of education under State responsibility for leadership and initiative, has available through it (for both its administration and

---

[1] Unofficial estimate as of June 1948.

362

its grants to States) approximately 1 percent of the total Federal funds in the fiscal year 1949 which go to schools and higher institutions in the States and students therein, to the operation or support of Federal educational institutions and programs, or for the administration of these programs. If we add to this Federal total the unclassified activities and those which do not concern regular educational institutions (category "B" activities), the percentage through the Office of Education would be considerably less.

In 1949 there is available something over $3,400,000,000 [2] of Federal moneys which will be used in educational activities which directly affect our regularly constituted schools and higher institutions, operate through them, furnish similar education, or assist students in these schools and institutions. As has been pointed out earlier, however, this is not direct general Federal aid to education although in some cases as a byproduct general assistance may result. A very large majority of these funds are dedicated to war- or defense-incurred educational activities such as education of veterans, schools in defense or military areas, military research and pre- or in-service education of military personnel through universities, raising the educational level of members of the armed forces, and so forth. Only the relatively small sums of money available to the Office of Education for its internal use in research, service, and leadership for the general development of education at all levels and in all parts of the country (in the vicinity of one and a quarter million dollars in 1949) mirrors the Federal concern for the over-all general development of education in this country.

Except for this small general interest in education expressed through the Office of Education, all Federal activities which deal with the regularly constituted schools are for specialized activities such as promotion of special areas of the curriculum, specialized educational services, assistance to special geographical areas, promotion of special fields of research, education for special groups of individuals, support for special types of higher institutions, or pre- or in-service education of specialized Government personnel. Although the educational institutions of the land are being utilized effectively for the promotion of many Federal causes, and although in general the schools and colleges of the land believe that the effect of any individual activity is beneficial to their programs, the emphasis in its totality on specialized phases of education favoring technical and scientific areas cannot fail to unbalance the educational institutions of the land. This is the type of indirect effect which we believe more dangerous than the threat of direct Federal control.

Additional factors give rise to further concern. The vast majority

---

[2] Includes in excess of $500,000,000 over official estimate for 1949 education of veterans appearing in appendix.

of these programs are administered by noneducational Federal agencies which are legitimately interested in the promotion of their own points of view and often permit their customary mode of direct operations to undermine State educational authority. The latter is particularly true in respect to elementary and secondary education. Sixteen executive departments and independent agencies of the Government through dozens of their subagencies conduct programs which concern elementary and secondary education. The previous chapter has told the story of the resultant bypassing of State departments of education, the overlapping of functions on the State or local level, and the effect on curricular balance. The Federal Government has neglected to build balanced strength in State departments of education. Nineteen Federal departments and independent agencies through scores of their subagencies have programs which concern higher education. It is not unusual for a university to operate federally sponsored programs with 25 Federal agencies and subagencies, each dealing independently and each with its own policies and procedures. The effect of these activities is also treated in the previous chapter.

The educational systems and institutions in the States have not been ungrateful for these Federal educational activities which concern them nor have they considered these activities other than valuable if not even essential in many cases. The complaint is that the Federal Government has never adopted an over-all policy in regard to its educational activities, that legislation has been piecemeal and programs uncoordinated. Lack of objective formulas in several programs for the distribution of funds or activities can permit abuses in favoritism to certain institutions or geographical areas. Aggressive groups or agencies have promoted their causes through education without regard to the over-all development of education. The Office of Education has been kept so weak that it has neither the governmental status nor the facilities to be an effective force in developing or coordinating a comprehensive Federal program or policy of education.

In addition to the educational programs of the Federal Government which concern the regularly constituted schools and educational institutions in the States there are a number of direct Federal activities or responsibilities in education, such as the education of children of Federal employees on Federal reservations and properties, education of Indians and other native peoples in possessions and occupied areas, "civilian" education of members of the armed forces, the conduct of the Military and Maritime Academies, the closely related programs for in-service training of governmental personnel, or education in the international interest. Particularly in respect to the first two types of these activities is there need of a definite Federal policy.

Even a cursory review of the previous chapters reveals that the Federal educational interest pervades practically all of the major departments and independent agencies of the executive branch. In summary, this rather confused situation is primarily the result of four factors operating on the Federal level:

1. Federal activities in education have developed on a piecemeal basis. They represent activities supported by various groups and special interests and at various times during our history in the absence of any over-all general Federal policy relative to education.

2. Education is a powerful force and method by which governmental services and departmental or agency points of view can be made to reach the people. Also its resources can be used effectively to perform governmental functions. For these reasons it is only natural that a given department or agency should desire to use education to further particular interests for which it has major concern.

3. The Government has found itself confronted with a number of direct education responsibilities which could not be shifted readily to the regularly constituted educational institutions in the States.

4. The basic desire of the people, expressed through Congress, to limit Federal control of education has resulted in a relatively subordinate Federal educational agency and a spread of educational functions in other Federal agencies in order to avoid Federal centralization of this function.

A Federal Policy for Education

The following generalized statements of policy are put forward as means of overcoming some of the major complications and inconsistencies in our allocation of educational functions throughout the Government and in our conduct of the activities involved.

RELATIONSHIP TO STATES AND EDUCATIONAL INSTITUTIONS IN STATES

1. Basic control of and responsibility for education should continue to be a State and local function.

2. Education is an essential service of major importance which must be well-organized and well-integrated to develop balanced activities stemming from needs of citizens and democracy. The Federal Government should recognize this rather than pursue a course of promoting unrelated educational specialties or special interests.

3. The Nation, as well as States and localities, is vitally concerned that education be effective. Thus Federal financial assistance and leadership of a noncoercive nature are often desirable. The Federal Government may use these for general assistance when needed, to pro-

mote desirable functions caused by changing national conditions and needs for which the regular schools and higher institutions in States may not have been sufficiently responsive in developing balanced services, or to equalize educational opportunity in States unable to provide proper education.

4. The goal of the Federal Government in its activities related to the regularly constituted schools and higher educational institutions in the States should be to develop self-reliance and self-sufficiency at the State or institutional level. When Federal assistance is given, either through fiscal or leadership means, it should be to this end.

5. When resources are available in the regularly constituted schools and higher institutions in the States through which Federal educational responsibilities or Federal purposes can be accomplished, these should be utilized and supported. Except in critical emergency situations, however, this should be done with due consideration to the well-rounded development and general welfare of schools and colleges throughout the country.

6. Grants-in-aid or other fiscal assistance to States for education should be as general as possible in nature consistent with the Federal obligation and necessity for ascertaining that funds are used for the purposes for which intended. When the purpose is other than emergency in nature, impartial objective formulas should be utilized in distribution of funds.

7. All Federal activities which concern elementary and secondary schools in the States should be the responsibility of one Federal educational agency unless the evidence is clear-cut to the contrary. In the latter case there should be legally required and specified coordination between the agency involved and the Federal educational agency to insure that operations are in accord with educational needs of schools and localities and that responsibilities are properly decentralized to State departments of education.

8. All Federal educational activities which concern higher educational institutions in the States, except those which are of a critical emergency nature, must be consistent with the policy stated in 2 above, and to this end there should be more dependence on the Federal educational agency for development of and advisement concerning these activities. Until more effective Federal policy and organization for these activities can be attained interagency coordination for activities which involve similar functions or purposes is necessary.

Special Federal Responsibilities for Education

1. The Federal Government should assure equal opportunity at public expense for elementary and secondary education of dependent children of Federal employees who live on special Federal properties,

reservations, construction projects, Federal overseas installations, and in occupied areas. Similarly this responsibility extends to cover situations where federally incurred activity creates an educational burden on communities which they cannot be expected to bear. One comprehensive Federal policy should cover all these situations.

2. The Federal Government should assure educational opportunity to Indians and other native peoples in Territories and possessions. One comprehensive policy should cover these situations.

3. As far as possible in connection with 1 and 2 above, use should be made of existing public educational facilities or if added facilities are needed they should be provided by the Government to State or local public educational agencies. All arrangements should be cleared through State departments of education.

FUNCTIONS OF THE FEDERAL EDUCATIONAL AGENCY

1. The historical functions of (*a*) collecting statistics and facts to show the conditions and progress of education; (*b*) diffusing information to aid in the establishment and maintenance of efficient school systems; and (*c*) otherwise promoting the cause of education throughout the country, should be retained with major emphasis. Among these three functions, the emphasis should be in the order listed.

2. The historical function should be expanded by congressional mandate to include the biennial collection of facts and objective description of all educational activities of the Federal Government which concern the regularly constituted schools and educational institutions of the country and the diffusion of this information. This should include research and diffusion of information concerning the effect of these activities on the regularly constituted schools and educational institutions in the States.

3. All Federal activities which concern elementary or secondary schools in the States should be the responsibility of the Federal educational agency unless the evidence is clear-cut to the contrary as stated in 7 above. This should include matters involved with instruction and educational services. It should extend to the basic responsibility for the comprehensive program for dependent children or Lanham Act type of assistance.

4. The Federal educational agency should be responsible for educational aspects of activities involving higher educational institutions which primarily concern more than the specialty of any individual noneducational department or independent agency. For instance, the ROTC is primarily concerned with the specialty of the Army and thus should remain there. On the other hand, the placement of exchange professors in American universities should be vested in the

Federal educational agency. This policy would not deny to the Department of State its logical noneducational part in the program.

5. When, because of the exceptions noted in 3 and 4 above, a Federal activity operates through or concerns the regularly constituted schools or higher educational institutions in the country with primary responsibility in other than the Federal educational agency, the latter should have a well-defined coordinating or educational service function in connection therewith. The certification of educational need by the Office of Education in the veterans' educational facilities program of the Federal Works Agency is a case in point.

6. The Federal educational agency should be a source for professional educational service to all agencies involved in educational matters whether having to do with in-service training or the promotion of their particular specialties. In general, duplication of professional educational personnel in noneducational departments and agencies should be avoided.

7. Cutting across several of these functions is that of strengthening responsibility, professional leadership, and educational initiative in schools and higher educational institutions in States, with particular reference to State departments of education. This should be a major function of the Federal educational agency.

8. Also implied above, but needing greater stress, is the function of aggressive research, diffusion of information, and of promotion concerning educational activities or services badly needed but often neglected by States. Such a function, properly performed, should encourage States to assume responsibility and may avoid some of the piecemeal demands for specialized Federal educational activities. It may result in Federal programs which are much more effective. The current move for a labor extension service is a case in point. This function may apply with equal force to such areas as need for school building construction and scholarships and fellowships. The Federal educational agency should be the first to detect these trends and to offer solutions based on research findings. Leadership and service of this type should be an important function of this agency. Lack of aggressiveness by the Office of Education may have been a factor in absence of comprehensive Federal programs and substitution of piecemeal activities in noneducational agencies.

9. The Federal educational agency should be a clearinghouse for service and information to educators, educational institutions, and scholars to insure that educational inquiries will be directed to the one or more Federal agencies, libraries, or individuals in the Government which are most expert in respect thereto.

10. Closely allied with this is the function of the Federal educational agency in respect to utilization of the rich resources of the Federal Government in a curricular service to schools.

Organization of the Federal Educational Agency

It is apparent from the materials presented previously that the United States Office of Education has not been properly equipped to perform the functions listed above. It has not been able to exert the educational leadership or render service either at the State or Federal level commensurate with the needs of education in States, the importance of education in our national life, or with the rapidly growing educational activities in the Federal Government. Considering all factors, we have been fortunate in having even the modicum of effectiveness which has been developed in this office. To some extent we believe this situation can be improved by proper organization which will better its professional status and give it more leadership stature.

The Federal educational agency is not primarily an operating office. Its major function is professional research, service, and leadership in the interests of education in the States. Thus, our first question must be: What type of organizational structure will permit this agency to perform this function most effectively? The question of what will look neat or streamlined in a Federal organization chart is secondary. It is fundamental that this agency should be nonpartisan both in its personnel and its point of view. It follows that every possible protection must be given to assure that it be protected from partisan politics and from those who desire to build power for the sake of power. This agency, in its organization, should be consistent with what is considered good organizational practice on the State and local level.

A National Board of Education

We believe that serious consideration should be given to the establishment of a National Board of Education. Such a board should be of a size small enough to assure compactness and not so large that it is unwieldy. Its members should be appointed for relatively long periods, and terms staggered in order to assure continuity in policy and to avoid "packing" by a President during any one term of office. Possibly 12 members, one appointed by the President each year for a 12-year term, would meet these qualifications.

Extremely high-type nonpartisan individuals with concern for the broad general welfare of society and individuals therein should be chosen. They should not be selected primarily because they represent any type of political, occupational, social, racial, religious, educational, or other special interest, but rather because they are our outstanding

369

citizens in their appreciation of education. It is to be expected, however, that in making selections the President will give some consideration to keeping the board reasonably representative.

No two members should come from any one State and probably no member should be appointed from a State which has been recently represented on the board. A majority of the members probably should be laymen as contrasted with professional educators. Memers should be removable from office only for cause specified in law.

Legal specification alone cannot insure the high type of board necessary. It is essential that those groups and individuals in this country who have major concern for the general welfare of education be a vital force in public opinion to assure proper appointments. In the last analysis this is our best guarantee for proper selection of members to this board, as well as for many other improvements suggested in this report.

Board members should not be paid, except for per diem and expenses when performing their official business. It is assumed that they would meet regularly four to six times a year and on call. The board should be primarily advisory in nature, but by specific mandate of Congress could, and probably should, be given a number of responsibilities such as determination of policy within legislative limitations regarding approval of State plans for education as related to Federal subsidies and the application of other standards which may be a consideration in making grants to States.

A number of functions of the old Federal Board for Vocational Education may well be assumed by this board. Certainly its most important function would be to advise the Commissioner of Education relative to needed research and promotional programs and to advise the Federal educational agency in developing its services in performing the functions outlined above. Its counsel should be a leavening force concerning educational matters in both the legislative and executive branches. It should review Federal policy in education from time to time to ascertain that the best interests of States and Nation are being advanced by Federal educational activities.

A number of considerations, some of which have already been discussed, prompt this suggestion:

1. The potential danger of using the Federal educational agency for partisan purposes or for the promotion of ideologies or educational programs inimical to the best State and national interest would be minimized by the National Board of Education. As it now stands, the Commissioner of Education can use his office, or, if he resists, his superiors can use his office, for improper or unwise purposes. The recent controversy between the Federal Security Administrator and the Office of Education at least demonstrates the potentialities of this

370

situation.[3] Education can be used to pervert the mind of a nation as has been done in certain other countries. Although this has not happened here, we must guard against the possibility that it could happen.

2. At both State and local level we insist that educational policy within constitutional or legislative limits be developed by a board of representative citizens. It is not logical that, at the one place where we fear undue control of education, we should neglect at least an opportunity for review of policy by such a group.

3. If the Federal Government is to encourage greater strength in State departments of education and proper organization therein, it must set an example for such departments. We have suggested a small grant to State departments of education which meet minimal federally determined standards. If this is done, or even if it should not be done, certainly the major function of encouraging proper organization to bring educational strength and initiative in States cannot be effective if the State finger of scorn can be pointed at Federal educational organization.

4. The Federal Government requires State boards for vocational education, yet on the Federal level we have abolished such a board, leading to situations which at least are alleged to have been federally "masterminded." Particularly in important matters of Federal determination of policy or standards within limits as prescribed by Congress, of discretionary power, or of State plan approval or disapproval the decision should not rest on the judgment of one individual. Such violates a Federal requirement in States as well as our best tradition of educational administration on State and local level.

5. The development of balanced Federal educational leadership and service to counter the present Federal imbalance, is a project which needs our best and most objective minds. It should not be entrusted to one individual regardless of the amount of wisdom he may possess. This is not the American way, particularly in education. We have no illusion that all the Federal problems in the field of education will be resolved by this report. Problems of the type indicated herein will be with us for a long time. It is essential that we have a continuing body of representative citizens which will be alert to see that the educational staff search out these problems, discover their significance, and make constructive suggestions relative to their solution.

6. The Federal educational agency must be alert to educational problems and difficulties from the grass roots of education in the

---

[3] See Congressional Record, August 2, 1948, Vol. 94, No. 123, 80th Cong., 2d sess., p. 9788 ; and Investigation of the Federal Security Agency, Hearings before the Subcommittee of the Committee on Appropriations, House of Representatives, 80th Cong., 2d sess., on the Department of Labor-Federal Security Agency Appropriation Bill for 1949, U. S. Government Printing Office, August 1948.

States. Although the professional staff in education of this agency will know of these problems from professional sources at State and local levels, it is assumed that this staff should also know of problems from the point of view of the educational layman. The board should help to keep it alert in this respect.

7. Educational administrators are accustomed to acting as executives to lay boards. They have learned the worth of such boards through training and experience. They resist being placed in positions where political considerations or one-man administrative control can exert undue influence over education. It is believed that a National Board of Education will enhance the opportunity to obtain strong professional educational leadership at the head as well as in subordinate positions in the Federal educational agency.

Thus we consider a National Board of Education an essential first in our reorganization of education on the Federal level. It should be without administrative functions, except as such may be given to it by specific act of Congress. It should safeguard the State and national educational interest. It should revitalize the Federal educational agency in its function of service to education in the States. The board should help the agency gain professional stature in the government so that it may better assume its position as an integrating and service force for the various educational activities of the Federal Government. It should help build balance into the Federal educational activities as they affect the schools and higher institutions of the country.

It is realized that, in spite of safeguards, appointments might be made with political considerations in mind. Again, public opinion is our best protection. During one term of office a President would be very unlikely to appoint a majority of the board. The public usually expresses itself more quickly and more vehemently concerning abuses in education than on other public matters. The mere whisper of scandal in school affairs will usually bring action from a community which may tolerate corruption elsewhere in its government. When an educator goes wrong it usually makes the headlines. Education is very close to the general public concern. Thus it is believed that a President would be diligent in making appointments.

Should Congress or the Senate have any part in confirmation of appointments? We are inclined to believe there will be less political consideration if the President has the final power of appointment, although we recognize that this is contrary to much precedent.

Even though the board's functions be primarily advisory, its caliber would tend to give it strong influence. Its closeness to public opinion in the States would be mirrored in its advisement and in its relay back to the people of anything contrary to the best public interest. This should result in better Federal policy and administration, and a quick check on faulty Federal conduct of educational activities.

Would this board tend to amass power or otherwise exert undue control over education? The potentialities of this type of abuse are considered to be much less than in the present placing of complete responsibility, without even advisory check, on administrative officials who can be politically appointed and in a political chain of command. Certainly, the Congress which brought such a board into being could regulate or even abolish it if its functions are abused.

There is no panacea in organization. We have tried another type of organization and its record of achievement has been disappointing. A National Board of Education, even for those who may consider it only an experiment, is a venture which has so much in its favor and is so much in the American educational tradition that it is worthy of a fair trial.

THE COMMISSIONER OF EDUCATION

The commissionership of education should be a professional career position. It should challenge the caliber of man drawn to our most responsible positions of educational administration at State, local, or institutional level. It is only by chance that such an individual can now be drawn to this position. What can be done to rectify this situation?

There are many valid arguments in favor of appointment of the Commissioner by the National Board of Education. Although we prefer this method of appointment we must admit certain justification for the belief that, if the President is to be responsible for the proper operation of the executive branch, he must select those who administer its activities. An alternate plan by which the President appoints from a panel of nominees submitted by the Board may be an appropriate meeting ground between these two points of view. This has the potential disadvantage of change in administration of the Federal educational agency with each change in the presidency. The position of Commissioner of Education must be nonpartisan in nature and every legal safeguard should be erected against the abuse of this principle. Again, public opinion concerning this matter will be a greater protection against abuse than matters which may be written into law. Appointmnt should be for an indefinite tenure determined by good behavior and effective administration.

INTERNAL ORGANIZATION OF THE FEDERAL EDUCATIONAL AGENCY

A number of matters which should be taken into consideration in the internal reorganization of the Federal educational agency have been discussed previously. These will not be repeated here, particularly as they are not the major concern of this report. Recommendations and suggestions concerning the transfer of certain activities to the office and the development of needed coordination have already been discussed.

Location of the Federal Educational Agency in the Executive Branch

The determination of the location of the Federal educational agency should be governed largely by its functions and its modes of operation. Where can it best perform its function of research, service, and leadership in the interest of education in States? Where can it best act as an integrating and service agency for the dispersed educational activities in the various departments and independent agencies of the Federal Government? Where can it operate most effectively without partisan influence or undue control of education in States? Where is it most likely to develop professional status commensurate with its importance?

There are three feasible places in the Government where the Federal educational agency could be located. First, a Federal department of education with a Cabinet officer at its head could be established. Such a recommendation was made by the National Advisory Committee on Education appointed by the President which rendered its report in 1931. This possibility is discarded primarily because it could subject education to political control. Other considerations in refusal to consider this solution favorably involve its incompatibility with good State and local educational organization, the needless increase of major governmental departments, the assumption of undue centralization of educational functions, and the regard for retaining basic control and responsibility for education in the States. Although education would gain governmental status by such a move, too high a price would be paid for it.

The second location, in a Federal department of health, welfare and education, has more to commend it. In suport of such a department it has been pointed out that all these functions are concerned with the welfare of the individual, the family, or the community. It follows the principle of centralization of functions by purpose. This would be a logical outgrowth of the present Federal Security Agency. By forming a united front, it is assumed that better presentations of over-all fiscal and other needs could be made to the President and to the Congress. Through the prestige of a secretary in the President's Cabinet, each concern of the department could be advanced more effectively and interdepartmental coordination implemented. Each of the services involves relationships with States usually in the form of

374

grants-in-aid, thus making for considerable compatibility in methods of operating. Efficiency and economy should result from such an organization.

On the negative side, and as related primarily to education, such an organization also has certain disadvantages:

1. The much-needed National Board of Education would not easily fit into the structure.

2. The secretary, and assistant secretaries, if such were in the picture, would almost of necessity be political appointees who could subject education to political pressures. Although such pressures would be damaging to the field of health, the damage to education could be much worse. Education deals with ideas in the minds of individuals, while health is concerned with their physical well-being.

3. The other agencies of the proposed department do not have the clear-cut tradition and record of placing responsibility on their counterparts in the States as has the United States Office of Education.

4. Education has more in common with activities of several other departments of the Government than with activities of the proposed department. Witness the educational activities of the Department of Agriculture, Atomic Energy Commission, Army, Navy, and the Veterans' Administration, all of which have larger programs which concern elementary, secondary, or higher education than the Office of Education itself.

5. The great need of developing the Federal educational agency as a professional servicing and integrating force for all educational activities of the Government, the large majority of which are outside the proposed department, has been pointed out. This may be used to support independent status rather than inclusion in a department.

6. There are those who fear that the interest of the present Office of Education would be overlooked as its activities are relatively small as compared with rapidly expanding activities, such as social security. Major consideration in determination of policy and allocation of budget would naturally favor the larger operating activities. They see little chance of obtaining a departmental secretary who has the vision or ability to weigh decisions which involve such diversified and specialized fields as would be represented in the department. A professional educator probably should not head such a department, as this associates education with partisan politics. It is also unlikely that such an individual would be appointed. The probability of either a professional medical or welfare individual in this position would tend to strengthen the special field of his interest possibly at the expense of education.

7. There are others who believe that association of education with these welfare activities would give to education the connotation of

charity and social service, an implication inconsistent with the important place of education in the life of a democratic nation.

8. It is the belief of many that the departmental structure adds a needless administrative level (or possibly two levels if assistant secretaries are included) to hinder direct representations to the President, to the Congress, or to the people in matters which involve education. Difficulties in this respect recently evident in the Federal Security Agency could easily become more aggravated in the departmental structure.

9. The too-prevalent tendency of a department to desire to amass power and control is antagonistic to Federal policy as it should concern education.

10. The proposed department to include education is contrary to accepted and best practice for organization of education on the State and local level.

11. In total, these factors might reduce public confidence in the Federal educational agency.

The third possible location for education is in a separate independent agency. Practically all the objections which have been raised in connection with incorporating the Federal educational agency in a department of health, welfare, and education are minimized or eliminated by such an organization. The National Board of Education would fit well into this plan. The opportunity for partisan controls and abuse is reduced. It may be in a better position to work with, integrate, and serve educational functions in other agencies of the Government. It would be less likely to come under noneducational domination. There is no implication that its services are involved with charity and social service. It should be able to make its representations to the President and to Congress directly without dilution of the professional education point of view by intervening administrators.

If there were any tendency to attempt to amass power and exert undue controls it would be in a position where responsibility could be easily established and proper corrective measures taken immediately by the President or the Congress. Such an organization is in line with accepted and best educational practice on state and local levels. Potentially the plan seems to offer greater chance of developing public confidence in the Federal educational agency. Professional competency in leadership and service should be able to develop more effectively.

But the argument is not all in favor of the independent agency. There is a substantial record of professional competency in a number of bureaus within departments. The record of competency within independent agencies has not always been good. The multiplying of governmental agencies reporting directly to the President is not good administrative policy unless the Office of the President is reorganized

376

to meet this contingency. Possibly a Cabinet officer might have more prestige and political ability in presenting needs of the agency to the President and the Congress than would the Commissioner of Education. The independent agency might tend to become too submerged or dissociated from the normal stream of responsibility of the executive branch.

In the last analysis the decision concerning the location of the Federal educational agency in the framework of the Government will have to be made in consideration of the total anticipated reorganization of the executive branch, a matter beyond the scope of the report. If education is thought of as "just another governmental function," the question can be answered in more routine manner. If, however, thought is given to the proper importance of education in the life of a democratic nation, its relationship and functions relative to education in States, its need for protection from partisanship, and the necessity for integration and service among the various educational activities throughout the Government, it is urgent to give special attention to the location of the Federal educational agency. These aspects may justify special treatment and exception from criteria developed for the more normal operating agencies. The balance of all the various arguments warrants giving serious consideration to the establishment of a separate independent agency.

If, in spite of what seems to be a majority of evidence in favor of the independent agency, it is considered essential to place the Federal educational agency in a departmental structure, the question arises as to how the National Board of Education could fit into this plan. It is believed that under no circumstances should this Board be sacrificed for the purpose of merely making the structure look neat. If the Board were placed at the bureau or agency level it would be so submerged that it might have little or no influence at the department level. It is thus suggested that the Board might better protect and foster education if it were advisory to the Secretary of the department, in which case the Commissioner of Education might well be its secretary or otherwise be delegated responsibility for its agenda and similar matters. It is apparent that neither of these solutions for locating the Board are as satisfactory as would be possible in the independent agency where no such problem would be encountered.

* * *

All the problems of the Federal Government in respect to education will not be solved by the recommendations and suggestions of this report. They suggest a general framework for Federal policy concerning education and an organization to execute it, as conditions for future progress. Moreover, it would be a mistake to expect the Federal educational agency, which through little fault of its own has played a very minor role in the Federal educational enterprise, to accept suddenly the full responsibility for solutions to all of the problems treated in this report. In a sense the Federal educational agency will have to win its right to be the integrating and service force, or the operating agency for added activities when justified, within the Government. Its major role of research, service, and leadership to strengthen educational responsibility and initiative in States is an increasing challenge. Implementing the Office so that it can grow in stature and service to perform these functions is necessary. The alternative is still further chaos in Federal educational activities and potential disregard for the best interests of schools and educational institutions in States.

Part Four

FEDERAL ACTIVITIES AND ORGANIZATION
IN THE FIELD OF EMPLOYMENT

Chapter I

SCOPE AND TRENDS OF FEDERAL EMPLOYMENT FUNCTIONS

The employment functions of the Federal Government in broadest terms may be defined as those of· supervising and regulating conditions of work in nongovernmental employment.. They include such activities as the conduct of research and dissemination of information concerning employment and variations in employment, wages, cost of living, conditions of work, and employment practices; the administration of regulatory statutes dealing with conditions of employment; development of sound and tested standards of employee relations and labor law administration; provision of job training and guidance facilities for potential and out-of-school workers to help them improve their prospects of gainful employment; the administration of public employment offices and unemployment insurance laws to compensate wage losses and to minimize periods of unemployment; the establishment of standards and procedures whereby public officials intervene to assist employers and labor organizations in preventing and adjusting disputes over conditions of employment.

At different points the Government's functions as supervisor of employment overlap its functions as provider of assistance to the unemployed, as educator, as protector of the health of the population, as stabilizer of the national economy, as administrator of national defense. Public assistance policies have historically been formulated and administered with a view to their effects on the supply and incentives of labor. The method of insurance originally applied to employment accidents has been extended to the protection of workers from the hazards of unemployment and old age, and is financed by a tax on pay rolls and in the case of old age on the worker's pay envelope.[1] The public employment offices register claimants for unemployment compensation and apply the provisions of law concerning their willingness and availability for work. The employment agency is vitally concerned with the standards and curriculum of vocational training and counselling activities in the schools.

In the enforcement of factory inspection laws concerning the health and safety of employees, the employment agency is compelled to rely

---

[1] In a few States, the employee pays an unemployment compensation tax.

on the medical and engineering professions and the health agency. Laws prescribing hours of work and overtime pay, minimum wages and prevailing rates, have to be considered in relation to their effects on costs, prices, employment, and purchasing power. The research and statistical functions of the employment agency are essential tools in the planning and timing of public works or other policies aimed at stabilizing employment at high levels and preventing violent fluctuations in the demand for labor. Finally, the public employment service is the natural agency to administer, with respect to civilian employment, selective service or national service legislation, both in order to establish orderly withdrawals from the civilian labor force and to direct workers from less to more esential industries and occupations.

The problems of structural organization and coordination in the field of employment are obviously complex. The democratic process of agitation, discussion, and compromise, here as elsewhere, has resulted in the recognition of economic and social responsibilities as governmental functions in piecemeal fashion. Regulation of the employment process involves issues as controversial as any in the relation of Government to the economic order. The past 10 years has witnessed in this field struggle over the issues as to who should administer these functions, how they should be coordinated and controlled, and how they should be coordinated with related activities. There has been frequent shuffling and transferring of functions, resulting in a high degree of functional dispersion. Many factors are involved here, including differences of opinion over the objectives of the Labor Department, the appropriate scope of its functions, conflicting ideas as to the requirements of congressional control and Presidential coordination, the pressures of influential groups with which employment and labor agencies have to deal, changing relationships with social security and national defense programs, and Federal-State relations. In the absence of deliberate consideration and action, these factors will operate to continue this wasteful peregrination of functions. It is highly desirable that fundamental consideration be given to the basic trends in governmental responsibility, and to the lessons of administrative experience, in formulating a concept of public purpose that will provide a focus of program supervision and policy coordination adequate to cope with the employment problems of the coming decades.

One basic trend in Federal responsibility and method with respect to employment and related functions is reflected in the congressional declaration of purpose in the Employment Act of 1946:

. . . to use all practicable means . . . to coordinate and utilize all its plans, functions, and resources for the purpose of creating and maintaining, in a manner calculated to foster and promote free competitive enterprise and the general welfare, conditions under which there will be afforded useful employment opportunities, including self-employment, for those able, willing, and seeking to work, and to promote maximum employment, production, and purchasing power.[2]

Clearly, however, achievement and maintenance of maximum employment is a national objective that comprises the activities of practically all Federal agencies. In establishing the Council of Economic Advisers in the Executive Office of the President, Congress recognized that it is too broad an assignment to be vested in the head of any single operating department. Below the central level of planning and coordination, however, several operating programs clearly assume a more interrelated aspect once Congress and the President think in terms of coordinating existing national policies so as to promote maximum employment, production, and purchasing power.

Changing Viewpoints on Employment Policy

Concept of the Labor Force

If high employment levels are successfully maintained the distinctions between programs dealing with the employed and the unemployed, between the employable and the unemployable, between those having or seeking employment and those unable or unwilling to work will be greatly reduced. The concept of guiding and developing the labor force as a whole, including the training, distribution, and utilization of the Nation's labor power will assume greater importance. Under the impact of depression and war, the Nation found it necessary to adopt and coordinate policies dealing with various parts of the working force—youth, employable unemployed, the physically handicapped, older workers, etc.—and the definition of employability changed almost overnight. In peacetime the Nation may consider neither necessary nor desirable the wartime centralization of responsibility for expanding the labor force, effecting controlled withdrawals for military service, and allocating manpower to essential industries and occupations, but it is increasingly clear that the most effective utilization of manpower requires thorough consideration of policies dealing with the training, placement and distribution, compensation, security, and satisfaction of workers in their jobs.

Coordination of Employment and Employment Security

Employment and employment security policies, so far as the latter are based on the employment relationship, should be formulated and evaluated in relation to each other. The nature of measures to be

---

[2] 60 Stat. 23.

383

adopted may vary as political and economic conditions change, but it is clearly desirable to encourage high levels of production which will permit the maintenance of adequate standards of life. Maintenance of high levels of production is a joint responsibility of employers and employees working in collaboration with the Government. Such policies may conceivably be discharged by collective-bargaining agreements or by statutory regulation and adjustment of social-insurance benefits. Fostering the sense of employer and labor responsibility for programs presents a problem radically different from giving direct assistance to individuals through health, educational, and social-welfare services or by outright financial payments. It is entirely possible that coordination of employment and security with social-welfare measures, and consideration of their effects upon the labor force and financial capacity of the economy as a whole, may be required at a supradepartmental level by Congress and the President.

Wage-Price Relationships and Industrial Disputes

In our national history it has been only in wartime that the Government has adopted policies controlling the general movement of wages. Experience with relatively high employment suggests that a situation could conceivably arise requiring the Federal Government to take action to regulate or control inflationary-deflationary price changes. Such action might entail the adoption of policies dealing directly with wages, and these policies would have to be coordinated with the machinery for handling labor disputes. The events attending the wage negotiations in such basic industries as coal, iron and steel, railroads, automobiles, and electrical manufacturing during the post-VJ-day period have since become almost routine annual occurrences, with sustained "follow-the-leader" effects that have been felt throughout the entire economy. In a free society, wage-stabilization measures of any kind would depend upon the practices and machinery of collective bargaining, but if public policies concerning wages should be adopted they should be administered in relation to the skills and information of the Government agencies continuously concerned with the supply and distribution of labor, and with the economic effects of industry, occupational, and geographical wage differentials.

The Interdependence of Employee, Employer, and Public Interests

Practically every Government function in the employment and welfare fields of the past 50 years has been adopted as a measure promoting the welfare of wage-earning and lower-income groups.

384

Such measures as accident and unemployment compensation, wage-hour and child-labor laws, collective bargaining, and social insurance generally, once so bitterly opposed, are now accepted basically as public policies although great difference of opinion still exists with respect to details. It is recognized that these policies have important economic effects in which both employer and employee groups and the general public have vital interests. As instruments, these policies will in all likelihood have to be modified or adapted to meet future needs effectively. Conflicts of real or presumed group interest will undoubtedly continue to arise. There is general consensus, however, that these conflicts should be restricted to the broad sphere of politics and legislation and that in general administrative departments should not seek to represent the interests of a single organized group as against others, nor restrict themselves to promoting the settlement of intergroup controversies through nongovernmental action without consideration of the public interest. Such concepts bring too narrow a perspective to bear upon the problems of achieving maximum employment and the national welfare. The interests of employers and labor organizations cannot be confined to or channeled through a single department. Efforts to do so have aggravated the complexities of governmental organization, and have immeasurably retarded the proper development of established functions. Proposals for departmental reorganization, therefore, should not be based upon protective or ideological affinities with influential groups in the population. As a problem of organizing to administer public policies most effectively, the approach should be to find a desirable focus of related functions for Congress and the President to rely upon for continuous study and coordination for purposes of administrative supervision and program development. From this standpoint, the appropriate method of relating the viewpoints of interest group organizations to administrative departments is through the maintenance of genuine advisory and consultative contacts at high policy levels. Both formal and informal devices of consultation, properly established, may be exploited to the mutual benefit both of the Government and outside groups.

PRESIDENTIAL COORDINATION AND DEPARTMENTAL COORDINATION

The foregoing trends have by no means secured full statutory or public recognition, but they perhaps provide guideposts for setting the course of administrative reorganization. One of the crucial factors in the field of employment policy as distinct from administration is the extent to which Congress and the President choose to place responsibility on one or more department heads for planning and coordination, or prefer to lift these activities up to the Executive Office level. As a general principle, the more widely scattered the operating functions, the greater the responsibility for coordination that is placed upon the President and the agencies under his immediate direction. The Employment Act makes no provision for coordination of operating programs beyond the utilization of statistical information and fixing of responsibility upon the Council of Economic Advisers for giving advice on national economic and fiscal policies. Supervision of operating programs requires an intermediate level, partly to prevent congestion at the center, and partly to encourage responsibility for handling congressional relations, settling inter-bureau disputes, maintaining outside consultative contacts, coordinating interrelated programs, and anticipating emerging needs by systematic study of operations. In order to lay the foundation for consideration of an appropriate structure of departmental coordination in the employment field, we turn now to identify the principal employment programs and to appraise their relative fiscal importance and administrative evolution.

Comparative Trends in Appropriations

Table XXV, page 387, presents a classification of Federal appropriations for activities specifically oriented toward the employment process and employer-employee relations. It extends Government employment, Government work and public assistance programs, and the social insurance other than unemployment compensation. It reveals the sharp rise in expenditures after each world war, the 20-fold increase during the thirties, and an apparent stabilization of appropriations for employment activities since 1945 close to $250,000,000. The total available funds for the Department of Labor are included at the bottom of the table, and show how small a part of the functions are now located in that Department. In 1949 comparison indicates a department restricted to statistical and regulatory functions, from which training, placement, and labor relations activities have been excluded.

Table XXVI, page 387, presents a functional classification of estimated expenditures, drawn from the Federal budget, using categories that are not strictly comparable with table XXV (particularly with respect to education and training). In this table the estimated expenditures for Government work and assistance programs and social security administration are included, to afford some idea of the relative size of employment functions compared with security and welfare.

[In thousands of dollars]

Major function	1915	1920	1930	1940	1945	1948	1949
1. Research and information [2]	204	309	359	1,012	3,985	3,473	4,073
2. Vocational training, rehabilitation and guidance [3]		22,050	3,829	3,865	95,505	25,587	32,162
3. Employment offices		672	217	3,480	82,037	69,043	[4] 207
4. Unemployment compensation				83,050	35,024	126,304	196,284
5. Regulation of employment conditions [5]				3,783	4,512	4,647	5,000
6. Promotion of labor standards		104	108	391	625	463	594
7. Labor disputes	300	246	422	3,895	[6] 21,546	9,583	13,353
8. General administration [7]	139	363	525	2,375	2,998	5,136	1,990
Total	643	23,744	5,460	101,851	246,232	244,236	253,663
Total Labor Department appropriations (estimated)	3,600		[8] 10,774	28,669	[9] 69,389	[10] 85,306	14,258

[1] Source: Estimates Division, Bureau of the Budget.
[2] Excludes employment statistical activities of Census Bureau, Bureau of Agricultural Economics, Interstate Commerce Commission, and Railroad Retirement Board.
[3] Excludes appropriations for Veterans' Administration, and includes only "trades and industries" part of the grants to States for vocational education.
[4] U. S. Employment Service appropriation merged with Bureau of Employment Security. The $207,000 was for the Veterans' Reemployment Rights Division. In 1940, part of the unemployment compensation funds went to support State employment offices.
[5] Excludes industrial hygiene functions of U. S. Public Health Service and Bureau of Mines Inspection activities.
[6] Excludes war agencies other than National War Labor Board.
[7] Offices of the Secretary and Solicitor of Labor, plus departmental appropriations for travel and contingent expenses until 1949.
[8] Includes Immigration and Naturalization Bureau.
[9] Includes $44,000,000 for Children's Bureau wartime EMIC program.
[10] Includes $65,000,000 for U. S. Employment Service.

TABLE XXVI.—*Functional classification of estimated expenditures for employment, security, and welfare activities, 1947, 1948, 1949* [1]

[In thousands of dollars]

	1947	1948	1949
Employment functions:			
Labor information, statistics, and general administration	10,713	8,734	8,216
Training and placement of workers	89,283	71,101	79,190
Unemployment and accident compensation	91,430	97,292	101,629
Mediation and regulation of employment conditions	19,682	17,432	22,642
Subtotal, employment functions	211,108	194,559	211,677
Security and welfare functions:			
Retirement and dependents' insurance	306,093	766,474	584,280
Assistance to aged and special groups	738,331	820,102	894,170
Work and direct relief	2,965	7,294	9,802
Social Security Administration	8,477	3,956	3,001
Subtotal, security and welfare	1,055,866	1,597,826	1,491,253
Grand total	1,266,974	1,792,385	1,702,930

[1] Source: U. S. Budget, 1949, pp. A25–26, A31–32.

Considering table XXV, it appears that by far the largest category in dollar terms is the item of grants to States covering 100 percent of the administrative costs for unemployment compensation and employment offices (the latter has been financed in large part by unemployment compensation funds since 1937, but not 100 percent until 1942). Next in size are the grants for vocational rehabilitation and education (veterans' rights and benefits are excluded). The statistical, promotional, and regulatory programs have always been comparatively small, none rising to as much as $10,000,000 in toto except the labor disputes agencies during the war and after the passage of the Labor Management Relations Act of 1947. Clearly, the programs of greatest cost are grants to States and the programs of direct money payments and services.

Expenditures for administration (personal services, travel, and other contingent expenses) of employment functions approximated $35,-000,000 in fiscal year 1948, slightly less than 20 percent of the total for that year. Administrative expenditures of approximately $15,000,000 constituted less than 1 percent of Federal expenditures for social security and public assistance. The relatively greater proportion of administrative costs in the employment field is due partly to the smaller amounts appropriated, but also to the fact that expenses for statistical, regulatory, and mediation functions fall practically 100 percent in the administrative category.

Centrifugal Tendencies

Down to 1933 the employment and welfare functions of the Federal Government were fairly well centralized in the Department of Labor. The Bureau of Labor Statistics, the Children's Bureau, the Women's Bureau, covered the research and informational field; the United States Employment Service was responsible for the placement, if not the training and educational, activities; the United States Conciliation Service handled labor relations except those in the railroad industry. The expansion of Federal functions beginning in 1933 resulted in setting up many new agencies and action programs outside the Department. The work and relief programs for adults and youth were established independently; the National Labor Relations Board, the Social Security Board, and the Railroad Retirement Board were made independent agencies. From 1933 to 1938 the Labor Department was enlarged by the creation of a Division of Labor Standards by administrative order of the Secretary (1935), the Apprentice Training Service (1937), and the Wage and Hour and Public Contracts Division (1936 and 1938).

In 1939 a process of attrition began. The Bureau of Immigration and Naturalization, which had been in the Department since 1913, was transferred to the Department of Justice by Reorganization Plan No. 1 of 1939. The Employment Service was transferred to the Social Security Board at the same time, and though it was returned to the Department of Labor in 1945 by Executive order, it was again transferred to the Federal Security Agency in 1948, this time by Congress in the Labor-Federal Security Appropriation Act of 1949. The Children's Bureau, except for its child labor and youth employment functions, was transferred to the Federal Security Agency in 1946, and in 1947

388

the Conciliation Service was abolished and reestablished as an independent agency in the Federal Mediation and Conciliation Service. The wartime manpower, wage control and labor disputes agencies were created organizationally independent of the Department of Labor, although they relied to a great extent on its statistical, inspection, and conciliation branches.

Viewed in the perspective of 15 years, covering the depths of depression and peaks of war and full employment, it was perhaps inevitable that the emergency programs and novel functions should apply unusual methods, nongovernmental personnel, and departure from established departmental routines. In emergency situations it may be desirable to set up short-run, temporary agencies outside the regular departmental structure. However, the present situation has gone much further and longer than this. The process of removing from the Department functions falling naturally within the scope of industrial and employment relations, that has continued now for 10 years, requires careful reexamination. In modern industrial civilization, the complex of labor, employment, and social security functions of government are so important that it is impossible for the political legislature and chief executive properly to carry forward their policy-making responsibilities without a focus of administrative leadership and supervision over the operating programs in these fields. From the standpoint of orderly administration, the problem is one of division and combination, unless it be assumed that these functions should all be combined in one department, grouping health and education welfare and social insurance.

TABLE XXVII.—*Personnel, by bureaus, Department of Labor, fiscal years 1939–41, 1946–48 actual, 1949 estimated* [1]

	1939	1940	1941	1946	1947	1948	1949
Office of the Secretary	135	222	188	293	324	259	242
Office of the Solicitor	(2)	(2)	(2)	240	238	225	210
Bureau of Apprenticeship	(3)	(3)	(3)	296	462	490	492
Bureau of Labor Standards	87	80	245	128	136	81	74
Bureau of Labor Statistics	700	603	892	1,734	1,713	1,006	1,043
Wage and Hour Division	704	1,776	2,589	1,267	1,365	1,123	1,141
Women's Bureau	79	89	67	63	73	67	61
U. S. Employment Service	825	(4)		[5] 1,322	1,558	1,000	(6)
Bureau of Veterans' Reemployment Rights						81	44
Immigration and Naturalization Service	3,773	3,817	(7)				
Children's Bureau	345	438	383	328	(8)		
U. S. Conciliation Service	83	107	160	488	449	(9)	
Retraining and Reemployment Rights Division				90	[10] 87		
National Wage Stabilization Board				799	[10] 413		
Total	6,731	7,132	4,524	7,048	6,818	4,332	3,307

[1] Source: Budget Office, Department of Labor.
[2] Not established as a separate entity—included in Secretary's Office, Wage and Hour Division, and Children's Bureau for those years.
[3] Not established as a separate entity. Included in the Division of Labor Standards in 1941 and prior years.
[4] Transferred to Social Security Board by Reorganization Plan No. 1, effective July 1, 1939.
[5] Does not include State and local office personnel paid from Employment Office Services and Facilities appropriation.
[6] Transferred to Federal Security Agency, effective July 1, 1948.
[7] Transferred to Department of Justice by Reorganization Plan No. 5, effective June 14, 1940.
[8] Transferred to Federal Security Agency by Reorganization Plan No. 3, effective July 16, 1946.
[9] Conciliation Service removed from Department, effective August 1947.
[10] Liquidated during 1947 fiscal year.

More than administrative considerations explain the centrifugal tendencies of the welfare, employment, and security agencies. One major factor has been the legislative mandate of the Department of Labor: "To foster, promote, and develop the welfare of the wage earners of the United States, to improve their working conditions, and to advance their opportunities for profitable employment." During all the agitation leading up to the creation of the Department in 1913, and ever since, this dedication of purpose has been interpreted widely as committing its administration to an irrevocable bias in favor of employees, and particularly of those employees who have joined labor organizations.

Organized labor has in many instances regarded the Department as its peculiar province and the Secretary of Labor as its representative in the President's cabinet. Employers and often substantial segments of the general public have shared this point of view. An opinion has existed that the Department could not be trusted to administer discretionary powers in fields involving controversies between management and labor. The very existence of these opinions has tended to prevent concentration in the Department of Labor of the activities of government designed specifically to advance the welfare of wage earners, even though the policies furthered by these activities have been adopted by the Congress.

A second factor in the dispersion of the employment functions is the emergence of the quasi-judicial board in the field of industrial relations. The National Labor Relations Board, covering disputes affecting interstate commerce generally, and the National Mediation Board in the field of railroad and air line transport are regarded as exercising judicial powers in the field of unfair labor practices and representation disputes, at least to the extent that adversary interests are keenly concerned that no single-headed administrative department should exercise control of any kind over the body deciding the issues. This fear of bias and political influence in single-headed departments responsible to the President underlies the development of independent regulatory tribunals primarily accountable to Congress and the courts.

Thirdly, operating administrative agencies, having tasted independence, do not look forward to being subordinated to a layer of departmental officials between them and the President or Congress. They enjoy the relative freedom of operation in carrying out their own special programs, without feeling too much responsibility for coordinating their policies with other agencies, or with outside groups upon whom the separate programs may be imposing conflicting obligations. Finally, labor organizations pay lip service to the idea of coordination of functions in a Labor Department, but are actually disturbed less by the dispersion of functions than by efforts to undermine and weaken them as separate programs.

390

All these factors help to explain the present scattering of Federal employment functions, plus the additional tendency of related security and welfare functions to draw employment agencies after them. Vocational education and rehabilitation, unemployment and old age security, and labor relations are all set up as independent functions, and then transferred to the Federal Security Agency, established in 1939. This process has resulted in a situation in which the FSA now includes a major segment of employment, along with health, education, and welfare functions. The major employment functions remaining in the Department of Labor constitute three sizable bureaus, the Bureau of Labor Statistics, the Wage and Hour Administration, and the Bureau of Apprenticeship. The Solicitor's office, the Bureau of Labor Standards, and the Women's Bureau together have less than 400 employees. Do these six agencies comprise a proper department? Should they be merged with other welfare programs in the Federal Security Agency? Or should a new concept and combination of functions be established which would provide emphasis and focus upon problems of the employed population, the labor market, and industrial relations separately from health, education, and welfare?

Before developing any proposals for meeting these problems, the principal areas of employment functions and their relations to health, education, and welfare programs will be examined.

Chapter II

STATISTICS OF EMPLOYMENT AND WORKING CONDITIONS

General Purpose Statistics and Operating Statistics

It has been estimated that two dozen Federal agencies collect and analyze some kind of statistics on employment. Most of these are operating or regulatory agencies which collect employment information because it is essential to or a simple byproduct of their statutory duties. Thus the Civil Service Commission obtains and publishes figures on Federal employment, the Bureau of Mines for the mining industry, the armed services for their military and civilian employees, the Office of Education for the schools, the Interstate Commerce Commission for railroads under its jurisdiction, and the Bureau of Agricultural Economics on farm labor and farm wage rates. The United States Employment Service collects from its affiliated State employment services the number of placements they make, which together with the number of registrations filed by job seekers affords to a limited extent a national picture of employment seekers and jobs filled through its facilities. It is generally recognized that nothing is likely to be gained by transferring to a single statistical agency collection and analysis functions which are designed primarily with a view to planning and controlling an agency's specialized operating program.

The quarterly employer wage reports under the old-age and survival insurance and unemployment compensation systems comprise parts of operating programs, but insofar as they approach universality of coverage they constitute the most inclusive data available on employment by establishments in covered industries and occupations. The OASI data are centralized; the unemployment compensation reports are in the files of the State employment security agencies, where they may be utilized by agreement with them and the Federal Bureau of Employment Security. Under the latter's regulations the State agencies collect, tabulate, and report information on their programs to build the statistical series on a comparable basis for the report on the system as a whole. Some States use part of their grants for employment security administration to publish estimates of employment for the State, by industry and local labor market areas.

392

The Census Bureau and the Bureau of Labor Statistics are the two Federal agencies which collect employment statistics on what may be called a general-purpose basis. The Census Bureau, in connection with the constitutional requirement for a decennial census of population, obtains information on employment status of each person gainfully employed, his occupation, and industry of employment. The Census of Manufactures (biennial), the Census of Agriculture (quinquennial), and the irregular Census of Distribution also produce information on total employment and wages, by industrial classification and employment status. Since 1941 the Bureau has conducted monthly population surveys on a sample of from 25,000 to 30,000 households in 68 areas throughout the Nation to obtain national estimates of the number of men and women employed, unemployed, or not in the labor force, for the week containing the 8th of each month. From time to time, on its own initiative and at the request of other Federal agencies, supplementary questions are included on the questionnaire to secure information on such matters as school attendance, housing status and equipment, and cash wages of farm workers. The program currently operates at a level of $1,300,000 annually.

The Bureau of Labor Statistics occupies what might be called the residual position in the employment statistics field. The statutory purpose of the Bureau is "to acquire and diffuse among the people of the United States useful information on subjects connected with labor, in the most general and comprehensive sense of that word, and especially upon its relation to capital, the hours of labor, the earnings of laboring men and women, and the means of promoting their material, social, intellectual, and moral prosperity." [1] Its formal employment statistics program consists of four activities:

1. In terms of cost, by far the largest is the monthly series of employment and pay rolls, hours worked, and average hourly and weekly earnings, by industry, based upon 125,000 employer or establishment reports, and collected in cooperation with some 30 State agencies.

2. Next in size are its occupational outlook studies, consisting of (a) surveys of the long-range employment prospects in occupations requiring planned preparation and training, (b) preparation of an Occupational Handbook for the Veterans' Administration containing a brief discussion of the trade, training requirements, and permanent prospects for employment in over 200 occupations, and (c) analyses of the effects of changes in the composition of the labor force on national labor supply, and of effects of economic factors affecting the national employment outlook (demand for labor).

3. A third program is the publication of monthly figures on hours, earnings and total employment in the construction industry.

---

[1] Subsequent legislation has expanded the scope of the Bureau specifically to include employment. 25 Stat. 182 ; 37 Stat. 737 ; 46 Stat. 1019.

4. The fourth activity is to provide monthly estimates of labor turn-over rates in selected industries.

The combined cost of these programs annually in 1948 was $770,000, compared with a total appropriation for the Bureau of $4,070,000. The Bureau also performs special studies for other agencies on somewhat of a "job-shop" basis, receiving from them on a working fund or reimbursable basis more than $500,000 annually.

The residual character of the Bureau of Labor Statistics program is further exemplified in the wide range of studies, series and reports in labor statistics other than employment. These include monthly indexes of prices paid by consumers for major commodities and services; wage-rate surveys for key occupations in selected industries and cities; reports on strikes, work stoppages, and analyses of collective-bargaining agreements; volume of construction expenditures nationally, building permits issued and housing units started; annual indexes of productivity and changes of man-hours per unit of product, by industry; studies of causes and rates of industrial accidents; and analyses of reports on labor conditions in foreign countries.

Intersecting Programs of Employment Statistics

POPULATION SAMPLING AND EMPLOYER REPORTING

The Census Bureau's monthly Report on the Labor Force (sometimes called Current Population Surveys) is a descendant of the sample surveys project undertaken by the Works Progress Administration when during the 1930's it was discovered that no adequate current information existed as to the amount of unemployment among individuals or households in the Nation. This operation was transferred by Executive order to the Bureau of the Census in 1941, where it was envisaged as a logical extension of the decennial enumeration into the current reporting field. Here the over-all concept of the labor force was developed, and made the basis for obtaining estimates not only of the employed, but the unemployed parts of the population's supply of manpower. It was also realized that a population sampling operation of this kind would give the Government the benefits of a Gallup poll of its own, not so much for reporting political opinion trends as for securing information of a socioeconomic character useful to practically all domestic agencies concerned with fiscal, economic, or welfare affairs.

Based upon a sample of households in the population, and including employment as well as unemployment, the Census Bureau's new series is more inclusive than the Bureau of Labor Statistics' employment index based upon a sample of employing establishments. The size of the sample and the source of information (housewives) prevent its use for producing information on employment by industries, or by localities and States without costly expansion, but it has become the primary source of information on the entire national labor force (supply). It could not be consolidated with the Bureau of Labor Statistics project because it is based on a different concept and collected by a different procedure. For the same reasons it is not a substitute for the Bureau of Labor Statistics series, but it raises problems of coordination which the Bureau of Labor Statistics was not slow to perceive. The Secretary of Labor has suggested at least three times the transfer of the project to the Department of Labor, in order to (1) avoid conflicts between the two series and assuring that they will be reconciled before publication, (2) centralize responsibility for the collection and reporting information on the volume and trend of employment, and (3) keep employment and labor functions grouped together for purposes of organizational responsibility and symmetry.

To these suggestions, the Department of Commerce has replied that the operation is a part of its unquestioned jurisdiction in the field of population research; that the project benefits from and in turn benefits the work of the Bureau's sampling experts in other lines of statistical research; and, very importantly, that the current population surveys are used to collect social and economic data that has nothing to do with employment or labor information. In these contentions the Census Bureau has been upheld by the Division of Statistical Standards in the Bureau of the Budget, which, since its establishment in 1939 and particularly since the passage of the Federal Reports Act of 1942, has exercised a general supervisory and coordinating function with respect to Federal statistical activities.

It seems to be generally agreed that the current population reports have to do with more than employment or labor information, and that if they were transferred to the Department of Labor they would have to be conducted separately so far as a collection and analysis are concerned. Probably no significant financial savings would be realized if consolidation is not feasible. The two activities serve different statistical purposes and each appears to be justified in its own right. From the standpoint of method, there is clearly a lesser degree of affinity to the employment statistics of the Labor Department than to the population statistics of the Commerce Department. To date no dramatic instances of conflict in the estimates of employment issued by the two agencies have received public notice, partly perhaps because the Bureau of Labor Statistics estimates are published in the Monthly Labor Review from 2 to 3 months later than the Report on the Labor Force. The labor force figures are made available by the Census Bureau to the Bureau of Labor Statistics for analysis and interpretation. The Budget Bureau is on the alert to assist in working out any interagency disputes that may arise. In short, there seems to be no pressing problem of a statistical or operating nature that requires coordination by means of transferring the operation to the Labor Department. In the longer run, however, if the population surveys were in the future to be expanded to enable the Census Bureau to make local and industrial break-downs of its data, it would then in effect be competing with the Bureau of Labor Statistics in the exercise of the latter's statutory function. From an organization standpoint, as long as the present conception of the two departments and bureaus remain, the apparent violation of major-purpose symmetry with respect to subject-matter (employment) is outweighed by the advantages of the project's present connection with population statistics as to method and purpose of collection. The principal unsettled matter in dispute is the control of release for publication, and this question can be settled through the Executive Office of the President.

CURRENT SAMPLING AND COMPULSORY REPORTING OF EMPLOYMENT

Enactment of the Social Security Act in 1935 provided, at least potentially, almost a complete census of employers and employment, because of the necessity of securing information from employing establishments on the workers and pay rolls subject to Federal and State taxes. The provisions of the State unemployment compensation laws, however, prevent the substitution of employer reports under them for the Bureau of Labor Statistics monthly series. The State laws vary as to the size of employing establishments subject to coverage; the reports are made quarterly; and the information is usually not available until 4 months after the end of the reporting quarter. Neither the States nor the Bureau of Employment Security have felt it necessary to spend the money required to make the tabulations available sooner. Strong sentiment exists in several States to reduce the frequency of employer reports to once or twice a year and to rely upon separation reports as the basis for determining eligibility for and the amount of benefits.

There are also limitations upon the usability of the Federal old age and survivors insurance data for current employment statistics reporting. The data are only for the last month in each quarter, are tabulated for only 1 month in each year, and become available usually about 1 year after the data on State-covered employment under unemployment compensation. The practical use, therefore, that has been made of the old age and survivors insurance and State employer reports by the Bureau of Labor Statistics has been to provide bench marks, or total figures, on employment by establishments, by which to improve the statistical reliability of the monthly sample. To this end, cooperative relations have been established and maintained between the Bureau of Labor Statistics and the two social security agencies.

396

The present arrangement under which the Bureau of Labor Statistics secures its employment statistics is to rely upon voluntary, direct employer returns of the Bureau of Labor Statistics schedules, except in 10 States (California, Illinois, Massachusetts, Montana, New Jersey, New York, Pennsylvania, Texas, Utah, and Wisconsin), where the State employment statistics agency uses forms similar to the Bureau of Labor Statistics and takes over the collection job (including the entire contact with the employer), simply sending copies of the schedule on the Bureau of Labor Statistics when they have taken off the information for their purposes.

A plan has been worked out under the sponsorship of the Budget Bureau for fully utilizing the State unemployment compensation reports and integrating them with the current Bureau of Labor Statistics' sample to obtain State employment estimates. Briefly, this plan calls for two steps. First, the Bureau of Labor Statistics would receive an appropriation for the purpose of reimbursing the States for the cost of personal services engaged in collecting and processing schedules prescribed by the Bureau of Labor Statistics and voluntarily submitted by employers to the State agency each month. (The size of the necessary appropriation was estimated at $300,000 for 1949, but this was not approved by the House Appropriations Committee.) The staff hired by State agencies through these enabling funds would permit the remaining 38 State agencies to assume the collection function already handled by the 10 named above; the report to the Bureau of Labor Statistics by the employer could be eliminated; and, if adequate employer cooperation with the State agency were forthcoming, a series of State estimates could be obtained within a month after the reporting date.

The second step calls for processing of the quarterly employer reports under unemployment compensation so that the classification of establishments is the same for the State and national series. (This work has been financed in the past by grants to the State by employment security agencies by the Bureau of Employment Security from title III funds under the Social Security Act, amounting in 1948 to $246,000 and projected in 1949 at $68,000 on the assumption that the Bureau of Labor Statistics would receive the $300,000.)

As the situation now stands, the Bureau of Labor Statistics continues to publish its national employment estimates relying upon State agencies in 10 States where the statistical work has been developed enough to meet the Bureau of Labor Statistics' standards and upon direct employer returns elsewhere. The Bureau has a cooperative arrangement with the Bureau of Old Age and Survivors Insurance and Bureau of Employment Security whereby it seeks to relate its estimates to the total employment reported by covered establishments. Limitations of the data reported under the Federal old age and surviv-

397

ors insurance and State unemployment compensation laws prevents their use as a substitute for the Bureau of Labor Statistics' monthly estimates, but under a series of cooperative interagency arrangements the information in the hands of the State agencies could be processed and developed as a basis for monthly employment estimates by the States as well as for the national Bureau of Labor Statistics series. The Bureau of Employment Security is not primarily a statistical agency, its main function being the supervision and review of State laws, policies, and financial operations, rather than in research and statistics of general economic interest. Nevertheless, it is the appropriate agent through which Federal funds to encourage adequate State statistical services should be administered. The prospects of statistical coordination and of the appropriate fiscal arrangement with the States would be improved and simplified if the two social insurance agencies, and Bureau of Employment Security in particular, were in the same Federal department as the Bureau of Labor Statistics.

LABOR MARKET INFORMATION

The operating reports of local and State employment offices to the United States Employment Service supplement the Bureau of Labor Statistics' estimates of employment by indicating trends in the size of the job-seeking portion of the labor force on a local, State, or national basis, as desired. Since the advent of unemployment compensation, the number of active job applicants at local employment offices is perhaps as close a count of actual job seekers as can be obtained. From the standpoint of employment statistics, however, the variation in State law coverage coupled with the normal limit on employers of eight or more workers means that the count is far from universal. Further, the distribution of skill in these registrations is not representative of the labor force either locally or for the country as a whole. Nevertheless, compared with the reports of claims payments and job orders received from employers, these figures provide the most concrete short-run picture of the labor market available within the over-all labor force estimates of the Census Bureau. However, as long as employers file only a small proportion of their labor requirements with the local offices, the picture of labor demand will remain less than satisfactory.

The job application and claim load reports derived from the State employment security agencies are primarily administrative tools, and are not reliable for research purposes. Nevertheless as such they contribute to the formulation of the national economic assumptions upon which forecasts of tax collections and benefit disbursements are made preparatory to formulating the annual program and budget requirements of the State employment security agencies. In terms of their fiscal impact upon purchasing power, they are also followed by the

398

Council of Economic Advisers in preparing annual and semiannual economic reports for submission by the President to Congress.

The active applicant and job-order files in local employment offices have their greatest potential usefulness in providing information about labor supply and demand in local labor-market areas. During the war, when practically all hiring was channeled through local employment offices, the Employment Service reports became the basis upon which labor market areas were classified as shortage, tight, or surplus, and thus provided (particularly after September 1943) the information upon which local area manpower production urgency committees instituted plant employment ceilings, allocated labor, and recommended cancellation or shifting of procurement contracts. When the wartime controls were relaxed or removed, the reliability of this information as a basis for employment estimates, even on a local basis, was impaired, but it remains as the major source of information about local labor supply and as a measure of operating accomplishment and as an instrument of administrative supervision.

The voluntary system of employer filing job orders, and the uncertainty attaching to the accumulation of placements reported by local and State employment offices, means that the Employment Service and Employment Security Agency operating statistics cannot be relied upon to yield adequate information concerning actual employment. They are unreliable for practically all research purposes. The Employment Service statistical program should be restricted to the level consistent with operating requirements in local labor market areas, and not expanded to compete with the Bureau of Labor Statistics in the national field, or with the Bureau of Labor Statistics—State Employment Security Agency ocooperative plan in the field of State employment estimates.

The role of the Bureau of Old Age and Survivors' Insurance in the employment statistics field remains indeterminate—an open question. Its employer wage reports approach as nearly universal coverage as can be obtained, although the law at present does not include all categories of employment. It is a Federal operation, and there is no incentive on its part to provide State estimates. As stated above, its information is secured for only the last month in each quarter, is tabulated for only 1 month in each year, and it becomes available only about a year later than the State reports on covered employment under unemployment compensation. The amount of money it would take to develop the appropriate sample and make the necessary tabulations available on a current basis is unknown. There is an unsettled question as to whether employer wage reports or some form of employee stamp book will ultimately become the evidence of right to old-age insurance benefits. Under the circumstances, it seems best to rely upon the Bureau of Labor Statistics-State Employment Security arrangement described above. Again, however, if the Bureau of Old Age and Survivors' Insurance and the Bureau of Labor Statistics were in the same over-all department, the planning and estimating work necessary to any primary reliance upon the former's information as the basis for employment statistics would probably be greatly facilitated.

OCCUPATIONAL OUTLOOK STUDIES

The Bureau of Labor Statistics, the United States Employment Service, and the Women's Bureau are all engaged in surveying employment prospects and opportunities for selected groups and occupations. The Veterans' Administration, the United States Office of Education, and the State educational and guidance agencies are important consumers of such information. By and large, an acceptable division of labor on the basis of sex has been worked out between the Bureau of Labor Statistics and the Women's Bureau, and necessary overlappings have been taken care of by letting the Bureau of Labor Statistics do the collection work in all but special research projects. With respect to the Employment Service, however, a very uncertain line of demarcation has been drawn, with the long-range occupational outlook field going to the Bureau of Labor Statistics and the short-range studies being performed by the Employment Service. The latter publishes two major types of outlook information.

A monthly publication, The Labor Market, summarizes the operating statistics and reports from the State and local offices, with special reports from time to time on the employment trends in selected localities, industries, occupations, or groups such as veterans or handicapped workers. Some of this material is prepared and written by the Bureau of Labor Statistics, and a useful publication has resulted. The Service also produces special studies of the employment outlook in particular industries, nationally and by localities. The justification for this type of information is that it is more useful to industry and school vocational counsellors than the long-range reports of the Bureau of Labor Statistics. On the whole, it would appear desirable to keep the Employment Service out of the research field and to concentrate its statistical energies upon the analysis and build-up of labor-market information on the local area basis. The Employment Service should stimulate the Bureau of Labor Statistics to plan and present its specific outlook studies in the light of the needs of vocational guidance counsellors. In this capacity it would join the Veterans' Administration and the Office of Education as advisers and consumers of the Bureau of Labor Statistics research.

Conclusions

1. The complexity of legislation and interagency relationships affecting employment statistics both on the Federal and State level is such that coordination cannot be achieved by a single act of legislation or administrative reorganization. It is a continuing process. Responsibility for this function is properly placed on the Division of Statistical Standards in the Bureau of the Budget, acting in consultation with the Federal agencies and appropriate representatives of the State agencies concerned.

2. From an operating standpoint, much would be gained if the Bureau of Labor Statistics, the Bureau of Employment Security, and Bureau of Old Age and Survivors' Insurance were placed within the same Federal department for purposes of interchanging information and working out the appropriate division of labor between operating agencies and general economic research in the employment statistics field. Relations with the States would be facilitated by reducing the spread and number of channels through which the latter have to deal. Perhaps the most productive result of such departmental supervision and coordination would be the prospective agreement on amendatory legislation whereby the conflicts in present legislative coverage might be removed, and the desirable division of labor at the Federal level and in Federal-State relationships could be implemented.

3. So far as reporting of employment by establishments is concerned, distinction should be made between the operating statistics of the Bureau of Employment Security (including the U. S. Employment Service) and the general statistical functions of the Bureau of Labor Statistics. Reports designed for operating purposes are not in general reliable tools for employment statistics, and the employer reports to the State agencies are not readily adaptable on a current basis for general employment statistics. When the variation in State legislation is taken into account, it seems desirable to rely upon the State Employment Security Agency to collect employer reports subject to the Bureau of Labor Statistics supervision with respect to the sample, the development and use of the bench mark, and the form of the schedule. Necessary contacts with the State agencies, and any Federal financial support for the State statistical operations, should be coordinated by and, to the extent necessary, channeled through the Bureau of Employment Security. The Bureau of Employment Security should not establish a general research jurisdiction in the field of employment statistics. No recommendation is made herein with respect to expansion of the present Federal employment statistics program, but it may be mentioned that the recommendation just made as to organizational responsibility provides a flexible pattern compatible with the extension or dominance of the establishment reporting into the field of State employment estimates.

4. No study has been made, and no recommendations are submitted, with respect to the reporting requirements imposed by the Bureau of Employment Security upon the States.

5. Apart from the question of jurisdictional conflict, there seems to be no compelling reason why the employment statistics produced by the Census Bureau through its population sampling procedures should be transferred to the same department dealing with employment relations and direct employer reports. A potential question may be involved as to whether establishment reporting should be continued as the basis for employment estimates if the Census Bureau is allowed to expand its sample to enable it to secure reliable employment estimates on a local or State basis (this has already been recommended by a staff study of the joint congressional committee on the economic report.) However, as long as the Census Bureau relies upon information given by housewives, it will presumably be some time before the Census Bureau will be able to publish reliable employment estimates by occupations, industries, or States.

6. The Employment Service should not be relied upon to collect general employment statistics. Assuming continuation of the voluntary system of filing job orders by employers, and the unrepresentative distribution of skills in the file of job applicants, the Service should restrict its statistical forms and requirements to administrative rather than general research purposes.

7. In the occupational outlook field at the Federal level, the Bureau of Labor Statistics should be recognized as having primary jurisdiction in making studies of occupational opportunity on a national basis, sharing this function on a cooperative basis with the Women's Bureau. The special Nation-wide industry studies of the United States Employment Service should be transferred to the Bureau of Labor Statistics, and the Service should restrict its economic research to local labor market areas and to the short-run analysis of the labor market that it can build up from its normal operating reports from State agencies. There should be a more cooperative relationship between the two agencies, particularly in the occupational outlook and employment statistics fields, and the Bureau of Labor Statistics studies should be designed so as to be useful for employment guidance and counseling interviewers in local employment offices. These interrelationships clearly suggest the advisability of placing the two agencies within the same department.

Chapter III

EDUCATION AND TRAINING FOR EMPLOYMENT

Introduction

In the United States the principal Federal function with respect to vocational training has never been administered by the employment or labor departments. The Smith-Hughes Act of 1917, providing for grants to the States in aid of vocational education, including training of workers and teacher training in agriculture, home economics, trades and industries, and distributive occupations, established an independent Federal Board of Vocational Education. The Board was composed of four Government officials (the Secretaries of Commerce, Labor, and Agriculture, and the Commissioner of Education) and three citizens representing agricultural, business, and labor interests. The Board was abolished in 1933, and the administration of grants transferred to the United States Office of Education (first in the Interior Department, and since 1939 in the Federal Security Agency).

Regardless of administrative changes at the Federal level, a consistent pattern of Federal-State relationships has been established throughout this period, now consisting of a direct line from the United States Office of Education to the State Director of Vocational Education or Supervisor of Trade and Industrial Education, who, under a Board of Vocational Education, allots funds within the States to the local school systems. The George-Deen Act of 1936 and George-Barden Act of 1946, under which the funds made available for grants were increased from less than $2,000,000 in 1918 to almost $20,000,000 in 1948, reflect a strong sentiment in the States for continuing the administration of vocational training through the State and local school systems. The wartime program of vocational training for war production workers, under which more than 4,000,000 persons were trained and retrained, was administered through this arrangement.

Under the George-Barden Act of 1946, the amount authorized for trades and industrial education annually is $8,243,150, distributed in proportion that the nonfarm population of each State bears to the total population of the United States and its Territories. Fifty percent of Federal funds must be matched by the States until 1951; the matching requirement is then increased by 10 percent annually until 1956, whereafter the States must match the Federal grant 100 percent. The 1946 law also included for vocational guidance an authorization of $1,500,000, to be distributed on the same basis as grants for industrial education. In 1947 the Federal expenditure for vocational training in trades and industries was approximately $7,325,000, providing for 727,900 enrollees.

Since 1920, Federal funds have been available to State boards of vocational rehabilitation to assist in the vocational adjustment of handicapped or disabled workers. This program has increased to a level of $18,000,000 in 1948 and 1949, but it is estimated that only about one-ninth of this amount goes for educational training. The larger portion provides for administrative costs, medical examinations and treatment, appliances and tools, transportation and maintenance.

The Office of Vocational Rehabilitation was formerly a part of the Office of Education, but Public Law 113, Seventy-eighth Congress (1943), assigned the functions of certifying eligibility of States for grants for vocational rehabilitation under approved State plans to the Federal Security Administrator, who has delegated them to the Office of Vocational Rehabilitation with separate bureau status. The statutory formula for disbursing funds to States provides that the Federal Government shall meet (1) 100 percent of the costs of administration, guidance, and placement (apparently as reported by the States), (2) 100 percent of the costs for providing services to war-disabled civilians, and (3) 50 percent of the costs of designated medical and training services. The States closed some 113,000 cases in 1947, of which approximately 44,000, or roughly 30 percent, were closed as employed.

The Apprentice Training Service in the Department of Labor was established pursuant to a congressional act of 1937 (Public Law 308, 75th Cong.), authorizing the Secretary of Labor to formulate and promote standards of apprenticeship, to encourage employers and labor organizations to set up apprenticeship programs, and to cooperate with State agencies to these ends. In 1948, 30 States had by law or gubernatorial action set up State apprenticeship councils. The Service both works through the States by advice and stimulation (no funds are available for grants), and also conducts direct local promotional campaigns through its own staff permanently stationed in the field. Over 5,500 local apprenticeship committees have been established. The program has expanded rapidly since the end of the war, the number of registered apprentices increasing from 22,000 in 1944 to almost 200,000 in 1947. The turn-over rate among apprentices is always high, and is estimated at approximately 35 to 40 percent. The annual appropriation for the Service in 1948 and 1949 has leveled off at about $2,400,000.

Of these three major programs, the two largest in point of size have always been outside the employment agency, and there has apparently never been any strong sentiment or pressing administrative reasons requiring their inclusion in the same agency. Organized labor has long accepted the fact that primary responsibility for free public education and vocational education in the United States is vested in State and local agencies, restricting its claims for recognition to demands for labor representation upon administrative school boards, with the twin objectives of maintaining adequate programs and preventing distortion of curriculum content. The American Federation of Labor, at its annual conventions during the 5 years following abolition of the Federal Board of Vocational Education in 1933, repeatedly attacked the elimination of the statutory requirement for authoritative labor representation in connection with the Federal Office of Education. Its lack of success in securing such recognition, plus its growing belief that the schools have failed to meet the educational requirements of the millions of workers who have never completed grade and high school have resulted in demands for corrective action. These trends and sentiments are reflected in the introduction of bills into the Eightieth Congress for a Labor Extension Service to meet the demand for adequate education for the adult wage-earning population, with the added conditions that grants for workers' education be administered on the Federal level by the Department of Labor and in the States by representative boards of school administrators and organized labor outside the existing departments of education and vocational training.

At present, however, the three Federal bureaus directly concerned with employment training have reached a relatively noncontroversial stage of administrative development. The Offices of Education and Vocational Rehabilitation review and approve State agencies and plans as a condition for receipt of Federal funds upon established practices in educational administration; the Apprentice Training Service formulates standards of apprentice training in industry and encourages State and local apprenticeship councils to collaborate with employers in setting up programs in conformity with these approved and tested standards. Over and above auditing the States' expenditure of funds (by the first two agencies), all three are continuously engaged in study and evaluation of the operation of existing plans and agencies, in publishing statistical and qualitative analyses in the form of bulletins and guides reporting the results of experience and exchange of ideas, in collaborating with professional organizations of administrators, teachers, and with employer and labor organizations. By and large, the agencies function through separate State, local, and industrial clientele groupings. The principal overlappings occur in the field of occupational outlook and guidance, in the placement of handicapped workers by State rehabilitation agencies, and in the utilization of vocational schools as a required part of the federally approved program of apprentice training.

Analysis of Employment Training Programs

The major areas of employment training may be arbitrarily distinguished as: (1) Occupational outlook, (2) vocational guidance and counseling, (3) vocational education in the schools, (4) vocational training in industry, and (5) adult education. This framework is useful in pointing up the major problems of program and organization.

Occupational Outlook

Training for employment should be based upon some preliminary estimate of employment opportunities in the field of the individual's preferences and aptitudes. It must also be predicated upon some fairly uniform terminology and understanding of the trades and skills for which training is to be given. These requirements involve the collaboration of the employer, the worker, the schools, and the employment office. The employer, the worker, and the employment office must use approximately the same terms to describe the job classification and the qualifications the worker must possess in order to lay claim to an occupational title. The schools should have some appreciation of these skills and the demand for them in setting up training programs, lest they train surplus numbers in unwanted skills for nonexistent jobs. Estimates of employment opportunity also must be based upon a common understanding of the nature of the occupation, or groups of occupations, the conditions of work associated with the job, and the character of the necessary preparation to gain the skill required, in order to calculate the numbers employed, the trend, and the prospective entrants for each occupation or trade.

The basic research in industrial processes and terminology necessary for developing a standard occupational classification has been performed by the national United States Employment Service staff. This work is embodied in a Dictionary of Occupational Titles. Containing over 20,000 distinct occupations, it is far too detailed for most educational programs outside the plant or shop. The list of "apprenticeable occupations" developed by the Federal Committee on Apprenticeship for industry and local apprentice committee use was, however, closely linked to the dictionary titles. The school programs quite properly use even broader classifications for purposes of vocational preparation, sometimes using a term as broad as an industry, for example, textile occupations, woodworking occupations, radio repairing, auto repairing. Other occupations may cut across industries, such as machinist, welder, printer.

The basic planning for vocational training programs is not a single agency operation. Research on industrial tasks and processes is an appropriate part of the screening (selection and referral) work of the employment service, and must be adapted by the school administrators for their respective purposes and standards. The long-run national employment outlook, as a problem of economic and industrial research, is handled by two Labor Department bureaus, the Bureau of Labor Statistics and the Women's Bureau. Research guides and bibliographies are developed by the Office of Education in cooperation with the Federal labor agencies for the use of the States. Local apprenticeship and school programs should be developed in close collaboration with the local employment office to avoid wasteful loss of students' time and energy. There is an outstanding challenge for local training programs to dovetail their work into the needs of industry and the placement experience of the employment service.

VOCATIONAL GUIDANCE AND COUNSELING

Inclusion of $1,500,000 for guidance work in the Vocational Education Act of 1946 reflects the widespread recognition today that proper provision for enabling the student to think and choose for himself in selecting his working career is a necessary part of every good school program. Such provision includes the development and administration of interest and aptitude tests, the stimulation of personal concern on the part of the individual about his future in terms of a recognition of the relation between abilities and preferences, and the development of a sense of social purpose and contribution. This process must, of course, be related to an awareness of areas and trends in vocational opportunity. Many children pass through or leave public school without conscious exposure to this phase of the formal educational process, and the employment service has developed a guidance program for out-of-school youth and older workers to meet problems of vocational adjustment arising at later stages in life.

The national office of the United States Employment Service has developed tests for measuring vocational aptitude among job applicants in connection with its work of selecting and referring qualified registrants to job openings. There is little evidence that either the Employment Service or the Office of Education in Washington, or their counterparts in the States, are interfering with each other or becoming involved in jurisdictional claims. There is a job to be done and a proper focus of emphasis for each in the distinction between the in-school and out-of-school population. What has come to attention as the source of greater actual ineffectiveness and harm is the lack of cooperative contact and activity between the school guidance officers and the employment office interviewers and counselors. On the national level where, aside from administration of grants, the problem is one of testing and technique development, location in different departments has not been an obstacle to collaboration between the Employment Service and the Office of Education.

During the 10 years from 1938 to 1947, enrollment in regular State trades and industrial education classes (excluding the vocational training for war production workers program) ranged from 543,000 to 850,000. The 7 million to 8 million dollars of Federal funds for training and industrial education goes for administrative salaries, physical facilities, and teacher training, as well as direct costs attributable to student instruction. This part of the present report is not concerned with the questions of the proper size and relation of the vocational education program to the rest of the educational program of the States. This subject is covered in the part dealing with education.

Trades and industrial education consists of four major types of classes:

1. *Evening trade extension.*—Supplementary training for workers desiring to improve or increase their daily vocational knowledge.

2. *All-day trade preparatory.*—Instruction of a general character designed to prepare youth of 14 years or over for manipulative skills and related subjects.

3. *Part-time trade preparatory and continuation.*—Training to increase civic and vocational intelligence of youth who have left full-time school and seek training other than in occupation in which employed.

4. *Part-time trade extension.*—Training for youth who have left full-time school and seek to extend their knowledge in the trade in which employed.

From the standpoint of the Employment Service and Labor Department, the principal concern with vocational education in the schools is the standards affecting employment relationships that are observed in the administration of vocational training. The age at which youth are permitted to drop general schooling and begin specific job preparation is one such problem. The Employment Service is not an enforcement agency, but it is influenced by the local standards as well as State and National policies with respect to the education and employment of child labor. Should the local office refer youth from 14 to 17 years of age in response to employer requests when its active file contains older workers perhaps with family responsibilities and better fitted for the job specifications submitted? Should schools continue to establish instruction in specific trades for 14 to 16 age children before they have completed their broader education? At present, the Fair Labor Standards Act permits employment of minors from 14 to 18 under regulations and specific exemptions by the administrator of the law (formerly the Chief of the Children's Bureau), so the legal situation now varies with State law and local industry practice with respect to the entrance age for employment. One proposal for dealing with this problem has been advanced by which a provision would be inserted in the Federal law and State plans that a minimum age of 17 be established for enrollment in any type of preparatory instruction for a specific trade or occupation, with school authorities being made responsible for its enforcement and with compulsory age records open to public and Labor Department inspection. Precedent for giving school officials authority to issue age certificates already exists in several States under procedures worked out by the Children's Bureau and Wage-Hour Administration.

Another problem of standards concerns the practice in some States of permitting vocational training programs to be established inside factories or shops that are really production lines, with the products going into commercial trade channels. A provision of the Federal law states that "no part of the appropriations herein authorized shall be expended in industrial plant-training programs, except such industrial plant-training be bona fide vocational training, and not a device to utilize the services of vocational trainees for private profit." The proviso, with enforcement left to local school authorities, leaves the determination of "bona fide vocational training" open to local pressures and practices. Here again the legal situation becomes indeterminate in the presence of conflict between local custom, local and industry-wide standards of business competition, strong or weak union agreements, and the lack of consensus concerning broader public policies with respect to employment training and the composition of the labor force.

Apprehension that vocational education in the schools will dilute and degrade genuine skilled craftsmanship is probably unfounded as long as both employers and unions maintain their standards of skill, and are willing to collaborate with a public apprenticeship agency in safeguarding agreed-upon standards for issuing certificates of apprenticeship. Long-established experience in advanced industrial States has shown that economic and vocational interests in maintaining standards are complementary here through the continuing intermediary of joint agreement and neutral administration. Vocational education in the schools cannot provide a substitute for training in industry under the supervision of skilled craftsmen; the motives and behavior patterns of student in each are different and easily detectable. The public interest here seems to consist in not merging the identities of vocational training and apprenticeship. There is, furthermore, no evidence of employer or union attacks on the principle of vocational education itself; criticisms for the most part are directed either at the failure to visualize vocational training in the proper sense, or at the inadequacy of facilities or available personnel.

409

The interest of employment agencies in standards of vocational school training clearly does not require administration of education by the general employment or labor department. Demands for such consolidation are not pressing, and they seem to emerge primarily as resultants from alleged blindness or deafness of educational administrators to desires of working people and to employment or labor standards that appear to deserve serious consideration. If our public schools did achieve a hard-and-fast distinction between general and vocational education, there might be a better case for transferring the latter to the employment department, but there is little indication of an early change in the traditional identification of "learning and labor" in our local public educational system. Only in the event of a major reorientation in policy or program would it seem desirable to disrupt established professional and administrative relationships by transfer at the Federal level.

VOCATIONAL TRAINING IN INDUSTRY

The Office of Vocational Rehabilitation in 1947 assisted the States to place upwards of 40,000 rehabilitated workers in remunerative employment. As already mentioned, only a minor portion of its funds are expended for direct employment or placement activities, but in a sense the major purpose of all medical and training attention is focused upon an ultimate satisfactory employment relationship for the disabled or handicapped worker. This orientation brings the Office of Vocational Rehabilitation, and its State counterpart, into immediate relationship with the Employment Service and its affiliated State services, which have a comprehensive knowledge and jurisdiction over the labor market and employment opportunities therein which it is important to maintain and expand. From this standpoint the handicapped compose a special group of potential workers whose employment prospects should be merged with, not separated from, those of veterans, women, racial minorities, youth, and elderly job seekers. Special employer contacts are usually necessary for the handicapped, but this does not justify splitting the group off for placement purposes. In the aftermath of war special attention is properly given to the needs of war disabled veterans, but in the normal course of events the emphasis upon placement indicates increasing collaboration with the agency containing the employment service. Since medical and training services constitute large segments of the program, fiscally speaking, there are definite relations with the health and educational agencies, but as the program sheds its welfare garments and becomes established as an economically practicable source of labor supply, upon which the disabled, their counselors, and employers may rely, necessity of coordination within the same department as the Employment Service is paramount.

The training program which typifies the primary role of industry in vocational preparation is apprenticeship. Production operations have to be learned on the job, perhaps even after years of vocational school, but most of these can be acquired in a matter of weeks. Even before the war many employers had begun to realize the effects of immigration laws in cutting down the skilled craftsmen coming from Europe, and the results of mass production and union policies in reducing the number of workers with a high degree of skill and understanding of technical industrial processes. True craft skill includes an attitude of mind and physical habit toward a calling as well as mechanical aptitude, and these are acquired only after long application to the many aspects of the trade under supervision of craftsmen who have mastered the process themselves. Guidance on the job and promotion through stages of increasing difficulty and responsibility is necessary, with oversight to insure that the training process is well-rounded and not subverted to the temporary allurements of high wages on production work. Supplementation of on-the-job training with general knowledge of industrial history and craft technology in night and part-time school is a feature of most programs, and the joint interest of employer and union must be enlisted in maintaining apprenticeship standards not merely for the welfare of the trainee but for the long-run productivity of industry. Finally, governmental supervision is necessary to protect apprenticeship programs against exploitation, and to assure unions that their agreement to a higher number of apprentices to be trained will not be abused.

The 1937 law authorizing the Secretary of Labor to initiate and promote apprenticeship specifically contemplated such action through the joint action of employer and labor organizations, and it is these contacts both nationally and in local communities that occupy the major attention of the Apprentice Training Service rather than simply encouraging, reviewing, and approving the work of State apprenticeship councils. Absence of Federal funds for grant-in-aid purposes, or of sustained attention by full-time State personnel, has reinforced this tendency as a matter of administrative policy. In this situation the States have not been stimulated to act vigorously or to appropriate necessary funds to take over the work begun by the Federal Government. Some 30 States and Territories have established apprenticeship agencies and councils, but excepting some 10 States where vigorous programs are under way, initiative and active responsibility have remained with the Federal service. Even in these States the Apprentice Training Service has maintained staffs as large or larger than those maintained by State funds. From an operating standpoint, the insistence of the Service in working in all directions, to national organizations of industry and labor, to the

States, and directly to the local community, has resulted in internal administrative difficulties and, on some occasions, in friction at State and local levels. These problems have not prevented the Service from establishing good relationships on the whole with employers and labor, a situation that has been reflected in Congress appropriating for the most part the funds requested by the agency and the President.

The principal interagency problem of the Apprentice Training Service lies in the vocational education side of the program, where it is reported unofficially that 30 percent of the registered apprentices have not received the supplemental training of 144 hours per year of related classroom instruction. This situation arises, it is said, because the schools have lacked the necessary facilities and personnel to provide the training required for the programs established by the Service. The present investigation has not ascertained the facts through actual field inquiries, but something would appear to be wrong either in local planning and coordination, or in the apportionment within the States of vocational-training funds.

The Veterans Administration has been much interested in apprenticeship, and several interagency arrangements have been worked out whereby veterans' allowances have been made available for time spent on apprentice training. State educational agencies certify individuals under training; State and local councils have permitted related war-service credit to apply to time required for training; and the United States Office of Education has collected and distributed information for the supplementary instruction of apprentices. A Federal Committee on Apprenticeship appointed by the Secretary of Labor includes a representative of the United States Office of Education. These arrangements indicate a division of labor whereby the Veterans Administration has financed a large number of those desiring to enter apprenticeship; the Apprentice Training Service has identified over 100 apprenticeable occupations, has established standards, and negotiated and sanctioned national and local projects; the Office of Education has assisted local and State agencies in developing curricular materials for related classroom instruction. At least on the Federal level, the primary problems of organizational responsibility seem to have been identified and grasped. There seems to be no problem or necessity requiring alteration of the present location of functions.

Conclusions

1. There are no compelling reasons for altering the existing location and division of responsibilities between the educational and employment agencies at the Federal level. The principal potential overlapping lies in the field of vocational rehabilitation, wherein the problem is whether State and local rehabilitation agencies should be

merged or more closely integrated with employment offices. The principal sources of economy in vocational rehabilitation lie in the alteration of the statutory formula to eliminate or lessen the weight given to State agency case-load estimates as a factor in allocating Federal funds, and in the elimination of grants for personnel primarily engaged in specific placement activities by the rehabilitation agency, on the assumption that such work should be handled through the employment service.

2. In the relation between vocational education and employment offices, it is not clear that the schools base their training programs to the extent desirable upon national, industrial, local, or occupational outlook opportunities evident to the Employment Service, the Women's Bureau and Bureau of Labor Statistics. A major hope of reform here lies with the appearance of vocational guidance officers in the schools, their recognition by school administrators, and close collaboration with the State employment service and State departments of education. The potentialities of constructive Federal influence upon local school planning and programming through the negative device of cutting or withholding funds seem negligible. Slight prospects of economy, but considerable benefit should emerge if heightened attention were focused upon the blurred lines between the Bureau of Labor Statistics and the United States Employment Service activities in the field of employment outlook.

3. A positive gap has appeared between the aprenticeship and vocational educational programs, again at local levels, in the failure of a third of the apprentices under the expanded postwar program to receive related classroom instruction in the vocational schools. Whether this situation is due to a lack of coordination, inadequate funds, or materials and manpower shortages, merits immediate investigation. With respect to the internal administration of the apprenticeship program, consideration should be given to the substitution of a matching grant-in-aid program, subject to present Federal standards, for the present policy of direct Federal servicing and encouragement of local apprentice committees. There seems to be little evidence that the States feel sufficiently the importance of a national policy calling for apprentice training as a condition of maintaining and increasing industrial productivity.

4. The vocational-education program of the Federal Government has settled down on an established, routine basis which has won two congressional increases in grant authorizations within the last 12 years.

Chapter IV

EMPLOYMENT OFFICES AND UNEMPLOYMENT COMPENSATION

Historical Background

The first public employment services in the United States were municipal agencies, established about 1860 and located in New York and San Francisco. In 1890 the State of Ohio passed a law establishing State-City employment offices in its five principal cities. By the beginning of the World War, some 10 States were operating employment services, with a total of some 96 local offices.

The Federal Government's activity in connection with an employment service began in 1907, with the creation of a Division of Information in the Bureau of Immigration, then in the Department of Commerce and Labor. With the creation of a separate Department of Labor in 1913, the Bureau and its Division of Information became part of it.

In 1918 the employment information program of the Bureau of Immigration and Naturalization was transferred to the United States Employment Service. That Service, financed during the war largely from President Wilson's defense and security fund, established some 850 local offices, federally operated but many being run in cooperation with State and city governments. In 1918 and 1919 direct appropriations for the Service were cut off and a Senate bill to give legislative authority to the Service failed to pass. The Federal offices were closed or turned over to the State and local governments, which in 1920 had reduced the number of offices to 269 in some 41 States. By 1933 there were 192 offices in 23 States.

Activity of the veterans' organizations led Congress in 1930 to appropriate funds to the United States Employment Service for the establishment of a special employment service for veterans. This money enabled the Service to open some 30 offices in different cities, most of them operating with one man and a clerk. In 1931 Congress passed the Wagner bill providing for the establishment of a Federal-State system of employment offices partly supported by grants-in-aid, but the bill was vetoed by President Hoover, who preferred a national employment service directly administered by the Federal Government. Congress then appropriated funds with which to set up Federal offices, of which about 150 were eventually opened. The system was not successful partly because of the political atmosphere of the period, partly because the State and local offices were disregarded in creating new offices, and partly because personnel was largely selected without regard to merit and experience. In April 1933, the Secretary of Labor abolished the Federal offices for veterans.

In June 1933, the Wagner-Peyser Act created the United States Employment Service as a bureau in the Department of Labor to administer a Federal-State system of employment offices. The law authorized appropriations of $1,500,000 for the new agency for the first year, and $4,000,000 for the following years. Three-fourths of this sum was set aside for apportionment among the States on the basis of population, to be disbursed only in amounts equal to those appropriated by the States and local governments for employment service purposes, and upon compliance with the provisions of the act. By the end of 1936, 34 States had employment offices functioning under the act; the following year the number had risen to 40, and by the end of 1938, 47 States had affiliated services functioning within the system.

From 1933 to 1938 emergency relief funds were utilized to establish a wholly Federal National Reemployment Service, which functioned separately from, but under the administrative direction of, the director of the United States Employment Service in certifying and referring applicants to jobs on public work projects.

In preparation for unemployment compensation benefit payments that began in 1938, the State employment services were expanded to meet the requirement of title III of the Social Security Act that State laws should provide for the payment of benefits solely through public employment offices or such other agencies as the Board may approve. (Sec. 303–a–2.) The act contains no specific provisions for grants for employment offices, but since the States provided for filing claims at such offices and for continued registration as evidence of availability for work, the Social Security Board in 1937 announced that it would make grants for the maintenance of employment services as an essential part of the cost of administering unemployment compensation. This interpretation was accepted by the Comptroller General in a letter to the Chairman of the Board of July 17, 1937.

State agencies thus dealt with two separate Federal agencies in securing funds to finance the costs of employment service operations. In reviewing and approving State agency budgets and operating plans, formulating regulations, and auditing expenditures, both the Employment Service and the Social Security Board were performing tasks with respect to interrelated operations in the State and local offices. An agreement between the Secretary of Labor and the Social Security Board in March 1937 failed to remove the difficulties of joint operation. On July 1, 1939, President Roosevelt through Reorganization Plan No. 1 transferred the Service to the Social Security Board, where it was combined with the Division of Unemployment Compensation into the Bureau of Employment Security.

The Social Security Board administered the United States Employment Service until September 1942. Pursuant to a telegraphic request from President Roosevelt, the State governors permitted transfer of the State employment offices to Federal operation on January 1 of that year, and on September 17, Executive Order 9247 transferred the United States Employment Service and the functions of the Federal Security Administrator with respect thereto to the War Manpower Commission. Executive Order 9617 (September 19, 1945) that abolished the War Manpower Commission also transferred the United States Employment Service back to the Department of Labor. The State and local offices of the United States Employment Service were not returned to the States until November 16, 1946, by direction of the Labor-Federal Security Appropriation Act for 1947 (Public Law 549, 79th Cong.). The United States Employment Service remained in the Department of Labor until July 1, 1948, when by special provision in the 1949 Labor-Federal Security Appropriation Act it was transferred to the Federal Security Agency.

The Major Employment Security Programs

Since 1933 the American employment security system has developed upon these three principles:

First, in its employment aspects, it is essentially a voluntary program. Some 1,800 free public employment offices have been established throughout the Nation at which job seekers may register in order to secure information as to such employment openings as may be voluntarily reported by employers. Compulsion was introduced in connection with unemployment compensation, where eligible or covered workers were required to register as unemployed and unable to find suitable work as a condition of receiving benefits, and employers must pay a 3-percent tax upon covered pay rolls subject to reductions.

Second, despite repeated attempts to establish a federally operated and financed system of employment offices and unemployment compensation payments, the States have successfully sustained their claim to responsibility for operating both the job-referral and benefit-paying functions, subject to Federal standards and supervision with respect to administration.

Third, although the Employment Service was partially financed by the States under the Wagner-Peyser Act on a matching basis down to 1942, since that time the Federal Government has paid 100 percent of its administrative costs just as it has paid 100 percent of unemployment compensation administration since 1935.

A fourth principle, which is not quite so clear in its application, but has become generally accepted as a lesson of experience, is that employment security consists of two distinguishable operations which must nevertheless be administered under unified control, namely, facilitating employment and unemployment insurance.

PUBLIC EMPLOYMENT OFFICES

The Federal Security Administrator, through the United States Employment Service, is authorized and directed by law [1] to promote and develop a national system of employment offices, and to assist in establishing and maintaining systems of public employment offices in the several States. In carrying out this function, the Service engaged in two types of activities: (1) Administrative control and supervision, and (2) program development and operations. The first category includes its formal statutory powers of prescribing minimum, and promoting improved, standards of efficiency and procedure, formulating necessary rules and regulations, determining eligibility of States for Federal grants and the amounts to which they are entitled, reviewing and approving State operating plans for conformity with Federal law and regulations, maintaining Federal standards through review of State agency budgets, inspecting and advising upon State operations, auditing expenditures and accounting systems, and finally, revoking State certificates of eligibility for receipt of Federal funds in cases of violation of Federal laws and standards.

Over and beyond the formal structure and exercise of authority, however, is the formulation of the technical goals and standards of administrative performance. The Service has sought to define its objectives in operating terms so that actual performance can be measured against work goals, but it has been found feasible to give these quantitative expression only to a limited extent. Broadly, the objective of employment service administration is to improve the organization of the labor market. This is carried on by:

1. Establishing an exchange of information upon available job openings and the qualifications of job seekers so that time, sacrifice, and effort in matching men with jobs are reduced to a minimum.

2. Increasing the efficiency of selecting and referring workers to jobs by developing job tests of qualifications and promoting a standard terminology for industrial occupations.

3. Guiding and movement of labor through a system of reporting on labor markets demand and supply, classified by location, occupation, or industry; maintaining a system of clearing labor not required locally to other States or labor market areas; and under emergency or wartime

---

[1] The principal statutory references, the Wagner-Peyser Act of 1933, title III of the Social Security Act of 1935, title IV of the Servicemen's Readjustment Act of 1944, and Public Law 646, 80th Cong.

conditions, to direct the movement of labor from less to more essential employment under national policies controlling the placement and allocation of the civilian labor force.

4. Providing specialized services of assistance, selection, and placement for particular classes of workers, for example, veterans, youth, migratory farm labor, and the physically handicapped.

5. Assisting in tiding over and reducing the strains of temporary unemployment by providing registration facilities and suitable work opportunities, if available, to applicants for unemployment benefits.[2]

Under a voluntary system of registering applications and openings for jobs, it is generally recognized that the Employment Service can never expect to make more than one-third of the hirings in private industry. In the United States the percentage of nonfarm hirings completed through the service has probably never been more than 20 except under the controlled hiring policies of the War Manpower Commission from 1943 to 1945, when the peak reached was 55. National totals of job applications in the postwar years have ranged between 7 and 8 millions; job openings received from employers in local offices during 1947–48 on the basis of a 6-month sample were running at an annual rate just below 7 million; placements have declined to about half the wartime peak, but still more than 5 million per year. Approximately one-fifth of total placements are on short-time jobs.

The most concrete impact of employment service administration is felt at the local level, and the service has stimulated a vigorous program of concentrating direct visits to employers on the larger ones in the area who account for 75 percent of its employment. Table XXVIII, page 419, indicates that there is an inverse relationship between the size of community and the percentage of placements to estimated hirings by the major market employers in the locality. Approximately one-third of all placements by local offices are in manufacturing industries, one-fourth in household or other service industries, one-fifth in wholesale and retail trade, and one-tenth in construction. By broad occupational grouping, about two-fifths of all placements are in unskilled work, one-fifth are in semiskilled and skilled jobs combined, one-fourth are in service occupations, slightly more than 10 percent are in clerical and professional work. By race, sex, and special minority group, about one-fourth of all placements are nonwhite, slightly more than one-third are women, slightly less than one-third are veterans. About 5 percent are physically handicapped.

Employment Service statistics do not reveal the potentialities of its role in providing encouragement and leadership, particularly in local

---

[2] This formulation does not follow precisely the U. S. Employment Service 6-point program, particularly in its listing of employer services, because the entire operation both services employers and promotes the welfare of wage earners.

City and State	Population	Gainfully employed	Major market			
			Gainfully employed	Estimated accessions	Local office placements	Penetration rate
Philadelphia	2,090,000	687,087	482,505	234,423	8,311	3.5
Washington, D. C	850,000	249,500	163,335	176,448	9,991	5.7
Total (over 500,000)	2,940,000	936,587	645,840	410,871	18,302	4.6
Atlanta, Ga	490,000	133,482	96,789	98,029	6,731	6.9
Indianpolis, Ind	450,000	152,500	108,500	49,257	5,644	11.4
Providence, R. I	364,000	136,000	90,326	20,774	1,434	6.9
Honolulu, T. H	360,274	95,709	58,957	40,990	1,892	4.5
Nashville, Tenn	287,000	95,612	66,929	23,176	2,819	12.2
Omaha, Nebr	252,000	63,000	47,973	57,310	4,114	7.2
Richmond, Va	251,871	88,155	53,970	28,053	2,969	10.6
Total (250,001–500,000)	2,455,145	764,458	523,444	317,589	25,603	8.1
Salt Lake City, Utah	240,800	56,100	28,888	13,032	2,350	18.0
Wichita, Kans	167,100	44,100	27,246	23,490	2,186	9.3
Total (150,001–250,000)	407,900	100,200	56,134	36,522	4,536	12.4
Erie, Pa	140,949	53,560	37,841	27,243	4,264	15.7
Reading, Pa	140,720	59,102	41,260	17,820	2,679	15.0
Kansas City, Kans	136,000	40,841	24,930	19,026	2,292	12.0
Pawtucket, R. I	135,000	48,000	33,521	10,391	703	6.8
Fort Wayne, Ind	135,000	43,800	34,200	16,065	1,392	8.7
Evansville, Ind	125,000	33,200	25,000	7,096	1,415	19.9
Total (100,001–150,000)	812,669	278,503	196,752	97,641	12,745	13.1
Columbus, Ga	100,000	33,169	24,766	34,992	2,966	8.4
York, Pa	97,096	40,780	30,814	14,697	1,695	11.5
Ogden, Utah	93,500	28,950	19,701	7,740	1,497	19.3
Topeka, Kans	91,247	28,936	19,506	13,851	2,342	16.9
Lincoln, Nebr	91,000	24,720	18,425	17,152	2,560	14.9
Jackson, Miss	90,000	26,400	18,724	20,760	1,726	8.3
Augusta, Ga	80,000	22,900	16,219	20,338	1,781	8.8
Manchester, N. H	80,000	29,600	22,260	16,200	2,629	16.2
Phoenix, Ariz	70,000	38,000	27,220	30,372	2,803	9.2
Provo, Utah	65,000	9,100	5,362	2,400	464	19.3
Williamsport, Pa	56,753	20,318	14,765	9,306	2,126	22.8
Total (50,001–100,000)	914,596	302,873	217,762	187,808	22,589	12.0
Newport, R. I	47,000	9,000	4,737	805	91	11.3
Lynchburg, Va	43,898	15,364	12,579	5,647	605	10.7
Newport News, Va	43,694	15,293	17,602	2,772	770	27.8
Tucson, Ariz	36,818	15,100	10,284	11,472	862	7.5
Great Falls, Mont	36,000	11,100	8,874	5,679	1,234	21.7
Hilo, T. H	29,111	7,914	6,087	3,076	187	6.1
Dover, N. H	27,215	9,525	7,098	6,564	910	13.8
Billings, Mont	26,200	7,870	5,784	3,702	502	13.6
Total (25,001–50,000)	289,936	91,166	73,045	39,717	5,161	13.0
Greenville, Miss	25,000	7,520	5,166	5,880	1,967	33.5
Keene, N. H	23,130	8,094	5,790	3,876	474	12.2
Missoula, Mont	21,500	5,525	5,308	3,397	740	21.8
Berlin, N. H	21,115	10,000	7,578	12,276	2,818	22.9
Vicksburg, Miss	21,000	7,405	5,483	6,260	1,671	26.7
Grand Island, Nebr	21,000	5,250	4,083	2,994	925	30.9
Helena, Mont	16,700	5,245	4,589	2,937	330	11.2
Harrisonburg, Va	9,000	3,150	2,933	894	122	13.6
Globe, Ariz	8,000	4,200	2,989	3,910	1,109	28.4
Flagstaff, Ariz	6,000	2,395	2,121	2,545	469	18.4
Total (25,000 and under)	172,445	58,784	46,040	44,969	10,625	23.62
Grand total	7,992,691	2,522,571	1,759,017	1,135,117	99,561	8.8

[1] U. S. Employment Service.

communities, for positive programs of maintaining high levels of employment and standards of personnel relations work. The United States Employment Service has sought to promote this conception

419

among State and local office managers by developing and maintaining uniform occupational classifications and job descriptions, by preparing general aptitude tests and specific occupational trade tests for improving the selection and counseling of job applicants, by establishing a uniform system of collecting and analyzing information on employment conditions and opportunities in each major labor-market area, and in providing staff training, materials, and guide manuals. The extent to which these technical aids increase the efficiency of labor-market organization by improving the quality of employment office

TABLE XXIX.—*Percentage of Employment Service placements, by industrial classification, October 1947–March 1948* [1]

Month	Total	All manufacturing	Wholesale and retail trade	Construction	Household and other services	All other
1947						
October	527,959	34.0	18.2	13.9	23.1	10.8
November	450,957	33.9	19.5	13.1	22.7	10.8
December	397,048	31.0	20.8	11.3	23.1	13.8
1948						
January	374,123	34.4	18.2	9.6	25.1	12.7
February	344,064	35.2	18.8	9.5	25.7	10.8
March	412,808	33.5	18.9	11.3	26.0	10.3
Total	2,506,956					

[1] Source: U. S. Employment Service, The Labor Market, December 1947–May 1948.

TABLE XXX.—*Percentage of Employment Service placements, by broad occupational grouping, October 1947–March 1948* [1]

Month	Total	Clerical and professional	Service	Unskilled	Skilled and semiskilled
1947					
October	527,959	11.6	22.4	45.9	20.1
November	450,957	12.5	22.6	44.4	20.5
December	397,048	16.5	23.6	40.7	19.2
1948					
January	374,123	15.1	25.6	37.2	22.1
February	344,064	14.1	25.8	37.2	22.9
March	412,808	13.1	26.6	38.1	22.2

[1] Source: U. S. Employment Service, The Labor Market, December 1947–May 1948.

TABLE XXXI.—*Percentage of employment service placements, by race, sex, and veteran status, October 1947–March 1948* [1]

Month	Total	Nonwhites	Women	Veterans
1947				
October	527,959	26.5	32.9	33.9
November	450,957	26.0	33.8	33.2
December	397,048	26.0	35.4	33.5
1948				
January	374,123	26.4	38.7	31.8
February	344,064	27.1	39.2	30.5
March	412,808	27.9	37.2	31.4

[1] Source: U. S. Employment Service, The Labor Market, December 1947–May 1948.

selection and referral is only partly measurable by such statistical indices as the number of job openings reported by employers. A major criterion in this field is the working relationships established with employer personnel men, their attitudes toward the local office manager, and their experience with the handling of job orders. On a higher level this evaluation involves the status and participation of the Service in joint programs with employer and labor organizations. As a means of establishing this the Employment Service has officially sponsored the use of formal representative advisory councils on local, State, and national levels, but excepting in certain States and special demonstration projects from time to time, the operating offices do not seem to have made effective use of this device.

Employer attitudes toward the Service are affected by the predisposition in favor of maintaining plant or gate hiring, by the experience of the past 15 years in which the Service was preoccupied first by processing applicants for public-works projects and then by working out the relationships with unemployment compensation. Added to this was the reaction from such wartime controls as plant ceilings, essential work classifications, and availability statements. In normal times employers tend to oppose positive central direction of the flow of labor except in the rare instance that consensus can be achieved among themselves on the principles controlling priority of referral. The principal way in which a voluntary public employment service can remove the frictional inefficiencies of the labor market, therefore, is through the completeness and accuracy with which it is able to collect and disseminate its information concerning employment conditions in the labor market area, and the Service emphasizes this aspect of its work. The interarea and interstate clearance system maintained by the United States Employment Service is an extension of this principle by establishing orderly procedures for the exchange of information about job openings and available job seekers.

Another aspect of employment office administration is the specialized counseling, information and selection services for groups of workers, such as the physically handicapped, youth, and migratory farm labor. It is well-recognized that these special groups can best be handled as a part of the total employment process, benefiting from professional standards and skills in employee testing and placement, and within the most comprehensive knowledge of labor-market conditions. A Federal Interagency Committee for the Physically Handicapped, under the chairmanship of the Deputy Director of the United States Employment Service has developed for the guidance of the State agencies a pattern of collaboration between the Veterans Administration and the Office of Vocational Rehabilitation with respect to counseling and placement procedures. During the 10 years of the National Youth Administration, a working agreement providing for

421

establishment of special youth services in local employment offices was established. This source of funds is no longer available, but many States still provide specialized divisions dealing with youth entering the labor market. The Farm Placement Service, a statutory responsibility of the United States Employment Service, was transferred to the Department of Agriculture's Extension Service during the war, but was returned to the United States Employment Service in January 1948. This function consists primarily in advising the State agencies as to the time and path of migratory labor movements, and in assisting the States to plan and set up mobile employment offices for handling the major seasonal shifts.

VETERANS

Congress gave special recognition to veterans in the organization of the United States Employment Service under title IV of the Servicemen's Readjustment Act of 1944. This title created a Veterans' Placement Service Board "to cooperate with and assist the United States Employment Service, and to determine all matters of policy relating to the administration of the Veterans' Employment Service of the United States Employment Service." This Board is composed of the Administrator of Veterans' Affairs, the Director of Selective Service, and whoever may have the responsibility for administering the United States Employment Service. The Chairman of the Board has authority and responsibility for carrying out its policies through veterans' employment representatives attached to the staffs of State employment services to which they are assigned by the United States Employment Service.

The Chairman of the Board may delegate his authority to an executive secretary of the Board appointed by him and who is thereupon designated as Chief of the Veterans' Employment Service of the United States Employment Service. Veterans' employment representatives must be veterans and residents for 2 years of the State in which they are appointed. They are recommended by the Chief of the Veterans' Employment Service for approval by the Board upon the advice of State veterans' administration representatives and concurrence of State directors of employment security and selective service. Upon approval by the Board, they are formally appointed through the civil-service and classification procedures of the United States Employment Service, and are paid as Federal employees under the Classification Act. Assistant veterans' employment representatives do not have to be approved by the Board. Veterans' employment representatives, attached to the staffs of the State employment services, are specifically made administratively responsible to the Board, through its executive secretary, for execution of the Board's veterans' placement policies through the State agency. They are also made functionally responsible for supervision of registration and placement of veterans, for promoting the interest of employers in employing veterans, obtaining information about employment prospects, and to maintain regular contact with employers' and veterans' organizations.

The law thus establishes a Federal employment service for veterans with a different Federal administrative head, and a distinct line of administrative responsibility to the field, although at the same time providing that the Veterans' Employment Service shall work with and through the United States Employment Service and State agencies. This imposes a difficult task of integration and coordination upon both Federal and State employment services. The Veterans' Placement Service Board Regulations, passed by the Board August 9, 1945, upon the joint recommendation of the Director of the United States Employment Service and the Chief of the Veterans' Employment Service, indicated however that an acceptable procedure had been worked out under the policy established by Congress. Frictions at the Federal level appear to have been resolved by the practice of formal appointment through the United States Employment Service upon the recommendation of the Veterans' Employment Service, and by establishing the general policy that the veterans' employment representatives shall concentrate upon developing job opportunities, providing special counseling services, and maintaining contacts with employer and veterans' organizations, restricting themselves to watchful observation of State procedures of registration, interviewing, and placement of veterans along with other groups of job applicants. It has not been possible to remove difficulties of operation entirely in the States. Administratively, of course, this arrangement is less desirable than if the veterans' employment representatives in the States were made wholly responsible to the State directors, and the Veterans' Placement Service Board relied upon the United States Employment Service to carry out its policies through the normal Federal-State relationship of supervision and maintenance of standards. In the special case of veterans, Congress has adopted the principle of a Federal employment service, leaving to the administrators of the two systems the problem of working out the necessary administrative adjustments. The Veterans' Employment Service of necessity will always present some difficulties under a Federal-State cooperative system. Under a cooperative system, the veterans' employment representatives should be turned over to the State employment security agencies and the Veterans' Employment Service should be merged with the United States Employment Service along with its other specialized service programs.

Public Law 26, Eightieth Congress, section 5 (a), transferred to the Secretary of Labor the functions of the Director of Selective Service under section 8 (g) of the Selective Training and Service Act of 1940

(54 Stat. 885), guaranteeing the reemployment of "members of the Reserve components of the land and naval forces of the United States who have satisfactorily completed any period of active duty, and persons who have satisfactorily completed any period of their training and service under this act." Public Law 87 provides similar assistance to merchant seamen, and by agreement with the Maritime Commission, the Veterans' Reemployment Rights Division performs this service for this group in addition to veterans.

Refusals of employers to rehire veterans or trainees are first sought to be adjusted by informal negotiations. Cases not settled are referred to the Solicitor of Labor and then to district attorneys, who may prosecute if they are satisfied that the veteran is entitled to reemployment under the statute.

The function might be regarded as within the area of the Veteran Employment Service in the United States Employment Service, but the officers of that Service, fearing that the enforcement and regulatory duties would conflict with their promotional work, preferred not to take it. It was therefore established as a separate unit in the Secretary's office with an intradepartmental committee composed of the Undersecretary, the Solicitor, the Directors of United States Employment Service and Veterans' Employment Service, the Director of Personnel and the Director of the Division to recommend policies governing the program to the Secretary of Labor. The transfer of the United States Employment Service to the Federal Security Agency leaves the function misplaced. It should be transferred to the Veterans' Administration, or alternatively, now that Selective Service has been reestablished, returned to the Selective Service System.

UNEMPLOYMENT COMPENSATION

The fifth major function of employment service at State and local levels is to register job applicants filing claims for unemployment compensation, to offer them suitable work for which they are qualified, and prepare the necessary papers for determination through the appeals machinery whether benefits should be denied when applicants reject jobs as not suited to their skill, training, or wage expectations. These are the operations which led to the financing of employment offices under the Social Security Act, and to the prevalent practice in the States of integrating State employment services with unemployment compensation activities under the same administrative head. The necessity for connecting the operations of registration and referral of job-seekers with disqualification proceedings and the processing of weekly claims requires no explanation. It is not so clear that the operations of applicant interviewing, classification, counseling, selection, and referral require a close connection with the operations of maintaining employer accounts, determining employer liability and contribution rates, tax collection, maintaining and processing wage records, computing and processing benefit payments, disbursement, and investigation of fraud.

The variations from State to State indicate the inadvisability of imposing uniformity by Federal mandate beyond certain standards intended to guarantee proper administrative performance. From 10 years of administrative experience, it is clear that the States have not emerged employment office functions with unemployment compensation procedures, but in different ways run them as a more or less integrated series of operations under unified direction at the State level.

It is sometimes assumed that there is an inverse relationship between the size of the continued claims for unemployment benefits and the number of placements made by the employment offices. This has been largely disproven by experience under the system. Employment service placements are not representative of the pattern of hiring in industry generally. In sustained periods of either full employment or depression placements are apt to be low and claims high, but seasonal or reconversion unemployment creates periods of high activity for both benefit and placement operations. Further, the necessity of matching qualifications to jobs prevents an automatic or necessary reduction of benefits by reason of employment service activities. While there is no necessary statistical relationship between placement and benefit operations, nevertheless the two programs are part of the same process of minimizing the effects of unemployment upon the individual worker, the economy, and the community. Each is essential to the other, and there are some opportunities for interchange of managerial and clerical personnel from one to the other.

The Federal Security Administrator, through the Bureau of Employment Security, exercises four functions under title III of the Social Security Act and section 1600 of the Internal Revenue Code. He approves State unemployment compensation laws for offset credit up to 2.7 percent of the 3 percent Federal pay-roll tax if they meet the standard requirements imposed by the Federal tax law. He certifies to the Secretary of the Treasury the States he finds eligible for grants for administration if their laws meet specified requirements under title III of the Social Security Act. He certifies to the Secretary of the Treasury amounts appropriate for grants to States for proper and efficient administration of their laws, and he may study and make recommendations as to the most effective methods of providing economic security through social insurance and related subjects by legislative and administrative policies.

The Treasury maintains separate State accounts in a Federal Unemployment Account that are credited with the amounts of tax collected in each State under tax-offset provisions, and invests all funds not required for withdrawals to meet benefit payments. At the end of

1947, the total fund was approximately 7.1 billion dollars. The Treasury also collects the 0.3 percent pay-roll tax (approximately $225,-000,000 in 1947) that goes into the general fund to cover appropriations for grants for administration of unemployment compensation and employment offices (amounting to $126,600,000 in 1947).

Under the Social Security Act, the State laws determine the scope of employment covered beyond the minimum definition established by the Unemployment Tax Act. For the most part, States determine the amount, waiting period, conditions of eligibility and disqualification, and duration of benefits. However, the Federal Security Administrator is empowered to refuse to approve State laws unless they contain basic provisions specified by the Social Security Act. Beyond approval of the State laws, he may, after reasonable notice and opportunity for hearing, find that in the administration of the State law a substantial number of individuals entitled to benefits have been denied them, or that the States have not complied substantially with such methods of administration as he (the Administrator) has found to be reasonably calculated to insure full payment of benefits when due. Having so found, he may notify the State that further payments for administration will not be made until he is satisfied that there is no longer such denial or failure to comply, and refrain from certifying any amounts for that State to the Secretary of the Treasury.

The significance of this authority lies in the moral persuasiveness it gives the Administrator to secure compliance with Federal administrative standards and procedures, rather than in the few times it has actually been invoked. Criticism emanating from the States with respect to Federal interference has been directed at the degree of detailed control over operating decisions, rather than against Federal dictation of coverage, amounts, and duration of benefits.

In terms of over-all effects, the first 10 years of full operation under the present system revealed a general, if varying, expansion in terms of coverage and size of benefits. Sixteen States in 1947 covered employers with 1 or more employees, and 29 covered employers of less than 8. The actual average weekly benefit for total unemployment had risen from approximately $11 to more than $18. The size of the unemployment trust fund seems to have been stabilized at approximately 7 billion dollars, although employer tax rates have been reduced through experience rating provisions to a national average of 1.4 percent instead of the original 3 percent. The major danger signal in the system is that some States have begun to pay benefits in excess of tax collections in any one year. This development suggests that studies be inaugurated of the tax structure in effect in the several States, partly to evaluate the actual effect of experience rating laws in producing stable, continuous employment, and partly to provide a program for adjusting tax rates to meet unfavorable tax collection—benefit payment ratios.

426

To a considerable extent, the Employment Service and the Federal Security Agency have collaborated in sending out joint regulations and in coordinating budgetary and auditing procedures, but this is possible only to a limited extent in establishing requirements and standards for separate field operations. Consolidation of the two agencies at the Federal level would result in simplification only if the scope and frequency of budgetary and administrative review were reduced and regional offices combined.

RECOVERSION BENEFITS FOR SEAMEN

Amendments to the Social Security Act in 1946 provided a temporary program of direct appropriations to reimburse the States for benefits paid to maritime workers employed by agents of the Maritime Commission or War Shipping Administration. This program has been extended twice (now to June 30, 1950) by congressional appropriation acts. For 1949 Congress estimated the cost at $750,000. Benefits are paid by allocating wages used as the basis for paying benefits to the State where the seaman files his claim. Funds for administration of this program are made available to the States under the same procedure as grants for unemployment compensation.

READJUSTMENT ALLOWANCES FOR VETERANS

Title V of the Servicemen's Readjustment Act of 1944 authorized the Administrator of Veterans' Affairs to reimburse cooperating States for allowances paid under the benefit provisions of the Federal law to unemployed veterans, and to certify to the Social Security Board (Federal Security Administrator) expenses for administration incurred under agreements between the Administrator and the cooperating States. It is estimated that in 1947, 1.4 million veterans were covered under this title, and that allowances totaling some $30,000,000 were made.

The program of the Bureau of Employment Security comprises systematic research and reporting upon State laws and their results, budgetary and administrative review of State tax-collecting and benefit-paying operations, and recommending desirable changes in the State and Federal legislation. (Auditing of State expenditures and supervision of personnel merit systems are performed by centralized bureaus in the Federal Security Agency). Fiscal standards based upon work loads for the several unemployment compensation operations have been developed, and these are used by the States to project cost estimates in line with national economic assumptions a full year in advance of the beginning of the fiscal year for which estimates are made. These estimates are first closely scrutinized by the Bureau's regional offices. The Bureau presents its own estimates of the sum required by the States to the Bureau of the Budget about 9 months in advance, and the President's estimates are submitted to Congress 6 months in advance. Congress thus enacts the necessary appropriations upon the basis of these preliminary estimates after four levels of review, including its own appropriations subcommittee. The States are also required to submit operating budgets in June, the month before actual appropriations become available, and in December, upon which the Bureau makes a semiannual allotment of the funds actually appropriated. The volume of work required by these procedures is considered extremely onerous by the State agencies, who have considered and proposed several plans for revising drastically the present method of 100 percent Federal financing of administrative costs.

Administrative review is carried on both by direct observation of State operations and by constant attention to compliance with reporting requirements. Review is carried on by detailed inspections, special surveys, and participation in the budget process by the Bureau's regional and Washington staff. Information, assistance, and advice is rendered State agencies through the comparison of experience in different jurisdictions, conferences, and issuance of field letters, bulletins, and reports on State activities.

Temporary Disability Insurance

Up to 1948 three States had adopted legislation providing for illness or temporary disability, and in 1947 such bills were pending in 14 State legislatures. The three States having such legislation, and most of the proposed bills, provide that the agency administering unemployment compensation shall administer temporary disability insurance. Coverage of workers, wage records, rate and duration of benefits, and administrative personnel are or can be largely identical under the two programs within a State, which makes for lower costs and simplified procedures than might be the case if sickness and disability were initiated under de novo administrative auspices.

Summary

The American system of employment security, with minimum standards established and supervised by the Federal Government, and with operating control over public employment services integrated with unemployment compensation at the State level, has established itself as an accepted, useful feature of labor-market organization in our private-enterprise economy. To the extent that employers notify employment offices of available job openings, and that employment offices are equipped to do an effective testing, counseling and referral job, registration of temporarily unemployed workers at employment offices for unemployment benefits makes it possible for them to find other suitable employment with a minimum loss of time and a partial replacement of wages. States have generally increased the amount and duration of benefits, and waiting periods have been reduced.

The Issue of Federal Organization

ADMINISTRATIVE FINANCING

Any system of Federal-State cooperation contains the seeds of mutual irritation and dissension between Federal and State legislators and administrative officials. Employment security has experienced many such conflicts, partly because of the frictions arising from the integration of State employment services with the new unemployment compensation agencies and partly because of the disputes arising out of the Federal Government's requirements in connection with its provision of all expenses for State administration. Several devices for meeting these problems have been proposed.

The two extremist views are: (1) Complete federalization, and (2) complete State responsibility. The former is supported by the arguments of greater adequacy of benefits, the greater solvency of benefit reserves pooled nationally rather than on a State basis, the desirability of having uniform standards of competence and salary in administration, the importance of having national policies and national administrative machinery to deal with national problems of unemployment and manpower utilization. The latter is supported by preferences for encouraging State initiative and responsibility, for retaining as many functions and as many powers as possible in the State governments, and for permitting variations in standards and policies according to State or regional opinions, and the conviction that employment security is a State and local problem that should be dealt with locally rather than nationally. The present system is a compromise between these views whereby the Federal Government levies the pay-roll tax, acts as custodian of the funds, prevents benefit reserves from being used for administration, establishes certain minimum standards for State laws, and supervises the administration of the system. At present the States are permitted to establish the variations in employer tax obligations, coverage, eligibility, amount and duration of benefits, and in appointing and fixing scales of payment for administrative personnel.

Complete federalization or complete State responsibility is not in issue. There is no serious consideration of eliminating the Federal pay-roll tax or custody and investment of the unemployment trust fund. The Federal Government should maintain certain minimum standards, review and report on the operation of State programs, and perform certain research, technical, and advisory services that it can usefully provide for all State employment security agencies. Since

1939, the question of whether unemployment is a National or State function has seemed relatively remote in view of the reduction of unemployment to minimum proportions. Reaction to Federal wartime manpower controls left little sentiment in favor of retaining the State employment services in Federal hands when the controls were removed. States already control the benefit structure and the quality of employment services rendered. Thus the major issue in the present Federal-State equilibrium of responsibility in employment security is whether Federal responsibility for maintaining adequate State administration (resulting in divided control over State administration, with States fixing the number and compensation of administrative employees, and the Federal Government determining the amount of money to be granted) should be terminated.

The unique method by which the Federal Government retains three-tenths of 1 percent of the pay-roll tax and finances 100 percent of administrative costs for employment security was adopted deliberately to secure certain results: (1) Adequacy of administrative funds in the initial stages of embarking upon a novel, untried program; (2) a pooled equalization fund for administration whereby smaller States would be assured of receiving administrative funds that might not be available if expenses were limited to the tax contributions from employers in those States; (3) flexibility in meeting needs growing out of violently fluctuating claim loads. Comparison of the totals in tables **XXXII** and **XXXIII**, pages 432 and 434, shows that tax collections have been more than sufficient to meet administrative expenses, and in general—though many States have complained that Federal estimates of need have been insufficient to meet requirements considered necessary by the States—there has been no evidence of break-down in State administration due to lack of funds. The size of grants has grown steadily, though since VJ-day the number of State and local employment office employees has declined from over 24,000 to approximately 20,500. In 1948 combined grants of approximately 65 million dollars each for unemployment compensation and employment offices exceeded 130 million dollars; for fiscal year 1949 Congress appropriated just that figure.

Appropriation hearings and other sources of information nevertheless disclose that the State agencies continually complain that amounts granted are inadequate, that the Federal agencies discriminate among States, and that they are subjected to too much detailed control both in the estimation and in the expenditure of funds. With respect to the first complaint, it is apparent that no automatic, objective measure of need is yet available. On the second point, it is equally clear that Congress deliberately gave the Federal agencies considerable discretionary authority in allocating grants among the States. The Administrator of title **III** of the Social Security Act is required to base his determination on (1) the population of each State; (2) an estimate of the number of persons covered by the State law and of the cost of proper and efficient administration; (3) such other factors as he finds relevant, for example, the proportion of claims or taxable pay rolls in each State to the total claim load or taxable pay rolls in the Nation. Annual appropriation acts have amended the old requirement of the Wagner-Peyser Act that grants for employment offices should be apportioned on a population basis to the effect that such grants shall be made in such amounts as the Administrator determines to be necessary for the proper and efficient administration of each State's unemployment compensation law and of its public employment offices (Public Law 646, 80th Cong.). Other elements that make "discrimination" of some kind inevitable are the wide variation in State laws with respect to administrative provisions and covered employment, with respect to workloads, the variation between States, and the variation in State salary and classification systems. Variations in costs per covered worker between States (table XXXIV, p. 438) reinfroce this conclusion. However, the high correlation between the percentage of combined grants going to each State and the percentage of covered workers in each State shows that the allocations have not been entirely capricious or arbitrary.

The crux of State criticisms of Federal administrative controls lies in the procedures and requirements of budgeting (described above) and in the detailed controls over expenditure. There is no question that the authority exists; responsibility for the manner of its exercise has deliberately been assumed by the Social Security Administration and Federal Security Administrator, who have in turn been governed by the procedural requirements of the Federal Budget and Accounting Act and congressional appropriations procedure. Given the Federal budgeting system, it is difficult to see how the long-range estimates of claim and work-load data that the States find so onerous, together with the record-keeping required, can be dispensed with, although undoubtedly some modifications could be worked out. Similarly, it is not unreasonable for the Federal agency to require the submission of operating budgets as the basis for apportioning appropriated funds and securing advance notice of anticipated deficiencies. Whether the established degree of expenditure control is necessary is also debatable, but in view of the tremendous sums involved a supervisory agency is scarcely to be blamed for taking every possible step to avoid charges of dishonesty or corruption.

Turning to alternative methods of financing State administration of employment security, we find that the major proposals under discussion are: (1) 100 percent offset by the States against the 3 percent Federal tax; (2) return to the States of the balance of tax collections left after grants have been made for administrative expenses, such

TABLE XXXII.—*Hypothetical distribution of collections under the Federal Unemployment Tax Act, by States, fiscal years 1938–47* [1]

[In thousands of dollars]

State	1938	1939	1940	1941	1942	1943	1944	1945	1946	1947	Total, 1938–47 [1]
Total	[2] 61,279	[2] 95,842	[2] 104,533	97,677	119,944	158,361	179,909	184,544	179,930	184,823	1,366,842
Alabama	484	733	885	911	1,309	1,980	2,052	2,168	2,201	2,029	14,752
Alaska	44	66	69	74	119	164	213	226	133	136	1,244
Arizona	179	249	249	234	284	459	519	492	496	517	3,678
Arkansas	225	364	370	347	433	732	677	673	840	771	5,432
California	3,838	6,745	7,151	6,574	8,333	12,339	15,470	15,959	14,809	15,215	106,433
Colorado	398	622	618	557	646	1,001	939	875	965	1,069	7,690
Connecticut	1,340	1,948	2,283	2,279	3,139	4,245	4,563	4,358	3,972	3,949	32,076
Delaware	155	264	288	265	319	420	482	481	442	467	3,583
District of Columbia	343	645	706	671	725	856	853	865	950	1,106	7,720
Florida	463	788	831	831	995	1,364	1,792	1,876	1,828	2,030	12,798
Georgia	697	1,056	1,125	1,084	1,408	1,771	2,127	2,316	2,296	2,474	16,354
Hawaii	138	213	229	205	315	504	418	392	442	487	3,343
Idaho	129	217	219	197	226	378	328	313	313	358	2,678
Illinois	5,264	8,422	9,037	8,303	9,792	12,019	13,325	14,158	14,161	14,931	109,412
Indiana	1,800	2,436	2,787	2,749	3,719	4,917	5,793	5,835	5,325	5,325	40,872
Iowa	626	1,029	1,011	924	1,108	1,367	1,521	1,606	1,643	1,785	12,620
Kansas	431	738	623	576	730	1,356	1,682	1,676	1,499	1,288	10,599
Kentucky	633	981	956	920	1,089	1,416	1,545	1,672	1,701	1,789	12,702
Louisiana	572	991	1,025	976	1,179	1,600	1,977	2,066	1,972	1,937	14,295
Maine	340	502	534	501	652	988	1,119	1,040	960	1,004	7,640
Maryland	886	1,392	1,551	1,546	2,074	2,991	3,427	3,212	2,997	2,870	22,946
Massachusetts	2,766	4,351	4,947	4,530	5,493	6,882	7,371	7,395	7,434	7,894	59,063
Michigan	3,802	4,775	5,874	5,959	7,555	9,855	12,076	12,055	10,494	10,524	82,969
Minnesota	880	1,623	1,661	1,402	1,560	2,030	2,316	2,413	2,480	2,575	18,940
Mississippi	197	314	323	338	445	637	633	690	710	796	5,083
Missouri	1,472	2,475	2,539	2,287	2,874	3,574	3,964	4,094	4,232	4,313	31,824
Montana	200	265	258	250	259	316	312	315	342	390	2,907
Nebraska	290	513	454	399	434	693	802	808	825	826	6,044
Nevada	54	99	96	92	106	268	237	177	170	225	1,524
New Hampshire	236	346	381	354	434	510	504	523	558	682	4,528
New Jersey	2,446	4,149	4,690	4,587	5,742	7,636	8,662	8,854	8,257	8,157	63,180
New Mexico	91	155	147	138	159	204	212	220	284	347	1,957
New York	9,728	15,954	17,563	15,284	17,187	20,936	23,228	24,333	25,065	26,615	195,893
North Carolina	775	1,297	1,468	1,386	1,737	2,247	2,353	2,415	2,504	2,977	19,159
North Dakota	76	136	110	104	110	119	127	142	156	196	1,276
Ohio	4,290	6,219	7,205	6,830	8,698	11,207	12,993	13,210	12,841	12,683	96,176
Oklahoma	504	875	866	751	842	1,260	1,514	1,544	1,531	1,465	11,152
Oregon	459	729	822	797	1,040	1,722	2,184	2,180	1,722	1,807	13,700
Pennsylvania	6,631	9,348	10,184	9,690	11,794	14,589	15,978	16,219	15,744	16,289	126,466
Rhode Island	474	708	840	771	1,050	1,403	1,427	1,392	1,330	1,377	10,772
South Carolina	353	538	602	605	801	1,023	1,041	1,055	1,123	1,360	8,501

South Dakota	75	145	139	131	136	186	166	168	192	235	1,573
Tennessee	672	1,072	1,101	1,067	1,402	1,866	2,273	2,636	2,705	2,525	17,319
Texas	1,631	2,926	2,890	2,605	3,168	4,600	5,643	5,973	5,794	6,001	41,231
Utah	212	320	308	290	340	578	661	523	510	542	4,284
Vermont	132	186	198	192	233	294	314	322	319	362	2,552
Virginia	729	1,214	1,276	1,288	1,775	2,436	2,326	2,250	2,291	2,500	18,055
Washington	815	1,273	1,372	1,340	1,709	2,879	3,556	3,827	3,333	2,855	22,959
West Virginia	860	1,191	1,290	1,277	1,555	1,930	2,071	2,134	2,217	2,352	16,877
Wisconsin	1,359	2,099	2,259	2,129	2,586	3,458	3,968	4,192	4,206	4,181	30,437
Wyoming	85	146	123	110	126	156	175	202	212	234	1,569

[1] Distributed according to taxable wages in each State covered by the Federal act for the calendar year ending during the fiscal year. Data adjusted for wages in small firms not covered by the act. With the exceptions noted, national totals agree with U. S. Treasury figures, including payments for penalties, interest, and delinquency. State distribution of collections based on States in which taxable wages earned rather than on the internal revenue district through which the tax return actually filed. Figures will not necessarily add to totals because of rounding.

[2] National totals shown for fiscal years 1938–40 are different from U. S. Treasury figures. The Treasury Department reported collections of 90.1 million dollars in 1938, 100.9 million dollars in 1939, and 107.5 million dollars in 1940. The 1939 and 1940 totals were adjusted to exclude collections from interstate railroads. The 1938 totals were derived by multiplying wages in calendar year 1937 subject to the Federal tax by 0.2 percent, the rate in effect during that year. The 90.1 million dollars reported by the Treasury Department for fiscal 1938 includes a substantial part of 40 million dollars subsequently transferred to unemployment trust fund accounts of States that did not have an unemployment insurance law in 1936 and whose employers, therefore, paid the full tax on 1936 wages into the Federal Treasury. The 61.3 million dollars figure shown for fiscal 1938 excludes payments for penalties, interest, and delinquency and any portion of the refunded 40 million dollars collected during that year.

Source: Bureau of Employment Security.

TABLE XXXIII.—*Obligations for State employment service and unemployment insurance administration, by States, fiscal years 1938–47* [1]

[In thousands of dollars]

State	1938	1939	1940	1941	1942	1943	1944	1945	1946	1947	Total 1938–47 [1]
Total	45,374	68,099	65,552	70,126	77,864	85,334	95,313	102,807	124,262	126,605	861,336
Alabama	830	856	717	786	889	1,025	1,336	1,639	1,884	1,946	11,909
Alaska	30	61	66	78	102	106	184	195	220	241	1,282
Arizona	323	317	265	303	358	401	469	564	680	727	4,406
Arkansas	173	455	477	540	809	899	883	925	1,078	1,109	7,349
California	3,836	4,649	4,494	5,046	5,757	6,687	7,834	8,581	12,235	13,688	72,809
Colorado	124	463	480	503	542	604	677	785	883	790	5,851
Connecticut	1,273	1,458	1,392	1,450	1,446	1,496	1,616	1,638	2,042	1,971	15,783
Delaware	130	248	241	240	241	231	263	280	322	307	2,502
District of Columbia	397	564	575	577	[2] 620	[2] 638	690	718	855	1,022	6,657
Florida	185	555	657	723	876	1,008	1,259	1,547	1,625	1,728	10,165
Georgia	223	870	955	1,045	1,176	1,215	1,518	1,941	1,886	1,826	12,657
Hawaii	91	163	169	151	174	214	270	316	303	269	2,119
Idaho	154	306	273	286	325	339	328	405	460	600	3,477
Illinois	313	1,459	3,715	4,949	5,524	5,975	6,512	6,241	7,839	7,548	50,077
Indiana	1,492	2,249	1,841	1,825	2,135	2,474	2,583	2,639	3,023	2,623	22,891
Iowa	360	858	748	555	662	858	905	1,089	1,345	1,345	9,493
Kansas	144	549	532	907	804	758	1,325	1,357	1,301	1,159	7,653
Kentucky	249	814	899	875	965	1,009	1,135	1,400	1,348	1,361	10,621
Louisiana	818	929	821	806	923	1,122	1,374	1,292	1,449	1,740	11,274
Maine	510	559	500	485	487	524	585	647	699	782	5,778
Maryland	889	1,108	933	873	1,011	742	916	1,629	1,691	2,117	12,884
Massachusetts	2,625	3,898	3,386	3,346	3,447	3,487	3,915	4,064	4,290	4,788	37,246
Michigan	1,426	3,981	3,264	3,232	4,088	4,252	4,727	5,340	7,646	7,325	45,280
Minnesota	1,256	1,652	1,283	1,426	1,507	1,689	1,877	2,125	1,915	1,193	17,390
Mississippi	332	475	449	489	624	742	916	1,130	1,152	1,193	7,502
Missouri	213	1,556	1,668	1,864	2,436	2,554	2,436	2,464	2,890	2,458	20,540
Montana	111	154	314	330	345	348	341	387	409	501	3,241
Nebraska	100	414	420	436	496	627	720	844	807	736	5,600
Nevada	105	179	172	190	209	193	250	279	323	348	2,248
New Hampshire	420	371	342	345	378	357	449	481	515	598	4,256
New Jersey	617	2,327	2,906	3,155	3,419	3,769	3,967	[2] 4,024	5,142	5,065	34,390
New Mexico	63	218	216	207	222	270	323	350	350	405	2,624
New York	7,654	9,909	8,548	9,027	9,756	10,184	11,181	[2] 11,903	[2] 14,932	[2] 16,400	108,667
North Carolina	1,220	1,425	1,158	1,230	1,325	1,521	1,792	1,903	2,046	2,180	15,301
North Dakota	110	197	213	243	265	246	283	382	380	356	2,676
Ohio	530	2,750	3,111	3,743	4,163	4,656	5,698	6,042	7,139	6,093	43,926
Oklahoma	283	760	742	728	899	995	1,043	1,191	1,340	1,340	9,271
Oregon	727	779	686	842	1,045	1,145	1,197	1,307	1,749	1,706	11,184
Pennsylvania	7,146	7,323	6,369	6,394	6,326	7,124	7,501	7,697	9,214	10,164	75,259
Rhode Island	782	809	689	755	738	779	807	937	1,026	954	8,275
South Carolina	354	631	613	615	691	789	949	1,076	1,096	1,225	8,039
South Dakota	87	165	170	191	213	272	335	415	351	295	2,493

Tennessee	756	1,035	956	1,060	1,189	1,293	1,528	1,761	1,932	2,053	13,563
Texas	2,103	2,545	2,429	2,432	2,761	3,073	3,290	3,994	4,538	4,364	31,528
Utah	288	335	304	326	398	449	540	645	691	798	4,775
Vermont	267	240	219	241	257	256	278	302	388	424	2,870
Virginia	824	987	962	989	983	1,212	1,533	1,773	1,662	1,604	12,530
Washington	141	767	925	1,081	1,496	1,690	1,871	2,075	2,690	2,874	15,611
West Virginia	920	1,225	926	911	855	900	954	1,002	1,225	1,224	10,142
Wisconsin	1,345	1,205	1,169	1,179	1,308	1,453	1,556	1,653	1,928	1,745	14,632
Wyoming	80	205	187	194	199	220	220	257	269	310	2,141

[1] Excludes the cost of operating national and regional offices of the Bureau of Employment Security, the U. S. Employment Service, and the War Manpower Commission; administrative costs connected with the servicemen's readjustment allowance programs, both State and National; costs related to the operation of the National Reemployment Service; and cost of operating the farm placement program carried on by the Department of Agriculture and State extension services during the period 1943–47. Penalty mail and postage charges prorated among States: Those relating to employment service operations for fiscal years 1945–47 are estimates. Excludes Puerto Rico. Estimates of liquidation costs (including terminal leave costs) involved in the return of the Employment Service from Federal to State operation prorated over fiscal years 1943–47. Figures will not necessarily add to totals because of rounding.

[2] Amounts for employment service estimated.

Sources: Bureau of Employment Security and U. S. Employment Service.

TABLE XXXIV.—*Administrative cost data on State unemployment compensation and employment service programs—fiscal year ended June 30 1947*

State, district or territory	Grants for unemployment compensation administration	Grants for employment service administration	Combined grants for unemployment compensation and employment service	Percent of combined grant		Employees covered June 1947	Coverage (June 1947) Percentage	Combined grants (unemployment compensation and employment service) distributions	Average cost per covered employee		
				Unemployment compensation	Employment service				Unemployment compensation	Employment service	Total
Alabama	$700,000	$1,246,000	$1,946,000	36.0	64.0	417,100	1.31	1.54	$1.68	$2.99	$4.67
Alaska	119,000	122,000	241,000	49.4	50.6	38,800	.11	.19	3.07	3.14	6.21
Arizona	262,000	465,000	727,000	36.0	64.0	96,600	.30	.57	2.71	4.81	7.52
Arkansas	526,000	583,000	1,109,000	47.4	52.6	204,500	.64	.88	2.57	2.85	5.42
California	7,442,000	6,246,000	13,688,000	54.4	45.6	2,378,500	7.47	10.80	3.13	2.63	5.76
Colorado	209,000	581,000	790,000	26.5	73.5	189,200	.59	.62	1.10	3.07	4.17
Connecticut	1,061,000	910,000	1,971,000	53.8	46.2	633,400	1.99	1.56	1.68	1.44	3.12
Delaware	155,000	152,000	307,000	50.5	49.5	90,200	.28	.24	1.72	1.69	3.41
District of Columbia	434,000	588,000	1,022,000	42.5	57.5	217,800	.68	.81	1.99	2.70	4.69
Florida	621,000	1,107,000	1,728,000	36.0	64.0	343,700	1.08	1.36	1.81	3.22	5.03
Georgia	704,000	1,122,000	1,826,000	38.6	61.4	497,100	1.55	1.44	1.42	2.26	3.68
Hawaii	123,000	146,000	269,000	45.7	54.3	100,000	.31	.21	1.23	1.46	2.69
Idaho	261,000	339,000	600,000	43.5	56.5	87,200	.27	.47	2.99	3.89	6.88
Illinois	3,741,000	3,807,000	7,548,000	49.6	50.4	2,360,500	7.41	5.96	1.58	1.61	3.19
Indiana	1,063,000	560,000	2,623,000	40.5	59.5	881,100	2.77	2.07	1.77	1.21	2.98
Iowa	395,000	950,000	1,345,000	29.4	70.6	329,600	1.03	1.06	1.20	2.88	4.08
Kansas	482,000	677,000	1,159,000	41.6	58.4	228,000	.72	.92	2.11	2.97	5.08
Kentucky	540,000	821,000	1,361,000	39.7	60.3	356,900	1.12	1.07	1.51	2.30	3.81
Louisiana	910,000	830,000	1,740,000	52.3	47.7	427,400	1.34	1.37	2.13	1.94	4.07
Maine	308,000	474,000	782,000	39.4	60.6	169,800	.53	.62	1.81	2.79	4.60
Maryland	970,000	1,147,000	2,117,000	45.8	54.2	543,200	1.71	1.67	1.79	2.11	3.90
Massachusetts	2,816,000	1,972,000	4,788,000	58.8	41.2	1,421,000	4.46	3.78	1.98	1.39	3.37
Michigan	3,596,000	3,728,000	7,324,000	49.1	50.9	1,565,000	4.91	5.78	2.30	2.38	4.68
Minnesota	735,000	1,441,000	2,176,000	33.8	66.2	520,800	1.64	1.72	1.41	2.77	4.18
Mississippi	372,000	821,000	1,193,000	31.2	68.8	171,400	.54	.94	2.17	4.79	6.96
Missouri	1,010,000	1,448,000	2,458,000	41.1	58.9	744,000	2.34	1.94	1.36	1.95	3.31
Montana	245,000	256,000	501,000	48.9	51.1	93,200	.29	.40	2.63	2.75	5.38
Nebraska	202,000	535,000	737,000	27.4	72.6	156,200	.49	.58	1.29	3.43	4.72
Nevada	144,000	204,000	348,000	41.4	58.6	37,500	.12	.27	3.84	5.44	9.28
New Hampshire	222,000	376,000	598,000	37.1	62.9	127,400	.40	.47	1.74	2.95	4.69
New Jersey	2,872,000	2,193,000	5,065,000	56.7	43.3	1,270,500	3.99	4.00	2.26	1.73	3.99
New Mexico	170,000	235,000	405,000	42.0	58.0	80,600	.25	.40	2.11	2.92	5.03
New York	8,530,000	7,873,000	16,403,000	52.0	48.0	4,274,100	13.42	12.96	2.00	1.84	3.84

North Carolina	823,000	1,357,000	2,180,000	37.8	62.2	605,700	1.90	1.72	1.36	2.24	3.60
North Dakota	89,000	267,000	356,000	25.0	75.0	38,900	.12	.28	2.29	6.86	9.15
Ohio	2,597,000	3,496,000	6,093,000	42.6	57.4	2,155,100	6.77	4.81	1.21	1.62	2.83
Oklahoma	539,000	801,000	1,340,000	40.2	59.8	252,600	.79	1.06	2.05	3.17	5.22
Oregon	786,000	920,000	1,706,000	46.1	53.9	310,200	.97	1.35	2.53	2.97	5.50
Pennsylvania	5,484,000	4,680,000	10,164,000	54.0	46.0	2,988,900	9.39	8.03	1.83	1.57	3.40
Rhode Island	395,000	559,000	954,000	41.4	58.6	234,200	.74	.75	1.69	2.39	4.08
South Carolina	390,000	835,000	1,225,000	31.8	68.2	296,400	.90	.97	1.32	2.82	4.14
South Dakota	78,000	217,000	295,000	26.4	73.6	47,300	.15	.23	1.65	4.59	6.24
Tennessee	849,000	1,204,000	2,053,000	41.4	58.6	477,700	1.50	1.62	1.78	2.52	4.30
Texas	1,585,000	2,779,000	4,364,000	36.3	63.7	1,079,300	3.39	3.45	1.47	2.57	4.04
Utah	301,000	497,000	798,000	37.7	62.3	121,400	.38	.63	2.48	4.09	6.57
Vermont	155,000	268,000	423,000	36.6	63.4	62,700	.20	.33	2.47	4.27	6.74
Virginia	512,000	1,092,000	1,604,000	31.9	68.1	475,000	1.49	1.27	1.08	2.30	3.38
Washington	1,504,000	1,371,000	2,875,000	52.3	47.7	503,900	1.58	2.27	2.98	2.72	5.70
West Virginia	620,000	604,000	1,224,000	50.7	49.3	375,400	1.18	.97	1.65	1.61	3.26
Wisconsin	565,000	1,180,000	1,745,000	32.4	67.6	717,100	2.25	1.38	.79	1.65	2.44
Wyoming	147,000	163,000	310,000	47.4	52.6	53,500	.17	.24	2.75	3.05	5.80
All States	59,359,000	67,246,000	126,605,000	---	---	31,847,600	100.00	100.00	1.86	2.11	3.97

Source: Unemployment Benefit Advisors, Inc.

Note.—For factors to be considered in an analysis of above costs, see accompanying advisor.

balance to be used for administration or for benefit payments; (3) raise the tax offset credit, say, from 2.7 to 2.9 or 2.95 percent; the one-tenth of 1 percent to be used to make a relatively small flat or matching grant to all States meeting Federal standards, to cover Federal administrative expenses, and to maintain the Federal loan fund for possible emergencies.

1. The 100 percent offset plan (H. R. 5736) would permit all collections under the 3 percent tax to be credited to State accounts in the unemployment trust fund, from which withdrawals could be made for both benefits and administrative expenses; the Federal Administrator would certify annually to the Secretary of the Treasury those States whose laws and administration meet the requirements of the Federal tax law and standards specified in the Federal unemployment compensation law. This proposal would turn complete financial responsibility for employment security over to the States, and would restrict Federal administrative control to inspection to assure that the States were meeting minimum statutory standards. It would eliminate the present flexibility of Federal appropriations procedure and the relative assurance that administrative funds would be available to meet emergencies arising from widespread unemployment or unforeseen claim loads; about a fourth of the States already receive less tax collections from the three-tenths of 1 percent than is required for administrative costs (there were 13 such States in 1945, 1946, and 1947); it would impose upon the Federal Government the burden of tax collection, accounting, determination of liability, statistical research, and maintenance of standards, without yielding any revenue for the Federal purposes.

2. Another plan (H. R. 6578), recommended by the Interstate Conference of Employment Security Administrators, would segregate tax collections from the three-tenths of 1 percent tax for administrative expenses in a Federal unemployment account in the unemployment trust fund; Congress would annually appropriate to this account the entire revenue from the three-tenths tax and authorize annual grants to States for administrative expenses found necessary by the Federal Administrator; after such withdrawals by the States in the first quarter of the fiscal year any surplus remaining in the unemployment account would be transferred to the accounts of the States in the trust fund; allocation of the surplus would be based on the ratio of taxable pay rolls in each State to total taxable pay rolls in the Nation; States would then be free, subject to State fiscal controls, to use their balances in the trust account for either administrative expenses or for benefits. This proposal would secure the advantages of adequate financing to all States, of flexibility in securing funds to meet either benefit or administrative requirements, and of eliminating budget controls over current State operations (long-range estimates for Fed-

eral budgetary purposes would still be necessary). The plan would require Federal budgetary review and determination of necessary amounts for State administration as a condition of allocating of the pooled administration account, so there would continue to be irritation over Federal budgetary procedures. The plan would give almost complete discretion to States in charging withdrawals from the trust fund either to benefit payments or to administrative expenses, once transfer from the unemployment account to the trust-fund accounts had been made. It would deprive the Federal Government of all revenues from the three-tenths percent pay-roll tax.

3. The third proposal that has received serious consideration has not been embodied in bill form. This would raise the State's tax offset credit from 2.7 percent of the 3-percent tax to 2.9 or 2.95 percent; the State legislatures would determine amounts actually necessary to be withdrawn from the unemployment trust fund for administration; the remaining 0.1 or 0.05 percent would go to the general fund of the Federal Treasury, where it would be used (a) for making flat grants to complying States to assure adequate appropriations for administration; (b) for paying Federal administrative costs; (c) for maintaining the Federal loan fund now scheduled to expire January 1, 1950. This plan would do away with the problem of finding an acceptable statutory formula for Federal grants; it would permit States to assume responsibility for determining administrative expenses over and above the Federal allowance; it would eliminate much detail in present Federal budgetary procedures, would restrict Federal control over expenditures to those necessary to secure the flat grant. Objections to the plan are the problem of determining the appropriate size and method of allocating the grant, the possibility that legislatures in poor States might refuse to supplement a fixed grant adequate to maintain a minimum employment security operations, and, finally, the inflexibility of State legislative procedures in meeting contingency needs.

There has been practically no serious discussion of transforming the method of financing administration of employment security to a Federal grant-in-aid basis, partly because of the lack of agreement on an appropriate statutory formula, and partly because of the relative success with which the Federal Government has discharged its responsibilities for paying 100 percent of the administrative cost of the system. The basic question of public policy for Congress to determine is whether the national interest in employment security requires the Federal Government to provide adequate administration and control over State expenditures for employment security.

Of the three methods described for turning over to the States the determination of expenditures for employment security, plan 1, providing for 100-percent tax offset credit to the States, would go furthest toward eliminating Federal controls and to remove assurance of flexibility and adequacy in financing State systems. It would provide no funds to cover the cost of Federal tax collection and administrative functions, and would provide Federal controls only to the extent that State laws would have to contain provisions necessary to comply with conditions specified in the Federal tax laws. Plan 2, providing for the annual merging of State benefit and administration accounts in the Federal unemployment trust fund, would retain Federal control to the extent of determining and appropriating the amount the Federal Government thought necessary for State administration, but once the balance in the administration account had been transferred to the benefit account, the States would be free to make their own final determination of withdrawals necessary for either benefit payments or administration. It also would make no provision to meet the cost of Federal tax and employment security administration. Plan 3, providing for raising the State tax offset credit to 2.9 or 2.95 percent and for a flat minimum Federal grant to all States, would allow such Federal controls as might be attached to the receipt of the flat minimum grant, and would meet the requirement of providing funds for Federal administrative expenses. From the standpoint of insuring adequacy of funds in all States, either 2 or 3 is preferable to 1. But plan 2 assumes that the Federal Government has no interest in maintaining the solvency of State benefit reserves by preventing withdrawal from such reserves for administrative purposes. Plan 2 is probably the most flexible and equitable of the three, but it permits use of benefit reserves for administration, and fails to provide funds to meet the costs of Federal administration. Plan 3 would combine the elements of major State financial responsibility on the one side, and the Federal interest in maintaining the minimum adequacy of administration, solvency of State funds, and in securing reimbursement for its own administrative expenses.

PROPER LOCATION OF THE UNITED STATES EMPLOYMENT SERVICE AND BUREAU OF EMPLOYMENT SECURITY

Apart from the issue of administrative financing, the principal source of Federal-State friction in employment security lies in the relation between unemployment compensation and employment service functions at the Federal level. It is now generally agreed by both Federal and State officials that it is desirable to integrate fiscal and administrative review of the two State programs under the supervision of the same Federal department. It is also generally understood by Federal and State officials that placement operations should not be subordinated or neglected in favor of paying unemployment compensation claims, and that certain employment service functions (notably occupational analysis, testing, reporting, counseling, and placement standards and procedures) should not be merged with unemployment compensation work.

These points of agreement emerged clearly during the hearings and debates over President Truman's Reorganization Plan No. 2 in 1947 and Plan No. 1 of 1948. The organizational issue is therefore primarily a question of location and coordination. The main points of controversy were (1) whether employment security should be administered in connection with other labor and employment relations, functions, rather than in connection with other social security, educational, and public health functions; (2) whether the Secretary of Labor should be entrusted with administering the certification and administrative functions under title III of the Social Security Act when he is charged with "fostering and promoting the welfare of wage earners and their opportunities for profitable employment."

With respect to the first point:

1. Employment offices and unemployment compensation are more closely related to each other than to other social security, educational, or public health programs. Both are Federal-State programs dealing with problems of employers and employees, hiring and lay-off, job stabilization, personnel, and labor-management relations. Neither has any comparable relation to public assistance or grants to States for education and public health. Old-age and survivors insurance is a completely Federal program, with different coverage and different administrative procedures from unemployment compensation. Insofar as old-age insurance might be merged with unemployment compensation as to coverage, it would have a closer administrative relation to wage experience and conditions of employment than to education, public health, or public assistance.

2. Employment security has close operating relationships with other employment and labor functions: in research with the Bureau of Labor Statistics and the Women's Bureau, in training with the Apprentice Training Service, in conditions of employment with the Wage and Hour Division and the Bureau of Labor Standards.

3. In the States, the employment security agency is not located in the State welfare, health, or education department, but is either located in the State industrial commission or labor department (15 States), in a department with other labor functions (6 States), or in an independent employment security or unemployment compensation commission (30 States). The States thus either consider employment security as an employment function requiring coordination with other such functions, or give it a separate status. They do not merge it with public assistance, health, or education.

4. Personnel engaged in employment service and unemployment compensation problems acquire the same basic training, familiarity,

and experience with labor and employee relations problems, and do not develop professional interest or concern with problems and techniques of public health, education, or welfare administration. Neither employers nor employees wish public policies concerning their interests to be administered from a professional social worker viewpoint.

5. The Employment Service (together with unemployment compensation) is a vital and necessary segment of the functions of any agency charged with administering Federal policies with respect to the labor market, working conditions, and labor-management relations.

Employment Security on the Railroads

The Railroad Unemployment Insurance Act of 1938, as amended, provides that the Railroad Retirement Board shall collect from employing carriers subject to the law and from individuals representing employees a 3-percent tax on pay rolls (up to $300 a month for each covered employee). The Board is required to deposit its collections with the Treasury. The Treasury disburses benefit payments as directed by the Board "prior to audit and settlement by the General Accounting Office," subject only to appeal by any claimant to a United States district court. Three-tenths of 1 percent of tax collections are made available for administration, subject to the requirement that the Board must turn over to the benefit (appropriated) account at the end of each fiscal year all money in excess of $6,000,000. The law also stipulates that all tax collections credited to the Board shall be permanently appropriated to the Board, and that the administration fund may include such amounts as Congress may appropriate for expenses necessary or additional to administration. The effect of these provisions is that while Congress each year reviews the Board's estimate of tax collections and necessary administrative expenses, its appropriation to the Board of all taxes collected does not prevent the Board from charging expenditures for administration up to the limits of the revenue from the three-tenths of 1-percent tax. The congressional appropriation for administration is simply a part of the larger appropriation of estimated total tax collections, to be accounted for each year by showing the estimate of obligations for administration in relation to the status of the entire appropriated account. Thus Congress has bound itself to finance the railroad employment security system as a separate revolving fund, independent of fiscal controls other than the annual appropriating procedure, and which is replenished each year by the amount of the Board's tax collections.

The jurisdiction of the Board and the coverage of the railroad retirement and unemployment insurance acts are identical and are restricted to the railroad industry. The system is therefore a special employment security system for this industry, merging the functions of permanent retirement and security from the risks of temporary unemployment. The administration of the two programs also has been merged, although the procedures of processing and determining retirement claims differ from those of unemployment and sickness compensation. The Board contracts with the carriers for the services of supervisory employees who take all types of claims. Retirement claims are sent to the Board's central offices in Chicago for processing and determination; unemployment compensation and sickness claims are sent to the Board's 9 regional offices; claimants for unemployment compensation are required to file applications for jobs which are sent to the nearest of the Board's 110 field offices.

The field offices investigate claims for all types of benefit, maintain an interviewing and information function for both claimants and carriers, and provide placement services for unemployment compensation claimants. In the central offices of the Board, the Division of Employment Service is a division of the Bureau of Employment and Claims. The Division prepares all instructions of the Bureau affecting field offices; supervises field office operations; and analyzes the field offices' operating reports. It thus performs the work of a division of field operations covering the taking, investigation, and processing of claims, and placement work of the Board. Thus in the central, regional, and field offices, the work of placement and compensation has been scrambled, and there is no segregation of work or cost figures between employment service and benefit payment operations.

Although during the war, when the Board controlled all hiring in the railroad industry, the number of placements rose to over 600,000, in 1948 this figure fell to less than 50,000. A few placements are made by referral to local State employment offices, but this is small because most railroad employees expect to be reemployed in the railroad industry. Seniority and rehiring provisions of union agreements limit to a relatively small number any placements that the State employment offices might make directly to railroads or by referral to the Railroad Retirement Board's field offices. Nothing would be gained in the way of efficiency by transferring the Board's employment service functions alone to the State employment services.

With respect to unemployment compensation, the proportion of covered pay roll subject to the 3 percent tax, and the benefit structure of the railroad system differ from the State laws. In its administration, the railroad system is completely Federal. The carriers perform services for the Board in taking and verifying claims but they do so under a Federal contract. The higher and broader scale of benefits under this separate industry arrangement than the State unemployment compensation laws would result in bitter opposition from labor organizations to breaking this system up and compelling railroad em-

443

ployees to seek benefits and placement service from the State employment security systems. While technically it would be feasible to have the railroads pay taxes to the States, it would be much more complicated, and would reverse the whole trend toward standardization in railroad operation and Federal regulatory legislation. Unless the retirement system were extended to universal coverage, and unemployment compensation were made a Federal function, the factors of efficiency, benefits, employee satisfaction, and tradition weigh heavily against transfer of responsibility for financing and administering railroad employment security legislation to old-age and survivors insurance and the States.

Other Relationships of Employment Service and Unemployment Compensation at the Federal Level

FULL EMPLOYMENT POLICY

Under section 4 (e) (2) of the Employment Act of 1946, the Council of Economic Advisers in the Executive Office of the President, in preparing and making recommendations to the President for his annual Economic Report, calls upon the Department of Labor among other Federal agencies for information and assistance. Much of this information is statistical, including data on wages, prices, and the distribution of employment by industry, occupation, and locality. The United States Employment Service and Bureau of Employment Security are the major sources of information on employment by labor market area and by States, and in two annual reports the council has drawn attention to the importance of improving the utilization of labor by improving the processes of employment training, counselling, and placement in relation to employment opportunities. The facilities of the Bureau of Labor Statistics, Employment Service, and Bureau of Employment Security are the primary sources of information about the industrial and geographical utilization of the labor force, and the relation of wage differentials to the distribution and movement of manpower. Although the labor force series of the Census Bureau may be the better information upon which to base the over-all objectives or goals of total employment, it is clearly desirable to coordinate the activities of the other agencies to follow up and observe actual trends and shifts in the distribution of the employed part of the labor force.

Summary and Conclusions

ORGANIZATION

1. The Director of the Employment Administration should establish a single Office of Field Operations, responsible for all functions

of administrative control and fiscal review, promulgation of standards and regulations, and handling formal relations with the State employment security agencies. This office would have direct supervision of regional offices. Separate staff divisions should be retained for carrying on specialized employment office standards and services.

2. The Veterans Employment Service should be abolished as such, and its functions transferred to the Employment Administration. Special attention to veterans' employment problems and liaison with the Veterans Administration should be delegated by the Director to an Assistant for Veterans' Affairs. The veterans' employment representatives in the States should be transferred to the State employment services.

3. The Veterans Reemployment Rights Division should be transferred to the Selective Service Administration or to the Department of Justice.

Financing

1. The tax offset method of financing the payment of unemployment benefits should be retained. It is effective in inducing the States to comply with Federal standards, and is compatible with a great degree of autonomy in fixing employer tax rates and in determining the amount and duration of benefits.

2. The issue as to whether the Federal Government should relinquish its interest in insuring adequate administration of employment security to the States is highly debatable. The extent of Federal control over budgetary, fiscal, and administrative procedures is perhaps excessive, but the State agencies continually complain that grants are insufficient and deficiency appropriations are practically an annual occurrence. On the other hand, State systems have not broken down for lack of funds, and the allocation of Federal grants seems to have followed, at least in result if not by intent, the proportion of covered workers in each State to the total covered workers in the Nation. No single-factor statutory formula appears to be feasible. If Congress should decide that it is more important to place financial responsibility for administration in the hands of State legislatures than to maintain Federal responsibility for adequate administration, two factors should be kept in mind:

a. The Federal Government should not permit the 2.7 percent tax to be diverted for administrative expenses by the States.

b. The Federal Government should retain some percentage of the 3 percent tax for Federal administrative expenses in connection with employment security, for operating a loan or contingency fund, and for making flat grants sufficient to meet the minimum needs of the

445

dozen States whose collections for administration do not meet administrative costs considered necessary by the Federal Government. These conditions would permit raising the offset to perhaps 2.9, and segregating the revenues from the difference between 2.7 and 2.9 in the Federal unemployment account to be available for withdrawal by the States for administrative expenses.

Chapter V

ENFORCEMENT AND PROMOTION OF EMPLOYMENT STANDARDS

Protection of the health, safety, and morals of wage earners was a subject of State legislation and constitutional controversy for 70 years before the Supreme Court decision in 1937 that finally upheld the Washington minimum-wage law. This decision seemed finally to confirm the power of the States to regulate conditions of employment, including industrial safety and health, workmen's compensation, hours of work, collection of wages, and child labor. The prevailing purpose and standard in State minimum-wage laws is to provide the amount necessary to support a single woman living alone according to minimum standards of health and decency, although many State laws permit variations from this standard by authorizing separate wage boards to set minima for different industries. Before the constitutional rights of the States were settled, however, the Federal Government had begun to seek national economic objectives through wage and hour legislation, on the several grounds that it was necessary (1) to raise living standards of low-wage groups in order to remove barriers to interstate commerce, (2) partly to prevent or modify extreme nation-wide economic fluctuations, and (3) to remove unfair competition in commerce through the establishment of legal minimum or prevailing wage rates.

Nullification of the National Industrial Recovery Act and the first Bituminous Coal (Guffey) Act seemed to deprive the Federal Government of any implied authority to control economic fluctuations by direct manipulation of wage levels. Nevertheless, congressional and judicial recognition of the other objective has given the Federal Government considerable power to stabilize money wages, both indirectly through the establishment of a national minimum, and directly in the case of wages in the construction industry on public works contracts.

Mandatory Standards of Employment

FEDERAL PUBLIC WORKS CONSTRUCTION

The Bacon-Davis Act of 1931 (46 Stat. 1494) requires that advertised specifications for every contract for the construction, alteration, or repair of Federal buildings and public works in excess of $2,000 shall contain a provision stating the minimum wages to be paid the various classes of mechanics and laborers employed on the project. These minimum wage scales must be based upon the wages determined by the Secretary of Labor to be prevailing for corresponding classes of laborers and mechanics employed on similar projects in the city, town, village, or other civil subdivision of the State, Territory, or District of Columbia. The Secretary is required to perform a similar function for construction financed under the National Housing Act (53 Stat. 807), the Tennessee Valley Authority Act (48 Stat. 59), and the Federal Airport Act (Public Law 377, c. 251, 79th Cong., 2d sess.).

Prevailing wage determinations thus vary by locality, and they include rates for all classes of skilled workers above the minimum. The agency contracting officer requests the Secretary to make such determinations in advance of the advertising of bids, and since the statute does not provide for review of his predeterminations they are apparently final. The Solicitor of Labor makes the necessary investigations, either into the records of the Department or other Federal agencies, or if the Solicitor considers such information insufficient to make a determination he may appoint a referee to conduct a field investigation in the locality of the project. The Secretary of Labor has delegated his functions of making the formal determinations to an assistant secretary. In 1947 determinations were made in over 9,000 cases, more than 3,600 above the number in 1946.

Enforcement of contracts based upon the wage determinations of the Secretary of Labor is a responsibility of the contracting agency, which may withhold so much of the accrued payments from the contractor as it deems necessary to reimburse employees for the difference between the contract wages and the received wages. This policy follows the pattern established in the 8-hour laws on Federal public works (37 Stat. 726) and the Copeland Act of 1934 (48 Stat. 948), which made the "kick-back" of wages by employees on Federal public works under force, intimidation, or threat of dismissal subject to $5,000 fine or 5 years' imprisonment. The latter law gave the Secretaries of Interior and Treasury, jointly, authority to make reasonable regulations for contractors on such work. Reorganization Plan No. 4 of 1940 transferred this power to the Secretary of Labor, who has in turn delegated his functions of interpretation and rulemaking under these laws to the Solicitor.

FEDERAL SUPPLY CONTRACTS

The Walsh-Healey Public Contracts Act of 1936 (49 Stat. 2036) requires that all Federal contracts for the manufacture or furnishing of materials, supplies, articles, and equipment in any amount exceeding $10,000 shall include stipulations providing that all persons employed under the contract shall receive no less than the minimum wages determined by the Secretary of Labor to be the prevailing minimum wages for similar work or in similar industries in the locality where the work is to be performed. No person shall be employed for more than 8 hours in any one day or 40 hours in any one week, except as the Secretary of Labor may by rule and regulation permit at the rate of one and one-half times the basic hourly rate of the affected employee. No male person under 16, female person under 18, or convict labor shall be employed. No part of the work under such contracts will be performed under conditions which are unsanitary or hazardous or dangerous to the health and safety of employees (compliance with the safety, sanitary, and factory inspection laws of the State in which the work is performed is made prima facie evidence of compliance with this provision).

Findings of violations are the responsibility of the Secretary of Labor. Violators are subject to cancellation of the contract by the contracting agency; they are liable for liquidated damages of $10 per day for each minor or convict laborer knowingly employed in performance of the contract; they are ineligible for other contracts for 3 years from the date of the determination of violation, and they are liable for any underpayment of wages through withholding of amounts due or through suits by the Attorney General. Minimum wages set under this law may and do vary by locality and industry. They may be above the minimum established by other State or Federal law, and are arrived at as the predominating rate in the area for common or unskilled labor. Public contracts determinations thus do not establish rates for grades of work above the minimum. The actual wage is not included in the contract under the Walsh-Healey Act; the law does not take effect until the administration establishes the minimum prevailing wage, either on his own initiative or upon information from a Government contracting agency. The definitions of "industry" and "locality" covered by wage determinations are both narrow and broad, and they do not follow a discernible pattern.

The Secretary of Labor has delegated general responsibility to the Administrator of the Wage and Hour Division; with respect to minimum wage determinations, exceptions, and modifications of contract terms, inspection of establishments for violation, and disbursements of recovered amounts to employees, the administrator alone makes recommendations to the secretary. In connection with formal legal actions and enforcement proceedings, however, the secretary has divided responsibility between the administrator and the Solicitor of Labor. The result is that these functions have come to be performed by members of the solicitor's staff. Regional attorneys under the solicitor initiate formal actions and perform the trial work. Trial examiners conduct the hearings and make the initial decision on the evidence. A bureau service section reviews the record and prepares the draft of the administrator's decisions. An interpretations section issues interpretive rulings. The Solicitor maintains an internal separation between the trial examiners and the staff attorneys, and has revised all procedures to conform with the Administrative Procedures Act of 1946.

EMPLOYEES ENGAGED IN COMMERCE OR IN THE PRODUCTION OF GOODS FOR COMMERCE

Since October 24, 1945, the Fair Labor Standards Act (52 Stat. 1060) has required all employers to pay each employee who is engaged in commerce or in the production of goods for commerce (except on 11 exempted classes of work) wages at not less than 40 cents an hour, except as an industry committee appointed by the administrator may recommend and he may find that a wage between 30 and 40 cents an hour may be necessary in order to prevent substantial curtailment of employment in the industry. Learners, apprentices, and handicapped workers may be employed at less than the minimum pursuant to regulations issued by the administrator.

Since October 24, 1940, all but exempted employers have been required to pay any employee thus engaged for a workweek in excess of 40 hours at a rate not less than one and one-half times the regular rate at which he is employed (exceptions are made in cases of annual wage guarantees or hours restrictions on a semiannual basis made pursuant to collective bargaining agreements with labor organizations certified by the National Labor Relations Board as bona fide, and in industries found by the administrator to be seasonal where the overtime payment provisions do not apply for a period not to exceed 14 weeks in the aggregate in any calendar year until the limits of 12 hours per day and 56 per workweek are reached. The same law prevents the shipment in commerce of goods produced in any establishment in which oppressive child labor has been employed. Oppressive child labor is defined as the employment of minors under 16 in manufacturing or mining industries, or of minors 16 or 17 years of age in occupations declared by the Secretary (formerly chief of the Children's Bureau) of Labor to be particularly hazardous or detrimental to their health and well-being.

The Secretary is permitted to make exemptions by certificates issued under appropriate regulations, and he is directed to provide by order or regulation that employment of minors aged 14 and 15 shall not be deemed to constitute oppressive child labor if and to the extent that the Secretary determines that such employment is confined to periods that will not interfere with their schooling and to conditions that will not interfere with their health and well-being. (The coverage of the child labor provisions of the law does not extend to establishments or

450

employers engaged in commerce.)   Violations of the law are subject to a $10,000 fine, 6 months' imprisonment (after second offense), and to employee liability suits for double the amount of unpaid wages or overtime compensation.

Although it is estimated that the Fair Labor Standards Act covers some 550,000 establishments and over 20,500,000 employees, it is estimated that in 1946 less than 1 percent of workers in manufacturing industries received less than 50 cents an hour. (By 1948 this had fallen to less than 0.1 of 1 percent, and less than 5 percent receive less than 65 cents an hour.) Nevertheless, over 3,600, or 9 percent of the 40,350 establishments inspected by the Wage and Hour Division in fiscal year 1947 were found in violation of the minimum-wage provisions. A much higher percentage, 47, were overtime violations, and 5 percent were violations of the child-labor provisions. Violations unadjusted by voluntary compliance are taken into Federal district court by regional attorneys on the Solicitor's staff, acting under the general direction of the Attorney General. Of the 450 actions brought during 1947 about 180 were criminal and 270 were civil. Of some $18,500,000 back wages reported due in 1947 almost $9,000,000 was ordered paid or agreed to by employers.

The principal interagency relationships of the Wage and Hour Division are with (1) the Apprentice Training Service, in formulating regulations for exemptions of learners and apprentices, (2) the Employment Service and Office of Vocational Rehabilitation on similar regulations, for handicapped workers, (3) the Women's and Children's Bureau in securing information upon working conditions of working women and child labor, (4) State labor departments and industrial commissions in working out cooperative arrangements for performing inspection services and issuing certificates for employment of minors under suitable protective regulations. Cooperative arrangements with States for making plant inspections have not proved successful, and have been terminated in all but two States.

The other Federal agency having mandatory authority over minimum wages in private employment is the Maritime Commission, which under title III of the Merchant Marine Act (49 Stat. 1985) is empowered to investigate working conditions on ocean-going vessels and to prescribe minimum wages, manning requirements and reasonable standards for working conditions of seamen. These standards are included in contracts whereby private owners and operators of shipping vessels receive "operating-differential" subsidy payments from the Government. The contracts fell into disuse when the Government requisitioned and operated the ships during the war, but have come into operation again with the return of shipping vessels to private operation. Working standards for seamen have become a matter of international negotiation carried on by the Labor Department through the International Labor Office, and are closely related to the wage determination work of the Labor Department on public contracts and minimum wages in commerce generally.

The question of whether to continue the segregation of responsibility for establishing minimum wages and working conditions for seamen in the foreign shipping industry depends upon (1) the degree to which the Maritime Commission exercises operating managerial responsibilities over the industry, (2) the extent to which minimum wages and working conditions in shipping are sufficiently different from the national minimum established in the Fair Labor Standards Act to justify differential treatment and determination. Restoration of ownership and operation to private hands would make it desirable to insure that wage standards at least, if not overtime, are not lower than the national minimum, which is the responsibility of the Wage and Hour Division.

Promotion of Improved Standards of Employment

COOPERATIVE RELATIONS WITH STATE AGENCIES

Under the authority of the organic law of the Department "to foster, promote, and develop the welfare of the wage earners of the United States (and) to improve their working conditions" the Secretary of Labor in 1934 established by administrative order a Division (now Bureau) of Labor Standards. Authority for the Bureau rests upon the annual appropriation act, the language of which for 1949 read: "For expenses necessary for the promotion of industrial safety, employment stabilization, and amicable industrial relations for labor and industry . . . including expenses for attendance of cooperating officials and consultants at conferences concerned with the work of the Bureau when called by the Bureau with the written approval of the Secretary . . ." The Bureau acts as the principal arm of the Department for developing cooperative relationships with the State departments of labor and industry. It arranges working agreements for joint activities in the fields of wage and hour, industrial safety, and homework inspections; promotes acceptance of the standards adopted by the International Labor Organization; prepares analyses and formulates standards of State labor legislation and administrative practice; promotes industrial safety programs by providing technical assistance to employers and State agencies in applying such standards.

The powers of the Bureau are voluntary,[1] and its methods of opera-

---

[1] The Bureau exercises the functions of the Secretary of Labor under secs. 9 (f) and (g) of the Labor-Management Relations Act (Public Law 101, 80th Cong.), requiring labor organizations seeking certification as collective-bargaining representatives to file certain information with respect to their organization and finances in such form as the Secretary may prescribe.

tion consist in research, acting as an educational agency and a clearinghouse for the dissemination of information, and in the conduct of an annual conference of State labor commissioners. It thus acts as a service agency, providing upon request information and technical assistance to State labor, employer, and civic groups interested in standards of good practice in improving conditions and relationships of employment.

Education in Industrial Relations

A major interest of the Bureau is the provision of materials and reports upon standards of employer-employee relations. It has developed manuals of good practice in grievance procedure for union stewards and personnel managers; working materials for university and union classes in collective bargaining and arbitration procedures; and methods of wage payment in industry, and administration of workmen's and unemployment compensation laws. Through the cooperative relationships established with States and universities, the Bureau has sought to expand these clearinghouse and research functions into a broad program of education in industrial relations by means of a grant-in-aid program operating through a State extension service.

Industrial Safety and Health [2]

Perhaps the oldest activity of labor departments in American States and in foreign countries is the administration of laws requiring employers to provide safe and sanitary conditions of employment. This responsibility as defined in legislation varies widely, but the activities involved include accident and disease prevention, hours and shifts of work, work clothing, sanitary facilities, methods of reducing fatigue, lighting and ventilation equipment, plant inspection, and standards of workmen's compensation. Accident and disease prevention in places of employment are closely related, and most factory legislation has given to the State labor department the authority to make rules and regulations and the right of entry to inspect plants to determine compliance with legal requirements of safe and healthful conditions of employment. A major portion of the research, standards, and technical services of the Bureau of Labor Standards has been devoted to the promotion of industrial safety and health in the States.

Title VI of the Social Security Act (now title III, part B of the Public Health Service Act of 1944) injected an element of conflict

---

[2] The responsibilities of the Interstate Commerce Commission and the Civil Aeronautics Board for safety promotion in the railroad and air transport industries are clearly established as desirable subjects for direct Federal supervision and specialization by the agencies dealing with the industry as a whole.

and friction at the State level between the labor and health departments. This title permitted the United States Public Health Service to make grants to the State health departments (amounting to approximately $1,000,000 a year) for industrial hygiene services without the necessity for the States to match Federal funds. Under these circumstances State legislatures have discontinued making substantial appropriations to labor departments for enforcement of factory inspection laws. Since the health department in most cases provides only those health services that are of a research, demonstration, and promotional character, the result has been not only to reduce the quality of enforcement work but to establish two overlapping departments at the State level dealing with management on plant working conditions.

Since 95 out of 100 work injuries are related to plant engineering and chemical conditions rather than medical factors, the Federal Public Health Service has encouraged the States to broaden their health activities to include accident prevention, safety organization, hours and other conditions of employment, without assuming responsibility for the unpopular task of enforcement. Efforts of the Bureau of Labor Standards to draw attention to these events, and to secure authorization for Federal grants for improving enforcement of occupational accident and disease prevention programs in the States, has resulted in the removal from the Bureau's appropriation language the words "and health" from its former authorization to promote "industrial safety and health."

A conceivable solution would be for Congress to transfer complete responsibility for accidents as well as disease prevention in industrial employment to the Public Health Service, and thereby suggest to the States that they transfer the entire function of accident and disease prevention to their health departments. Presumably, however, this would involve coercion in an internal matter of State administrative organization, and would run counter to the whole tendency in the advanced industrial States to centralize responsibility for inspection and law enforcement in the labor department. The alternative solution, which has seemed reasonable to the State of California (by informal agreement between the directors of industrial relations and public health), the Bureau of the Budget, to the Public Health Service (at one time) and to the Bureau of Labor Standards, would be to establish a functional division of labor.

Such a division of functions would make the labor department responsible for the formulation of rules and regulations concerning the safety and health of employees in consultation with the health department, and for inspection of plants for violation of industrial safety and sanitary laws, while the health department would be responsible for research and laboratory tests in industrial hygiene,

454

specific plant surveys and formulation of plant health programs, educational activities in industrial hygiene, and for providing technical services upon request of the labor department.

This arrangement would be enforced by a restriction upon the use of Public Health Service grants for law-enforcement activities in connection with accident prevention, and by provision of funds for grants to State labor departments for recruitment and training of personnel in industrial accident and disease prevention, and for the improved administration of State laws regulating conditions of employment. This plan does not impose an impracticable distinction between working conditions having to do with employee safety and health; it confines the two agencies to the activities they both properly, and formally, seek to perform; it clarifies the responsibility and provides for consultation and mutual cooperation in the processes of enforcement.

The Coal Mines Inspection Act of 1941 (55 Stat. 177) provided for direct Federal inspection of coal mines by the Bureau of Mines (Interior Department), with the power to notify employers, employees, and State officials of the existence of safety or health hazards. This law was passed at the urging of the United Mine Workers, who insisted that most of the 30 States with mine-inspection commissions or bureaus had failed in the enforcement of mine safety laws, largely because of the ability of mine operators to persuade State inspection officials to adopt extremely lax standards in inspection and application of penalties.

The Federal law, under which approximately $4,000,000 is appropriated annually, insures no greater application of penalties but is intended to provide assurance at least that the operators will be put on advance notice that specific hazards to safety and health should be removed. The administrative effects of this law have varied. In States where there is a strong, nonpolitical, mine safety division the Federal activity only duplicate its work; in other States, Federal inspection removes the incentive to eliminate political appointments and to raise standards of inspection and enforcement. Although there is little basis for questioning the validity of the congressional decision that mine workers' safety and health required Federal assumption of responsibility for inspection, as long as the enforcement responsibility remains with the States it would seem desirable to strengthen State administrations rather than provide a supplement or substitute for it.

On the State level, there is a clear parallel here with the problem of the Bureau of Labor Standards in improving administration of State safety and health laws in industries other than mining, although there has never been any suggestion that the Bureau undertake inspection functions directly. From the standpoint of conformity with the established pattern in Federal-State relations, strengthening of State administration would call for Federal matching grants-in-aid, subject to Federal supervision of standards providing that State personnel be appointed and removable only on a strict merit basis.

If such a grant-in-aid program were adopted, the Bureau of Mines inspection functions should be merged with it, placed on the same basis, and the entire program administered by the Department of Labor. As long as the Department of Labor has no fiscal or administrative responsibilities other than those of a research and educational character, the Federal Government's direct relations with the mining industry may just as well be centralized in the Department of Interior (along with other energy resources) and Bureau of Mines.

CHILD LABOR AND YOUTH EMPLOYMENT

The act of 1912 (37 Stat. 79) creating the Children's Bureau made that agency responsible for investigating, reporting, and coordinating activities of the Federal Government with respect to problems of children and child life. The Fair Labor Standards Act of 1938 made the Chief of the Children's Bureau responsible for promulgating rules and regulations with respect to the exemption provisions of the law permitting children less than 16 to work in occupations other than manufacturing and mining, and those of 16 and 17 in nonhazardous occupations, and for making administrative determinations of violations that should be prosecuted in the courts. Down to 1946 these activities (except factory-inspection work which was given to the Wage and Hour Administration) were performed in the Industrial Division of the Children's Bureau. The President's Reorganization Plan No. 2 of that year transferred the Bureau to the Federal Security Agency, leaving the research, rule-making, and enforcement functions of the Industrial Division in the Department of Labor.

The Secretary of Labor separated the research and standards-setting functions from the formal rule-making and enforcement responsibilities, delegating the former to the Bureau of Labor Standards and the latter to the Wage and Hour Division. The Department of Labor Appropriation Act of 1948 eliminated funds for research and promotional work from appropriation item for the Bureau of Labor Standards, necessitating transfer of all child-labor and youth-employment responsibilities to the Wage and Hour Division.

The accompanying over-all reduction in appropriations necessitated further elimination of personnel, so that from the subsequent reorganization there emerged a Child Labor Division under the Wage and Hour Administrator with fact-finding functions limited to supervision of the enforcement of the child-labor provisions of the Fair Labor Standards Act. The net effect of these events has been to eliminate the basic research and standards-setting work formerly done by the Children's Bureau in the field of youth employment.

456

The present administrative situation places responsibility for fact finding, formulation of standards and programs in the field of youth employment, and enforcement of the Federal child-labor law in the Secretary of Labor. Under financial pressure, the Secretary has consolidated all three functions in the Wage and Hour Administration as a part of the enforcement program. An enforcement program in general does not provide a proper atmosphere or environment for the conduct of basic research.

There are two places where such research and formulation of standards might be done: (1) The Children's Bureau in the Federal Security Agency, (2) the Bureau of Labor Standards. The latter agency is engaged primarily in working with State labor departments on all types of problems in labor-law administration, and its research work in child labor consists in collaborative projects to determine the most satisfactory forms and methods of State administration. The Children's Bureau is more accustomed to the operations of design, collection, and analysis involved in basic research projects, but its approach is the much broader one of studying the child's economic relations along with other aspects of his environment, biological, psychological, and cultural. Should research be carried on in this framework, or should special emphasis be given to the problems of youth employment in the context of the employment situation in the Nation or the community, and of employer-employee relations? If it be granted that problems of study be from the standpoint of employment relations rather than the individual child, this program should remain in the Department of Labor.

WOMEN IN INDUSTRY

The Women's Bureau was established by law in the Department of Labor in 1920 (41 Stat. 987) with authority to investigate and report to the Secretary of Labor upon all matters pertaining to the welfare of women in industry and to publish the results of such investigations in such manner as the Secretary of Labor may prescribe. The Bureau's studies and publications include occupational opportunities for women, wages and hours in various industries, occupations, and localities, and standards of legislation and administrative practice for the improvement of their economic, civil, and political status. The Bureau has no enforcement or financial authority. Organized on a clientele, or population group, basis it overlaps in function the Bureau of Labor Statistics, Labor Standards, Employment Service, and Wage and Hour Division, to perhaps the greatest extent in the case of Labor Standards, of which it is a logical subdivision. These potential overlappings have for the most part been avoided by intradepartmental coordination.

457

Recognition of the bureau as a major operating division in the Department reflects efforts of certain women's organizations to focus attention on the problems of securing legislation to eliminate discrimination against working women in wages and employment opportunities, rather than by the more remote, symbolic method of constitutional amendment. Given this orientation, the location of the Department of Labor has never been brought into question.

INTERNATIONAL LABOR AFFAIRS

The Secretary of Labor was instrumental in securing American membership in the International Labor Organization, and down to the formation of the United Nations Economic and Social Council was the principal American delegate to international conference on labor problems. He still makes the nominations of American employer, employee, and government delegates to the ILO; he nominates advisers to the Council and to its subordinate commissions on social matters, human rights, the status of women, and the Economic and Employment Commission. The secretary has established a Trade Union Advisory Committee on International Affairs, composed of top officials of the AFL, CIO, Railway Labor Executives Association, and independent organizations, through which he is able to communicate the views of American labor on foreign affairs to the State and Defense Departments.

The Department of Labor is represented on the State Department's Executive Committee on Economic Foreign Policy. Under the Foreign Service Act of 1946 the Department is represented on the Foreign Service Board of the State Department, through which it assists in the examination, appointment and training Reserve officer labor attachés to American embassies abroad.

The Labor Department is also represented on the State Department's Committee on Occupied Areas Affairs, where it has helped to develop labor programs for occupied areas and to advise the Civil Affairs Division of the War Department on labor problems arising in administration. The Bureau of Labor Statistics is responsible for the analysis and dissemination of materials on foreign labor conditions and labor relations, the Bureau of Labor Standards and the Women's Bureau provide training facilities and materials to exchange representatives from foreign governments (principally Latin America and the Philippines) interested in American labor policy and administration.

Coordination of these activities has been vested in an Assistant Secretary of Labor, who speaks for the Department on all international matters and directs and supervises the international work of all bureaus, including formulation of policy, representation on interdepartmental committees, and clearance of all policy communications.

458

Liaison with the State Department has been established at the secretarial level, the secretariat of interdepartmental committees, and the Division of International Labor, Health and Social Affairs, to the end that the Department's participation in policy matters affecting labor and employment, and provision of technical services, is facilitated to the maximum extent.

The Department's assumption of responsibility for providing technical services of research, training and advice on labor questions, establishing liaison with the labor movement on foreign labor conditions and policies, and for participation on committees on matters involving foreign policy, appears to be the appropriate administrative relationship between a subject-matter department and the department responsible for the conduct and coordination of foreign affairs.

Summary

1. Regulation of employment standards is an established function of the Federal Government, partly as a means of preserving prevailing wage rates in the construction industry on Federal public works contracts, and partly to promote economic stability by establishing a national wage floor for economic competition. These functions are centralized in the Labor Department, with the exception of the enforcement responsibilities in connection with contract violations, and the Maritime Commission's function of setting minimum wages in operating-differential subsidy contracts with private American companies engaged in foreign shipping. These are appropriate functions of the Labor Department, to which they should be transferred in connection with clarifying amendments to the coverage and exemptive provisions of the Fair Labor Standards Act.

2. Federal regulation and promotion of employee safety and health has followed four varying patterns. The Interstate Commerce Commission and the Civil Aeronautics Board directly supervise and enforce safety and health standards in the railroad and air transport industries without regard to the States. The Bureau of Mines inspects all properties in the mining industries, with power to notify and publish all cases of safety and health hazards. The Public Health Service makes unmatched grants to the States to establish industrial hygiene services in State health departments, and the Bureau of Labor Standards in the Labor Department formulates advisory standards and furnishes technical assistance to State labor departments in the administration of State safety and health laws.

a. The nature of the responsibilities of the ICC and the CAB over their respective industries makes it desirable for them to retain jurisdiction over employee, as well as traveler, safety and health.

b. In the absence of a general program of Federal regulation of employee safety and health, the jurisdiction of the Interior Department and the Bureau of Mines over the mining industry in matters of research, technology, production, and marketing properly includes inspection of working conditions. Enforcement responsibilities remain in the hands of the States, where in all but a few cases administration of safety and health laws has been weak, there would be no point in transferring the Federal mine inspection function to the Department of Labor. Transfer would be meaningful only as a part of a broad Federal program for improving State safety and health laws, with supervision and maintenance of strong standards of merit in appointment, promotion, and tenure. In this case the Bureau of Mines inspection duties could be turned back to the States, and its supervisory work transferred to the Labor Department.

c. Industrial hygiene is inseparably associated with accident prevention and enforcement programs of the Federal and State labor departments, and its promotion is more a problem of plant engineering and sanitary working conditions established by labor laws and industrial relations policies than by techniques of general public health, such as venereal disease and tuberculosis. The State labor departments should be enabled to develop their enforcement functions of employee safety and health, and the State health departments encouraged to confine their responsibilities for industrial hygiene to the areas of research, demonstration, and health education.

Part Five

RELIEF AND SOCIAL SECURITY

INTRODUCTION

Prior to 1929 the National Government played a very small part in relief and it had adopted no Nation-wide formal systems for assuring reasonable social security to individuals either directly or through Federal grants-in-aid to the States. The major developments in national activities have taken place within the past 18 years.

In the United States, as in foreign countries, the national activities were developed piecemeal by categories or programs with very little consideration of interrelationships and the problem as a whole. The National Government in the thirties was under heavy pressure because of the depression and the resulting demand for immediate action. With thousands of people in need, time did not permit of the analysis and mature deliberation that is essential to see the problem as a whole and to develop an integrated program that is well adapted to the American form of government and the American economic and social system.

The American Federal system of government was moreover a complicating factor, especially in the early days of the period. According to the constitutional law as it had been previously interpreted by the courts, the National Government had no direct authority in the fields of relief and social security. National legislation had therefore to be framed with careful consideration of the probable attitude of the Federal courts, especially of the Supreme Court. As that court reinterpreted the Constitution, especially with respect to the clauses relating to interstate commerce and the general welfare, the National Government gained greater authority and freedom. As a result the various laws establishing programs were not drafted upon a reasonably uniform concept of the division of powers between the Federal Government and the States.

State governments and their subordinate county and municipal governments in the depression were moreover often in great financial difficulties whereas the National Government with its almost unlimited borrowing power could proceed for years, as it did, on a basis of deficit financing. The situation was one highly conducive to opportunism at all levels of government and to experimentation, often without much consideration of the relationships between the experiments.

The Commission on Organization of the Executive Branch of the Government was created to review and appraise. Its mandate requires not only elimination of overstaffing and duplication among Federal agencies but also curtailing and limiting the functions, activities, and services of the National Government. A major way of curtailing and limiting the functions and activities of the National Government obviously lies in reconsideration of Federal-State relationships and in studying the interrelationships and coverage of legislation adopted piecemeal with respect to special categories.

In the field of relief and social security the problems of organizational structure within the Federal Government itself is a matter of relatively minor significance. The real issues relate to the programs themselves and, in the case of relief, not only to the programs but also to the relationships between the Federal Government and the States. As a matter of fact few definitive recommendations regarding changes in structural organization can be made until issues of broad policy are settled. This necessity for decisions with respect to policies is widely recognized.

This report on relief and social security is therefore largely concerned with these broad issues of policy. No attempt has been made to go into detailed facts with respect to the several programs. Such an effort would have resulted in an impossibly voluminous manuscript. Perhaps more important reasonably complete descriptions of the various programs can generally be supplied by the several agencies involved. The major issues, it is believed, can be broadly defined without the myriad of minute detail that is necessary in drafting laws and administrative rules and regulations.

The report will be primarily concerned with old-age and survivors insurance and with the three public-assistance categories of the Social Security Act. The opinion is very widely held, however, that if old-age and survivors insurance is retained without substantial change in basic concepts, its coverage should be made almost universal. If it should be so extended, it will present the difficult problem of how other systems are to be adjusted to it or whether they can be continued in anything like their present form. Among these systems are the Railroad Retirement System, the private systems that are being created through collective bargaining, the various systems for employees of the National Government or agencies under its general direction, including the District of Columbia, and the systems of State and local governments. The relationship between veterans' benefits and old-age and survivors insurance likewise present great difficulties.

The report deals briefly with these other systems in the effort to bring out the nature of the major issues in relation to old-age and survivors insurance. No attempt has been made to describe the veterans' benefits or the various retirement systems, public or private, in detail. Such an undertaking would have consumed far more time than was available for the study and it would have been difficult for the Commission to have passed upon the minutae.

This chapter of the report does not deal with unemployment compensation.

464

Chapter I

OLD-AGE AND SURVIVORS INSURANCE

With these words from the concluding sentence of the Eighth Annual Report of the Board of Trustees of the Federal Old-Age and Survivors Insurance Trust Fund [1] practically all students of the subject will be in agreement:

. . . there is need for a review of the old-age and survivors insurance program, covering not only the benefit formula, the coverage of the system, and the scope of protection afforded, but also contributions and financial policy. . . .[2]

The need for a thoroughgoing, comprehensive review is indeed so great that it seems as if no sound conclusions as to organization and procedures can be reached until the substantive issues of policy have been reconsidered and redefined by the Congress. The present section will therefore be primarily concerned with the origin and nature of the major issues.

The Origins of the System

The present old age and survivors insurance system had its beginnings in "title II—Federal Old-Age Benefits" of the Social Security Act, approved August 14, 1935.[3] The amendments to title II, adopted in 1939, virtually revolutionized the original plan and introduced many of the current issues with respect to coverage, insured status, benefits, and finance.

The original act bore many resemblances to a modern retirement system operated by an employer, public or private, as part of the personnel system. The money to pay for the benefits was to come from contributions from the employer and the employee, although for constitutional reasons contributions were taxes paid into the general treasury and Congress was authorized to appropriate into the "Old-Age Reserve Account" the sums necessary on an actuarial reserve basis to finance the system. President Roosevelt in recommending legislation had said:

---

[1] The trustees who transmitted the report were John W. Snyder, Secretary of the Treasury, L. B. Schwellenbach, Secretary of Labor, and Oscar R. Ewing, Federal Security Administrator. The trustees are required to make an annual report to Congress under section 201 (b) of the Social Security Act as amended.

[2] Federal Old-Age and Survivors Insurance Trust Fund, 80th Cong., 2d sess., S. Doc. No. 160, May 25, 1948, p. 32.

[3] 49 Stat. 620-48.

In the first place the system adopted, except for the money necessary to initiate it, should be self sustaining in the sense that funds for the insurance benefits should not come from the proceeds of general taxation.[4]

The original system, adopted in accordance with recommendations of the Executive, had the following characteristics that are germane to the consideration of present problems.

1. The money necessary to pay the benefits was to come from special pay-roll taxes levied against covered employers and employees. No large contributions from general revenues toward benefit costs were provided.

2. The pay-roll taxes, starting at 1 percent each on covered employers and employees, were to be advanced, according to schedules set forth in the act, until on December 31, 1948, they were to be 3 percent each on covered employees and employers.[5] The resulting 6 percent taxes on covered wages was estimated to be approximately a level premium which, on an actuarial basis, would accumulate an "Old Age Reserve Account,"[6] adequate with the interest it earned to pay all benefit costs.

3. The benefits to be paid covered workers who retired in the initial years of the system were to be very small. Benefits under the original act were based on total covered wages earned under the system.[7] Hence they would be very small at the outset but would advance progressively on the average as the system matured and the totals of covered wages paid to workers increased with the number of years they had served under the system. Aggregate annual benefit payments under the system would not reach their approximate maximum for somewhere in the neighborhood of 80 years.

4. The system was relatively free from forfeitures. If the employee died before attaining the age of 65, his estate was to receive 3½ percent of his total covered wages. If he had been covered under the system but had not attained an insured status, he was entitled on attaining age 65 to a lump-sum payment of 3½ percent of total covered wages.

5. The system was concerned primarily with provision of benefits for the aged retired covered worker himself. Only incidental provision for widows, children, parents, and others was made through death benefits payable to the estate. Covered men and women, regardless of marital condition and status as to dependents, paid the same premiums and were entitled to the same benefits.

With provisions such as these the covered workers were not to any appreciable extent made a specially privileged class, in that (a) they

---

[4] Economic Security Act, Hearings before the House Committee on Ways and Means, 74th Cong., 1st sess., p. 14.
[5] 49 Stat. 636–37.
[6] 49 Stat. 622.
[7] For the benefit formula see 49 Stat. 623.

were not to receive benefits which would ultimately be paid for in part by the proceeds of general taxation, and (*b*) there were no large windfall benefits for those who retired in the early years of the system, as benefits were directly related to total covered wages received during service under the system.

It was true that passage of the law forced all covered employers to contribute to this general retirement system. Some of them already were contributing to retirement systems. More important the exclusion from the system of large groups already provided for under other systems involved no serious discrimination as general tax revenues were not being used. The distinct system for railway employees, the numerous systems for public employees of State and municipal governments and for employees of private educational institutions were not affected. The National Government was of course using tax revenues for its retirement systems for its own employees, but it was in this case the employer.

Principles in the 1939 Amendments

The concepts of the original 1935 act did not long survive. Entirely different fundamental concepts were substituted. Among the most important were:

1. The principle of a true actuarial reserve system was abandoned and a non-actuarial Federal old-age and survivors insurance trust fund was substituted. How large that fund shall be is a matter of legislative and administrative determination and it is not based on the amount of benefits ultimately to be paid from it.

2. The Congress adopted legislation that prevented the gradual increase of the pay-roll taxes to the level premium deemed necessary to make the system self-supporting. On December 31, 1948, it will be recalled, the pay-roll tax was to have been 6 percent, or 3 percent on the employee and 3 percent on the employer. It has remained at 2 percent, one on each of the two parties. Thus had 6 percent been the true required level premium, only one-third of it was actually being paid and an actuarial deficit was accumulating at the rate of 4 percent of pay roll each year, plus interest.[8]

3. Abandonment of the actuarial reserve, failure to increase the taxes to an actuarial level premium, and the development of a huge actuarial deficit mean

[8] The benefit formula of the 1939 act paid benefits of 40 percent of the first $50 of average monthly wages and of 10 percent with respect to the remaining $200 of covered wages, with certain minimum provisions applicable to those with average monthly wages of less than $50. Taxes were uniform on all wages up to $250 a month. Under such a system a general increase in wages operates to reduce the actuarial level premium which would be necessary to support it. The benefits on the first $50 or less are the high-cost benefits per dollar of tax receipts, with respect to them, whereas the benefits on $200 are the low-cost ones per dollar of such tax receipts. Thus as the number of workers at $50 per month or under decreases and the number at $50 or over increases, the cost of benefits diminishes per dollar of tax receipts. As a result of increases in wages the actuarial level premium which would support the present Old Age and Survivors Insurance has fallen. According to the Advisory Council on Social Security it is at present 3.26 according to the low estimates and 5.66 according to the high. For discussion of the low-cost and high-cost estimates see "Costs of Present Program Revised and Expanded," in this chapter.

that ultimately the Government will have to make huge contributions from general revenues to pay the promised benefits. This fact was clearly recognized in 1943 when a provision was included in the Revenue Act of 1943: "There is also authorized to be appropriated to the trust fund such additional sums as may be required to finance the benefits and payments required under this title." [9] For several years, however, no appropriations will be required because benefits can be paid from that excess of receipts over benefit payments which is characteristic of any old age retirement system that starts with all paying in and none or relatively few actually drawing benefits.

4. The benefit formula was so changed that relatively large benefits were payable to persons who attained an insured status and retired or died in the early years of the system. Benefits were no longer based on total covered wages received in the whole time under the system but on average monthly wages. Thus employees who had paid or occasioned the payment of only a few hundred dollars would receive benefits which would cost several thousand dollars.

5. The original system had made no provision for wives, widows, dependent children, and parents except indirectly through the death benefit of 3½ percent of total covered wages. The new system introduced benefits for wives 65 years of age or over, widows 65 years of age or over, widows under 65 who were responsible for dependent children, dependent children, and, under certain circumstances, dependent parents. Lump-sum death benefits became payable in small amounts only if at the time of death no beneficiary was immediately eligible for a benefit under any of the other categories. Benefits for wives 65 years of age or over, dependent children of retired workers, and for survivors obviously were more expensive than a death benefit which amounted to not much more than a return of contributions.

6. Costs of the system were, however, reduced by the introduction of new and fairly intricate provisions with respect to an insured status. Under this plan workers under the system could be divided into four classes:

a. Persons could be covered but not in any way insured. If they died, or for any other reason withdrew from covered employment, the contributions which they had made to the system were forfeited. The cause of withdrawal was immaterial. No benefit was paid even if the worker died leaving dependents or if he was totally and permanently disabled.

b. Currently insured was the first protection actually attained. It gave protection to such eligible dependents as the worker might have if the worker died in covered employment or very shortly after withdrawing from it.

c. Temporarily fully insured constituted the second stage in actual protection. If the worker withdrew from covered employment temporarily fully insured his eligible dependents, if any, were protected until such time as his status as temporarily fully insured expired. He had no protection for his own old age unless he returned to covered employment.

d. Permanently fully insured represented the real protection. If the employee withdrew from covered employment with that status he had the full protection that the system provided, an old-age benefit for himself on retiring at age 65 or over, for his wife, if he had one, if she was 65 or over or when she attained that age, and for such dependent children as he might have. If he died, either before or after retirement, eligible dependents would receive benefits by virtue of his permanently fully insured status. For young workers entering covered employment after the system was established this status could be obtained by 10 years of continuous service. For them the requirement was 40 quarters of covered employment.

[9] 58 Stat. 93.

Forfeitures are fairly numerous under this system. They occur:

1. If an employee dies or for any cause withdraws without having attained an insured status. Neither he nor his dependents get anything.

2. If an employee with an insured status dies leaving no eligible dependent or no dependent who lives to become eligible, his estate forfeits all his contributions excepting the amount that is paid as a lump-sum death benefit, practically funeral expenses. Dependents and eligible dependents, it should be noted, are not synonymous. A widow under 65 years of age is not eligible unless she has the care of an eligible child of the deceased, regardless of her physical and mental condition or her employability. She does not attain eligibility until she reaches the age of 65. A child over 18 years of age is not eligible even if an invalid. Dependent married children under 18, brothers or sisters, nephews or nieces, or grandchildren are not eligible.

Forfeitures are more probable among women than among men. The childless single woman has no eligible dependents except possibly one or more parents "chiefly dependent upon and supported by such individual at the time of such individual's death."[10] The child of an insured married woman is eligible to take from her "only if at the time of her death (or retirement on age benefit) no parent other than such individual was contributing to such child and such child was not living with its father or adopting father."[11] The covered and insured married woman is entitled to a primary benefit on retirement, but if she is also entitled to a wife's benefit by virtue of her husband's insurance, the amount of her wife's benefit is reduced by the amount of her own primary benefit. The married woman does not protect her husband under this system even if he was as a matter of fact entirely or mainly dependent upon her for support.

An element of forfeiture is involved in the fact that the insured worker who withdraws with only a currently insured or temporary fully insured status has only the equivalent of term insurance for his eligible dependents if any. He does not attain old-age protection for himself even to the extent of the taxes paid by him or on his account and he loses the privilege of having the Government contribute heavily to the costs of his old-age protection.

Possible Changes in Present System

As was pointed out at the beginning of this section, few if any students of the subject advocate standing pat on the existing system

---

[10] See act, title II, sec. 202–f.
[11] The same, sec. 202–c–4.

of old-age and survivors insurance. The alternatives are the extension and the modification of the existing system to remove its anomalies, inconsistencies, and inequities, or the development of a system based on radically different basic principles. The arguments in favor of an entirely different system will not be given at this point as they arise largely from the financial, economic, and administrative aspects of the problem, immediate consideration will be given to what would have to be done to the present system on the coverage and benefit sides if its basic principles are to be retained.

EQUALITY OF TREATMENT

It seems perfectly clear that if general revenues of the Government are to be used to pay benefits granted without reference to need, or in other words without any means test, all the workers of the Nation and those dependent upon them have a right to equal treatment under the law. Special privileges to persons engaged in selected occupations can hardly be defended when well-to-do persons engaged in them receive windfall benefits while persons with very modest means in other occupations get nothing and very poor people have to depend on means test public assistance. Forfeitures in event of disability are likewise indefensible. Thus certain reforms are essential if the present basic principles are to be retained, despite the fact that they will be costly, a matter to be considered later. The major reforms would be:

Coverage.

The system would be extended to cover practiclly all gainful occupations, notably agricultural labor, domestic service in private homes, the self-employed, Government service and service in private education, religious, and eleemosynary institutions. Thus almost everyone would share in the distribution of general tax revenues and in the proceeds of pay-roll taxes on employers, which insofar as they are shifted to consumers are a disguised or hidden sales tax.

Universal coverage would also eliminate those forfeitures which now result on movement from a covered to an uncovered occupation. They would make less arbitrary the present provisions with respect to an insured status, although the wisdom of retaining these status requirements at all requires careful consideration in any system in which the Government contributes heavily and underwrites the whole load.

Universal coverage would likewise eliminate the present twilight zone that separate the two definite statuses of (1) the covered employee of a covered employer and (2) the individual worker uncovered because he is working on his own account. In numerous instances a relationship exists between a corporation or business and persons who represent it, typically as salesmen, under contracts that at common law make them independent businessmen working on their own account.

An issue has arisen as to (*a*) whether these so-called independent salesmen are entitled to social security benefits by virtue of their services rendered after the passage of the act and (*b*) whether the corporation or business should pay the tax. The two issues are separable because under existing law the employee who renders service to an employer who should have been covered is entitled to benefits even if his employer did not pay the tax or withhold the tax from the employee's pay envelope. The Supreme Court in a recent decision held that these relationships constituted employment within the meaning of the law, but the Congress passed over the President's veto a bill which operated to suspend giving effect to the decision in the expectation that it would in the coming session give consideration to extension of coverage.[12]

Disability Benefits

Benefits with respect to total disability, either permanent or temporary, would probably have to be provided.[13] These provisions would necessarily be fairly intricate, for doubtless a distinction would have to be made between a disability which renders a person unfit for any gainful employment and one which unfits him for his present occupation but does not render him unemployable in any gainful occupation. Forfeitures in event of disability are indefensible and a disabled employee and his dependents should not have to wait until he has attained age 65 to be eligible for benefits.

Immediate Insurance

If general taxes and pay-roll taxes on employers are used to finance the system it is questionable whether protection against death and disability should not be immediately effective upon entering covered employment.

Unemployment

Careful consideration should be given to provisions with respect to prolonged and involuntary unemployment. Under the present system it may result in loss of old-age protection or a material decrease in the amount of benefit. It may prevent attaining either a currently insured status or a temporary fully insured status. The American system,

---

[12] Public Law 642, 80th Cong.

[13] Some persons maintain that disability benefits should only be paid to persons who are in need. Such a provision does not seem consistent with survivors benefits paid regardless of need. It would mean that the mother and children get benefits if the father dies, but do not if he is totally and permanently disabled and requires support and care.

471

which is based on percentage deductions from wages earned in covered employment, does not readily permit of excusal of contributions when unemployment is involuntary. In this connection it will be remembered that unemployment compensation pays benefits only for a limited number of weeks and that time on unemployment compensation does not count in determining benefits under old-age and survivors insurance.

Adjustment of Other Retirement Systems

Making old-age and survivors insurance universal would probably necessitate far-reaching changes in many existing retirement systems, public and private. In many instances these systems have been established on the basis that they constituted the only formal organized protection. It seems questionable whether employers and employees could continue to pay present contributions and in addition pay the pay-roll taxes and general taxes necessary to support the universal system as it begins to pick up something approaching full load. It seems probable that most existing public and private systems for employees not now covered under old-age and survivors insurance would have to be either entirely abandoned or radically revised so that they would be supplemental to the universal system.

This issue would be extremely important for the National Government because several retirement systems are established and operate through laws passed by Congress. The two largest ones are the general Federal retirement system and the railroad retirement system, but there are numerous others, including the Foreign Service, the provisions for retired pay in the armed services and other services paid under army pay tables, and teachers, policemen, and firemen in the employ of the District of Columbia.

Veterans' Benefits

The relationship of veterans' benefits to social security benefits would also present serious problems for the National Government. Two or three illustrations may be helpful here.

Assume that the universal system provides disability benefits. A veteran after working in a covered occupation for several years is forced to withdraw because of a disability which is determined to be service connected. Does he get both a veterans' benefit and the full universal social security benefit?

When the veterans of a particular war as a class reach the retirement age, a movement arises for service pensions. Is the veteran to receive both a service pension and the no-means test benefit from the general system?

In general, are persons to be permitted to draw benefits under two or more systems?

472

The increase in the cost of living that has taken place since 1935 is another important factor in leading to a general belief that the existing system of old-age and survivors insurance requires thorough reconsideration. Two economic facts are self evident:

1. The social security of the individual depends on his ability to obtain the necessaries in food, shelter, clothing, medical care, etc. If prices advance so that his money benefits lack the necessary purchasing power the system has lost much of its social utility.

2. Man is largely dependent upon practically current production for food, clothing, and medical care. The recent war has demonstrated that even a few years interference with residential construction creates a serious problem with respect to shelter.

When the laws of 1935 and 1939 were passed it was assumed that price levels were sufficiently stable and that changes were so gradual that a contributory insurance system was practicable. Events have proved that if the system is to be effective benefits must be adjusted upward to meet increased living costs. Several important points must be raised in connection with this fact.

1. An actuarial reserve system of insurance, public or private, operates on a money basis, with money premiums and money benefits. The insured carries the risk of advancing prices and diminished purchasing power of money and reaps the benefit of a possible fall in prices. If stable purchasing power is to be guaranteed, the Government in the event of substantial increases must provide it at the expense of general taxpayers.

2. It is entirely practicable politically to get an increase in money benefits in the face of rising prices. Is it politically practicable to have a decrease in money benefits in the face of falling prices? Could a cost of living factor be introduced into the benefit formula so that the promised benefits would have the purchasing power of the dollars of say 1939 or of the dollars at the time of amendment of the act? As noted in the preceding paragraph, the Government would have to increase its contributions in times of high prices but if benefits were tied to prices it would reduce them in periods of low prices.

3. The United States has been experimenting with an old-age insurance system that relates the amount of benefit to earnings in covered employment—total earnings during coverage in the 1935 act and average earnings in covered employment in the 1939 amendments. It was not assumed at the time that there would be a sudden sharp step up from one level of wages and prices to another so that the size of the total of the average would depend so much on the actual years during which the insured was covered.

473

In any retirement system relating benefits directly to earnings commonly involves the use of a benefit formula or several different alternative plans. If persons with small earnings are included, it is rarely practicable to make benefits a fixed uniform percentage of earnings alike for all. Although a benefit of half or even quarter pay might be adequate in the later years of life for upper-bracket employees, even half pay would be insufficient for the employee who has never earned much more than a minimum of subsistence. Under the 1939 amendments to the Social Security Act, the primary benefit is 40 percent of the first $50 of average monthly earnings in covered employment plus 10 percent of the remainder. Earnings of over $250 are neither taxed nor counted for benefits. The total of the amount derived from the use of these two percentages is increased by 1 percent of that total for each year of covered service. This formula gives from an actuarial standpoint a marked advantage to the low-paid worker over the high-paid worker and to the short-service worker over the long-service worker per dollar of contribution and interest earned by contributions. In addition to this advantage, minimum provisions are included in the 1939 amendments which make more adequate provisions for persons with low average covered earnings.

A marked increase in wages and prices obviously makes such a benefit forrmula and such minimum provisions obsolete. It likewise makes questionable the provisions with respect to the maximum amount of wages to be taxed and to be used in determining benefits. The maximum limitations on the amount of benefits which may be paid with respect to a single insured individual also are outmoded. The entire benefit formula has to be recast to make the system socially effective.

If benefits are raised for workers who retire after the effective date of a new act and much of the cost of this liberalization is ultimately to come from general revenues, is it fair for the Government to refuse to make like increases in the benefits paid to workers already retired? Refusal might be politically inexpedient. A substantial number of beneficiaries already retired under the existing law, moreover, lack resources to maintain a reasonable level of living and unless benefits are raised will have to resort to means-test public assistance.[14]

It must be remembered, however, that old-age and survivors' benefits are now being paid to many who were not in need when they became eligible and are not in need now. Neither they nor their employers on their account contributed more than a small fraction of the cost of these benefits. Are these windfall benefits to be increased at

---

[14] For statistical evidence on this point see Adequacy of the Income of Beneficiaries Under Old-Age and Survivors Insurance, Social Security Bulletin, February 1948, pp. 12–22.

general expense and the special privileges of this particular group be still further enhanced?

A question is pertinent as to whether such a system is properly designated as insurance unless that term is stripped of all its old financial meaning. In 1935 when President Roosevelt said that the system should be self sustaining in the sense that funds for the payment of insurance benefits should not come from the proceeds of general taxation, the term insurance had its old financial connotations but now they are largely gone as heavy commitments of general revenues become necessary.

The upward spiraling of wages and prices and the abandonment of the insurance concepts of the 1935 act might well result in a reconsideration of the original decision to relate benefits to wages. The question should be faced as to whether a universal, comprehensive no-means test system requiring ultimately heavy contributions from general taxes should do more than provide a modest uniform benefit for the worker and for each type of dependent who received support from the retired or deceased worker—wife or widow, children, or dependent parents. If the Government itself is to be a heavy contributor, variation in amount of benefit in accordance with length of service is questionable. Justification for it lies in insurance concepts but if they are largely abandoned for the system as a whole the Congress might well consider abolishing them here too.

The administrative costs of relating benefits to earnings in covered employments should be considered in this connection. The system necessitates maintaining detailed records of the earnings of each covered worker throughout the whole period of his covered employment and using the resulting data in figuring benefits. It is obviously impossible to have a perfect record for every person. A large staff of clerical employees is necessary for this work in the Old-Age and Survivors Bureau of the Social Security Agency and covered employers are put to substantial expense in making the basic returns and supplying employees with information. Should a new law change the benefit formula and make it applicable to all living beneficiaries, all existing cases would have to be refigured and new cards made for issuance of checks. A question exists as to whether the social and economic advantages of a relationship between benefits and average earnings is sufficient to warrant the costs of administration and the difficulties of adjusting to meet changes in wages and prices.

The cost of administration of old-age and survivors insurance charged against the trust fund was 27 million dollars in 1944–45, 37 million dollars in 1945–46, and 41 million dollars in 1946–47. These figures do not reflect actual expenses in the respective years because of bookkeeping adjustments.[15] According to the report of the Advisory

---

[15] Annual Report Federal Security Agency, 1947, p. 160.